Professional
Interviewing

PROFESSIONAL INTERVIEWING

CAL W. DOWNS
University of Kansas

G. PAUL SMEYAK
University of Florida, Gainesville

ERNEST MARTIN
Cox Broadcasting Corporation

HARPER & ROW PUBLISHERS, New York
Cambridge, Hagerstown, Philadelphia, San Francisco,
London, Mexico City, São Paulo, Sydney

Sponsoring Editor: Alan M. Spiegel
Production Manager: Jeanie Berke
Compositor: Lexigraphics Inc.
Art Studio: Vantage Art Inc.

PROFESSIONAL INTERVIEWING

Library of Congress Cataloging in Publication Data

Downs, Cal W   1936-
  Professional interviewing.

    Includes index.
    1. Interviewing. 2. Interviews.
3. Employment interviewing. 4. Decision-making.
I. Smeyak, G. Paul, joint author. II. Martin,
Ernest, 1945–   joint author. III. Title.
HN29.D69   158'.3   79–20597
ISBN 0–06–041739–0
ISBN 0–06–041736–6 pbk.

Contents

Preface

Interviewing and being interviewed are common experiences for most of us. The purpose of this book is to describe some considerations which will enable you to be more "professional" in conducting interviews and more effective in achieving the desired results—without merely relying on a trial-and-error approach.

From this book, we hope that you can develop the skill of analyzing a situation while you are participating in it. Various alternatives in relation to the specific person with whom you are dealing should be thought about and the most effective one should be chosen. Adapting to an individual situation is a deterrent to reducing the interview to a pat formula.

Our goal in this book is to make you aware of some of the most important decisions that need to be made in conducting an interview. Behind every decision that you make lies some kind of rationale. For this reason, we have tried to report some basic behavioral research findings that will be useful to you. The philosophy and the techniques are also based on years of actual experience, on original research about interviewing procedures, and on extensive training of interviewers.

The main emphasis of the book is aimed at developing some very practical skills—skills in planning interviews, skills in managing interviews, and skills in interpreting data. These skills can be applied in many different contexts; this becomes obvious when you look at the organization of the book. There are four parts. The first develops a number of basic skills and decisive points applicable to all kinds of interviews. Part II describes the interview as a management tool. This includes discussions of selection, appraisal, counseling, discipline, exit and persuasive interviews. In Part III, we treat interviews in mass-media contexts. This will be useful to people in various phases of journalism. It will also be helpful to managers who find themselves being interviewed by journalists or who conduct news conferences themselves. In the final part, IV, interviews are described as research tools. In addition, to the topics normally discussed about surveys, there are two unusual and important chapters about focused interviews and organizational analysis. This section should be useful not only to marketing departments and academic researchers but also to managers who need to collect data about employee attitudes, products or service, and their organizations. Even though a manager may not collect the data, he or she should be knowledgeable about the ways of acquiring it.

In organizing the book this way, we have made available to you a cafeteria approach to interviewing. You may pick and choose those aspects of special concern to you. Although not everybody will need to know all aspects equally well, there is an advantage, however, in having it all available—as is indicated by the following true story. A young man took some training in interviewing while working on an M.A. in broadcast journalism. After graduation, he took a job as a manager in a radio station. He later reported that in school he had not been particularly interested in talking about the interview as a management tool, because he was a journalist—interested in journalistic interviews. During his first two months on the job, however, he had to discipline and then fire three people. His training suddenly became very relevant not only to his position as a journalist but also as a manager.

In a number of instances, the role of the interviewee is explored along with that of the interviewer. Whenever this is not done explicitly, we feel that it is done implicitly. After all, a thorough acquaintance with the interviewing process is perhaps the best kind of preparation that any interviewee can have.

Since this is a book about strategies of dealing with other people, there are serious questions about the ethical considerations that ought to guide your behavior. It would be impossible for us to present a code of ethics that would suit every person in every circumstance—although there is such a code listed for broadcasters. Nevertheless, we hope that readers will be aware of the ethical guidelines that they set for themselves. Furthermore, our emphasis upon building strategy should never be construed as negative manipulation of the person with whom you are dealing.

Finally, interviewing requires that you refine a number of important communication skills. In this sense, this book is only the beginning of your search. No skill can be developed merely by reading about it. You must still transfer the ideas from the printed page into your verbal and nonverbal behavior. This will require analysis and practice. For this reason, projects, discussion questions, and transcripts are included at the end of the chapters. Remember that it is useful to know what works effectively for others, but in the final analysis you are searching for what works best for you. All "professionals" are not alike. Good luck in your search.

CAL W. DOWNS
G. PAUL SMEYAK
ERNEST MARTIN

Professional
Interviewing

Part I
BASIC PROCESSES
OF INTERVIEWING

The six chapters in Part I are designed to present a broad outline on which
the rest of this book is based. Many of the guidelines will be repeated
in the different parts of this book, but it will be helpful for readers
to come back periodically to these initial chapters for review because
the guidelines will be covered in the most depth here. It is assumed that
once you have read these chapters, you will be able to apply them to
the different contexts.

The basic processes that are covered in Part I include: (1) preparing
for the interview, (2) managing the interview, (3) interpreting the
content and the relationship in an interview, and (4) judging your
own effectiveness. In a sense, these are behavioral objectives, because
when you finish reading these initial chapters, you should be able to
accomplish each one of the objectives with ease.

Because we believe in the utility of a good orientation for any
communication endeavor, the following overview is presented so that you
will know what to expect in this part.

An interview is a specialized form of oral, face-to-face communication
between people in an interpersonal relationship that is entered into

for a specific reason associated with a particular subject matter.
Its effectiveness can be judged in terms of the purpose of the interview, the techniques used, the time frame, the perspective of the person doing the evaluation, and the reliability and validity of the information obtained. These are covered in Chapter 1.

The things that affect the interviewer's interpretation of messages are: motivations, purposes, perceptions, thinking patterns, language expertise, biases, attitudes, and memory. These also affect the interviewee's interpretation of the content of the interview. These are covered in Chapter 2.

Those aspects of the interview that can be planned are the purposes, agenda, questions, structure, setting, and reaction to special problems. Such planning can prepare the interviewer for any contingency that might arise within an interview. These are discussed in Chapters 3 and 4.

The processes pertinent to managing the interview are setting the climate, listening, probing, motivating, and controlling the interview. These involve a high degree of communication technique, and relevant guidelines are suggested for each in Chapters 5 and 6.

Finally, this part is addressed to the interviewer. Nevertheless, if understanding a situation helps a person interact in that situation better, any person can read Part I with the potential of becoming a better interviewee, too.

Chapter 1
The Nature of Effective Interviewing

Most readers of this book already will have participated many times with another person in an interaction called "an interview." Probably, they have been successful at it, too.

The word "professional" as applied to interviewing implies that there are varying degrees of proficiency in those skills necessary for effective interviewing. Felix Lopez compares the professional interviewer to a professional musician.

> Interviewing is very much like piano playing—a fair degree of skill can be acquired without the necessity of formal instruction. But there is a world of difference in craftsmanship, in technique, and in finesse between the amateur who plays "by ear" and the accomplished concert pianist. The self-instructed player mechanically reproduces on the keyboard certain melodies that have been committed to memory; the artist, by skillfully blending mastery of musical theory, countless hours of practice, and personal interpretation, creates an effect that is technically precise, pleasing to the audience, and expressive to the pianist's inner feeling.[1]

[1] Felix M. Lopez, *Personnel Interviewing* (New York, McGraw-Hill Book Company, 1975), p. 1.

Sometimes, the interviewer "plays by ear" and is successful. For example, an assistant dean of a business school confessed recently that she had had no training as an interviewer and that she just relied on intuition and her natural inclinations but had been so successful in her interviews that it had been decided that no one would be hired for any position in the school without being interviewed by her. What was she doing? She did not know, but she was doing it effectively. Could she teach it to others? No. Does this one experience indicate that training in interviewing is not necessary? Not at all. Just as there are some individuals who develop an effective tennis swing naturally, there are some individuals who are lucky enough to pick up effective communication skills quite naturally. You can always do a better job, however, if you know *what* you are doing and *why* you are doing it. In fact, our approach in this book is not necessarily to give you a plan of how to conduct an interview. We feel, instead, that the greatest skill that you can pick up from reading a book like this is *how to analyze* a situation, determine what your alternatives are, and then choose how you wish to proceed. We will provide you with a very basic frame of reference for your consideration.

WHAT IS AN INTERVIEW?

Despite the way we sometimes talk, there is no such thing as "the" interview. There are a lot of different situations in which two people interact that can be called an interview. In this book, we will describe a basic framework that cuts across all of the following types of interviews, but each one has some subtle differences from all the rest.

selection	public research
appraisal	telephone
counseling	focus
disciplinary	journalistic
exit	broadcast
internal research	press conference
negotiation	medical

It is a mistake to identify one kind of interview as being relevant to only one kind of job. While journalists, for example, may be interested primarily in learning how to get information from others, they may also find themselves hiring new reporters and appraising their performances. This fact was demonstrated by a broadcast manager who recently visited us. His interest had always been in broadcast interviewing, but in the first month on the job he had to fire three people, a type of interview that he had never even considered relevant to his job. Similarly, personnel managers who normally conduct selection and appraisal interviews may find themselves taking an in-house survey or meeting the press to announce some major organizational development in the company.

Another common misconception is that an interview is just conversation. Although a good interview may appear to be highly conversational, there are some important points that distinguish it from mere conversation. Interviewing has been defined in different ways. In their classic book on interviewing, Robert Kahn and Charles Cannell define an interview as "a specialized pattern of verbal interaction—initiated for a specific purpose, and focused on some specific content area, with consequent elimination of extraneous material."[2] Charles Stewart and W. B. Cash define it as "a process of dyadic communication with a predetermined and serious purpose designed to interchange behavior and involve the asking and answering of questions."[3] Since the word "interviewing" in common usage refers to so many different kinds of interactions, it is difficult to write one definition that will accommodate all of them. Nevertheless, it is important that we establish a basic definition as a frame of reference. Consequently, we define an interview *as a specialized form of oral, face-to-face communication between people in an interpersonal relationship that is entered into for a specific task related purpose associated with a particular subject matter.* A discussion of some of the key terms of this definition will make it more meaningful.

1. An interview is *usually* an oral, face-to-face exchange. The people involved are in one another's presence and verbalize their messages aloud. This gives the interview some real advantages over questionnaires, because (a) respondents are more likely to say more than they will write, (b) people are motivated by the mere presence of another person, and (c) oral exchanges offer more immediate opportunities for probing, clarifying answers, and providing feedback.

This definition, however, is not without its exceptions or limitations. While the interview is *basically* an oral exchange, questionnaires and resumes are often used within an interview as supplements.

Even more important, however, is the fact that the face-to-face situation allows visual, nonverbal messages to be a very important aspect of the interview. They must not be overlooked. Sometimes, these visual messages reinforce the verbal ones; at other times, they contradict them. For example, a person may be saying, "I'm quite comfortable, thank you" at the same time that she is twisting a handkerchief and looking anxiously around the room. Research has emphasized the relative importance of the

[2]Robert Kahn and Charles Cannell, *Dynamics of Interviewing* (New York: John Wiley & Sons, Inc., 1963), p. 16.
[3]Charles Stewart and William B. Cash, *Interviewing* (Dubuque, Iowa: William C. Brown Company, Publishers, 1978), p. 5.

visual cues and suggests that when people receive contradictory messages, they are more likely to believe the visual ones.

Finally, this part of the definition overlooks the telephone interview, which plays a very important role in marketing surveys and public opinion polls. With the telephone, two people are in one another's "presence" only orally.

2. The people in an interview are in an *interpersonal relationship*. This differentiates it from other face-to-face situations such as lectures and group meetings. Nevertheless, certain variations of the interview may include groups of people. The most notable examples are focused interviews, multiple interviewers in selection interviews, and press conferences. In its most popular form, however, an interview involves two people, and several major considerations for analyzing such interpersonal communication will be explored later.

Finally, the word "relationship" suggests that there is a certain structure that relates the two individuals to one another. This structured relationship is often described in terms of a role. A role includes the *behaviors that are associated with a position.* In other words, certain actions are associated with a given position, regardless of who the individual is in that position. The two roles that people occupy in an interview are that of the interviewer and the interviewee. Most of this book focuses on the interviewer role and behaviors that can be legitimately expected in good interviews. Nevertheless, it must be stressed that the interviewer and interviewee roles are supplementary and that you can only view the interviewer role in terms of its relationship to the interviewee role. Furthermore, each role often is shaped by very personal interpretations. Generally, the interviewer role will be developed in terms of its three major functions: (1) planning strategies, (2) conducting or managing the interview, and (3) measuring the results. Each of these are developed more fully in Chapters 2 through 6.

3. People interview for task related purposes; they have something they want to accomplish, that is, select a person for a job, collect research data, admit a patient, or write a news story. It is this task related purpose that differentiates an interview from mere conversation. A conversation can go anywhere; an interview, however, must be focused on content that is relevant to your purpose. Figure 1.1, adapted from Kahn and Cannell, attempts to illustrate the difference between the two. The X's represent communication exchanges that are relevant to the interviewer's purpose. The O's, H's, F's, and D's are topics or subjects that are irrelevant.

Figure 1.1 suggests that it is desirable to weed out irrelevant subject matter and to keep the discussion relevant. In order to do this, the interviewer will have to exercise *controls* over the interaction. However, the amount of control must be decided on in the context of a given situation.

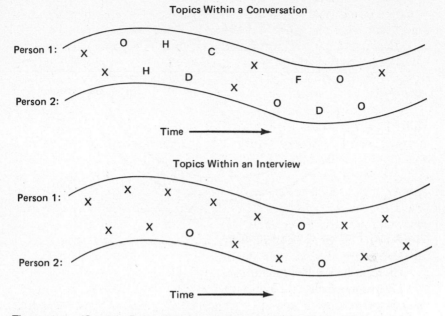

Figure 1.1   (Source: Robert Kahn and Charles Cannell, *Dynamics of Interviewing,* Copyright © 1963 John Wiley & Sons, Inc., p. 15. Adapted by permission of John Wiley & Sons, Inc.)

THE INTERVIEW AS INTERPERSONAL COMMUNICATION

Since an interview is basically a unique form of interpersonal communication, it is useful to begin our analysis with a general model of communication. There are many of these, with each trying to capture a dimension of this illusive process called "communication." One of the simplest definitions or descriptions was originated by David Berlo.[4] He identified communication as a source sending a message through a channel to a receiver. George Gerbner then tried to develop a model that would take into account more of the complexities of communication.[5] The Gerbner model describes communication in terms of

1. someone
2. perceiving an event, person, or stimulus
3. and reacting
4. in a situation
5. through some means

[4]David Berlo, *The Process of Communication* (New York: Holt, Rinehart and Winston, 1960).
[5]George Gerbner, "Toward a General Model of Communication," *Audio-Visual Communication Review* 4 (Summer 1956): 73.

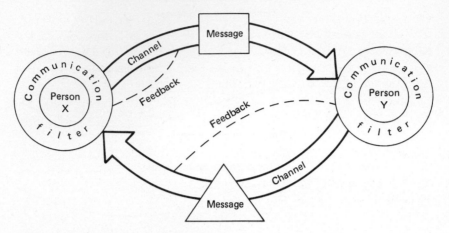

Figure 1.2   Process of communication.

6. to make available materials
7. in some form
8. and context
9. conveying content
10. of some consequence

The elements in most communication systems include people, messages, channels, and results or consequences. Consequently, we shall focus on communication as *people in a relationship sharing messages by exchanging them through some channel in order to produce some consequence.* This statement about communication has a number of ramifications that shall be explored throughout this book. There are several that should be identified here, however, as a basic framework for later discussions.

1. *Communication in the interview is a mutual process.* Both people in an interview contribute to the interaction, and the effectiveness of their efforts depends on their mutual cooperation. Neither person has exclusive control over the communication behavior of the other, and either can choose to block communication. In Figure 1.2, person X can communicate to person Y only if Y will listen or read the message. Y will share only those messages with X that Y wants X to have. This joint process is essential for you to remember when you try to accomplish your interviewing objectives.

The mutuality of the communication process also reinforces the idea that some effort must be expended to create a climate in which the interviewee is willing to communicate. Even in boss-subordinate interviews there is a limit to which the boss can accomplish his or her objectives based on the cooperation of the subordinate.

2. *Two-way communication is generally more effective than one-way*

communication. One-way communication is characterized by messages that go in basically one direction, for example, from the boss to the subordinate or from the interviewer to the interviewee. The sender is not particularly interested in the responses, questions, comments, or reactions of the receiver. Consequently, in a one-way situation the interviewer can never be certain that there is mutual understanding or that the message has been effective because there is no feedback. Feedback refers to

> the process of correction through incorporation of information about effects received. When a person perceives the results produced by his own actions, the information so derived will influence subsequent actions. Feedback thus becomes a steering device upon which learning and the correction of errors are based.[6]

Many people are comfortable in a one-way situation because it is efficient in terms of saving time and also they do not have to worry about reacting to questions or comments.

Two-way communication, on the other hand, involves feedback. Messages are sent in both directions, so both individuals participate as senders and receivers, and each must be receptive to the responses, or feedback, received from the other. Two-way communication takes time. Hundreds of experiments and exercises, however, have demonstrated that the extra effort and time, and the willingness to receive feedback are instrumental in increasing the likelihood that the people involved will understand one another. The reason for this will become clearer later as we describe the different influences on the way that people interpret messages. For the moment, it may be useful to examine a couple of real cases.

> In preparation for a meeting with a customer, I needed a list of computer equipment that was proposed for his system. Not having this list in my file, I called one of my subordinates in and asked him to provide me with a list of computer equipment in system XYZ. He returned a few minutes later with a copy of the purchase order for the equipment which did include a list of the equipment, but it was also cluttered with other information. This would not serve my purpose. I then explained to my subordinate why I needed this list and the general format that I wanted it in. The next list I got from him suited my purpose perfectly.

The moral to this story asserts the necessity of feedback. Communicators often erroneously assume that since they know exactly the results they want, the receiver will also. Thus, they often neglect to provide clarifying details.

Whether or not someone gets feedback is often determined by the

[6]J. Reusch, et al., *Non-Verbal Communication* (Berkeley: University of California Press, 1954), p. 4.

kind of climate in which the interview takes place. Sometimes the expectations of feedback are never articulated, and people do not give it. For example, a subordinate once listened to some instructions from a supervisor. The subordinate's only comment was, "Yes, sir." Later, someone asked whether or not the subordinate understood the supervisor. His comment was very revealing: "No, but you don't think that I was going to ask him, do you?" In this case, the interviewee apparently preferred to risk making a mistake than raise a question or show that he did not understand. People often react this way, so as an interviewer, you may have to make a very explicit request for feedback and build the kind of climate that permits the interviewee to give it. Examine what happens in the following case.

> SUPERVISOR: Bob, will you accept responsibility for these two-dimensional calculations for our contract project?
>
> BOB: O.K. What's involved?
>
> SUPERVISOR: Here is a detailed list of the results requested. We need to have the job finished for the July review meeting. Does that sound reasonable to you?
>
> BOB: I guess so. Maybe I should try some one-dimensional problems first to get a feel for the effect of material properties on the results.
>
> SUPERVISOR: That would be fine. In fact, it is a good idea so long as you are not diverted from the main question and from making the deadline late.
>
> BOB: Do you think it would be a good idea to take a trip to ACME Corp. and find out how they are handling some of the difficulties that I can see coming up?
>
> SUPERVISOR: If you feel that would be beneficial, then do it, but it should be this week or next week at the latest. I am concerned about your getting started on the problem promptly so we can meet the target date.
>
> BOB: I can't get started before the parameters for the material models are established, so I should have plenty of time to make the trip next week.
>
> SUPERVISOR: That's right. You can't get started until the material models are ready, but they should be finished next week. I would like to see you set up and waiting rather than starting after you get the information. It's important for us to have this job completed by July 1.
>
> BOB: O.K. I'll get started on it.

In this case, both people were exploring the thinking of the other, and neither left with a vague impression of what was important to the other.

As important as the concept of feedback is, people do superimpose some limitations or qualifications on it. For example, if you answer the following questions, you will get an insight into some of the limitations that you can place upon feedback.

About what are you willing to receive feedback?
From whom will you receive it?
Is everybody from whom you will receive feedback equal?
Under what conditions or when will you receive it?
Are positive and negative feedback equally welcome?

Interviews occur for a purpose, and they focus on certain kinds of information. One of the characteristics of being a good interviewer is the ability to *control* the interaction so that the purpose of the interview is achieved. This means that not all comments or responses are relevant. Therefore, you may need to set limits on the kind of response that is appropriate.

The degree of control necessary in an interview varies widely. One important factor involves the amount of authority you have over the interviewee. In certain medical, research, and business interviews control may be quite easy to maintain and quite necessary; in journalistic and information getting interviews, where the interviewee does not necessarily have to cooperate with you, control may be almost impossible to maintain. The necessity of control is illustrated by the report of an orthopedic surgeon. While there are many patients who are somewhat timid with doctors, others like to talk about a number of things unrelated to their immediate illness. The surgeon found herself getting into all kinds of time pressures because the interviews were becoming too lengthy. Therefore, she decided to cut her interview times in half in order to see all her patients. In her explanation, the surgeon said that she wanted to empathize and to have a good relationship with her patients, but the interview time "just was not a social hour." Consequently, she became very directive in the interviews and in weeding out irrelevant subject matter.

Since feedback is an important dimension of an interview, you will need to make a very conscious, concerted effort to obtain it if it is not volunteered. The following suggestions are useful techniques to generate feedback: (1) ask for it; (2) listen when it is given; (3) train people to expect you to be receptive; and (4) keep a climate that allows feedback.

3. *Each communicator needs a balance of sending and receiving skills.* Often when people think of communication in terms of sending and receiving, they think of one person as the sender and the other person as the receiver. This is unfortunate because one person is then designated as the talker and the other is designated as the listener. This is particularly dangerous in a working situation because it is common practice for a manager to be identified as the sender or supplier of information and a subordinate to be characterized as the listener.

If you believe in the mutuality of communication and the importance

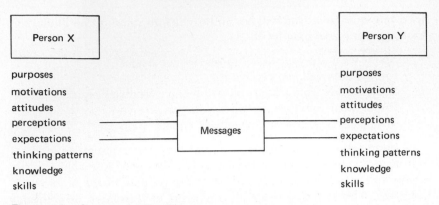

Figure 1.3   Communication filters.

of feedback, and that people are both senders and receivers, then you should agree that communicators need adequate sending *and* receiving skills. Obviously, you need a good facility with language in order to express your ideas well. Unfortunately, however, most people have had more training in expression than they have had in listening. Consequently, we underscore listening as one of the key communicating and interviewing skills.

4. *Each person is a unique filter of communication; therefore, expect differences.* In some ways each person is unlike every other person; no two are exactly alike. This is what makes communication so challenging: two people who are different in important ways, who have different goals, who use language differently, and who have different styles of communicating then share what they have in common.

Obviously, people are not completely different from one another; they are alike, too, in some important ways. They do have some common learnings, some shared experiences, and some common goals. To the extent that this is true in an interview, communication becomes easier. However, one of the greatest causes of communication problems is that we expect people to be like ourselves instead of being tuned in to the fact that they may be different in some important ways. When we expect people to be like us, we often take shortcuts or make assumptions that turn out to be erroneous and inefficient. Therefore, it is our purpose to challenge you to begin to expect people to be different from yourself, rather than like you. If you expect differences, you will seek ways to clarify your own point of view and you will also realize the necessity of discovering what the other person's understanding is.

Finally, some of the factors on which people may be alike or different are listed in Figure 1.3. Remember that each one of these factors operates as a kind of filter or screen through which a person's messages are sent and through which another person's messages are interpreted. Several of these factors exert a major influence on the interview and will be treated more thoroughly in Chapter 2.

5. *Effectiveness is measured in terms of a number of different yardsticks.* If you examine our definition, you will discover that it describes what happens in an interview very generally but never gives any explicit criteria for judging whether or not the interview is successful. How is effectiveness measured? We have asked hundreds of interviewers how they know when their interviews have been effective, and their answers are quite revealing.

By far, the most frequent answer to this question is "when I get the results I want" or "when I achieve my purpose." This is one of the most important points we want to make: you should judge your effectiveness in terms of the results. This implies, of course, that you are able to identify exactly what your purposes are. Unfortunately, it is easy to go into an interview with only the vaguest notion of what you are trying to do. The professional interviewer automatically identifies a purpose.

Sometimes, interviewers judge effectiveness in terms of the *techniques* that they have used. We feel less strongly that this should be so. Of course, the learner needs to focus on techniques, as well as to learn how to avoid leading questions, to structure the interview, and to have an impact upon the interviewee. Success does not come just from avoiding technical problems, however. It is possible, for example, for an interviewer to lose control of an interview or to have a tense period with the interviewee and still have an effective interview if the interviewer overcomes the problems and achieves his or her purposes. Therefore, we emphasize that success is not judged by the absence of problems; every interviewer may face unexpected reactions or interpretations that create real problems. The professional will not be overcome by the problem, but will quickly adapt to work through them.

In judging effectiveness, the interviewer needs *to keep a time frame in mind.* Every communication interaction can be examined in terms of its *immediate* impact or its *long-range* impact. Consider the sales representative who has dozens of interviews with a potential client over a six-month period and never makes a sale and then at the end of the six months walks in and receives a large order. When did this sales representative suddenly become effective? Ultimately he was not effective until the deal was closed. At the same time, the sale probably was not culminated in one day either. Everything that happened in the previous interviews influenced the final outcome. Since a number of interviews that we will consider involve long-term relationships, that is, job performance reviews, counseling, discipline, journalistic reports, and press conferences, it is useful to assess effectiveness in terms of long-term implications as well as short-term implications.

Any interview is made up of two important dimensions that can be analyzed for effectiveness: content and relationship. The one on which we will tend to focus most often is the *content*. We conduct interviews to get information or to give information. Therefore, at one level, the content or information exchanged occupies our attention.

It is our contention, however, that the *relationship* between the interviewer and interviewee is equally important in most circumstances. In fact, the nature of the relationship may determine whether or not certain information gets passed on during the interview. For example, many interviewees are very wary of revealing negative information about themselves. A high degree of interpersonal trust may be a precondition for such revelations to be made. Consequently, the professional interviewer may build a certain relationship as a means of getting certain content introduced into the interview. There are a number of transcripts provided in this book. As you analyze them, try to examine the apparent relationship as well as the content of the interview.

An interview may also have several purposes and, therefore, mixed results. It is possible, for example, to get the content that you want and yet ruin the relationship or to accomplish one purpose and not accomplish a second. This simply underscores that effectiveness is often a matter of degree—a mixed bag, if you will—rather than being an absolute. Your degree of effectiveness may be useful to examine.

In order to judge effectiveness, you also have to ask "from whose perspective?" Communicators often have different, incompatible goals, making it virtually impossible for all to succeed. The salesperson may try to sell you something when your purpose is to resist buying. The recruiter may try to identify your weaknesses when your purpose is to prevent her or him from finding out any negative information. The journalist may need to probe areas about which you are determined to say, "no comment." Realizing that people have different purposes in an interview will make you aware of what is actually going on in the interview. This is another reason why effectiveness must often be judged in terms of degree.

A vital criterion for judging effectiveness is the concept of *validity*. This refers to the extent to which you are observing, receiving, or measuring what you think you are observing, receiving, or measuring. Another way of looking at validity is to ask, "Am I really getting truthful information?" Sometimes validity is low because people choose to lie, to deceive, or to answer only partially. At other times validity is hampered by inadequacies of techniques and tendencies toward biased interpretations of the information that is being received. This means, then, that any real communication barrier encountered in the interview may decrease the accuracy in getting or giving information and, therefore, reduces the validity of the interview. This has ramifications for any interview but is particularly crucial for scientific investigations. Finally, it is the importance of validity that makes interviewers feel the need for improving their roles as interviewers.

Somewhat akin to validity is the concept of *reliability* as a factor in judging effectiveness. Reliability is the extent to which you would get the same results if you or another interviewer were to conduct a similar interview with the same individual. If two people interview the same person on the same topic and do not get consistent information, something is wrong, and the results of both interviews would be questioned. Again, the discrepancies may occur because of a willful change by the interviewee or because of some inconsistency or inadequacy on the part of the interviewer.

For example, Herbert Hyman reported a number of studies that question the reliability of the data.[7] In one study white and black interviewers surveyed a sample of blacks and obtained different information. The black interviewers reported more resentment about discrimination than did the whites. Why? We cannot be certain. Were the blacks purposely withholding information, or were the whites just perceptually blinded or biased? We do not know. The fact that the two groups differed, however, calls into question the reliability of the data. There are many studies like Hyman's. Similarly, when two recruiters have widely different estimates of the same candidate, the reliability is low. Since the interviewee's answers cannot be controlled entirely, the emphasis in this book is upon those things that you can do to make your interviews as reliable as possible.

THIS CHAPTER IN PERSPECTIVE

The purpose for any beginning chapter is to provide a general orientation to a book. In this chapter several key ideas have been set out as the foundation on which the rest of the book will be based.

First, an interview cannot be reduced to a formula. People just are not predictable. At best, you can learn a variety of strategies and techniques that can be used. It is up to you to analyze a situation and to decide what strategy and technique are most appropriate.

Second, your ability to analyze an interview while participating in it is perhaps the greatest and most fundamental skill that you can develop. The discussions that follow are designed to make you aware of the relationship as well as the content factors in an interview. These two are so interwoven that you cannot separate them easily.

Third, the interview is a special form of communication. There are, of course, many books that have been written trying to explain this pro-

[7]Herbert Hyman et al., *Interviewing for Social Research* (Chicago: University of Chicago Press, 1954).

cess. All the things that are included in those books may apply to the interview in some way. On the other hand, you have already learned a great deal about communication through your own experiences. If you can bring your experiences into awareness, they can be the basic foundation for your interaction in an interview.

Fourth, you cannot improve your skills in anything unless you have some criteria for judging effectiveness. One of the basic purposes of this chapter has been to get you to think about the several different criteria that may apply. It is particularly important that you remember that communication in any interview is a joint process and that therefore people might be using different criteria to measure their effectiveness.

Finally, this chapter introduced you to three different roles that an interviewer has: a planner or strategist, a manager or controller of the interaction, and a measurer or interpreter. The next three chapters amplify these concepts. Because measurement is the ultimate objective, it is discussed first so that the planning and managing aspects of your role can be viewed in terms of the things that affect your interpretations.

PROJECTS

1. Feedback is one of the most important concepts in this chapter. Think of your own experiences. What are some of the ways in which you have been successful in getting other people to give you feedback? What are some of the reasons why you were reluctant to *give* feedback to others? In those cases in which you were reluctant to give feedback, was there anything that the other person could have done to get you to give feedback?

2. Make a list of the most important factors that you think affect interpersonal relationships. Be able to explain each and then discuss them with other people.

3. Which of the criteria for effectiveness have you used most often? Why? Were there some mentioned that you have not used? In the future, which criteria will be most useful to you?

4. What should you do if you realize that you and the other person have different purposes for an interview and are using different criteria to judge its effectiveness?

5. Think of a specific communication situation or investigate the tape or transcript of an interview. Describe the way in which the content of the messages is related to the relationship itself.

6. To what extent are you a filter of communication?

Chapter 2
Communication Influences on the Interviewer and the Interviewee

One of the main points of Chapter 1 is that interviewers filter all messages that come to them through their purposes, motives, perceptions, and attitudes. This means that interviewers are doing something to the information that comes to them and that they are actively involved with it. In this chapter our objective is to explore the ways in which you as an interviewer can operate upon that information, both consciously and unconsciously. In many ways this chapter will focus on your role as a *measurer* of information, of people, and of circumstances, because you are constantly involved in judging the adequacy of information or the image of the other person. Perhaps it would be advantageous for you to examine your role as a measurer before we examine your role as a strategist or controller of the interview. By doing so there will be a number of strategic decisions that you might make to account for the ways in which you habitually process the information received in an interview.

The specific influences upon you that we will examine are your (1) purposes, (2) motivations, (3) perceptions, (4) thinking patterns, (5) language expertise, (6) bias, (7) attitudes, and (8) memory.

PURPOSES OF COMMUNICATING

People communicate or resist communicating in order to achieve their own personal goals; they communicate, in other words, for a purpose. This is a basic assumption that has two very important implications for an interview.

First, an interview is a *special event*, and you ought to be quite clear about what you are trying to accomplish. The more concretely you can refine the statement of your purpose, the more carefully you can plan to achieve it. For example, "to get information" is not as useful a statement of purpose as "to get information about how person X makes decisions."

Second, it is useful to remember that *each* person in the interview has a purpose. When these purposes are congruent, things may work out well. At times, however, the purposes are not congruent or even compatible. If a journalist interviews you, you may cooperate in giving information so that you can get certain publicity. In such a case, the purposes are different, but they are still compatible. In a selection interview, you may want to discover a person's weaknesses or discover reasons for rejection; the candidate, on the other hand, wants not to identify weaknesses but to concentrate on strengths. In such a case the purposes are diametrically opposed. As these examples illustrate, you should always be aware that the interviewee is trying to achieve certain goals and that his or her answers are not given aimlessly. Recognition of this fact will have an impact upon how you evaluate the information that you receive.

Purposes can be a major part of filtering in another way. We have spoken to people who have said that their purposes were basically to get information. In analyzing their actions, however, it has been quite apparent that it was not just information that they were looking for, because they tended to reject any information that was not consistent with their point of view. These people did not want information but reinforcement. Consequently, their filtering would reject anything that did not comply with this purpose. This point has been demonstrated many times with people who have decided on a political candidate, bought a specific product, or stated a new idea. Once they have made their decisions, they do not want to be bothered by contrary evidence.

Finally, your purposes determine the way you listen and probe. They become the basic guide for most of your interviewing behavior.

MOTIVATIONS FOR COMMUNICATING

Your communication is influenced by your specific motivations and needs, which are frequently related to your purposes. You need not be a mentalist or amateur psychologist to detect the differences in motivations among people; you need only be a careful listener to the way people talk about themselves and their situations. Once you have picked up some trends, you can use them in tailoring an interview to the interviewee's particular needs and interests. The following list identifies some of the most basic needs that various theorists have identified. They exist in many different degrees, and not everyone will have all of them. Furthermore, priorities change over time.

1. physiological needs—to have enough air, food; to possess healthy body functions
2. social needs—to be around other people; to be included in their activities
3. ego needs—to feel good about oneself; self-respect; self-confidence
4. security—to be free from want or fear; to avoid unpleasantness or danger
5. achievement—to make progress; to attain goals
6. affection—to love and to be loved
7. control/power—to influence one's own surroundings
8. dependency—to have others make decisions for oneself
9. individualism—to be different; perhaps to work alone
10. status—to have respect from others; to attain position; to be important; to be recognized
11. growth—to be stimulated and challenged
12. altruism—to be helpful to others without personal benefit
13. economic—to have money; to be in a healthy financial state
14. health—to be absent of disease

As an interviewer, detection of the needs relevant to a particular individual is helpful in several ways. First, you can appeal to relevant needs to get the person to participate in the interview. You may have to pay some people for an interview; some will grant you an interview to get publicity; others will enjoy talking to you; and still others will grant an interview in order to try to control the flow of information about a topic or a situation. It is useful to detect the differences so that you can appeal to the different individuals.

Second, you can tailor what you say in the interview to the interviewee's needs. For example, if you are trying to get someone to accept an idea, show how it is related to that person's individual needs. Conversely, when interviewees resist an idea, it may be because they can see no concrete relationship between the idea and their needs. Probe until you are able to establish such a link.

Perhaps one of the best ways of showing how motivation can be applied is to use examples from two different theories. William Schutz has developed a means of analyzing people's basic interpersonal orientations.[1]

[1]William C. Schutz, *The Interpersonal Underworld* (Palo Alto: Science and Behavior Books, Inc., 1966).

He has isolated three different orientations that people tend to have toward others: (1) inclusion, (2) affection, and (3) control. Figure 2.1 explains each of these orientations. People may score low or high on each dimension, yet no value judgments are placed upon them. In other words, people are just different, and it is not more preferable, for example, to be highly sociable than to like to work alone.

Schutz's work points out how motivations may contribute to compatible or incompatible relationships within an interview. For example, if someone who has a high inclusion need is interviewing someone with a high inclusion need, you might expect a lot of socializing and interaction. Other things being equal, these people will fill each other's needs and get along well. On the other hand, suppose the interviewee is low on inclusion but the interviewer is high. This could easily become an incompatible situation. The more the interviewer tries to include the interviewee in a social relationship, the more uncomfortable the interviewee will become and the more resistance the interviewee will demonstrate. The interviewer may well wonder why the resistance occurs and press harder. If this situation continues, the interviewer will likely end up with the impression that something is wrong with the interviewee, and the interviewee might feel that the interviewer is aggressive. Neither person is having his or her own needs met.

Control is another basic orientation that has some interesting ramifications. People high in control on the Schutz scale like to lead, to make decisions, to influence their destinies, and to exercise power over others. If you put two of them together in an interview you may well develop a power struggle. People low in control like to be led, to follow, to have decisions made for them. If you put two of them together they probably will spend a lot of time encouraging each other to make a decision. You might find them talking like this:

PERSON X: What would you like to do tonight?
PERSON Y: Oh, I don't care. You make the decision.
PERSON X: But I really want to do what you want.
PERSON Y: But it doesn't really matter to me.

The most compatible situation is for one person to want to control (lead) and the other to want to follow. This works particularly well if the one high on control happens to be the interviewer or the supervisor.

The Schutz theory offers an excellent framework for analyzing what is going on in an interview between two people. First, by examining the *comments* in terms of showing affection, exercising control, or building a social relationship, you can find out what their basic orientations toward one another are. Second, it allows you to examine the relationship to determine how they are responding to one another. As the interviewer,

INCLUSION

Expressed: I make efforts to include other people in my activities and to get them to include me in theirs. I try to belong, to join social groups, to be with people as much as possible.

Wanted: I want other people to include me in their activities and to invite me to belong, even if I do not make an effort to be included.

AFFECTION

Expressed: I make efforts to become close to people. I express friendly and affectionate feelings and try to be personal and intimate.

Wanted: I want others to express friendly and affectionate feelings toward me and to try to become close to me.

CONTROL

Expressed: I try to exert control and influence over things. I take charge of things and tell other people what to do.

Wanted: I want other people to control and influence me. I want other people to tell me what to do.

Figure 2.1   Names and definitions for Schutz scales.

you can analyze the interaction in these terms and then increase your own flexibility in order to adapt to the basic orientations of the other person. For example, if you know that the interviewee is high on inclusion, you may spend time socializing or talking about his or her importance to the "team." If you know that the person is a loner, who works better alone and resists being included in a lot of activities, you might curtail the socializing and emphasize the importance of the interviewee as an individual. If you know that the interviewee has high control needs, you may permit him or her to take a greater role in the interview; if he or she is low on control, then you may not push very hard for participation. If the person has high affection needs, then you can fill these by making the person feel very appreciated.

David McClelland offers a second way of looking at motivation. He identifies three basic needs that people have: (1) affiliation, (2) power, and (3) achievement.[2]

Affiliation is similar to inclusion in Schutz's theory. The person who is high in it will tend to define most situations as social situations. Consequently, in attempting to satisfy this person's needs in the interview, you will need to demonstrate a concern for the personal relationship between the two of you as well as the interviewee's relationship with others in the family as well as at work. With this type of person you should constantly stress the person's affiliative contribution toward the work effort, be

[2]David McClelland, *Motivational Management* (The Forum Corporation of North America, 1976).

friendly, and take care to observe all the interpersonal niceties for building rapport. If you are a manager who must give this person negative feedback, take special precautions to separate the evaluation of the person's behavior from the evaluation of the total person. Any action that is the reverse of the ones described will demotivate the affiliative person.

The need for power is the need to engage in powerful actions that bring reputation and position. People who have it are concerned with public evaluation, and they often elicit a strong emotional reaction from others. Any way that you can provide status and control in dealing with such people is likely to satisfy their needs.

The need for achievement is the need to set realistic goals and then to attain them. Growth and competition are necessary for this type of individual. Consequently, the actions that satisfy such a person include careful planning, frequent feedback, emphasis upon the person's unique contributions, letting the person know when he or she outperforms others, and keeping the interaction interesting and challenging. It is also important to make this kind of person feel that he or she is a part of the goal-setting. Consequently, interacting with this kind of person in an interview must involve an emphasis upon goals and achievement.

In what sense then do your motivations filter communication behavior? You behave in ways that make sense to you, and what makes sense to you is generally related to your own needs. Therefore, you can be expected to send messages that will accomplish or fulfill your needs, and you will, in turn, interpret messages in terms of how they relate to your needs. Taking this into account, the wise interviewer will rarely assume that all people are motivated in the same way or that their needs are just like his or her own.

Finally, most people have one overriding need: to protect and enhance the self-image. People have images of what they are, and it does not matter that others do not share them. The self-image is one of the most important psychological constructs that a person has, and most people will react in whatever way is necessary to defend it. Thus, this defense often exercises a tremendous influence over the way a person communicates. Defensiveness sometimes blinds a person, and this is one of the reasons that supportive climates enhance communication whereas defensive ones inhibit cooperation.

PERCEPTIONS

One of the more interesting parts of your filtering role is the way that you perceive your communication.[3] Perception involves the selecting, or-

[3]Much of this discussion is based on material from William V. Haney, *Communication and Organizational Behavior* (Homewood, Ill.: Richard D. Irwin, Inc., 1973).

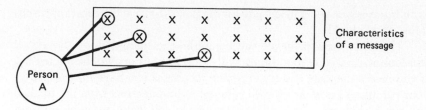

Figure 2.2   One person abstracting.

ganizing, and interpreting of messages in ways that make sense to you or suit your purposes. It is essentially an unconscious activity, often dominated by learned habits. In this section it is our aim to make you conscious of some of our patterns of perception so that you can evaluate them in terms of how they affect communicative behavior.

First, there are so many cues in any communication situation that it is impossible to pay attention to all of them. Yet, any one of them can be a vital message to be interpreted. Examine the following list.

> *Nonverbal Communication Cues*
> appearance
> gestures
> facial expression
> posture
> movement
> voice quality
> eye contact
>
> *Verbal Communication Cues*
> words used
> way of organizing
> several ideas in one sentence
> way words are said

This is only a partial list, but it illustrates the number of cues that are available for your analysis at any one moment. We can complicate this even more by suggesting that ideas do not all get equal attention; you pay more attention to some than to others.

Since you cannot pay attention to all communication cues, or messages, you select some and leave more out. This process of selection is sometimes called *abstracting*. Figure 2.2 illustrates how this works. A person perceives a message (for example, a person, an idea, or a statement) but actually only sees or hears a few characteristics of that message. This means that the parts always represent the whole. It is important that

as an interviewer you concentrate on the parts that are the most representative and valuable.

The abstracting principle can be applied to many different levels. If
you look at a room, certain things will stand out; others will be neglected.
If you read a message and try to repeat it, unless you have memorized it,
your paraphrase is what you will remember and abstract from the total. If
you summarize an interview, your summary will leave out a lot of things
that actually were said and emphasize what you think were the key points.

The relevance of this principle to the interview is that everybody is
abstracting or selecting out those items that are most vital to them or that
make the most sense in their worlds. Consequently, when two people
hear the same message, they may hear some of the same characteristics,
but often they will focus on some different ones, too. Their experiences
are not identical and their definitions of the message are also not identical.
Therefore, one of the major communication lessons that you can learn is
to *expect differences in perception.* In order to do this, you have to overcome past habits. Since perceptions constitute realities, people assume
that if an experience is real to them, then it must be real for other people,
too. This is an assumption that must be overcome, and you can do it when
you realize how you shape what it is that you see or hear. In the abstracting process, people create their realities by choosing what they want to
focus on. This is not undesirable; in fact, it is inevitable. However, it is
important to recognize that people are *creating* different realities out of
the same materials. This point receives special emphasis because the
success of so many interviews hinges on whether or not the interviewer
discovers what the interviewee's perceptions really are.

Figure 2.3 illustrates graphically how two people can focus on the
"same" message, see or hear some features in common, but still focus on
some different characteristics, too. Focusing on the different characteristics naturally changes the perception and thus the reality of each.

One of the best ways of demonstrating this point is to show different
stimuli and identify what different people see. This can be fun, but it also
provides a valuable lesson. Figure 2.4, for example, has a number of lines

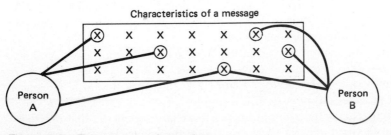

Figure 2.3   Two persons abstracting.

Figure 2.4   (Source: E. G. Boring, 1930 from Richard J. Gregory, *The Intelligent Eye* (New York: McGraw-Hill Book Company, 1970). Used with permission from the McGraw-Hill Book Company.

that make up a picture. Before you read further, identify what the picture looks like to you. When people see it for the first time, they perceive the lines as a woman. However, there is a great difference in their perceptions. Some see an old woman or a witch; others see a glamorous young woman dressed in stylish clothes. Which is it? Well, if you look closely, it can be either, depending on how you structure the lines. For most of us, it is difficult to keep changing our focus from an old woman to a young woman. This illustrates how difficult it is to change our perceptions after we have defined a situation. Note that the stimulus in this case is the pattern of the lines, but people organize them differently, so they actually see different pictures. This is an interpersonal perceptual problem. If we do this with pictures, how much more likely are we to do the same thing with verbal messages, where we have even greater latitude of interpretation? It has been demonstrated, for example, that the same answers on a test may be evaluated differently by different professors and that recruiters who hear the same interview will judge the person differently. In both instances, their measurements differ because their perceptions differ.

Why do we select, organize, and interpret communications as we do? There is no easy explanation to this, but it is a good question for each one of you to raise. Consequently, some of the most general influences are explored in the following pages.

Influences on Perception

Motives are one influence on perception. In the preceding discussion of motivation it was emphasized that people often see what they want to see and hear what they need to hear to fulfill their needs. Since motives influence perceptions greatly, it is almost impossible to talk about either motivation or perception without pointing out how powerfully they interact. For example, if I do not like you, I may have a need to keep your messages from agreeing with mine; consequently, I may receive a message from you and interpret it so that I "know" that you did not really mean what you said. In work situations it is commonplace to talk about an employee's need to misunderstand in order to protect the person's own self-image because the person would be uncomfortable if the messages were interpreted any other way. These are merely suggestions of how motives affect perception in detrimental ways. Motives can also facilitate perception in constructive ways. The need to understand and be understood may enable a person to look at situations from several different angles, for example, to see both the old woman and the young woman in Figure 2.4. The point is not that all perceptions are limited by a person's motives but that they *can* be; when they are, motivation is a powerful influence.

Past experience is another major influence on perception, because experience conditions people to make sense out of their worlds in certain ways. Over time this conditioning develops patterns. Since no two people have exactly the same past experiences, you can expect some differences in perceptions. For example, past experiences with interviewers will determine how people interact with you initially. If the experiences have been good, they may be receptive to you. If they have been bad, stressful, or a waste of time, the person will not be as open to your interview.

Frame of reference is another perceptual influence. We are all part of groups that have learned to perceive in certain ways. The optimists see a bottle as half full; the pessimists see it as half empty. Republicans tend to look at the role of government quite differently from Democrats. Management and labor differ in objectives and perceptions of one another. Therefore, your reference groups play an important role in affecting your perceptions.

Environments differ for most people, causing subtle differences in perception. Many interviews involve managers and subordinates, and here is where many differences can be pinpointed. While managers and subordinates nominally are in the same organization, their perspectives differ because they hold different positions in the organization, and, consequently, they are aware of different circumstances and influences. In sum, their environments actually differ. It has been demonstrated, for example, that in describing a subordinate's job, a boss and a subordinate may disagree on an average of 25 percent of the time. The two can communicate, but invariably their perspectives differ. A manager almost always has a more general perspective than the subordinate. For example, the subordinate may be basically concerned about the immediate work environment, but the manager may need to be concerned about coordinating several work units. In this sense they are operating in different environments.

Internal states also influence perceptions. The degree of emotional involvement is a powerful influence. Fear, for example, sometimes makes a person see things temporarily in shadows that are not really there. Anger or rage keeps a person from seeing things objectively. Apathy keeps a person from paying attention.

Mental sets influence perception because they allow for only one interpretation despite the evidence. These sets seem to be rigid or frozen interpretations. Sometimes the set can be general, such as always looking at things through "rose-colored glasses." At other times it can be very specific. The following example demonstrates a number of things about communication, but one of the most important things it demonstrates is the mental set of the manager. It has a blinding impact on the manager, and he was not open to other interpretations. Furthermore, it shows that sets have great longevity. In this case it took several days to woo the manager out of his interpretation.

> A new laboratory manager was assigned to head the systems engineering laboratory. A senior systems engineer, who had known the new manager only three months, wanted to impress him. Therefore, she went into the manager's office and said, "I have some time, since the job I have does not occupy me full time, and I could help you with some new assignments."
>
> The manager answered, "Oh, you have nothing to do?"
>
> The senior systems engineer hastily replied, "Yes, I do, but it doesn't occupy me full time."
>
> The manager then asked, "What are you charging your time to if you have nothing to do?"
>
> At this point, the senior systems engineer lost her temper, and an angry interaction occurred.

This example demonstrates quite clearly that the message sent was not necessarily the message received. Apparently, the culprit in this case is a mental set. Once the laboratory manager had defined the offer of help as "nothing to do," there was almost nothing that anyone could do to change his definition.

THINKING PATTERNS

There do seem to be consistent thinking patterns that evolve in each of us, and they affect the way we communicate. Some people, for example, handle concrete relationships very well but have difficulty with very abstract theoretical materials. Others have no trouble at all with the theoretical materials. Some get into habits of inductive reasoning; others use a deductive reasoning. All of these patterns have legitimate value; they are just different. Attention will now be turned to two rather common problems associated with the way people think, and it will be very relevant to your role in the interview as a measurer or an interpreter of communication.

Inferences and Observations

The first problem is confusing inferences with observations. There is often a failure to differentiate between the two. An *inference* is a mental leap—a statement or a conclusion made about the unknown on the basis of what is already known, whereas an *observation* is a verifiable experience through one of the five senses. Obviously, all reasoning involves an ability to make inferences, but there is a distinct advantage of knowing what you are doing when you make one. William V. Haney is the leading authority on this point, and his books and films have been used by thousands. Haney contrasts observations and inferences in the following way.[4]

Statements of Observation	Statements of Inference
1. can be made only *after* or *during* observation	1. can be made at any time
2. must stay with what one has observed and must not go beyond (I observed a man *wearing* a tie; his *buying* it, if he did so, was beyond my observation.)	2. can go well beyond observation to the limit of imagination
3. can be made only by the observer (The observational statements of another person are still my inferences, assuming that I have not observed what the person has.)	3. can be made by anyone
4. only *approach* certainty	4. involve degrees of probability

In order to determine whether or not you can distinguish between observation and inference, look at the following story and answer the questions following it. Read the story as often as you wish. Then for each of the statements about the story, circle the "T" if the statement is true, the "F" if it is false, or the "?" if you do not know whether it is true or false.

[4]Ibid., p. 222.

THE STORY

Barbara Record, a campus recruiter for the Pittsfield *Herald,* was filling out forms behind a desk when Pat came rushing into the room 10 minutes late for a prescreening interview. While reaching out to shake hands, Pat accidentally knocked an ashtray off the table. Apologizing, Pat explained that the coach had kept the team longer than usual. Barbara pointed across the desk to a chair for Pat to sit in and said, "Well, we better get started to make up for lost time." The total interview lasted 20 minutes.

1. Barbara Record was irritated by Pat's lateness.	T	F	?
2. The man who knocked the ashtray over was the job candidate.	T	F	?
3. Pat was late because the coach kept the team over-time.	T	F	?
4. Barbara is a campus recruiter.	T	F	?
5. Pat will not get the job because of a bad impression.	T	F	?

If you have answered all the questions, the correct answers may be instructive. You should have circled all with "?" except question 4. Question 1 should be "?" because the story does not say what Barbara's internal state was. Many people would be irritated, but Barbara may not be. The story does not describe Barbara's internal state. Question 2 should be "?" because the sex of the job candidate is never mentioned. Pat is a common name for males as well as females. Furthermore, female athletic teams are on the increase. Question 3 should be "?" because it involves hearsay. Pat *said* that the coach kept them overtime, but we do not know that this report is accurate. Many people give false excuses. Question 4 should be "T" because it restates specifically what is in the story. Question 5 should be "?" because it asks us to make a prediction that goes beyond what the story says. No one can observe the future.

This discussion reemphasizes that any statement that goes beyond what is actually known is an inference. Furthermore, certain kinds of statements are always statements of inference. Any statement about the future cannot be an observation; only inferences (predictions) can be made about the future. Any statement about a person's motivation is an inference; behavior can be observed, only inferences about motivation can be made from it. Finally, any statement that involves a second-hand report involves inferences that the person is *capable* of telling you the truth (review the discussion on perception) and is *willing* to tell you the truth (review the discussion on motivation).

Why can the confusion between inferences and observations be detrimental? First of all, inferences involve probabilities, so there is always a degree of risk of being wrong. Sometimes the risk is greater than at other times. At any rate, you will be on more solid ground if you calculate the risk of being wrong and be prepared. Second, inferences often allow the interviewer to fill in information that has not really been covered or stated. A recognition of the tendency to make inferences will encourage you to double-check information and not make important inferences unconsciously or haphazardly. This is why a summary is such a useful means of double-checking.

Discrimination Patterns

All people and events are unique in some important ways, and it is a healthy thinking pattern to concentrate on their uniqueness. Let us demonstrate now three ways in which the failure to discriminate leads to some problems.

First, there is often a tendency to lump people, events, or situations together because of their similarities. This is all right *unless it obscures any differences.* If you forget the possibility of uniqueness, then you are likely to stereotype people and situations. Our society is fighting a battle against stereotypes of *people* on the basis of race or sex, but there still is a tendency to stereotype *situations.* All situations are not alike, and you as the interviewer need to base your behavior on the differences among situations rather than on the similarities. The objective is to *discriminate among, not against.*

A second type of discrimination failure occurs when you do not recognize that people and things change over time. A time bound stereotype is a kind of frozen evaluation. To prevent this, some companies insist that each new appraisal must have a definite time frame; happenings previous to the time frame are not germane.

The third type of discrimination failure is to think only in terms of bipolar opposites. There are a lot of times when we find it easy to think in only two ways: agree-disagree; black-white; honest-dishonest; loyal-disloyal; or competent-incompetent. Often such bipolar fixations do not represent all the choices that really exist. For example, there are many degrees of agreement and disagreement. A person may be neutral or indecisive rather than in agreement or disagreement.

Defense of the Status Quo

One of the most frustrating thinking patterns is a closed mind. There are many people who apparently have a basic resistance to change. This resistance often takes the form of not wanting to explore the possibility that something new might work. The frustration that can occur between a proposer and a resister is demonstrated in the following example.

> On the first day of my new position in California, I called my assistant in to discuss several ideas that I had regarding changes in procedures, reports, and programs. It seemed that each time I would propose something, her response was, "That can't be done." Sometimes, she would say, "We tried that before, and it won't work." My reaction to this was to reply, "Nothing is impossible; it only takes a bit longer." I was very emphatic, and the interview ended on a somewhat emotional level. The next day my supervisor called me in to state that my assistant's husband had called him to inform him that he did not appreciate "the new tornado in the office" giving his wife "a hard time."

We can see from this example just how emotional resistance can become.

To a certain extent, perhaps all of us have some resistance to new ideas. Furthermore, an idea is not necessarily good because it is new. On the other hand, communication thrives on mutual exploration of ideas. Ultimately, you may reject an idea, but it is useful from a communication point of view to at least listen to what the other person wishes to say. In other words, openness as a thinking pattern facilitates interpersonal communication.

LANGUAGE EXPERTISE

Language problems are the ones encountered most frequently in interviews. The two people involved use a common language, but the meanings associated with that language are often quite different. Examples like the following are legion.

> During a budget meeting with my supervisor and district managers, the supervisor outlined a zero-based budget format to be used by both the operating and staff functions. This format was discussed by all parties, and it was agreed that we would follow the method. There were ten individuals at this meeting who would carry this information back to their offices and implement the system.
>
> The first budget was submitted, and no two of the budget formats were the same. My own budget did meet the supervisor's expectations, but only because my job location was next to his and I could ask him questions.

This example highlights the fact that people often bypass each other with their messages and also that feedback can be very beneficial.

In order to overcome some of the problems with language we need to make several important points. We will start with the following principle:

| Message ≠ Meaning |

1. Discriminate between message and meaning; they are not the same even though the words are sometimes used interchangeably. There is always something physical about the message, for example, type on a page or air waves. These exist outside the body and can be sent from place to place.

2. Meanings, on the other hand, are inside people. They are the interpretations of the message. Communication is most effective when two people have similar meanings associated with a common message, but you can never send your meaning somewhere else. You send messages that are constructed in such a way that you try to *elicit* a similar meaning within the other person.

3. Meanings are learned through experience. There is no inherent connection between a word and its meaning. In order to demonstrate this, we need to list only one word from a foreign language. Lets take the German word "pferd," for example. Anyone who knows German will know that this word means "horse"; anyone who does not know German would not know what is meant because he or she has not *learned* to make the connection between the word and the object. This point is obvious when we talk about foreign languages, but it is so easy to forget when we are using a native language. People come to expect that everyone uses language in the same way, but experience teaches us that they do not.

The fact that meanings are learned also has other implications. If they are learned, they change over time. Consider what has happened to the word "cool" in the United States. Further, people may learn *many* meanings for the same word. Consider the number of different ways in which "communication" has been defined. Consequently, you should not assume that a word has only one meaning.

4. The communication problem that frequently occurs when people forget that we do not all have the same meaning for a given word is *bypassing*. We think that we mean the same thing because we share common messages or words, but we do not and this causes problems. In fact, *one of the greatest communication lessons that you can learn is that you do not have control over how others interpret your messages.*

5. The potential for this bypassing problem existing is one of the soundest reasons for getting feedback to your messages. Regardless of how clear you think your messages are, check them with the other person. Clarity is not a characteristic of a message; it is determined by the receiver's interpretation.

6. Giving feedback readily is also desirable because not only do you realize that others misunderstand you, but you realize that you also may be misinterpreting what someone else means.

7. Finally, it is possible to bypass not only in terms of words but also in terms of the way messages are conveyed. For example, a supervisor reports that his superior has told him how to select new electronic technicians. One of the requirements is to score above 50 on a test. However, the superior "did this verbally and appeared very casual and indifferent in what he was saying." After interviewing a person who had a score of only 35 on the test, the supervisor liked the candidate's answers and decided to hire her anyway. The supervisor told us what happened then: "As I

casually mentioned this to my boss, he hit the roof and reprimanded me for ignoring his specific instructions. He concluded by saying that he meant what he said. I had been misled by the mood in which he gave the instructions."

Such problems as just described happen more frequently than we care to admit. Therefore, you can make progress if you come to expect differences in interpretations, just as you should come to expect differences in perceptions.

BIAS

No discussion of communication filtering in an interview would be complete without a discussion of bias, because it certainly shapes how people react to messages and how people measure information and other people. Kahn and Cannell define bias as "any *unplanned* or *unwanted* influence in the interview."[5] Generally, bias can be described as having a systematic influence on the communicators. It can stem from fixed attitudes, mental sets for perceiving the world, expectations, motivations, reactions to certain language, or certain patterns of making inferences. It is important that you differentiate between bias and judgment because some would claim that anytime you make up your mind you are biased. Remember that judgment involves a critical examination of something; bias is an unwanted, systematic error that leads to dysfunctional interviewing behavior.

Kahn and Cannell offer the following model of bias in Figure 2.5. The background characteristics of both the interviewer and the respondent are important because they affect the general filtering system of the communicators; they determine how a person learns to filter. The psychological factors are important because they are the mediating patterns that determine behavior. Finally, the behavioral factors are important because they determine the actual content and relationships within the interview. Much of the remainder of this book will focus on ways of overcoming some of the errors in behavior.

The greatest means of alleviating bias is to be aware of how it might occur.

> What does the interviewer require in order to function effectively and without bias? We have answered this question by saying that he requires techniques for question formulation, for inducing respondent motivation, and for focusing the communication on the content objectives of the interview. We believe, however, that the interviewer needs also a deep understanding and insight into the dynamics of the interaction process of which he is a part. The

[5]Robert L. Kahn and Charles F. Cannell, *Dynamics of Interviewing* (New York: John Wiley & Sons, Inc., 1963), p. 176.

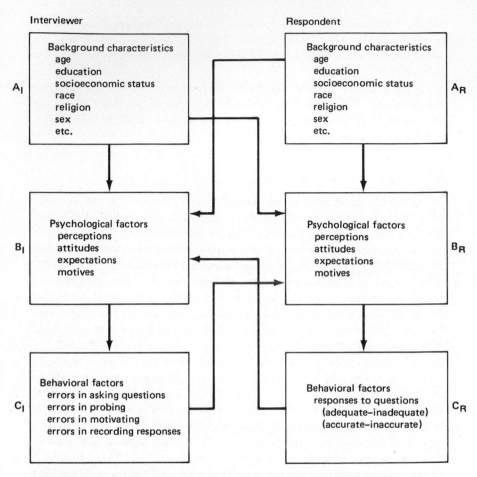

Figure 2.5 Sources of bias. (Source: Robert Kahn and Charles Cannell, *Dynamics of Interviewing*, p. 194, Copyright © 1963 John Wiley & Sons, Inc. Reprinted by permission of John Wiley & Sons, Inc.)

interview process itself is complex, and each case sufficiently idiosyncratic so that no set of rules and procedures will suffice unless the interviewer has such insight into the psychology of the interaction.[6]

ATTITUDES

Attitudes comprise one of the most important filters, both in terms of shaping messages to be sent and in interpreting the messages from other people. There are four attitudes that are particularly relevant.

First, attitude toward the other person is very important. There are

[6]Ibid., p. 202.

some people whom you like and others whom you dislike, and your attitude determines to a great extent how much time and energy you are willing to expend on the interview. You tend to devote more time and energy to those about whom you have a favorable attitude. Sometimes it also determines how much you say in the interview. In order to demonstrate the working of attitudes, we asked many managers if they ever had to communicate with someone when they hoped that the other person would fail. Generally, they were reluctant at first to admit it, but most of them recount experiences where this was true. Then we asked how this attitude shaped their behavior, and they listed such things as cutting the communication short, leaving important details out, not listening to the person, or not being patient. But when attitudes were favorable, they would go to extraordinary lengths to make certain that the messages were understood, and they also devoted more time to the communication.

From a receiving point of view, you may need to recognize that the interviewee's attitude toward you may inhibit communication. People have difficulty accepting ideas from someone whom they dislike, distrust, or oppose. Sometimes in a work situation you may need to ask yourself whether or not you are the best person to conduct an interview with the interviewee. You may not be (in terms of securing acceptance of the message). In such cases, if there is a legitimate alternative, use it.

Second, attitudes toward the message influence your behavior. When you like or support the content of a message, you may demonstrate this enthusiasm in expressing the message. When you dislike or do not support the message, you are likely to pass the buck or show by your behavior that you do not believe it. Some people even invite the other person not to believe the message with an attitude of "I don't want to tell you this, but. . . ."

Similarly, it works the same way for an interviewee. The interviewee will accept some messages and reject others because of his or her attitudes toward the content. This is why criticism is often so difficult to take. If you are planning an information giving interview, one of the best things you can consider is, "How will the interviewee feel toward this message?" Your answer to this question may dictate the strategies you will choose to complete the interview successfully.

Third, attitudes toward personal, face-to-face communication are a factor. Some people enjoy oral communication, but others would much prefer impersonal writing. It is our hope that your experiences with this book will enable you to enter into these interviews with confidence and with positive attitudes. Your interviewees, however, may still be nervous. Recognizing this will help you to do things within the interview that may make them appreciate the experience more.

Finally, attitude toward self is a very great filter in communication. It shapes a lot of communication behavior. When you are confident, it shows by your enthusiasm and your manner of expression. On the other hand, when you are not self-confident, you may experience anxiety in trying to articulate your ideas. From a receiving point of view, you may select out of your environment those messages that tend to reinforce your current self-image. Anybody can find some kind of information that contradicts any criticism that is received. In such a case the person would find himself or herself disregarding any messages that are not supportive. Unfortunately, this attitude often causes people to filter out information that could have great utility for them, both in terms of productivity and in relationships. Therefore, it may be useful simply to ask yourself, "How am I doing as a communicator?" and "How would others rate me as a communicator?"

MEMORY

Abstracting is a continuous communication phenomenon that is highly dependent upon your ability to remember. The farther you get away from an event, the more things you will forget about it and the more you will focus your recall on just a few items. Thus, memory is an important part of your personal filtering. Because interviewees are bombarded with lots of information, both verbal and nonverbal, they need some means of facilitating accurate memory.

The most common way to remember is to take notes during an interview. This practice helps document your immediate perceptions of important points, and frequently a review of your notes will call to mind things that were quickly forgotten at the end of the interview. Thus, notes—particularly verbatim comments—can be invaluable in remembering. The major liability in taking notes concerns their impact upon the interaction between the interviewer and the interviewee. As the interviewer, you may find that taking copious notes sometimes inhibits the flow of communication, and you may need to change your pattern. Furthermore, interviewees are often curious about what you are writing and may even request to see it.

A second means of remembering is to eliminate note-taking during the interview and to write out a comprehensive summary immediately after the interview is finished. This is a technique used by many recruiters. How well this succeeds depends upon your ability to discipline your listening and your ability to retain important points. By all means, if you use this method, force yourself to complete the summary immediately after each interview. Sometimes, interviewers who are rushed put it off until later, often with disastrous results.

A third way is to tape-record the interview, provided that the interviewee is consulted and agrees. This might be particularly important in training, as you seek to improve your techniques, or in counseling, where you want to return to analyze the interaction in depth. We have also used it in conducting focus groups because we wanted verbatim comments and it would have been impossible to write them all down during the interview. The great liability, however, for taping interviews is that it takes as long to listen to them afterwards as it does to conduct the interview. Therefore, it is limited by time considerations.

The final means of stirring the memory is to have a second person interview with you. A discussion between the two of you is likely to call to mind most of the important things, and you can test for agreement in your assessments.

These four ways are merely options that you have, and you will need to determine which works best for you. In order to make this choice, however, you may wish to experiment with something other than the method you have been using. On the other hand, if your current method works well for you, stick with it.

THIS CHAPTER IN PERSPECTIVE

Whenever you receive information, you are not merely a passive recipient. On the contrary, you are very active in sorting out, arranging, organizing, and interpreting what you hear. For this reason, people operate as communication filters; that is, they keep some things out and let other things in. In this chapter eight aspects of your filtering have been identified and discussed:

> purposes
> motivations
> perceptions
> thinking patterns
> language expertise
> bias
> attitudes
> memory

Obviously, there are other factors that influence your communication behavior, but these are ones that have the greatest impact. In discussing each of these factors, we have found it impossible to apply them in all the different ways that they can be applied to the various types of interviews. Instead, we have made you aware of them so that you can be aware of how they influence you.

Finally, these eight factors play a major role in your interpreting and measuring information. They explain what you do with information when you receive it. Therefore, they need to be taken into account as you plan your strategies and control your specific interviews. Then you will be in a better position to judge your own filtering behaviors and modify, or compensate for, them whenever necessary. When you control an interview, perhaps the most basic rule to remember is to analyze your own communication behavior and to control yourself.

PROJECTS

1. There are a great many pictures that have been used to demonstrate how people perceive the same picture in different ways. Make a collection of them. Then discuss with others the validity of the points that they make.

2. Identify your own chief motivations. Review the discussion of motivation in this chapter and discuss how you might fit into either of these analyses. Recall some incidents that have demonstrated this motivation in you.

3. To what extent is the notion of *filtering* a useful communication concept? Is it inevitable? If so, why should people be concerned with it?

4. Have several ten-minute conversations with someone in which you explore different ways of taking notes. Find out which one works best for you. How did each one affect the interaction with the other person?

5. Look at a transcript of an interview and try to identify all the examples that you can in which filtering is taking place between the interviewer and the interviewee.

6. Collect several actual examples of bypassing. Try to determine why it happened. What could have been done to circumvent it?

7. "Bias" is a very abstract word that has many evaluative connotations. Frequently, someone will say that you are biased just because they disagree with your conclusion. Do an in-depth study of this concept, trying first to list other people's definitions and then to mold your own.

Chapter 3
Planning Strategies

PART I

An interviewer can be a strategist, that is, make skillful plans before the interaction that will maximize the chances of achieving the desired results. This is not meant to imply that an interviewer can or should anticipate everything that is going to happen in an interview, try to be Machiavellian, or play the role of an amateur psychologist. It does stress, however, that careful planning sets the interviewer on a definite course and makes her or him more aware of options. The interviewer then becomes a better master of the situation.

In general, there are six broad areas of strategy that can be used in most interviews. The first three are covered in detail in this chapter, and the last three are discussed in detail in Chapter 4.

1. State your purpose(s) as explicitly as possible.
2. Prepare an agenda.
3. Identify the best approach to raising questions and formulate some tentative questions.
4. Structure the interview.
5. Plan the physical setting.
6. Anticipate problems.

STATING YOUR PURPOSE

Have you ever been so troubled by something that you just needed to talk to a certain person about it? You did not know exactly what you wanted to accomplish, but you felt something would be accomplished. Well, that is the way a lot of people have approached interviewing. It is not something they planned; it is something they just did. Frequently, they felt indefinite or uneasy about what really had been accomplished.

Before you start an interview, it is wise to set some definite objectives. Ask yourself what your purpose is. What do you want to be the results of the interview in terms of (1) the content and (2) the relationship with the other person?

Often there is a need to set several objectives and to refine them because the way they are stated can influence the way you behave. For example, we have used the same role playing situation with hundreds of practicing managers who must deal with a given problem with a subordinate. Many of them will define their purposes in terms of counseling the employee; others will define it in terms of discipline. The important point to be stressed is that both groups behave quite differently toward the subordinate and that the content of the interviews differ drastically between the two groups. The way the problem was defined dictated the kinds of solutions the managers had. This example reinforces the importance of deciding exactly what you are trying to accomplish.

Furthermore, you should not let general labels inhibit you. Sometimes terms like "selection," "information getting," "sales," "counseling," and "appraisal" actually get in the way. There is a tendency to feel that once you have identified your general purpose, everything else will fall in line. This is not necessarily true. There can be many specific purposes associated with each of them, and these need to be identified as concretely as possible. If you are going to review someone's performance, for example, it may be helpful for you to balance negative with positive comments. Unless you identify this as a purpose, you may forget to do it.

PREPARING AN AGENDA

The specific task related purpose usually demands that each interview explore certain specific content areas. These areas will form your agenda for the interview. The exactness with which an agenda can be prepared will vary greatly from interview to interview, but it is very important that you think about the kinds of information that must be exchanged in order to meet your purposes.

In some cases, preparing an agenda may involve a lot of background research. The manager who is going to talk with a subordinate about absenteeism may profit from a little research about absenteeism. She or he could talk with other supervisors, read some professional literature, and also review her or his own hunches as to why people are absent. Experience has shown that just asking someone "Why have you been absent?" may not get reliable information. The manager who has done some homework is in a much better position, because the manager knows several reasons why people tend to be absent and can probe every one if necessary. Similarly, the professional journalist will be so thoroughly grounded in a topic that she or he often will know as much about it as the person being interviewed. In other words, well-prepared agendas can yield excellent interviews.

At the same time, however, agendas need not be set in concrete. They can be modified. A common practice is to identify certain topics to be covered but have no preference as to order. We have done this with focused groups and attitude surveys. Nonetheless, you ought to assess the priority for each type of topic so that you can make certain that the ones you have given the highest priority will certainly be covered.

RAISING QUESTIONS

Questions are basic to most interviews, whether you are conducting a survey, selecting an employee, evaluating a worker, making a sale, or collecting information for a newspaper story. Consequently, the ability to use questions *effectively* is a key communication skill you should cultivate constantly.

There is a great difference between (1) merely asking questions and (2) making questions work for you effectively. Anybody can ask questions; it is an easy activity. Unfortunately, the problem with many questions is that they often elicit answers that cannot be used because the questioning techniques are not very refined. The following discussion highlights some of the subtle considerations that can make a real difference in the way questions are asked. Basically, the criteria for evaluating questioning techniques are three: (1) How does it affect the respondent emotionally and psychologically? (2) How does it affect your relationship? (3) Does it give you the kind of response for which you are looking?

1. *Decide on the response you want; then frame the question.* Some people often put the cart before the horse. They frame a question that they like and do not consider the kind of response it might bring. Remember that the primary reason for asking a question is to get a response that is usable to you in some way. This thought should under ie all other decisions you will make concerning asking questions.

2. *Plan preliminary questions to cover the entire range of your agenda.* To many interviewers this seems obvious. For example, such careful planning is standard operating procedure for any survey research. Planning also can be useful in preparation for any interview, and it ac-

complishes two things: (a) the individual interview is likely to be better, and (b) planning elevates questioning techniques to such a conscious level that the interviewer becomes more aware of what he or she is doing.

We have already focused on the necessity of identifying purposes and planning an agenda. This guideline is just another way of saying that the questions need to be such that all agenda items are covered. It would be useful to make a list of topics on the left and write out the questions pertinent to each topic on the right.

Planned Topic	*Question*
1. Background	1. What were the greatest influences on you as you grew up?

3. *Refine the wording of each question.* The way a question is phrased has a tremendous impact upon the way an interviewee answers. Your techniques can be improved by keeping the following points in mind.

a. The words must be understandable to the interviewee. Most interviewers would never intentionally ask a question that the interviewee does not understand; nevertheless, sometimes they do so unintentionally with negative results. What happens when certain words in the question are not clear? Generally, two kinds of problems are created. There is a *communication* problem, because a person cannot really answer a question that has not been understood. Many people will not ask what a word means because it suggests ignorance on their part. Lack of clarity also creates a *motivational* problem. A person tends to avoid risky situations, and there is a risk of exposing his or her lack of understanding. Consequently, many people in this situation will try to change the subject, leave the interview physically if they can, or bluff their way through. None of these alternatives gives the interviewer what is wanted most— valid information.

Knowing the potential problems should stimulate you to make the effort necessary for making your questions understandable. Some methods that can be effective are the following:

1. Tailor the question to the individual's vocabulary and depth of understanding.
2. Pretest the question on other people to see what kinds of interpretations they give.
3. Set the climate so that the person will not be defensive and will feel free to ask clarifying questions.

For example, suppose you were interviewing a manager about her interviewing behaviors in her exit interviews. (Experience has taught us that some managers think of dismissal interviews as exit interviews.) If you want to avoid the possibility that she may talk about a dismissal

interview, you might ask, "Would you describe how you personally conduct exit interviews? By exit interview, I'm referring to the final interview
you have with employees who have decided to leave the organization
voluntarily." Make it a practice to define key terms.

b. Be sensitive to the possibility that you might inadvertently load a
question in favor of a particular response by using highly evaluative
words. Students often raise the following question with their professors:
"Am I going to miss anything important by being absent tomorrow?"
There are certainly better ways of asking this question so that a teacher
will think that what he or she is presenting on any given day will be
important. Similarly, the researcher would be tilting the scale if he or she
asked someone how they felt about foreigners taking over so many American banks. "Taking over" is not a neutral concept. In the same way a
manager would not be wise in asking a subordinate, "How is the department reacting to the radical new demands by the union?" or "What have
been the employees' reactions to the burdensome increase in social security taxes?" since the inadvertent use of the word "radical" or "burdensome" is likely to influence the answers.

c. When consistency or tabulation is important, you should ask each
interviewee the same questions in the same way. In other words, be
careful about paraphrasing. It might be a good communication strategy to
adapt to the receiver most of the time, but here is an exception.
Whenever you begin to paraphrase or change the words, the actual content of the question may be changed. Therefore, different interviewees
would not be answering identical questions. It is not often that such rigor
must be used, but it will be important anytime that answers are to be
tabulated or compared.

d. The wording of the question also dictates the subjectivity of response that you are going to get. There are three questions listed below
that at first glance may appear to be asking for the same information. See
if you can pick out the subtle differences.

1. What does your co-worker do that upsets you?
2. What is it about your co-worker that you do not like?
3. What causes the friction between you and your co-worker?

We are not asking you to suggest which of these questions is best but
to point out two areas of difference. First, there is a difference in how
much of the relationship is included. Questions 1 and 2 seem to point to
the co-worker as the cause of the problem, whereas Question 3 includes
both "you and your co-worker" in the problem. Second, there is a subtle
difference in the kind of information requested in Questions 1 and 2.
Question 1 is asking for concrete, verifiable behaviors. If the respondent
says, "She's the most offensive person I've ever known," he has not
answered the question because he has not related how the co-worker

actually behaves. On the other hand, Question 2 leaves room for feelings as well as facts in the answer. Whereas Question 1 seems to ask for objective information, Questions 2 and 3 allow the interviewee to answer in either subjective or objective terms. This distinction is an important one to keep in mind as you evaluate whether or not interviewees have actually answered the questions they have been asked.

4. *Determine the scope and the depth of response that you need.* This is done primarily by selecting between *open* and *closed questions.* Because this is the most important decision you will make about your questions, we shall dwell at length on the nature and implications of them.

Open questions ask for broad or general information; they put few restrictions on how the interviewee might answer. The following are some examples of open questions.

> Tell me about yourself.
> What were your most memorable experiences on your first job?
> How do you feel about the neutron bomb?
> How would you evaluate the local newspaper?
> What kind of working relationship did you have with your co-workers?
> What kinds of differences, if any, has moving around a lot made in your life?
> In what ways do you think we could curb inflation?
> How have you been able to use the information from the supervisory training last year?
> What is your reaction to this commercial (or article or statement)?

Such open questions have a great value in many circumstances.

a. They help you discover the interviewee's *priorities.* You might assume, for example, that whatever the interviewee begins to say in response to "Tell me about yourself" will reflect what the interviewee feels is most important or significant about herself, or himself.

b. They help you discover the interviewee's *frame of reference.* In answer to the question, "How would you evaluate the local newspaper?" the interviewee is likely to talk about parts of the newspaper in comparison to similar parts of other newspapers with which he or she is familiar. The interviewee will also identify certain criteria used in the evaluation. Therefore, this answer may reveal his or her frame of reference in terms of parts of the newspaper, other newspaper experiences, and criteria used in judgment.

c. They often give *recognition* to the interviewee and satisfy a communication need by letting the individual talk through his or her ideas while you listen. Most people react well to someone who shows an interest in what they have to say. There are few things more frustrating than not being allowed to complete a story you want to tell.

d. They tend to be *easy to answer* and pose little ego threat. Furthermore, there is little risk of the interviewee being wrong because there are usually no right or wrong answers. When you ask "What is your reaction to this commercial?" the interviewee may ultimately disagree with you, but there is no rightness or wrongness in such opinions.

e. By definition open questions give the interviewee the *freedom to structure an answer* as he or she wishes. Therefore, with an open question you do not structure the answer in terms of your own vocabulary or idea of the chronology of events. This has the distinct advantage of permitting the interviewee to volunteer information about which you might never think of asking.

f. They *encourage catharsis*. The interviewee can only get things "off his (or her) chest" if the interviewee is allowed to talk about them, at length if necessary. If you determine that catharsis is productive—and it may not always be—then open questions will facilitate it.

g. They *reveal the interviewee's emotional state* as well as the facts present in the answer. For example, in selection interviews the specific experiences a person has had may often be less important than the perspective the person has about those experiences.

h. They reveal *how articulate a person is* and how well the person is able to think out loud or how much the person has thought about the topic. In selection interviews, for example, it may be very important to make this assessment.

i. They reveal the *depth of a person's knowledge* and perhaps how certain the person is about this knowledge. Anyone can be against inflation, for example, but if a person begins to support ways of curbing it, he or she will automatically reveal his or her level of knowledge about economics.

Open questions also have some distinct limitations.

a. They consume a lot of your time and energy. In some cases you may feel that the time is warranted; in others, you may feel it is wasted. For example, a journalist who knows exactly what information she or he needs may feel that long answers lack merit.

b. They may make it more difficult to control the interview. Some interviewers are reluctant to cut off an interviewee even when there is a digression, because they feel that the break might inhibit the interviewee later.

c. Recording and tabulating answers is more difficult. This is particularly true if the answers are long, rambling, or sometimes seem to be contradictory. For example, suppose we ask a person the question, "How do you feel about the neutron bomb?" Person A answers, "I try not to think about it because it is too terrible. Anything that kills people without destroying property puts the emphasis on the wrong side. Nevertheless, if the defenses in Europe need to be strengthened, as the reports indicate, I suspect that we'll develop it. It's a tough problem." How would you code this answer? Does it support its use strategically? Is person A against it altogether? You would not know yet. To code this answer you would have to obtain more information and get person A to make some choices because the answer as it stands has not given a clear decision.

d. Open questions make it difficult to verify results when more than one interviewer is used. Different interviewers may interpret the answers with somewhat different emphasis.

e. Interviewees often are uncertain as to how much detail is wanted. Consequently, they feel inhibited about covering much territory.

Closed questions, in contrast to open questions, are very specific and frequently restrict the options available to the interviewee. There are three types of closed questions that can be identified. The most extreme form of a closed question is the *multiple-choice question* so often used on academic tests, public-opinion surveys, and application forms. In this type of question, all the alternatives are listed, and the interviewee simply checks one. Several examples follow.

How much do you earn a year?	*Of which party are you a member?*
_____ $5,000	_____ Republican
_____ $5,000–10,000	_____ Democrat
_____ $10,001–20,000	_____ Independent
_____ $20,001–30,000	_____ American
_____ $30,000 +	_____ Prohibition
	_____ Socialist
	_____ Other

How satisfied are you in your job?

Satisfied <u>1</u>   <u>2</u>   <u>3</u>   <u>4</u>   <u>5</u> Dissatisfied

If you voted "no" on the recent bond issue for X, which of the follow-ing influenced your vote?

_____ X is not a high priority with me.
_____ I did not like the specific proposal.
_____ I was influenced by the newspaper reports.
_____ There has got to be a stop somewhere.
_____ I do not trust the people associated with X.
_____ Other _____.

Second, there are many closed questions that can be categorized as *bipolar;* that is, two options are built into the question itself. The most common form of this type of question is the Yes-No option. Examples are given below.

Did you vote in the last election?
Did you take the medicine just as prescribed?

Did you find the training helpful in your job?
Did you report this to your supervisor?
Are you applying for other jobs?
Do you mind working weekends?

Another common form of bipolar question that is often misused is illustrated by the following examples. It is misused when it does not represent all the options.

Do you agree or disagree with President Carter's energy proposals?
Do you favor or oppose passing the bond issues?
Would you rather work alone or in a group?
Do you experience more pain here or there?

The third type of question is one in which the interviewer searches for a specific answer and may not be aware of all the options, yet only one answer is correct.

Where did you go to college?
How old are you?
How long have you been in this job?
When did you have your prescription changed?
How often do you listen to a radio news broadcast?
When did the conflict first begin?

Closed questions have particular merit under the following conditions: (1) when you want to save time and energy (and money), (2) when you want to maximize your control over the interview, (3) when you know exactly what information you want, (4) when classification and tabulation of results is more important than the amount or the depth of information, (5) when you are dealing with a crew of interviewers who need training, (6) when you are trying to help a person reconstruct an event, (7) when the interviewee is shy and reluctant to talk, (8) when you have many questions that must be asked in a few minutes, and (9) when the answer does not require an explanation.

On the other hand, closed questions also have limitations. First, the amount of information that can be obtained is limited. For example, you cannot ascertain how much information the interviewee has or how strongly he or she feels about it, or what the interviewee's frame of reference for the answer is. Second, closed questions sometimes thwart an interviewee's need to explain or to talk about the answers. Therefore, the interview may not be a satisfying communication experience. Sometimes witnesses in court, for example, are extremely frustrated because they are asked to answer "yes" or "no" when they would like to supply a lot of information to help interpret the answer. Third, falsification is easy. It is sometimes possible to check out some answers by asking additional questions, but it may be impossible to check out others. For example, if someone asks you whether you agree or disagree with the president's energy proposals, you need not even know what those proposals are in order to give an answer. You can merely agree or disagree with the president.

Now that we have given a brief overview of both open and closed questions, we must reemphasize that whichever form you use should depend upon the kind of information that you desire. Neither form is inherently preferable to the other. In fact, they can often be quite complementary. The following example from a job performance review illustrates this point:

> INTERVIEWER: Have you found the supervisory training seminar to be useful to you in your job? (closed)
> INTERVIEWEE: Yes, I have. In a lot of ways.
> INTERVIEWER: In what ways? (open)
> INTERVIEWEE: Well, it made me think about some things I'd never thought about. For example, I'd never given much consideration to giving positive feedback to my subordinates. Now I make a special effort to recognize their achievements.
> INTERVIEWER: Has this changed the way in which they respond to you? (closed)
> INTERVIEWEE: Yes, I think the whole atmosphere is more congenial now.
> INTERVIEWER: Since you said that the training has been helpful in a lot of ways, can you tell me about some of the other ways? (open)

This example demonstrates that it is not always necessary to make a choice between open or closed questions. The best policy may be to have them work together.

5. *Determine whether the information can be obtained best through direct or indirect questions.* By far most of the questions that are asked in an interview tend to be rather direct. All of the illustrations used in the section on open and closed questions are quite direct. They ask the respondent exactly what the interviewer wants to know. With the direct question, we assume that the interviewee is both capable and willing to answer the question, and this assumption is probably correct most of the time. The direct approach, therefore, needs no greater justification and support. Indirect questions will be used less frequently, but under certain circumstances they may be very helpful. The following discussion illustrates three ways of developing indirect approaches.

a. You can permit the interviewee to camouflage a response. Suppose you were a member of a team auditing communications in a university and you want to ask the faculty, "How do you evaluate the dean as a communicator?" Many people will volunteer an answer. In some cases, however, faculty members may feel their security to be threatened. After all, they may not be certain that the dean will not hear of their response. If any nervousness is detected, you may choose to ask, "How would most people here evaluate the dean as a communicator?" The assumption is that individuals will still tend to answer the question in line with their personal feelings, but now they can answer the question with less fear because it is couched in terms of "most people." Many interviewers ask an indirect question in order to initiate the discussion and then try to turn the focus on the interviewee's direct response later.

b. Sometimes the information can be obtained indirectly through a test. A bank recruiter, for example, hires a lot of tellers, and one of the criteria useful in making selection decisions is how closely the applicant pays attention to detail. The rationale is that a teller needs to pay very close attention to exact numbers and decimal places. If she were to ask candidates directly, "How good are you at paying attention to detail?" most of the answers probably would be positive. The recruiter knows that people can tell how they *feel* about doing detail work, but they may not always know how well they *do* it. Consequently, the recruiter has a series of pictures that she asks the applicants to describe. Their responses demonstrate how much detail they notice. Such an indirect approach is used by counselors, psychologists, market analysts, advertisers, and focus groups, as well as recruiters.

c. How a person talks about a topic may be an indirect gauge of what the person actually thinks or feels. In Chapter 5 we will note that recruiters are interested in a person's level of confidence, enthusiasm, and oral communication skills. An analysis of actual transcripts shows that recruiters seldom ask, "How enthusiastic are you?" or "How much leadership ability do you have?" If they did, again the answers would be positive because the interviewees want jobs and there is a certain social acceptability associated with each of these traits. Rather, recruiters ask the interviewees to talk about themselves and their experiences. The answers actually demonstrate a level of confidence, enthusiasm, and communication skills. In such instances, this is a very useful but indirect means of assessing important characteristics.

In conclusion, we suggest that it might be useful for you to select some indirect means of obtaining the following information. For practice, change the direct form to an indirect form.

1. How do you feel about your boss? (attitude survey)
2. How honest are you? (selection)
3. Why do you feel this way? (counseling)
4. What can be done about X? (public opinion survey)
5. What hinders you most in your job? (performance review)

6. *Use a variety of questions.* It is amazing how frequently interviewers develop an apparent preference for one particular kind of question and

learn to depend on it almost exclusively. For example, some recruiters develop a bad habit of asking closed questions. While they may be appropriate for a telephone survey, this pattern is not useful at all for a selection interview.

It has been demonstrated already that open and closed questions can be used well to supplement one another. Varying the types of questions can help you obtain information of different types and also make for a more interesting and more fulfilling communication experience.

In building variety there is a particular type of question that is often underused. It is the hypothetical situation question. They are immensely useful because the answers to them usually are less abstract and deal with a very specific situation. They are the closest thing to actual job behavior that can be observed in an interview. An airline, for example, asks the following hypothetical situation question in selecting ticket agents: "Suppose that it is Christmas eve and the airport is packed with people. You've been working feverishly for five hours and there is still a line at your counter. All of a sudden, a woman with a small child runs up to the front of the line yelling loudly that she is about to miss her plane." In a job performance review, a boss wants to discover his subordinate's own supervisory orientation so he asks the following question: "Suppose you asked one of your subordinates to prepare a report for a particular meeting. A week later, just before the meeting, this subordinate rushes in and tells you that she just hasn't had time to finish the report and isn't prepared. How would you react?" Hypothetical questions are also frequently used in surveys to people so they can make choices: "If you could afford any car that you want, which one would you buy?" The Harris and Gallup polls periodically ask people to say how they would vote today if the current president were running for reelection against a prominent member of the opposite party. It is a way of testing public sentiment.

There is no guarantee that how people say they would respond in these situations is the way they would actually respond. Nevertheless, occasional use of hypothetical questions can enrich both the information you can obtain and make the interview a more pleasant experience.

7. *Keep the questions relevant to the purpose of the interview.* In the final analysis, purpose needs to guide what you do as an interviewer. Even the initial question "How are you today?" may not be as irrelevant as it might appear. To the physician or the counselor it would be central to the purpose of the interview, but in any other kind of interview it fulfills a purpose of building rapport or helping to establish a relationship.

In the personnel situation, we are in the process of dealing with the problem of relevance. We are moving toward addressing questions specifically related to job requirements. Legal guidelines help in getting interviewers to focus on the relevance of the questions asked. But aside from the legal aspect, it is merely good practice to tailor the questions to the purpose. If it accomplishes nothing else, it saves time and effort.

Relevancy, however, is not always an easy matter to decide. For example, a group of observers thought the question "What work does your father do?" was irrelevant in a selection interview. Maybe what the father actually does was irrelevant, but the observers failed to see how the interviewer was using it. The candidate had already admitted that he had had no work experience and was having difficulty talking about himself. When the interviewer asked this question, the candidate became more articulate because there was something concrete about which he could talk. So the question contributed something to the interview *process.* Furthermore, the man's answer led to some interesting follow-up questions regarding work related travel experiences that the interviewer probably would not have anticipated if the question had not been asked. This example shows how an apparently irrelevant question can be useful to the interviewing process. Not all are so valuable. In fact, there are many instances in which the irrelevancy of the question causes embarrassment or hinders the interview. For example, a nurse criticized the following practice among some medical professionals. Specifically, she described the embarrassment of a shy young man when he was asked about his sexual habits. There was no apparent connection between this question and the hernia problem he was having, and the result was some needless embarrassment.

Perhaps the most useful point to be made here is that too many interviewers develop a pat set of questions often borrowed from a list that they have seen somewhere. They grow comfortable asking them because they have asked them before and also lose sight of how they actually relate to their purposes.

COMMON PROBLEMS ASSOCIATED WITH ASKING QUESTIONS

The previous guidelines can be of immense help in framing good questions. Nevertheless, one of the best ways of overcoming certain problems is to focus directly on those problems. We have found it useful to call attention to the following pitfalls that commonly occur in all kinds of interviews.

Double-barreled Questions

The double-barreled question creates a common problem. In essence, it occurs when the interviewer asks two or more questions before the interviewee has had a chance to answer the first question. The following examples were taken from actual transcripts.

Example A
Tell me why you want to work for our bank and what you know about our bank.

In this case, neither question was answered fully, because the interviewee tried to handle both at once. Furthermore, the interviewer did not seem to know where to go with the two answers. She finally focused on one part of the question and never returned to the other.

Example B
What are the advantages and disadvantages of being a nurse?

The interviewer lumped the disadvantages with the advantages, and it seemed that the respondent was interested primarily in giving one of each in order to answer this question satisfactorily. These two areas would need to be completely separated in order to get a full discussion.

Example C
When did you first notice this feeling of depression? Was it before or after you took this new job? And what have you been doing to control it?

Taken separately, there is nothing wrong with any of the three questions. In fact, they may even follow well in this sequence. However, it would not be wise to ask the three together. Frequently, an interviewee will be confused or overlook one of them. Occasionally, the interviewee will see the problem and ask, "Which of these do you want me to answer first?"

Two-in-one Questions

Occasionally, an interviewer will connect two things in one question so that it will appear to be one question rather than actually two.

Example
How can we make our employees happier so they will be productive?

In the United States it is commonly assumed that there is a relationship between worker satisfaction and productivity, but our studies have not borne this out. For example, there are many workers who are very happy but who are not very productive. Consequently, the interviewer in this case is making an unwarranted assumption about the relationship between satisfaction and productivity.

Example
We're taking a neighborhood poll. How do you feel about the recent defeat of the bond issue and the failure to make Cleveland a more progressive city?

In this case, there is a strong value orientation connected with the bond issue. The interviewer apparently assumes that the bond issue was necessary for progress. Others may not agree. Therefore, this question, too, blends two questions together that might well be handled separately.

Bipolar Questions

Bipolar questions limit the interviewee to one of two choices. There are many occasions when it is entirely appropriate. However, it is misused when (1) there are in actuality more than two choices available, so the middle ground is neglected and (2) it reduces the answer to an over-simplification.

Example
Do you approve or disapprove of the new teacher contract?

If the purpose of this question is to make the interviewee give a general reaction, this question may do just that. However, it is useful to keep in mind that there are degrees of approval, and some people would like some aspects of the contract but dislike other aspects of it. Furthermore, there may be some who would be undecided or have no opinion yet. This closed question would not present them with these options. Consequently, you must be careful about using polarized alternatives such as agree or disagree, approve or disapprove, and yes or no. A good rule to keep in mind is to give interviewees as many options as possible. For example, "Are you a Republican or a Democrat?" is not a good question, because it leaves out many options that thousands of people have taken, such as the Prohibition, the Socialist, and the American parties. Furthermore, many have selected to remain independent of any party affiliation.

Leading Questions

A question becomes a leading question when it is phrased so that it is easier or more tempting for the interviewee to answer it in one way rather than another. Frequently, they include explicit or implicit references to the answer that the interviewer expects.

Of all the problems that we have discussed, this one is perhaps the most universal. While we expect that competent interviewers avoid using them, Stephan Richardson and his colleagues have found that "trained interviewers do in fact make considerable use of leading questions, despite the proscription in the interviewing literature. . . ."[1] Many writers urge interviewers to avoid leading questions altogether, but we do not take this position. We recognize that they are not very useful in securing valid, reliable data in any information getting interview, but there are many times when an interviewer chooses deliberately to use leading questions in order to produce stress, to sell a product, or to get reinforcement for an idea. Consequently, leading questions become a serious

[1]Stephan Richardson, et al., *Interviewing* (New York: Basic Books, Inc., Publishers, 1965), p. 184.

problem only when this interviewer does not know that he or she is in fact leading the interviewee to distort responses.

It is not always easy to take a question out of the context of the interview and identify it as leading or nonleading. Vocal inflection and what has gone on in the interview prior to it certainly can shape the interpretation. Nevertheless, the following are several methods by which respondents can be led.

IDENTIFICATION OF THE EXPECTED ANSWER

It is easy to give the interviewee an idea of what the appropriate response should be. Consider the recruiter who urged, "This job calls for a lot of travel. You don't mind traveling, do you?" Of course, the interviewee does not, if she or he wants the job. A subtler form of asking this question would be: "How do you feel about traveling in your job?"

A similar example occurs when questions are phrased in such a way that an answer would contradict the interviewer. For example, a boss might say, "Didn't you think that Mary's latest commercial was about the best we've had?" It would be difficult to disagree with this type of question, even among friends, and the chance that a subordinate would feel comfortable contradicting a boss with a "no" is very slim. After all, the boss has indicated that reinforcement is wanted, not a truthful opinion.

PRIOR STATEMENTS

Often the verbal comments made just before a question is asked can influence the way an interviewee answers.

Example

The president has recently come out in favor of deregulation of natural gas. Do you favor or oppose eliminating these controls and possibly increasing inflation?

Not only is this question a double-barreled question with loaded words such as "inflation" thrown in, but the initial comment runs a risk of leading the interviewee. Some people may know nothing about the gas market but have strong feelings about the president. Therefore, they may choose to answer on the basis of their sympathy—or lack of it—for the president.

EMOTIONALLY LOADED WORDS

The journalist who asks, "Would you favor or oppose the sending of our surplus wheat to feed the starving people of _____?" is likely to get a higher percentage of respondents who favor this idea than the pollster who asks it in a far more neutral form.

ASSOCIATING A RESPONSE WITH A DESIRABLE GOAL

Sometimes the questioner is looking for a way to make it difficult for a respondent to say "no" to a particular question. The association can occur implicitly, as in "You do want to get the most for your money, don't you?" or "Surely you would not want your child to suffer in school because she does not have this set of reference books." The important point of this discussion is that questions can, in fact, sell the interviewee on a given response. This is an extraordinary kind of control for an interviewer to have. In some cases an interviewer may want to exercise this kind of control skillfully. In many cases, however, interviewers hope to get honest opinions; in such cases they need to avoid any possibility of directing the interviewee's responses.

THIS CHAPTER IN PERSPECTIVE

This chapter discussed three of the six strategies that can be planned for an interview: the purpose, the agenda, and the preliminary questions. Basically, we have attempted to reinforce the idea that most interviewers could do more planning than they do. Furthermore, it has been suggested that planning is often related to effectiveness. While planning in terms of purpose and agenda is fairly obvious, the influence of the phrasing of questions has not always been that obvious to people. Therefore, it is particularly useful for you to spend more time experimenting with asking a question in different ways. You also might have someone else ask you a question in different ways in order to see how your own response is affected.

PROJECTS

1. Make a list of questions that you have heard in an interview or have seen in a transcript that should have been revised. Then revise them.

2. Observe several different kinds of interviews on television, such as an interview by Johnny Carson, a news interview by Barbara Walters, and an interview in some commercials. Pay particular attention to the questioning techniques. Were there ways in which they were loaded or leading?

3. How can questioning techniques affect the relationship between two individuals?

4. What is your own preference between open and closed questions? Why?

5. Take a question and practice changing it from an open question to a closed question. Then practice making it direct and indirect. The easier this is for you, the more flexibility you will have in an interview.

6. Think of times when you have been an interviewee. Compile a list of things about your interviewer's questions that you liked. Then make a list of the things that you did not like.

7. To what extent is it fair for you as an interviewer to manipulate an interviewee through subtle phrasing of questions?

Chapter 4
Planning Strategies

PART II

In the previous chapter we examined strategy in terms of purpose, agenda, and formulating questions. In this chapter our objective is to discuss those aspects that structure the content and the relationship between the interviewer and the interviewee. The three strategies that will be discussed include: (1) structuring the interview, (2) planning the physical setting, and (3) anticipating problems.

STRUCTURING THE INTERVIEW

Every interview has a basic framework. Even if the structure is not planned, it develops during the interaction. The exact structure that you build will depend upon the situation and the type of interview. In surveys, for example, the structure is often rigid. Sales interviews often follow a basic pattern that has been found to be effective. In employment interviews the structure may be tailored to fit the job. In journalistic, counseling, or medical interviews, each new interview may be unique. Even though you would not structure all of these interviews alike, there are some basic guidelines that should be considered.

The Introduction

No time is more crucial to the success of an interview than the first few minutes. This is the time to build whatever relationship is going to exist. Yet, frequently everything about the interview is carefully planned *except* the opening; what happens then is often left to chance, sometimes with mixed results. The opening can be planned generally, and it should be. The objective is to do whatever is necessary to motivate the interviewee to interact freely and accurately with you. The following guidelines are designed to accommodate this objective.

1. *Start with a realistic greeting.* This is the time when the basic interviewer-interviewee relationship is going to be established, and research has shown that people form their basic impressions of one another during the first few minutes of an interview.[1]

There is a certain significance about the word "realistic." It suggests that interviewers attempt to create different kinds of atmospheres for different kinds of interviews. For example, it is often desirable to create *rapport* with the interviewee during the opening. Rapport involves building a degree of comfortableness together, of trust in one another, and of basic goodwill that will permit nondefensive interaction. Rapport is particularly necessary when you interact with strangers; therefore, it is most appropriate in surveys and in medical, journalistic, and selection interviews. Furthermore, rapport may be particularly useful when the interviewee is in unfamiliar surroundings. The applicant who goes to a new company to apply for a job or the subordinate who is called into the boss's office is likely to experience some nervousness because the person is out of his or her own turf. Therefore, the interviewer can do some of the following things to allay nervousness and create rapport.

> self-introduction
> enthusiastic welcome through nonverbal messages (like a smile and a warm handshake)
> courteous offers of coffee or other refreshment
> informal, banal exchanges (about the weather, traffic, or current event)
> personal inquiry (such as "How are things going?")
> humor

Actually, rapport builds or wanes throughout the course of the interview. Since the kind of information given is related to how comfortable the interviewee is with the interviewer, it may take a long period of time or even another interview for the interviewee to open up.

Not everyone appreciates attempts to build rapport, however. One

---

[1]L. Qunin and N. Zunin, *Contact: The First Four Minutes* (Los Angeles, Nash Publishing Co., 1972), pp. 8–14.

person was given the following message in preparation for a survey interview that had been carefully arranged:

> Don _____ indicated to me that he wanted to get right to the point in the interview and not "waste time" with rhetoric designed to establish a constructive atmosphere.

The interviewer did not try to build rapport. He acknowledged the interviewee's request and told him that it was important that a brief orientation be given. After three minutes, the body of the interview was being covered. As this message would suggest, it is not always appropriate to make an elaborate effort at building rapport. In fact, there are times when it becomes quite dysfunctional. A great many mistakes have been made in this regard by supervisors, for example, who have scheduled an interview with an employee. The purpose is often to counsel, discipline, or dismiss, and the employee knows that something is wrong. Therefore, talking about the weather would be seen as irrelevant and "beating around the bush" and could actually increase, rather than decrease, anxiety, since the employee is waiting for the inevitable "bomb" to drop.

In conclusion, an interviewer should know the importance of rapport and how to build it, and perhaps it should become a natural thing to do. However, the interviewer should also know how to get to the point quickly in a very business-like way when the rapport stage is unnecessary or dysfunctional.

2. *Try to motivate the interviewee in specific ways.* Ask for help or assistance. This is a very common opening and works well because most people have a need to be needed. It is hard to turn down a sincere request.

Mention any rewards that may come as a result of the interview. Researchers offer monetary rewards or a copy of the results. Personnel representatives offer a position, and bosses often hold out a raise or a promotion. Sales representatives offer a premium of some kind for participation. The strategy works for all of them.

Make the interviewee feel important. You can refer to the importance of the person's position or the amount of influence that the person has. Another way of making the interviewee feel important is to emphasize the problem and the kind of impact the interviewee's answers can have. Simply stressing that his or her answers are unique is a way of making the person feel important.

Explain how the interviewee was selected. People are often very suspicious as to why they were chosen.

Refer to others who have participated or who have recommended that this particular interviewee be contacted. People tend to be more comfortable if they know that peers have also been involved. This is why a salesperson often drops names of others who have bought their products.

3. *Give the interviewee an orientation to the interview.* Generally, the interviewee should be given three pieces of information as part of the orientation. First, the interviewee should be told the purpose of the interview. This sets the course that the interview will follow, and generally people are more comfortable and cooperative when they know what to expect. Many people are suspicious or cautious in ambiguous situations. You can alleviate this problem by giving a clear orientation. This is helpful to the interviewer as well as to the interviewee. In training hundreds of interviewers, we have found that they need constant reminding of what the purpose actually is, and it is useful for them to be able to state it. Examine the following introduction.

> Jane, I wanted to talk to you today about a problem that has been reported to me. Let me explain it and how it was described to me and maybe you can shed some light on the situation, so we can get this cleared up. Yesterday your manager reported that you were disturbing another worker and when he said something about it to you, you gave him a lot of back talk—that you were insolent in front of all the other workers. Now what do you have to say for yourself?

Many managers when they looked at this introduction have picked out different emphases. There is a desire "to talk . . . about a problem," and the interviewee's ability to "shed some light" seems to imply that her input is being sought. The interviewer said that he was trying to get Jane's side of the story. However, most of the managers who looked at this introduction suggested that the last statement seems to show that Jane already has been indicted and that this statement is likely to produce a very defensive response. The point is that this last statement seems to negate the earlier statement of wanting to hear Jane's side. Furthermore, it colors everything that the interviewer has said up until then. This example demonstrates how careful you need to be in determining the purpose for your own benefit and how carefully this purpose needs to be stated to the interviewee.

Second, the interviewee should be told what his or her role will be in the interview. One of the most common ways this is done in a selection interview is to suggest, "I have a few questions that I'd like to ask you. Later in the interview I'll give you an opportunity to ask me some questions." Statements like these are helpful because they give a concrete definition to the relationship and alleviate any confusion of how the interviewee ought to operate. Another important item here is that they should know how much time the interview will take.

Third, the interviewee ought to be told how the information is going to be used. Specifically, the interviewee needs to know whether or not the information given is to remain confidential, in what form it is going to be reported, and what is likely to happen as a result of it. An interviewee needs this information in order to determine how much he or she wants to cooperate in giving you information. Sometimes, an interviewee may have a lot at stake. Perhaps, it is needless to suggest that whatever the interviewee is told in this regard should be honored.

Finally, the orientation should lead quite naturally into the main body of the interview.

The Body of the Interview

The body of the interview is where the main content is shared. It is the reason for the interview in the first place. To make it as beneficial as possible, three things affect the overall structure of the interview: (1) whether to use a directive or nondirective approach, (2) an outline of the topics to be covered, and (3) the sequence of the questions.

DIRECTIVE VERSUS NONDIRECTIVE APPROACH

The choice between a directive and nondirective approach reflects the basic interviewing style of the interviewer, and most types of interviews can be approached in either of these two ways. Each has a profound impact on the structure of the interview.

Basically, the directive style is rather straightforward and deductive in form. The interviewer knows exactly what he or she wants to cover and introduces the topics. The interviewer uses direct closed questions, and the interviewee may not have an opportunity to introduce other topics. This directive structure is most characteristic of standardized surveys, but it can apply to any type of interview.

The nondirective style, by contrast, is rather inductive in form. The interviewer may toss the lead to the interviewee and follow wherever he or she takes it. This is often used in counseling interviews and is one of Norman Maier's suggested forms for a job performance appraisal.[2] It is also the style that many supervisors try when problems come up. The rationale is that it decreases defensiveness when a client or a subordinate is the one to initiate the definition and discussion of a problem.

USE OF AN INTERVIEW GUIDE OR SCHEDULE

When the choice has already been made to be directive, an interview guide may be an important aid to the interviewer. Basically it is an outline listing all the topics and subtopics that the interviewer wants to cover in the interview. It comes in three forms: nonscheduled, highly scheduled, or moderately scheduled.

When the order or sequence of the topics is unimportant, the interview is frequently referred to as a *nonscheduled* interview. Attitude surveys and press conferences frequently are designed in this way, because

[2]Norman R. F. Maier, *The Appraisal Interview* (New York: John Wiley & Sons, Inc., 1963).

so much depends on what the interviewee actually says. Nonscheduled interviews give great flexibility or freedom in adapting to the particular respondent or the needs of the moment. They also permit the use of open questions and probing. Used by a skilled interviewer, the nonscheduled interview does not have any real disadvantages because it can be organized spontaneously. A problem does come up, however, when there are multiple interviewers and there is a need to pool or to replicate their findings. The very flexibility which they enjoyed then makes it difficult to tabulate their findings in exactly the same way. Answers do not always come out as a specific "yes," "no," or "maybe." Some researchers try to overcome this problem by taking verbatim comments that can be compared. These also add a bit of "spice" to any report.

Frequently, it is wise to plan not only the topics to be covered, but also the order in which they are to be covered. The most completely structured interview is called a *highly scheduled interview.* In its extreme form the interview outline is *standardized* so that it contains all of the questions and probes to be asked in the interview. They are asked in the same wording and in the same order for every respondent, and the answers are immediately recorded. This type of interview is particularly useful in public opinion polls, attitude surveys in companies, telephone surveys, and academic research.

Since many of the questions in a highly scheduled interview tend to be closed, the obvious advantage is that the answers will be easily tabulated and replication will be easy. Furthermore, an interviewer does not have to be particularly skilled to get results. The procedures for building these kinds of outlines have been thoroughly worked out, and the outlines do exactly what they are designed to do. They are, however, entirely inappropriate for most interviews other than polling, research, or surveys because of the rigorous measurement desired. They cannot be used with much success, for example, with a group of job candidates.

Fortunately, there are degrees of structure between the nonscheduled and the highly scheduled interview. Those interviews in between these two extremes are called *moderately scheduled* interviews, and they come in many varieties. Basically, the interview outline contains a list of the topics to be covered in a *suggested* order with possible probes for each. In some cases, it might be advisable to maximize interviewee participation at the very beginning by starting off with the easiest (least threatening) or the most recent topics. The rationale for starting with the least threatening material is that trust is more likely to grow during the interview so that the interviewee will be open then to respond to sensitive topics. If you begin with a threatening question, the interviewee is likely to balk and the interview will suffer. Therefore, the structuring of the interview is a way to ensure that you get answers to the more innocuous questions first.

We should point out that "it is difficult, if not impossible to develop a sequence of questions that will have the same emotional meaning for most respondents."[3] Consequently, putting the least threatening questions last will give you the ability to adapt to individual respondents. On the other hand, there may be a certain inherent relationship that dictates the order, such as (1) the time sequence, (2) the spatial relationship, (3) cause and effect, (4) parts of the whole, (5) problem solutions. Finally, the topics might be arranged in order of the interviewer's priorities in an attempt to allow the most time for the things that are the most important.

Even moderately scheduled interviews require some planning, and they are particularly useful as a training tool for beginning interviewers. If you can still remain flexible by using the outline as a tool rather than becoming a slave to it, then the detailed preparation can be of immense value. It combines the advantages of preparation and freedom to adapt to individuals and to probe broad topics with spontaneity.

Most of the time discussions of schedules focus on interviews that are going to be used with multiple interviewees. However, the same principle of planning can be very useful in preparing for a one-time interview with an individual. Whether you are involved in a job performance, discipline, or counseling interview, the basic question is still what sequence the topics ought to be in. It can make a real difference in the interviewee's reactions.

SEQUENCE OF QUESTIONS

In the last section we were concerned primarily with the overall organization of topics for the entire interview. We will now focus on the relationship within those parts. In other words, we will focus on the basic structural development for each subtopic.

• *Funnel Sequence.* The *funnel sequence* starts with the most general or broad questions at the top of the funnel, and each succeeding question narrows the focus and becomes more specific. All the questions may be open and the most open questions would come first. If closed questions are used, they would come at the bottom of the funnel. An example of the funnel sequence is given below.

Example A
What do you think are the most important problems facing the company? Of these, which do you feel is the most important? How does it affect you in your job?

This sequence was taken from an attitude survey that was planned to allow the interviewee a completely free rein in identifying problems. His

[3]Stephan Richardson et al., *Interviewing* (New York: Basic Books, Inc., Publishers, 1965), p. 44.

reply is likely to relate his general frame of reference about the company and also the kinds of things he sees as being problematic. Had the interviewer started with questions on specific topics, such as economic conditions, management decisions, or job security, the interviewer might have inadvertently structured the interviewee's thinking so that topics of real concern would be passed over.

Example B
Would you please tell the court what happened? Exactly how much of this did you see? What was the injured party doing? How fast would you say the defendant was driving? In your opinion could the accident have been prevented?

This sequence was taken from a legal interview about an accident. The interviewer asks the interviewee to give the overall context. Knowing that what happened may include hearsay, assumptions, opinions, and facts, the interviewer asks the second question in order to discover which details were seen. Finally, there are very specific bits of information that would have to be clarified.

Example C
What is your reaction to this recording? How would you evaluate the music? The lyrics? Would you buy it?

In this telephone interview, an excerpt from a record was played for the interviewee. The interviewer was interested in two things: (1) the subjective evaluation by the interviewee and (2) the interviewee's behavioral responses so that she could predict an amount of sales. She felt that she should obtain general reactions before getting to the bottom line. The last question has a note of finality about it, suggesting that the interview has come to an end.

These examples not only demonstrate the nature of the funnel sequence but also suggest conditions when it might be most useful.

1. It lets the interviewer discover the interviewee's frame of reference.
2. It avoids leading the interviewee or shaping the interviewee's responses.
3. It satisfies a need for the interviewee to communicate opinions.
4. It maximizes the interviewer's options about what can be probed.
5. It can be used by supervisors in order to get their subordinates to bring up specific problems.

• *Inverted Funnel Sequence.* The *inverted funnel sequence* is the exact reverse of the funnel sequence just described. It starts with specific questions, proceeds to more general questions, and concludes with the most general questions.

Example D

What interviewing procedures were used in your last job performance review? How did these differ from the procedures used in your previous reviews? How typical are your reviews in comparison with those given generally throughout the company?

In this example, a consultant had been assigned the task of evaluating the job performance reviews in a particular company. Although she asked many very specific questions, there was one segment in which she used these three questions. The reason they were put in an inverted funnel sequence was that the interviewer felt it was necessary in order to get people to think very concretely about a given appraisal before they really would be able to make comparisons. So the sequence was based on a constantly enlarging scope: think about one appraisal; compare it with your own appraisal; and, finally, make some judgments about all the appraisals.

Example E

You've read both proposals. Which of the two benefit plans do you favor? What are its strengths? Are there any things you'd like that are not included in either of the programs.

In Example E it is important to get a commitment from the interviewee initially in the interview. Then his or her thinking can be probed.

Example F

Where were you when you first heard the news? What were you doing at the time? How did it affect you? What are your plans now?

The questions in Example F could be transcribed from many journalistic interviews. The initial questions are closed investigations about a past event. They are there because (1) the reader or the audience needs a review of the circumstances as a frame of reference, or (2) it may be important to get the interviewee to remember the specifics in order for her or him to talk about general reactions and plans.

You may use the following characteristics of the inverted funnel sequence in determining whether or not to use it.

1. It forces the interviewee to think through specific attitudes or facts before articulating a general reaction or a conclusion. In this way, it follows an inductive thinking pattern.
2. It motivates the reluctant interviewee to communicate. Shyness or the reluctance to relive a bad experience makes a person reluctant to talk. However, answering some specific questions often opens a person to greater expression later.
3. It primes the interviewee's memory. When a person has forgotten an event, specific questions can help reconstruct the event and perhaps "jog the memory."

4. An initial commitment (yes or no) can be invaluable in interpreting the more general responses that come later.

• *Alternative Sequences.* Not all questions are related in terms of narrowing or enlarging the scope of the answer. It might be difficult, for example, to put the journalistic inquiries of who, what, when, where, and why in either the funnel or inverted funnel pattern. They are related, but it may not matter in what order they come. Similarly, there may be times when you may have five or six similar or equal questions (all open or all closed, for example) that need to be asked. The result may be a kind of tunnel sequence.

Example G
I'm going to read off several items and I'd like for you to tell me why each one is not important to your job satisfaction.

1. pay
2. your relationship with your supervisor
3. your family
4. the company's image
5. fringe benefits
6. your own productivity
7. your peers
8. recognition of your efforts

In this example matters other than the scope of the questions will be used to determine the sequence.

TRANSITIONS
Much of the structure of an interview can be planned, but it is virtually impossible to plan the exact nature of the transitions. Even though they cannot be planned, the professional interviewer should develop skills to make the flow from one point to the next as smooth as possible. Although they are often overlooked, transitions are an integral part of the structure of any interview. Because they are interconnecting links between points and topics and serve several important functions, they deserve attention of their own.

One of the chief functions of transitions is to give a constant orientation to both the interviewer and the interviewee about where the interview is going. You will notice how the ease of communication is momentarily halted when abrupt changes are made in an interview. This comes from a disorientation as the interviewee wonders how the past discussion is related to the old or tries to develop a new perspective. At any rate, it takes a while to get back on course. People need a sense of direction and a sense of progress in moving in that direction. The type of transitions that do this well are the *summary* and a *brief explanation* of where, and perhaps why, you are moving from one topic to another. For example, a simple statement by a recruiter that "we've covered those questions that I wanted to ask of you; now let me answer any questions that you have," explains that the interview is moving into a new stage. Another example is the statement, "We've covered the major questions in the survey; now I'd like to ask you some demographic questions that will be used simply to group all respondents into certain categories. No individuals will be identified." Hopefully, such a transition explains why the coming questions are necessary and this explanation may be absolutely necessary to get people to cooperate.

Another important function of transitions is to control the topic discussed, which is often linked to time control. In a counseling interview a subordinate may keep leading the discussion to his or her poor relationship with another employee. In this case, the interview may not move in the desired direction; furthermore, the interviewee may become more and more emotional. Finally, the supervisor will have to exert some control in order to move from the topic to a more productive one. The transitional statement may be: "Well, Alison, I'm really not particularly interested in this, uh, problem with Rachel any further. I know it's important to you, but I don't think that we can explore it very productively today. What I'm most interested in is determining how much of a problem scheduling is for you and what kinds of things we can do to reduce it."

CONCLUSIONS

Like transitions, conclusions are rarely planned in terms of specific content; however, it is useful to consider what they should accomplish.

First, the interview should be brought to a very definite close even though another interview may be wanted later. The interviewee should not have to wonder or to ask as some do, "Is that all?" or "Are we finished?" The interviewer can end it verbally with a statement such as "Well, I guess that about wraps it up for me," and nonverbally by making an appropriate gesture such as standing up, shaking hands, or opening the door. Second, the conclusion should leave both people with a sense of accomplishment. A final summary helps to do this. Third, the conclusion should forecast what is going to happen as a result of the interview. New meetings are scheduled, future correspondence is planned, a report on the survey is sent, or the time for publication of a study is scheduled. It is a good rule to keep all promises that are made. Finally, the conclusion should have a positive impact upon the relationship. It is always proper to express appreciation for the interviewee's time and cooperation and to refer to the importance of the interviewee's contribution. In situations when the interviewer and the interviewee have a continuing relationship, as with bosses and subordinates, it is useful to end in a way that is going to keep the relationship sound and productive. The interview should not be viewed as a complete unit that has ended but as merely one interaction that may influence all other interactions that the two people involved might have.

PLANNING THE PHYSICAL SETTING

In recent years the general area of nonverbal communication has received a great deal of attention as researchers have tried to measure the impact on human communication of physical appearance, dress, arrangement of furniture, vocal cues, physical environment, and personal space.[4] The overwhelming evidence supports the conclusion that the environment in which an interview is held contributes to the overall outcome of the interview. Consequently, it is naive to think that the physical setting cannot be used deliberately to accomplish the interviewer's objectives. We make this statement without any kind of value judgment as to how much and in what ways the environment should be manipulated. Consider the following.

A manager had a long rectangular desk in his office with one end pushed against the wall. A subordinate once suggested that if they were to pull the desk out from the wall, one more person could be accommodated around it. The boss replied, "In this office, there is only one head of the table." Upon hearing this story, people often groan in opposition to the manager's feeling. You may not agree with his objective, but the truth is that the manager knew exactly what he wanted to accomplish and he arranged his environment to send a nonverbal message, which most people had probably already sensed. Similarly, it is not infrequently that workers vie for larger offices, a certain position at a table, or a seat next to a certain person, because it *means something.* In 1978 Midge Constanza's office was changed from next to President Carter's office to a small office in the White House basement. Immediately, reporters drew all kinds of implications about what the president was "saying" by this move. Soon afterwards she resigned.

These are not isolated happenings, and we want to examine some strategic decisions that interviewers can make about the physical setting of an interview.

1. Where the interview takes place may have some profound implications. You may choose between a work environment and a more neutral setting like a restaurant, cafeteria, or lounge. You can expect the work situation to create a more formal, business-like atmosphere and the more neutral environment to decrease substantially the prevalence of work pressures. You can make this choice to accomplish your purposes. If you

[4]For an excellent review and synthesis of this literature, we recommend the following book: Mark Knapp, *Non-Verbal Communication* (New York: Holt, Rinehart and Winston, 1972).

want to enhance your own authority, you may have the interaction in your own office; in those instances when you want to reduce social distance with an employee, you might go to his or her office or invite him or her to a neutral, more relaxed setting. Many journalists would much prefer a more neutral setting because the interviewee is more likely to "open up" with a story.

2. The interior of an office or a room can be "landscaped" to achieve certain effects. One of the most interesting topics focuses on the desk. Common folklore suggests that if you want to create a formal situation that enhances your authority, you will sit behind a desk while the interviewee is seated across from you. If you want to set the interviewee at ease and build a more friendly climate, you can move from behind the desk and sit beside the interviewee. There is some evidence that this is more than just folklore. In an experiment by A. G. White in a doctor's office, "with the desk separating doctor and patient, only 10% of the patients were perceived 'at ease,' whereas removal of the desk brought the figure of 'at ease' patients up to 55%.[5] The ultimate question here is how at ease do you want the interviewee to be. Some people respond by placing their desk so that it can never be between. There are some situations, such as in discipline interviews, where you may not want a desk at all. Perhaps the best situation is to arrange your office so that either alternative is available to you. Then you can make it formal or informal.

The concept of personal space may have an impact also on the way that office furniture is arranged. Edward T. Hall has studied this over a long period, and his observations suggest that the physical distance between people affect the way they interact; space speaks. Intimate distance ranges from touching to 20 inches. Casual-personal distance or neutral distance is from 1½ feet to 5 feet. Impersonal-business distance ranges from 4 to 12 feet. Public distance covers areas beyond 12 feet.[6] These distances not only communicate something about the relationship but also affect the vocal shifts by which people communicate.

We do not really want to be prescriptive about how far chairs should be placed from one another, but we do want to emphasize that there exists a conversational distance. Locate your own conversational distance by experimenting with chairs and couches at certain distances. Beyond a certain distance, people tend to be inhibited and formal and want to move closer. However, if they are moved too close, they become uncomfortable and defensive. Obviously, the topics being discussed and the kind of interview being held will also have a strong influence on the appropriateness of the setting. Remember, however, that the setting does influence your interactions.

[5]Ibid., p. 33.
[6]Edward T. Hall, *The Silent Language* (New York: Fawcett World Library, 1965), p. 163.

3. There is an influence that the room's "landscaping" can have on the interaction. This stems from the general decor of the room. Knapp describes an expensive living room as saying, "This room is for show purposes only; sit, walk, and touch carefully." Other rooms tend to suggest that you can "sit down and make yourself comfortable." It is difficult to generalize here, but it seems reasonable that the greater the difference is between a person's normal surroundings and what is encountered in the interview situation, the more uneasy the interviewee will be. Therefore, this may be a factor in deciding where to have the interview.

4. The presence of other people at the interview will influence the interviewee. A young man with an MBA said that his decision to find a new job came when his boss walked into a meeting in his office and "yelled" out some criticisms. He felt that the boss's criticism might have been accurate but that he had been grossly unfair in embarrassing him in front of his peers. A good rule to follow is to make certain that criticism is always given in private and praise is given in front of others.

5. Interruptions are generally taboo in important interviews. They not only interrupt the flow of information but also suggest that the interview itself may not be important. Therefore, for important interactions, a designated power should hold all calls or screen out other people. One of the most effective ways to avoid interruptions is to leave your regular office altogether.

6. Eye contact between you and the interviewee is generally desirable, and the room can be arranged to facilitate this. For example, avoid having the interviewee face directly into a window behind you; the glare may hurt the person's eyes or you may be inviting distractions. Recognize also that there are times when eye contact makes people uncomfortable. Many counselors dim the lights in order to make people more comfortable when they are discussing personal matters. One manager invites her subordinate to a walk around the block when she has to have some negative exchanges. She is uncomfortable in conflict and feels better when she does not have to look at the person during these periods.

ANTICIPATING PROBLEMS

Once again, we stress that anticipation is not designed to turn you into an amateur psychologist. Sometimes, problems do not occur. At other times, you may be confounded because things happen that you never anticipated. The fact is that the kind of potential problems encountered are far too numerous to be catalogued here. Perhaps we can illustrate the point with some examples. The supervisor who is going to give a negative appraisal to a subordinate can anticipate some defensiveness and perhaps hostility. How is the supervisor going to handle it? The investigative reporter who is going to interview a public figure about some sensitive personal materials may anticipate some digressions and attempts to skirt the issues. How is the reporter going to handle this? The lawyer can expect a client to be one-sided in the interpretation of an event. What can be done to draw out as many facts as possible?

Since the kinds of problems encountered in an interview will vary among different kinds of interviews, we will deal with them in each discussion of a particular kind of interview. Nevertheless, it is worth mentioning here that you should think enough about the interviewing relationship with a specific person that you will be prepared for whatever problems you might encounter.

THIS CHAPTER IN PERSPECTIVE

Interviewers should plan more than they generally do. If the planning takes the form of consideration of alternatives, it will be an excellent prelude to the actual interaction. The six strategies that have been presented in the previous two chapters include the following:

1. State the purpose.
2. Prepare the agenda.
3. Identify preliminary questions.
4. Structure the interview.
5. Plan the setting.
6. Anticipate problems.

These points will be amplified in each of the chapters that deal with specific types of interviews, since effective planning needs to take place before every interview. As you increase your expertise in the interviewing process, many of these things will become habitual. Nevertheless, if you ever find yourself having a problem, it would be a useful process to go back to the drawing board and begin to plan in detail.

When you look at the six steps above, it becomes evident that what you do in regard to each determines your basic approach to the interview. It is your interviewing style. Most of these can be linked to either a directive or nondirective approach. Therefore, you can begin to look at your own philosophy in these terms.

PROJECTS

1. Look at several offices or pictures of offices with an eye toward evaluating how the "landscaping" of the offices will affect communication.

2. Figure 4.1 has an outline of a room with a door. Draw in a desk, two chairs, and a table so that you can have the greatest impact upon communication in an interview. Try several different sketches to explore several possibilities.

Figure 4.1   A room to be arranged.

3. Evaluate your own attempts at planning. For the next interview that you have, spend a half-hour filling out the interview preparation form (Figure 4.2). After the interview, analyze in what ways the elaborate planning was beneficial.

4. To what extent is planning akin to manipulation?

5. What kinds of planning can you do if you are the interviewee?

6. Discuss the relative merits of the directive approach in contrast with the nondirective approach in several different kinds of interviews.

7. To what extent do you prefer organizing your interviews?

8. Review all of the six areas covered in the last two chapters on planning an interview. Are there aspects of planning that have not been discussed?

A. State the purpose for the face-to-face interaction.

    1. What is the exact result that I want from this interview?

        (a) Information

        (b) Attitude

        (c) Behavior

B. How should I arrange this setting?

    1. Time

    2. Place

    3. Other

C. What are the topics that I want to be certain to cover?

    1. Is there a special order that they should be in?

D. What are some questions that I should ask?

E. Are there potential problems that I can anticipate in conducting this interview?

    1. How can I best motivate this interviewee?

Figure 4.2 Interview preparation form

Chapter 5
Conducting the Interview

PART I

Regardless of how well you have planned your strategies, each new interviewee presents a challenge. Every person is different in some important ways, and even the same individual will behave differently as circumstances change. In other words, no one is completely predictable, and your plans are the best ones only until the interview actually begins. The plans will fortify you as you enter the interview. Nevertheless, you must be flexible enough to adapt to the other individual and to any anticipated or unanticipated problems that occur. This adaptation requires a special kind of analytic ability, that is, *the ability to analyze what is happening while you are participating in the interaction itself.* It is not always easy to be both an observer and a participant, but with practice this ability can be developed. When you learn to analyze in this way, it will become easy to assess the situation, calculate your alternatives to meet the situation, and then choose the one alternative that is going to move you toward your purpose. It is this kind of analysis and adaptation that is characteristic of your role, and there are five tactical areas that are particularly important.

1. establishing and maintaining a productive climate
2. listening analytically
3. probing thoughtfully
4. motivating the interviewee continually
5. controlling the interview

ESTABLISHING A PRODUCTIVE CLIMATE

Interpersonal climate represents the general atmosphere, mood, or tone in which the interaction takes place. It is a rather broad term that describes how the interviewer and the interviewee feel about their relationship. So far no researchers have been able to measure all of its basic components, but it will be instructive to examine a number of ways that climate has been conceptualized. Keep in mind that it is being described basically from the viewpoint of the interviewer in order to examine some things that an interviewer might do to achieve the kind of climate that suits his or her purposes. While most interviewers approach climate as something to be set in the introduction, it is also useful to remember that climate may shift subtly and quickly and that a conscious effort must be expended to maintain a good climate throughout the interview.

Comfort Versus Stress

Perhaps the most common way of thinking about climate in an interview is in terms of comfort or stress. Comfort represents the degree to which an interviewee can be made to feel at ease. Stress is often anxiety imposed internally by the interviewees themselves. They may come to the interview with a large amount of internal anxiety in anticipation of things such as "What if the interviewer asks something I don't know?" "What's going to happen?" "I really need to make a good impression." "Can I do it?" or "I wish that I had not agreed to this." There is tension created also when the interviewee is in unfamiliar surroundings such as the interviewer's office or a new building. Some of the most frequently used ways of building a comfortable climate include the following:

Spend a few minutes in small talk about the weather or about some current event.
Offer coffee, water, or a drink.
Sit beside the interviewee in a comfortable chair.
Use a warm, friendly tone of voice.
Give a full orientation.

As these points would suggest, perhaps the overriding principle for building a comfortable climate is to show a genuine consideration for the other person's needs.

There is a productive reason for establishing a comfortable climate. People tend to be less guarded and more talkative and communicative under relaxed circumstances. Since several kinds of interviews are covered in this book, however, we must disagree with those who say that the interviewer must *always* make the interviewee comfortable. You should if it suits your purposes. One condition in which this is nearly always useful is when you are interviewing strangers for research, selection, or journalistic interviews. In a superior-subordinate relationship, it may be useful in most instances to set a comfortable climate, but in others it could be dysfunctional. For example, it is perhaps quite unrealistic to expect anyone to experience comfort in a disciplinary interview; to start off with small talk would only increase the interviewee's anxiety. In selection interviews there are interviewers who sometimes like to put interviewees under stress to test their reactions, and they find this useful.

Formality Versus Informality

Formality is characterized by (1) a business-like atmosphere, with the content and processes carefully monitored, (2) formal address, such as Mr., Ms., or Senator instead of first names, and (3) the interviewer dominating the structure of the interview. Informality is characterized by the exact opposites of these.

Since form of address plays a major role in setting a climate, it warrants special examination here. As the interviewer, you will set the tone to a great extent. It is particularly important for you not to be hesitant in introducing yourself in a way that suggests what you expect. To introduce yourself as Ellen Ross when you would prefer to be called Ms. Ross or Dr. Ross only gives the interviewee a misleading cue.

People sometimes make a mistake when they assume that informal climate and comfort go together. This is not necessarily the case. Interviewees can be comfortable in either formal or informal situations, provided that it meets their expectations. Subordinates, for example, expect a certain distance with their bosses, and some elected officials expect a certain distance from journalists; distance is simply built into the situation. Consequently, the degree of formality may vary considerably among productive interviews. One basic consideration is what kind of climate the interviewee expects.

Another important consideration is the degree of formality that suits you, the interviewer. Over a period of time you will develop some preferences about how you relate to others and what works best for you. In fact, you may prefer to relate informally with some interviewees and to be formal with others. Decide on the climate that permits you to achieve your objectives and build it.

Open Versus Closed Climate

The distinctive features of an open climate are a great willingness to trust, an avoidance of evaluation, and an apparent willingness to accept whatever information the interviewee wants to give. Essentially, the interviewee experiences a certain freedom of expression. This climate is particularly useful for any information getting interview. In the special circumstances surrounding superior-subordinate interviews, it is important to distinguish between openness in (1) message sending, such as a candid disclosure of feelings or information by the interviewer and (2) message receiving, or encouraging and permitting the frank expression of views divergent from your own. Furthermore, openness needs to be defined in terms of task related openness or nontask related openness. You may, for example, be willing to hear anything about nontask related topics, but you may also be more closed or limited as to what you will accept about task related topics. Others prefer to exclude the nontask related topics but will accept any task related information. In other words, openness exists as a matter of degree and everyone sets limits. A supervisor may accept "Would you clarify that last instruction?" but may rule out "I don't want to do it." as a legitimate response.

Openness is really an attitude. If you say that you want to have an open relationship, your behaviors must not contradict what you say. There are many people who will tell you that they want your honest opinion and then cut you off before you have sufficient opportunity to express it. The ultimate expression of openness is for a healthy two-way communication to take place, with both you and the interviewee conversing freely.

A closed climate is the antithesis of an open one. Communication basically goes in one direction, with the interviewer being highly directive. There is little desire on the part of the interviewer to create rapport or a cohesive relationship, and participation is highly controlled. Normally, we do not advocate developing a closed climate because it breeds defensiveness and stifles revealing expressions. Nevertheless, there may be times in a work situation when you choose deliberately to impose limits. In one instance a supervisor grew tired of hearing the same idea expressed again and again by a subordinate. To overcome this, he closed the interview climate by regulating the topics about which the subordinate could talk. In the same sense, a journalist will "close" the atmosphere a bit when she sees that the interviewee is taking her in a direction that she does not want to go.

Defensive Versus Supportive Climate

Jack Gibb delineates the characteristics of the two types of interpersonal communication climates as shown in Table 5.1.

Table 5.1 THE CHARACTERISTICS OF TWO DIFFERENT CLIMATES

DEFENSIVE	SUPPORTIVE
Evaluation. To pass judgment on another; to blame or praise; to make moral assessments of another; to question another's standards, values, and motives.	*Description.* To be nonjudgmental; to ask questions that are perceived as genuine requests for information; to present "feelings, events, perceptions, or processes that do not ask or imply that the receiver change behavior or attitude."
Control. To try to do something to another; to attempt to change an attitude or the behavior of another; to try to restrict another's field of activity; "implicit in all attempts to alter another person is the assumption of the change agent that the person to be altered is inadequate."	*Problem orientation.* The antithesis of persuasion; to communicate "a desire to collaborate in defining a mutual problem and seeking its solution" (thus tending to create the same problem orientation in the other); to imply that the other person has no preconceived solution, attitude, or method to impose upon the other; to allow "the receiver to set his own goals, make his own decisions, and evaluate his own progress—or to share with the sender in doing so."
Strategy. To manipulate others; to use tricks to "involve" another; to make another think he or she is making his or her own decision; to make another feel that the speaker has a genuine interest in her or him; to engage in a stratagem involving ambiguous and multiple motivations.	*Spontaneity.* To express guilelessness, natural simplicity; to be free of deception; to have a "clean id"; to have unhidden, uncomplicated motives; to be straightforward and honest.
Neutrality. To express lack of concern for the welfare of another ("the clinical, detached, person-is-an-object attitude").	*Empathy.* To express respect for the worth of another; to identify with another's problems, share his or her feelings, and accept his or her emotional values.
Superiority. To communicate the attitude that one is "superior in position, power, wealth, intellectual ability, physical characteristics, or other ways" to another; to tend to arouse feelings of inadequacy in another; to impress another that the speaker "is not willing to enter into a shared problem-solving relationship, that he probably does not desire feedback, that he does not require help and/or that he will be likely to try to reduce the power, the status, or the worth of the receiver."	*Equality.* To be willing to enter into participative planning with mutual trust and respect; to attach little importance to differences in talent, ability, worth, appearance, status, and power.

Table 5.1 *(continued)*

DEFENSIVE	SUPPORTIVE
Certainty. To appear dogmatic; "to seem to know the answers, to require no additional data"; to regard the self as teacher rather than as co-worker; to manifest inferiority by *needing to be right;* to want to win an argument rather than to solve a problem; to see one's ideas as truths to be defended.	*Provisionalism.* To be willing to experiment with one's own behavior, attitudes, and ideas; to investigate issues rather than to take sides on them; to problem-solve rather than to debate; to communicate that another may have some control over the shared quest or investigation of ideas. ("If a person is genuinely searching for information and data, he does not resent help or company along the way.")

SOURCE: Jack R. Gibb, "Defensive Communication," *Journal of Communication,* (September 1961): 142–148. Reproduced by permission of the International Communication Association.

The descriptions in Table 5.1 demonstrate that it is easy for people to do things unconsciously that contribute to another person's defensiveness. Our purpose by describing them is to emphasize that you can consciously build a good climate if you work at it.

Finally, it is important to recognize that assessment of the interviewing climate is a very subjective process. The descriptions or labels are really perceptions that people have. Furthermore, just because you try to be informal, supportive, or open does not mean that the interviewee will necessarily perceive it as such. Therefore, you will need to stay keenly aware of how the interviewee is responding to you, and then perhaps this will suggest to you how he or she is thinking at that moment in response to the climate of the interview.

LISTENING ANALYTICALLY

Your questioning technique is one of the most important skills that you can develop. Our focus, however, must now be enlarged to examine another important skill: listening to the interviewee's answers and analyzing them. The reason for asking a good question is to get a response, and your success as an interviewer depends on how valuable that response is to you. You must learn to make an immediate evaluation of a response; in fact, your analysis must begin while the interviewee is answering you. This combination of listening, analyzing, and asking probing questions differentiates the best interviewers from the more mediocre ones. Before you can be good at probing, however, you must become a good listener.

The sad fact is that many people do not listen very well. There is a temptation to be so concerned with your questions or what you are going to say that the amount of analytic listening you do is minimal. Novice interviewers frequently fall into the trap of treating any verbal response as a complete answer to a question and then move on to their next planned question. This failure to listen has been identified as one of the greatest barriers to communication in all kinds of situations, but it is particularly important that it not be allowed to become a barrier in an interview.

The Value of Listening

A first step in improving your listening ability is to become convinced of its values to the interview interaction. Basically, the values of listening can be grouped into two general areas: its impact upon the content of the interview and its impact upon the relationship between the interviewer and the interviewee.

In terms of content your ultimate success in achieving your objectives in any information collecting interview will depend upon how well you are able to receive information. Listening not only helps you determine what should follow each of the interviewee's responses but also is necessary to avoid making errors in recording and interpreting the data.

In terms of the relationship, the impact of analytic listening is perhaps even more profound. (1) Listening allows you to determine exactly the other person's frame of reference. (2) Listening often reduces emotional tension. It becomes a particularly useful tool for curtailing the pendulum effect that often occurs when one person feels that he or she must counterbalance the other person's anger or aggression. Taking time to listen breaks this pattern. (3) Listening conveys a sense of importance to the interviewee. Most people tend to respond favorably to those who will listen to them. This point was illustrated pointedly by a participant in a focus group who said, "Sure, I'll cooperate. No one ever asked my opinion before." (4) Listening is persuasive. People have to refine their thinking while trying to articulate their ideas. By listening carefully and asking an occasional question, you can help them in this refinement process. Frequently, they have to change their initial opinions as they work through their own ideas. (5) Listening is also a form of effectively relating to others. Hopefully, your listening will convince the other person to reciprocate by listening to you.

Barriers to Listening

A second step in overcoming poor listening habits is to become aware of some of the most common obstacles to listening so that you can rid yourself of any that you may have.

The *tendency to evaluate* is a kind of intolerance, described by Carl Rogers and F. Roethlisberger as the most detrimental obstacle to listening. It is "our very natural tendency to judge, to evaluate, to approve (or disapprove) the statement of the other person of the other group.[1] In such a situation a person makes no attempt to find out what the other person really means or why the person accepts a particular point of view. If the evaluation is negative, then the choice is either to tune the interviewer out or to cut the interviewee off. In either case, the flow of information is ended and the relationship may be impaired.

Somewhat akin to the tendency to evaluate is the characteristic of some interviewers *to be impulsive*. They jump in and interrupt before an idea is sufficiently developed, or they ask questions to change the subject before the interviewee is ready. Experienced interviewers know the value of waiting; they get a maximum of information.

Never *responding* (verbally or physically) is another bad habit. It leaves the interviewee in limbo, not knowing whether he or she has been understood. The interviewee feels that you do not care. This practice can also be very intimidating. For example, a manager recently asked what he could do to keep job candidates from being so afraid of him. A videotape of one of his interviews revealed that he tended not to react to people. Consequently, he came across as a very cold individual, and people were unsure of how to interact with him. Effective listening involves giving some feedback to the interviewee in an apparent natural reaction.

There are also several *nonverbal habits* that irritate interviewees. If you catch yourself in such actions, try to overcome them, because they are distracting to the other person.

> avoiding eye contact; most people expect eye contact
> looking at your watch or out the window
> playing with a pencil or other object
> doodling
> obviously concentrating on your next question rather than on the answer to your current one
> writing too many notes

Finally, one of the worst listening habits is *allowing interruptions* either in person or by the telephone. Interruptions introduce distractions that make it very difficult to sustain a train of thought. In short, they make listening very difficult.

The Nature of Listening

Anyone can improve as a listener if the person is willing to work at it. In most cases, a person's potential exceeds practice. Therefore, there is a

---

[1]Carl Rogers and F. Roethlisberger, "Barriers and Gateways to Communication," *Harvard Business Review* (1952): 46.

need to discriminate between the *ability* to listen, which most people have and the *willingness* to listen, which more people need. If you need to improve your listening, there are several points about the nature of listening that may help you begin.

First, listening is not the same as hearing. It is easy to become adept at carrying on a conversation without remembering what has been said. This is listening at a very superficial level.

Second, listening occurs at different levels. You can focus on the explicit content of an interview by listening to those messages that are actually verbalized. This is very important. Sometimes, however, you can tell much by what is *not* said if you are listening for it. You also need to pay attention to those things that are implied but are never stated outright.

Third, as an interviewer, you have the power to decide what you want to listen to. These are the areas that you decide to probe. In other words, your probing is a means of directing your listening. If you are going to be a good prober, you must listen analytically.

Fourth, Carl Weaver has suggested that listening involves a number of subskills. These are listed below.[2]

    to get main ideas
    to hear the facts
    to make valid inferences
    to get the central theme
    to retain pertinent content
    to identify the main and supporting ideas
    to perceive differences between similarly worded statements
    to identify correct English usage
    to use contextual clues to determine "word meanings"
    to comprehend oral instructions
    to hear details
    to hear difficult material
    to adjust to the speaker
    to listen under bad conditions
    to resist the influence of emotion laden words and arguments
    to take notes
    to structuralize a speech
    to prevent the facts from interfering with hearing the main idea
    to improve concentration by use of special techniques
    to hear the speaker's words
    to develop curiosity
    to follow directions

[2]Carl Weaver, *Human Listening* (Indianapolis: The Bobbs-Merrill Co., Inc., 1972), pp. 9–10.

to judge relevancy

to recognize topic sentences and to associate each topic sentence
with some previous bit of knowledge

to recognize what the speaker wants the listener to do

to understand how words can create a mood

to understand connotative meanings

to predict what will happen next

to understand denotative meanings

to identify speaker attitudes

to get meaning from imagery

to notice sequences of ideas and details

to check for the accuracy of new information

to avoid the effects of projection

to evaluate and apply material presented

to introspect and analyze one's own listening disabilities

to judge validity and adequacy of main ideas

to discriminate between fact and fancy

to judge whether the speaker has accomplished his or her purpose

to recognize self-contradictions by the speaker

to be aware of persuasive devices used by the speaker

Developing Listening Skills

There are no simple formulas for making listening easy. We have laid the
groundwork, however, by pointing to the value of close, precise listening.
Now we call attention to several positive steps that can assist you in
becoming a better listener. These suggestions are based on work by Felix
Lopez.[3]

1. *Prepare.* Be fully informed so that you can appreciate the special
nuances and implications of the answers you get.

2. *Involve yourself in the interaction.* Lack of interest dilutes attention. To listen well you must be convinced that the interaction is important. If you search, you can find something of interest about almost anyone or any topic. If the content is of no real consequence to you, be
motivated to listen by reminding yourself that your relationship with the
interviewer is important and that you must listen if you are to sustain the
relationship.

3. *Concentrate.* Being attentive requires expending a lot of energy
and self-discipline. You can weed out some distractions by preventing
interruptions, but the mental disruptions and wanderings are still tempting. Inexperienced interviewers are often so worried about their structure

[3]Felix Lopez, *Personnel Interviewing* (New York: McGraw-Hill Book Company, 1975), pp.
58–63.

or their next question that they find themselves concentrating on what they are doing rather than on the interviewee's behavior. It is also tempting to anticipate what the interviewee is going to say with such certainty that you may tune out momentarily. In doing so, you risk being caught when your comments do not fit what the interviewee has been saying. Concentration is difficult, but it can be mastered. Focus on what the interviewee is saying, how it is being said, the gestures that accompany it, and what relevance it has for things that have already been said. Practice this often and periodically give yourself a mental examination to determine how well you are doing.

4. *Link information together.* There should be a natural or logical connection between the questions, answers, and new questions. Making mental links between what is going on with what has gone on before is one of the best ways of maintaining your concentration. As you do this, there will be a natural free-flowing interaction that will transform the interview into a conversation with a purpose.

5. *Integrate messages so that you listen for total meaning.* Listening in depth requires an integration of all the messages that you see and hear into patterns or trends. This will enable you to view information from a general·perspective instead of examining only the bits and pieces. Integrating involves organizing or arranging all the parts so that you get the total picture. When the organization is attempted, any gaps in the information become readily apparent, and you can probe for these.

Ralph Nichols has been one of the most popular proponents of effective listening, and people have found his advice very instrumental in developing their listening skills. The following eight guidelines have been adapted from his writing.[4]

> *Find areas of interest . . .* The key to the whole matter of interest in a topic is use. Whenever we wish to listen efficiently, we ought to say to ourselves: "What's he saying that I can use? What worthwhile ideas has he? Is he reporting any workable procedures? Anything that I can cash in, or with which I can make myself happier?"
>
> *Hold your fire . . .* We must learn not to get too excited about a speaker's point until we are certain we thoroughly understand it. The secret is contained in the principle that we must always withhold evaluation until our comprehension is complete.
>
> *Listen for ideas . . .* Good listeners focus on central ideas. . . .
>
> *Be flexible . . .* Note-taking may help or may become a distraction. Few of us have memories good enough to remember even the salient points we hear. If we can obtain brief, meaningful records

[4]Ralph G. Nichols, "Do We Know How to Listen?," *The Speech Teacher,* 10 (March 1961): 120–124.

of them for later review, we definitely improve our ability to learn and to remember.

Resist distractions . . . A good listener instinctively fights distractions.

Exercise your mind . . . Poor listeners are inexperienced in hearing difficult, expository material. Good listeners apparently develop an appetite for hearing a variety of presentations difficult enough to challenge their mental capacities.

Keep your mind open . . . Try to identify and to rationalize the words or phrases most upsetting emotionally. Often the emotional impact of such words can be decreased through a free and open discussion of them with friends or associates.

Capitalize on thought speed . . . Most persons talk at a speed of about 125 words per minute. There is good evidence that if thought were measured in words per minute, most of us could think easily at about four times that rate. It is difficult—almost painful—to try to slow down our thinking speed. Thus we normally have about 400 words of thinking time to spare during every minute a person talks to us. . . . Not capitalizing on thought speed is our greatest single handicap.

In conclusion, effective listening is not a passive activity. It requires work, dedication, concentration, and self-discipline. The rewards are worth it, however. As you develop your abilities to listen and to analyze, conducting an interview will become much easier.

THIS CHAPTER IN PERSPECTIVE

Only two of the five tactics set out at the beginning of this chapter have been discussed. The others will be included in the next chapter. Nevertheless, these two will represent a great challenge for you. Climate is the foundation for everything else. As you examined the different types of climate described, you were aware that they describe the kind of relationships that can be developed between two people. You also became aware that the kind of climate, or relationship, may indeed determine the kind of messages and content that can be shared between two people. Therefore, it is a factor that is preliminary to everything else.

Listening, on the other hand, is a skill that is very important to communication. If you are to begin to analyze what is going on in an interview, you must listen, not only with your ear but also with your eye. Before you can determine which of your alternatives is best, you must listen. It is ironic that less time is probably spent training people how to listen than is spent on any other communication skill. Nevertheless, we hope that this discussion has stimulated your desire to begin to train yourself to be a better listener, because listening is necessary if you are to develop the three tactics that are discussed in the following chapter.

PROJECTS

1. Examine each of the types of climate and try to determine when each particular type would be appropriate. Even though some of the descriptions have negative connotations, they may be appropriate under certain circumstances.

2. How realistic is Jack Gibb's dichotomy in Table 5.1? Are there times when his descriptions need some qualifications?

3. "Openness" is a popular concept today. What do people mean when they say that you ought to be "open"? How is this related to the idea that protecting the self-image is a basic motivation?

4. Make a list of as many irritating listening (or nonlistening) habits that you can. What makes people engage in these?

5. Whose responsibility is listening? Should a listener listen regardless of what is going on, or should the speaker be required to make it "interesting"?

6. If you have been able to improve your own listening habits, identify some of the procedures. Make a specific plan whereby you will continue this improvement.

7. How do you feel when people do not listen to you?

8. In order to work on listening, get into groups of three individuals. Designate one person as the listener, another as the speaker, and a third as the observer. Enforce the rule that the speaker must present something for five minutes with only interruptions of questions of clarification allowed. The observer should enforce the rule. At the end of five minutes, talk about the difficulties presented to the listener.

Chapter 6
Conducting the Interview

PART II

In this chapter we will discuss the final three strategies for conducting an interview: (1) probing thoughtfully, (2) continually motivating the interviewee, and (3) controlling the interview. Before you begin reading this chapter, it might be well for you to review the two tactics we explored in Chapter 5 so that the relationship between the two chapters will be evident.

PROBING THOUGHTFULLY

The rationale for probing is that for the majority of topics secondary questions must supplement primary questions. Probing is an important skill because most answers, particularly to open questions, are inadequate or deficient in some way. They simply do not cover exactly what the interviewer wants to know in exactly the right amount of detail. This observation is not meant to be a negative assessment of an interviewee, because there can be several good reasons for an incomplete response: You and the interviewee may be operating at different levels, with different expectations, with a different understanding of words, or with different kinds of things at stake.

The ability to probe well is perhaps the one skill that discriminates between the best interviewers and those who are merely adequate. To probe thoughtfully, of course, depends upon your ability to listen analytically. In order to develop this important skill, the following section covers the nature of inadequate responses, the reasons why they are given, the different types of probing, and some guidelines for probing.

Inadequate Responses

"The first requirement of an interviewer in handling successfully the problems of inadequate response is that he [or she] be able to recognize response inadequacy in its various forms."[1] Basically, a response may be inadequate in any of the following ways.

1. *There may be no response.* Some interviewees choose not to answer a question, and they remain silent; others may even articulate their refusal to answer. For example, a recent telephone interviewer asked several questions of an interviewee and received good responses until she asked the question, "How much do you earn?" The interviewee immediately responded, "I don't think that I care to answer any more of these questions. After all, I don't really know who you are." The interview was then ended politely but firmly.

2. *The response may be incomplete.* What an interviewee tells you may be useful, but you may also need additional information about the topic. If you ask someone to tell you about her work experience, for example, she may identify her work in a department store, in a restaurant, and on an internship in a hospital at different periods of her life. This just whets your appetite for more information, and you will need more extensive information about each of these areas for it to be of value. In other words, the initial response provided only general information that needed to be probed more thoroughly.

3. *An answer may be irrelevant to the question.* It may be a digression or may even completely change the subject. This problem becomes particularly acute when the interviewee is very articulate. The interviewer always faces the question of whether to interrupt the interviewee or to get the conversation back on track.

4. *Inaccurate information sometimes is given.* It could be that the information given contradicts known fact or that the interviewee is making unwarranted assumptions. Should you correct the interviewee or not? This depends upon your purposes. It might be revealing, however, to discover the interviewee's reasons for the inaccurate information.

5. *Some responses are so poorly organized that they are difficult to follow.* Inarticulate interviewees commonly leave out information, so that

---

[1] Robert Kahn and Charles Cannell, *Dynamics of Interviewing* (New York: John Wiley & Sons, Inc., 1963), p. 218.

there are gaps in your interpretations, or they may explain things in ways that make it very difficult for you to see the connecting links. When you probe, you may find that the interviewee feels that he or she is being forced to be repetitive. Nevertheless, it is still necessary for you to get the correct information.

6. *The answer may contain words, the meaning of which are uncertain to you.*

Reasons for Giving Inadequate Responses

Recognizing the forms of the inadequate responses listed may be helpful to you in determining what kind of probing you should use. As part of the analysis process, however, you may also need to assess why the interviewee gave a deficient answer in the first place. The following reasons are common ones.

> does not understand the purpose of the question or how you might use the information
> does not understand the kind of answer desired
> is uncertain about how much of an answer to give
> does not understand the language in the question
> is unwilling to give information that is personal, threatening, or endangering to self
> may not know the answer
> may not remember
> finds it difficult to articulate feelings
> thinks you will not accept or understand the answer
> does not care about you or the interview
> fears the results of giving an answer
> has competing thoughts, so concentration lags

These reasons can be grouped into three general areas: (1) those involving unwillingness on the part of the interviewee to answer, (2) those involving confusion about what you want, and (3) those involving an inability to answer due to a lack of knowledge or a faulty memory. These categories offer some direction in determining what kind of probing you should use.

Types of Probing

Probing can be classified generally as either direct or nondirective. Direct probing focuses on exactly what you want to know, whereas *nondirective probing* focuses on merely keeping the interviewee talking without any coaching as to what areas to include. First, we will explore the types of direct probing.

ELABORATION

Your most consistent need will be for additional information. Therefore, you should ask the interviewee to extend, to amplify, or to build up the response. Some examples of probing for elaboration are

> Tell me more about that.
> What else can you tell me about_____?
> Was anything else happening at this time?
> How did you feel about that?
> Was there more to the incident than that?

CLARIFICATION

When you do not understand the words an interviewee uses or how certain events are related, you will need to obtain some explanations. Note the following example:

> INTERVIEWER: How do you feel about the new organization?
> INTERVIEWEE: Ummmh, it's OK, I guess.

In this case, the question is open and does not put any limits on the interviewee's answers. Not knowing what the options are, interviewees typically use words like "OK" or "interesting." Such answers are too indefinite to be very meaningful. Is the response positive, or is it negative? In order for you to interpret this response adequately, you would need some clarifying information.

Similarly, a response may give several bits of information that are vague or ambiguous. The following exchange took place in a screening interview.

> RECRUITER: What was your major at the university?
> CANDIDATE: I majored in personnel administration because I'm basically people oriented and like to work with people.

In this case, the recruiter was given two areas that needed probing, and he had to make a choice as to which should be probed first. He then immediately asked the question, "What did personnel administration involve at your university? What did you study?" Then later he probed, "Earlier, you described yourself as being people oriented. Would you tell me what that means to you?"

REPETITION

Interviewees often evade questions. When this happens, one option you have is to repeat the question exactly or to ask a reasonable facsimile.

> JOURNALIST: What do you think should be done to curb inflation?
> POLITICIAN: That's a difficult question, but there are a lot of suggestions that ought to be considered. We've got to stop it; that's for certain, or we're going to have real problems.

In this example, the politician clearly does not answer the question; she merely talks around it, suggesting that it is indeed an important topic. Skillful probing is necessary to make this politician commit herself on a specific proposal. One possibility is to ask the same question again to show that you know that she has not answered it.

CONFRONTATION

Many interviewers shy away from confrontation, but this desire to avoid an unpleasant situation creates a bias in the interview. Confrontations may be useful in calling attention to an apparent inconsistency or a contradiction among items of information in the answers. If the interviewee is actually contradicting himself or herself, he or she ought to be made aware that you recognize this. Unfortunately, some interviewees do lie. There is a more important reason, however, for confrontation. Often what appears to be a contradiction can be explained rationally if you explore it. Things sometimes get left out inadvertently, and it is easy to give wrong dates or to have a slip of the tongue. In such cases, it is more equitable to give the interviewee an opportunity to clarify the situation than for you to leave the interview convinced that the interviewee was lying or was incompetent. Finally, it is important to confront an interviewee because he or she may feel embarrassed to volunteer important information. If the interviewee seems reluctant to commit himself or herself, you may have to test the interviewee's sentiments explicitly.

Not all confrontations need to be emotionally wrecking interactions. In the following example from a counseling interview, the subordinate would not introduce or admit a problem existed until the manager confronted him in the following way.

> INTERVIEWER: It seems to me that what you have been saying, Perry, implies that any solution to this problem of coordination has to come from other departments? Is this the way you feel?
>
> INTERVIEWEE: Well, (silence for ten seconds) maybe it sounds that way. I don't know. You know, when people pressure you . . . well, it's not easy to decide what to do . . . what's best or fair for everybody. Maybe there are one or two things that we could be doing . . . You know, I'm certainly willing to do my share, to meet others half-way. But they need to understand our problems, too.
>
> INTERVIEWER: OK. I really didn't mean to overstate your case. But it did seem to me that all of the things you said earlier indicated that Tom and George were going to have to do the adjusting, and I just wanted to check it out to see if I am reading you correctly.
>
> INTERVIEWEE: Well, you know, when you put it that way, I guess it sounds kinda harsh . . . and maybe selfish. I don't want it to sound that way. Still, I must admit that it would be easier . . . and a lot

cheaper and simpler . . . if they would make some changes. I realize everybody has to work together. I just don't want to be the one who gets pressured all the time.

In the final sentence the subordinate admits to some feelings that he has been unable or unwilling to express until now. Perhaps it is unlikely that he would have ever done so if his boss had not confronted him quite directly with the implications of his own statements.

In addition to direct probing, there are also several kinds of *nondirective probing*. There are many instances when you will want just to keep your interviewee talking. You may not have any specific questions, but you may want to encourage the interviewee to continue giving you information. In such cases, nondirective probing is very useful. There are four types of nondirective probing that you can use skillfully and unobtrusively. In many cases, the interviewee is not aware of them.

SILENCE

Novice interviewers often have a low tolerance for silence; they often feel that unless someone is talking, nothing is happening. This certainly is not the case. Still, one of the hardest lessons to learn is to use silence deliberately and productively. In fact, the lack of any pauses may be an indication that you are nervous or insecure.

Silence has several functions. It allows interviewees time for reflection and thinking. Not every answer will fall into place quickly, and generally people need some time just to think. Silence may also communicate a mood. Research "indicates that there is a positive correlation between the amount of silence used by the interviewer and the respondent's general level of spontaneity."[2] A pause slows the pace a bit and keeps you from interrupting your interviewee's chain of thought.

In what sense can silence function as probing? It merely communicates that more is expected. If it is accompanied by a nonverbal expression of interest, such as a nod of the head, it also indicates a willingness to listen. Since the interviewee is likely to have less tolerance for silence than you, he or she probably will experience some pressure to fill the gap and will keep on talking.

Obviously, long periods of silence can also be dysfunctional. There are people who like to play games to see how long they can outlast the other person. Therefore, in exploring the use of silence as probing, it must be understood that we are talking about occasional brief periods of silence lasting perhaps 10 to 20 seconds. If, after waiting this long, the interviewee has not begun to talk, you may need to use other means of securing information.

[2] Raymond Gorden, *Interviewing* (Homewood, Ill.: Dorsey Press, 1969), p. 188.

NEUTRAL PHRASES

Verbal spurts such as "I see," "Hmmmm," "Un huh," "Yes?" "OK," and "You don't say" tend to encourage interviewees to keep talking. These phrases are actually uttered while the interviewee is talking, but they do not really interrupt the interviewee. In fact, if you pay attention to the way people converse almost anywhere, you will hear them using phrases such as these to show that they are listening and to encourage the conversation to continue.

REFLECTIVE STATEMENTS

Sometimes you can repeat back to the interviewee a statement that the interviewee already has made to indicate that further clarification or elaboration is needed. For this reason, they are often called mirror statements.

> DOCTOR: How are you today?
> PATIENT: Well, to tell you the truth, I don't feel too well.
> DOCTOR: You don't feel well?

The doctor has used the patient's exact words but has turned them into a question. This is an excellent means of getting interviewees to tell you more without structuring their answers. The same technique is used in the following examples.

> PROFESSOR: Mary, you didn't do as well on this test as before. What happened?
> MARY: I just didn't have the time I needed to study.
> PROFESSOR: You didn't have time?

> POLLSTER: How do you feel about the president's tax proposals?
> CLIENT: I'm against any tax increases; they're way too high already.
> POLLSTER: You think taxes are too high?
> CLIENT: I sure do. There's a general tax revolt developing in this country. The more you make, the more they take. You never get ahead. It's got to stop somewhere. I sure hope this proposal gets killed quickly.

INTERNAL SUMMARIES

Periodic reviews of the most important points you have covered in an interviewee serve a triple function. First, they act as a probe by allowing the interviewee to check the adequacy of your interpretation of what has taken place. In fact, it is often wise to preface your summaries with a remark that suggests that you are probing. For example, a manager was trying to secure suggestions from her subordinate. After a while she said, "Okay, Jim, let me see if I understand your recommendation." She then went on to summarize what she thought Jim had been saying. Such a tactic is very helpful, because it is not infrequent that the interviewee will need to correct an interpretation with a comment like "That's not quite what I meant." Your summaries can be an open invitation to more discussion or a search for more accurate understanding. Second, accurate summaries demonstrates that you have been listening. This has a motivational impact upon your relationship with the interviewee. Third, summaries are an excellent means of building transitions from one topic to another. They give people a sense of direction and a sense of progress.

Guidelines for Probing

Skill in probing comes by developing a sensitivity to the communication process and an ability to analyze almost instantaneously what additional information you need. It can never be reduced to mere technique. The following guidelines, however, focus on some of the most important considerations for probing effectively.

EXERCISING CONTROL OF THE TOPIC

Organize so that you will stay on track. Probing is the way that you can direct the interviewee toward giving you the kind of information that you want. As we pointed out earlier, it is also your way of indicating what you are willing to listen to, that is, of weeding out the relevant from the irrelevant information. For this reason you must have a clear idea of what you want to accomplish. Examine the following examples to determine what area could be probed.

> SUBORDINATE: If I have to start this new project without adequate supplies, I'm really going to raise hell!

You have several options here. If you want to keep the discussion on an informational and somewhat rational level, you might ask, "What supplies are you short of?" If, on the other hand, you analyze the situation and feel that there may be more to the reaction than is evident, you might want to focus on the subordinate's feelings by asking, "You're angry, aren't you?" Neither of these probes are inherently better than the other, and you probably can identify some other alternatives. What you do depends upon what you are trying to accomplish.

The following situation presents similar options.

> INTERVIEWER: As far as you are concerned, how do you feel the new system is working out?
> INTERVIEWEE: Well, there's a lot of grumbling going on because a lot of people don't like it. They say it's just too impractical and takes too much time. It was probably dreamed up by people who never did this kind of work.

What is the most appropriate response to the comments in this conversation? What alternatives can you list? We presented this example to hundreds of supervisors, and their responses tended to fall into two groups. One large group said that they would repeat the question, "How do *you* feel?" or ask, "Is that the way you feel?" According to this group, the original question specifically asked for a description of the interviewee's feelings or attitudes and not someone else's feelings. Therefore, they viewed the response as inadequate. The other group viewed the interviewee's response as very relevant. Therefore, they said that they would ask, "What is impractical or unrealistic about the system?" or "What are the problems with them?" This group felt that the interviewee obviously did not want to commit himself or herself to a personal answer for a particular reason; therefore, the interviewee answered indirectly. To this group it was more important to find out what the problems are than to press for the interviewee's feelings. Furthermore, they inferred that the indirect response was so strong that it' probably reflected the interviewee's own feelings anyway. Remember that neither of these two groups is wrong or right; they merely differ in what they were willing to listen to.

KNOWING WHEN TO STOP
Not everything has to be probed in depth. Do not drag out an interview needlessly. Even in-depth interviews have a point of diminishing returns. Consequently, assess your priorities and quit when you have everything you need.

SENSITIVITY TO THE INTERVIEWEE'S NEEDS
Remember that the interviewee has purposes and needs that he or she wants to fulfill. In a survey, for example, some people have a need to articulate their feelings; therefore, you should perhaps listen more than you want to in order to keep a pleasant atmosphere and be able to get other information that you want. In a manager-subordinate relationship, a subordinate often needs to protect his or her self-image. Therefore, the person may choose to answer indirectly rather than directly. Furthermore, in all types of interviews there may be a need for the interviewer to justify why certain questions are being asked; the respondent may need to know the interviewer's purpose before giving an answer.

EVALUATING YOUR OPTIONS
The following example illustrates the necessity for training yourself to evaluate your options. Suppose you are a personnel manager who is giving an exit interview to an employee who is leaving the company. You ask, "John, we're sorry that we are losing you, and we wonder if you could tell us why you decided to leave." John answers, "I've got this job at Nolan,

and it's just time to move on." Since the interviewee's response does not give you reasons for his departure, your next question could be any one of the following:

1. "What made you decide to do that?" This is an open question that essentially repeats the original question. It could be useful, because John may have misunderstood what was being asked of him.
2. "Of course, we're particularly interested in why you were willing to leave your job here and move to Nolan. Can you tell me something about that?" This is very similar to the probing question above. Its primary difference is that it contains a preliminary comment that is an attempt to show interest and perhaps motivate John to respond with some specifics.
3. "Are you getting more money there?" This is a closed question that amounts to a "fishing expedition." Coming so early in the interview, it is a mark of an unrefined interviewer who uses a specific question when a general one would be better. Unfortunately, many interviewers try to use specific, probing questions too early.
4. "Didn't you like it here?" This is a poor closed question, because it sounds as if the interviewer is defensive or is begging for a compliment. People often leave organizations that they like because the opportunities are better elsewhere. This is not a very desirable probe.
5. "What do you mean by 'it's just time to move on?' " The interviewer here has picked up a hint of why the interviewee wants to move and asks for some clarification. This could be an excellent means of getting specific information.

USING CUES FROM THE INTERVIEWEE
Watch for covert as well as overt cues from the interviewee. Sometimes, the fact that the interviewee has left something out may call attention to it; therefore, you would want to probe. The choice of certain words also may indicate that there is more behind the verbalization than is being expressed.

DISTINGUISHING FACT, OPINION, HEARSAY, AND FEELINGS
You need to know exactly what type of information you are getting. Consider the police officer who is interviewing a witness to an accident. She might begin with "What happened?" However, experience teaches that people often fill in a lot of gaps in their stories by making up or inferring things. Consequently, she may probe the answer with "Exactly how much of this did you see?" It is important to remember that all information getting interviews need a clearly connected factual base that can be

weeded out from opinions or feelings. Inexperienced interviewers, however, tend to excel more in obtaining opinions than in obtaining facts or feelings.[3]

MOTIVATING THE INTERVIEWEE

Behavior is influenced by the kind of reward and the intensity of threats anticipated. The concept of motivation includes the process of furnishing incentives or inducements to move the interviewee in accordance with your objectives. Previously we have talked about motivation in terms of fulfilling a need that the interviewee has. This was explored in Chapter 2. In this section we will focus on the need for you to motivate the interviewee to participate fully and cooperatively in the interview process. Six motivators are examined, and then six recurring problems are described.

Motivators

ORIENTATION
People often hesitate or are reluctant to commit themselves in ambiguous situations; they participate more fully when they know what is expected of them and have some direction. Therefore, it is appropriate for you to give some orienting cues throughout the interview. For example, you may explain the rationale for a question, you may discuss how the information is going to be used, or you may provide a summary so that the interviewee will be aware of how you are moving from one point to the next. The important point is that orientation is a powerful motivator, if the interviewee is willing to go in the direction you are trying to take her or him.

RECOGNITION
Most people respond favorably to someone who makes them feel important in some way. This technique is used by pollsters when they tell people that their opinions are important: supervisors use it in appraisal interviews when they tell employees that they need to improve because they play an important role in the organization. Recognition satisfies the ego or self-actualizing needs.

CATHARSIS
Nearly all people have times when they must get things "off their chests" before they can deal rationally with an issue. They seem to feel relieved of

[3]William Banaka, *Training in Depth Interviewing* (New York: Harper & Row, Publishers, 1971), p. 100.

some burden and are more attentive after they have rid themselves of the anger or the anxiety that they have been harboring inside. You probably have heard someone say, "There, I've said it, and I feel better already." You may not always feel that catharsis is appropriate, and you may not want to take the time for an interviewee to go through this process. It is your option as an interviewer to tolerate it or to shut it off. It can be a motivator, however, because the person may have emptied himself or herself of certain emotional barriers that were preventing effective participation in the interview and may now be ready to become a cooperative partner.

CONGENIAL RELATIONSHIP

Establishing a rewarding relationship with another human being is an enjoyable experience. Therefore, many interviewers will cooperate because they like the interviewee, find him or her stimulating, or trust him or her. Whatever you can do to build this kind of relationship will be a powerful motivator in the interview. For example, an interviewee may be persuaded to cooperate and answer questions completely more by who you are than by the topic or the idea being discussed. Such a relationship may take time to build. One of us once interviewed someone for 45 minutes in an attitude survey and was ready to end the interview and leave. Suddenly, the interviewee asked him to sit down again and began to give honest answers that he was unwilling to give earlier. Apparently, it had taken this long for the interviewee to be certain that the interviewer could really be trusted.

CHALLENGE AND GROWTH

People often look for positive challenges or ways to extend themselves. Therefore, you should look for ways to stimulate the interviewee.

EXTERNAL REWARDS OR THREATS

All of the motivators just described are intrinsic to the interview in the sense that they bring inherent satisfaction to the interviewee through participation. There are motivators, however, that are extrinsic to the interview. In research surveys, for example, the respondents are frequently paid $4−$10 per interview, and the only reason some of the interviewees volunteer is for the money. A politician's reward may be the publicity he or she receives. A manager may promise a subordinate a promotion or may threaten the subordinate with disciplinary action in order to get the person to cooperate. These extrinsic motivators are very effective when intrinsic ones are not enough. They constitute an effective tool, but intrinsic motivators need to be present, too, for the most effective communication experience.

Problems in Motivation

The problems that you can expect to encounter are far too numerous to be treated comprehensively here. Some of these will be covered in later chapters as they occur in specific kinds of interviews. However, there are a few inhibitors that cut across all kinds of interviews, and these can be treated profitably here.

TIMIDITY

Shy people find it difficult to respond easily in an interview. Their answers tend to be brief and underdeveloped. Many are so ill at ease that they want to get out of the situation as quickly as possible. If you are interacting with someone who behaves timidly, the first thing you should do is try to ascertain why the person is behaving this way. Is it a personality trait? Might it be caused by the fact that your surroundings or status are greater than the interviewee is accustomed to? There may not be much you can do if the former is the case except to be pleasant and reassuring. In the latter case, however, it would be useful to change surroundings, to create a more relaxed atmosphere, and to assure the person of his or her own worth. In either case, it might be useful to start out with easy topics or questions whose answers do not require much elaboration. The objective is to get the interviewee to start talking about anything. Hopefully, the interviewee will gradually lose part of his or her timidity. Caution must be exercised so that you do not appear to be too aggressive in trying to get the interviewee's participation. The situation can best be handled if you invite, not demand, the interviewee to participate.

EGO THREAT

The self-image is one of the most important psychological constructs for any person. When it is threatened the individual has a natural inclination to defend it. It is predictable, therefore, that most respondents will withhold information that threatens their ego or that they will misunderstand threatening information that they receive. The need for security may cause them to repress or evade so that the free flow of honest, valid information is inhibited. Such a reaction to ego threat may take many forms: some say they have forgotten; others deny; some defend themselves; and some write off the whole episode with a "no comment."

Ego threats arise in an interview for different reasons. Sometimes they are conscious ploys on the part of the interviewer. A journalist may challenge, apply pressure, and even bait a potential interviewee in order to get a story. A manager may use them to convince an employee to accept a certain idea or behavior. Some people delight in using this technique; others rule it out ethically as an element of trickery or force.

The truth is, however, that it can work for people in a very persuasive way.

On the other hand, there are many times when ego threats become barriers to communication, and this would be a matter of concern. An assurance of anonymity may help overcome it in research as well as in discipline interviews. Thorough explanations sometimes are successful in getting people to examine themselves less defensively and more logically. Separating a criticism of a behavior from an evaluation of the total person is often successful. In this case, you would try to reduce the ego threat by letting the person feel good about himself or herself generally while looking at one characteristic in which the person may need to improve. Finally, you may be surprised sometimes when an interviewee reacts in a threatened way if you had no intention of creating such a reaction. If this occurs, a simple explanation of your intention may be instrumental in getting the person to perceive your comment or question differently.

ETIQUETTE

Raymond Gorden describes an etiquette barrier as being a reluctance on the part of an interviewee to answer a question because it contains "information perceived by the respondent as inappropriate to give to the type of person doing the interview."[4] It occurs when a candid answer would be considered in poor taste. There are things, for example, that subordinates do not say to their bosses, church members do not say to their ministers, or foreigners do not say to members of the host country. To do so would violate a norm and shock the interviewer. Therefore, there is a qualitative filter operating that makes the respondent withhold certain facts or modify the way he or she talks about a subject.

You can often anticipate an etiquette barrier whenever you and the interviewee have a vastly different positional, social, or cultural background. You can imagine what barriers might exist if a white, middle-class, college educated social worker tried to deal with a black, disadvantaged, uneducated family. Answers would probably be doctored so that they would appear socially acceptable to the interviewer. If you anticipate that there might be an etiquette barrier operating, there are several alternatives by which you can try to overcome it.

Select interviewers similar to the interviewees.

Use a questionnaire instead of an interview.

Use multiple-choice questions with options that show that you would not be surprised by the choice of any response.

Make a statement prior to the question to show that you would not be shocked. For example, you might say, "I know that sometimes

[4]Gorden, *Interviewing*, p. 76.

people_____. Have you had a problem with _____?"
Never register shock, even if you are shocked. Keep your reactions
  under control.
If you want information, be very unevaluative of the answers that you
  get. Do not agree or disagree or make moral judgments.

DEFENSIVENESS

The barrier of defensiveness has been covered more completely in the
discussion of climate in Chapter 5. Still, it is such a common barrier that it
is worth mentioning again.

People generally become defensive under any of the following conditions.

1. Serious evaluation or criticism, particularly when it is thought to
   be unjustified, makes people rush to defend themselves. This is
   one reason for not trying to correct all problems with an interviewee at once. In some cases, a person might deal effectively
   with one complaint, but the introduction of several may overload
   the person's circuits and cause him or her to try to defend himself
   or herself against all of them.
2. Manipulative strategies are not conducive to effective communication. For example, a manager described how she and her superior
   had both read the same material about nonverbal communication;
   therefore, in their meetings they each tried to stare the other
   down. For the manager, it became a form of defense against what
   she thought was manipulation on the part of her superior. Their
   meetings were rarely productive when this happened.
3. An attitude of superiority—not considered to be legitimate—often
   brings out a response of trying to put the other person "in his or
   her place."
4. Dogmatic statements or attitudes breed defensive reactions because the interviewer will try to make the interviewee "see the
   light."
5. Any statement perceived as untrue is an invitation to defend
   against falsehood.
6. An attack on an interviewee or a lack of concern for him or her as a
   person may necessitate defense in order to preserve honor or
   dignity. Actually, you may feel the need to attack an interviewee
   on occasion or to defend yourself. In either case, if you react too
   aggressively you may risk starting a vicious cycle in which both of
   you may become increasingly defensive, so that communication in
   its fullest sense becomes impossible. This is a very unproductive
   situation. If you are attacked, avoid a defensive reaction; perhaps

your own stability will motivate the other person to participate in the interview less aggressively.

PRIOR RELATIONSHIP

A prior negative relationship is a very common barrier to communication. A manager and a subordinate or a husband and wife may have a long history of not getting along together; a public figure may have a basic distrust of members of certain television networks; a homemaker may have had bad experiences with door-to-door sales representatives. All of these situations have one thing in common: the interviewee will not be enthusiastic about the interview, and the interviewee's consequent behavior may inhibit communication.

In a work situation you will need to be aware that you may not always be the best person to conduct a particular interview with a given individual. If information sharing is important, the interviewee may be more motivated to give the information to someone else than to you. Similarly, a particular journalist may have raised the ire of a certain public figure; therefore, a different journalist may be more successful in getting a full story from this public figure. The point is that you need to be aware of how your previous relationship with someone might affect your interview.

Of course, it is not always possible or desirable to send someone else. In such cases, give much thought to how you can secure the cooperation of the interviewee. Generally, you will need to provide the interviewee with an expectation of intrinsic or extrinsic reward, and the reward may need to be commensurate with the pain of interacting in an unpleasant relationship.

FORGETFULNESS

Forgetting is another frequent barrier to communication. Whereas the five barriers previously mentioned deal with people's willingness to interact in an interview, the failure to remember is a matter of ability. Everybody forgets at times, and you cannot really anticipate when this is going to happen. There is no way of planning for it. There are some things that you can do, however, to help an interviewee remember when it happens.

First, recognize that people forget for one of many reasons. Events that were not particularly meaningful are not recalled very vividly. Traumatic experiences, on the other hand, may be too painful to recall. A lapse of considerable time causes a person to forget a number of details and to focus attention on just a few. Furthermore, the pressure of an interview itself may frustrate the interviewee's memory. Sometimes, people have even been known to forget for strategic reasons, like protecting themselves. If you develop some insight into why people cannot remember, you are in a good position to help them.

Second, be aware that remembering often takes time and effort.

Memory is not something that people switch off and on easily. Furthermore, the fact that a person is trying hard to remember can be frustrating, and this may make it even more difficult to remember. Sometimes, you may feel that you can help an interviewee remember by urging the person on with phrases like, "Come on; you can remember. I know you can do it." This kind of urging, however, probably will make the person more anxious. Your best tactic is to give the respondent time; decrease the presssure. Be patient and allow some silence.

Third, switch topics; talk about something else for awhile. This is one of the best means of reducing the pressure and focusing attention away from the memory barrier. After you have talked about other matters, you may wish to come back to the forgotten material later. Surprisingly, people often have no difficulty recalling things at this point.

Fourth, if you are trying to reconstruct an event, you can facilitate memory by asking very direct questions. For example, if you were interviewing someone about a sequence of events, you might want to probe whether X came before or after Y. As you try to get all the facts in their proper sequence, double-check your findings. Be particularly careful to watch for possible inconsistencies. You are trying to help the other person, so you must also be very cautious about superimposing your own structure or thoughts on the interviewee.

CONTROLLING THE INTERVIEW

In nearly all interviewing situations the locus of control rests with the interviewer. It is part of your role, and only an occasional interviewee will challenge it. There are degrees in the amount of control that you may choose to exercise, but one of the worst criticisms that can be leveled at you as an interviewer is that you have lost control of an interview.

Actually, most of the things that have been discussed in Chapter 5 and this chapter are related to ways that you can control the interview: by setting a climate, by probing, and by motivating the interviewee to respond.

The greatest source of control, however, is for you to control yourself. Following the guidelines in this book should help you to become a well-disciplined interviewer who keeps yourself under control and who is analytic enough to exercise options in a way that will accomplish your purposes.

THIS CHAPTER IN PERSPECTIVE

All the planning in the world is useless if you cannot implement your plans. In Chapter 5 and in this chapter five tactics have been described that will enable you to accomplish your purposes.

1. Set the climate.
2. Listen analytically.
3. Probe thoughtfully.
4. Motivate the interviewee.
5. Control the interview.

It is hoped that the relationship among these five factors are evident. Listening is a part of setting a particular climate. It is also a prerequisite to being able to probe thoughtfully. The desire to probe, however, is not enough; it takes a great deal of skill. Furthermore, there are many alternative ways of probing, and you must be able to determine which one is suited for obtaining your information from a particular interviewee. The more you understand why responses are inadequate, the better you will be able to make decisions among your alternative ways of probing.

The material about motivating respondents in this chapter is directly related to the discussion on motivation in Chapter 2. It would be well for you to review that material. As you attempt to motivate the interviewee, keep in mind that this individual must be offered a valuable reason to cooperate with you, since communication in the interview is a joint process. Therefore, your basic aim is to provide an intrinsic or extrinsic reward to the interviewee for participating in the interview. Finally, all of the guidelines discussed have been designed to give you some measure of control over the proceedings.

This chapter concludes the presentation of materials about basic interviewing processes. Now you are ready to begin to examine specific types of interviews in terms of these processes.

PROJECTS

1. Why do you think many interviewers do not probe as well as they ought to? List as many reasons as you can. A good place to begin is with your own probing techniques.

2. What are the relative advantages of direct probing in contrast to indirect probing?

3. Critique any transcript of an interview in terms of the probing techniques used.

4. How can you know what will motivate another person to participate in an interview?

5. Make a list of the most frequent problems that make it difficult for an interviewer to control an interview.

Part II
THE INTERVIEW
AS A MANAGEMENT
TOOL

There is no more important relationship within an organization than the one that exists between a subordinate and a superior. This relationship affects both the job satisfaction and the productivity of each of them. Consequently, it is useful to explore the nature of this relationship in several different kinds of interview situations. In this part we will analyze the interaction between them from the initial selection interview to the final exit interview when the employee decides to move to another job. In a sense, covering all of the possible relationships enlarges the definition of "interview" for many managers who have thought of it traditionally in terms of only selection and appraisal. Nevertheless, we feel that different kinds of interviews do take place between a superior and a subordinate, and this section has been written in the hope that it will enrich the style by which you manage.

Chapter 7 explores the means by which managers make selection decisions. There is still a lot of subjectivity involved, but the procedures themselves can be analyzed and skills improved. In Chapter 8 the role of the interviewee in a selection interview is addressed specifically. This is the only time that we have devoted a chapter entirely to the interviewee.

It was written because there are some very specific steps that a person can take to improve his or her chances of making a favorable impression in an interview and of selecting a good organization to work for.

Chapter 9 outlines a number of alternative means of conducting appraisal interviews. The entire appraisal process is of great concern today. Unfortunately, many organizations have adopted systems without training their managers to use them well. Consequently, this can be an important chapter for any manager to read.

Chapter 10 is an attempt to explore a philosophy of counseling. The decision to counsel someone involves considerable risk, and you should never elect to counsel someone if the problem is outside your expertise. One of the important points made in this chapter is that you must distinguish between counseling and discipline (which is explored in Chapter 11). Many managers shy away from discipline because of its negative connotation. Chapter 11 attempts to present it as a positive force within the organization.

Chapter 12 presents a means of maximizing the information that you can get from exit interviews. Many organizations conduct them unprofitably as ritual. As they are often practiced, they are a waste of time. However, they need not be if they are done with a purpose.

Finally, Chapter 13 explores some of the important considerations in a negotiation or a persuasive interview. In Chapter 13 we break out of the superior-subordinate limits, although the materials apply there, too.

Chapter 7
The Selection Interview

At its best, a selection interview is a pleasant communication interaction in which two people meet one another in order to exchange information. The candidate tells about himself or herself, and the interviewer describes the company and the specific job available. It is the selection process that most people think of immediately when they hear the word "interview," because almost everyone who works has participated in several interviews. A 1957 survey by Spriegel and James revealed that 99 percent of the 872 firms surveyed required that job applicants be interviewed.[1] According to a report in 1977,

> Many employers no longer require job applicants to take tests. Interviews and application blanks are a much more common means of screening employees. . . . Over 96% of the companies surveyed said either an interview or an applicant's previous experience were the most important factors to them when it came to selecting employees.[2]

[1] Orman R. Wright, Jr., "Summary of Research on the Selection Interview Since 1964," *Personnel Psychology* 22 (1969): 394.
[2] "Survey Finds Testing Less Important in Employee Selection," *Personnel Management-Policies and Practices* 24 (January 1977): 3.

As this survey indicates, interviews play a crucial but supplementary role in the hiring process. The interviewer obtains critical information that can then be weighed along with information from application forms, resumes, letters of recommendation, psychological tests, grade records, and whatever else an organization chooses to collect.

Hiring procedures vary widely. Their complexity depends upon (1) the level of the job and (2) the status of the job market. There will be obvious differences in the hiring of a top executive, a middle manager, and a production line worker. The higher the level, the larger the dossier that will be needed to make a selection. On the other hand, one personnel representative described her interviews as a mere ritual when the labor market is tight because she would hire "anybody" that applied.

Since hiring practices differ among jobs, the selection interview is a misnomer. There is just no such thing as *the* basic selection interview, because there are many different formats. A prescreening interview will have some major differences from an in-depth interview. Nevertheless, this chapter attempts to describe some of the things that most selection interviews have in common.

UNIQUE CONTRIBUTIONS OF THE INTERVIEW

From time to time people have questioned the value of the interview to the selection process. It is important that you know that it does make some specific and very unique contributions. Listed below are some of the things that are accomplished in an interview that cannot be accomplished through written materials.

The Interviewee

1. The interviewer can assess communication abilities, appearance, personality factors, thinking patterns, and level of motivation. None of these factors can be judged from resumes or questionnaires.
2. It provides an opportunity to obtain information about the candidate that might not be obtained otherwise. Most people will say more about themselves than they will write down. Furthermore, probing often yields more depth to the answers: the "why" is often more important than the "what." Therefore, the interview facilitates a more thorough familiarization with the candidate.
3. In talking with the interviewer, the interviewee is likely to reveal the real extent of his or her interest in the job and the company. It is not infrequent that in the course of exchanging information the interviewee will realize that expectations about the company or the job are not consistent with the real situation.

The Company

1. An interview personalizes the company. As the representative of the company, you provide the image that the interviewee has of the company. Through you the interviewee gets a sense of the working atmosphere and of the people in the organization.
2. The interview supplements and expands any written materials. It provides an opportunity to give more detailed explanations about the local offices, the personal aspects of jobs available, career and advancement opportunities, and corporate philosophy. One recruiter was very specific about this when he said, "We have never been able to design a brochure that adequately represents our company."
3. The interview allows the tailoring of information to a specific interviewee. Not every interviewee is interested in the same things about a job or a company. Consequently, their questions may vary considerably.

RESEARCH PERSPECTIVES

More research has probably been done about selection interviews than any other type of interview, and it will be instructive to look at some of the conclusions that have been drawn from two syntheses of this research.[3] Keep in mind that the studies being reported vary widely in terms of the kinds of jobs and the nature of the interviews described.

1. An interviewer is consistent in the approach to different interviewees; the techniques remain fairly constant.
2. In an unstructured interview, material is not consistently covered.
3. When interviewers obtain the same information, they are likely to interpret it differently.
4. Structured interviews, in general, provide a higher interrater reliability than do unstructured interviews.
5. The form of the question does affect the answer obtained.
6. Although the reliabilities of interviews may be high in given situations, the validities obtained are usually low.
7. The attitude of the interviewer does affect his or her interpretation of what the interviewee says.
8. In the usual, unstructured employment interview, the interviewer talks more than the interviewee does.

[3]Eugene Mayfield, "The Selection Interview—A Re-evaluation of Published Research," *Personnel Psychology* 17 (Autumn 1964), and Orman R. Wright, Jr., "Summary of Research on Selection Interview."

9. Interviewers appear to be influenced more by unfavorable than favorable information.
10. Interviewers tend to make their decisions early in an unstructured interview.
11. Interview decisions are made on the basis of behaviors in the interview as well as on verbal cues.
12. Judgments of an interviewee are affected by the characteristics assessed about previous applicants.

Research conclusions can be useful information for anyone who is eager to improve interviewing skills. They point out weaknesses, needed directions for improvement, and raise new questions. Consequently, it is wise for you to make use of the findings presented in the rest of this chapter.

Nevertheless, you ought to have a healthy skepticism about and recognize the limitations of any given research. For example, look at the second conclusion above. Material is not covered consistently in an unstructured interview. In comparing a number of interviewers, this apparently seemed to be true; however, this conclusion washes out the few interviewers who have perfected their technique of holding unstructured interviews so that they can in fact cover the same materials in each.

PLANNING THE INTERVIEW

Two different phenomena have created a tremendous need for better planning of selection interviews. As described above, academic researchers have for years challenged the reliability and validity of some interviewing procedures. Many interviewers apparently had no training on how to conduct an effective interview, and they relied on intuition, with questionable results. These results were not taken too seriously, however, until legal regulations began to challenge what is appropriate for an interview. With such attention focused on their procedures, people who had to conduct selection interviews started investigating ways to make them better. Consequently, we want to outline some considerations for *planning* an effective interview.

Tailoring the Interview to the Job

It is critical to tailor the interview to the job. For purposes of analysis, make two columns on a sheet of paper. On the left, enumerate the job skills needed for a particular position. Consult any job descriptions in order to make this list as complete as possible. Then rank them according to their priority. On the right, list the characteristics needed by anyone who would fill that position. The following lists represent the responsibilities and qualities that one company listed for a sales position.

Job Responsibilities

initiate contact with potential customers

present oneself well, orally and physically

be punctual

keep displays attractive

keep accurate sales records

react pleasantly with different types of people

close as many sales as possible

be convincing without being pushy

be promotable

Qualities Needed

be able to analyze situations

possess self-assurance

be articulate; have good communication skills

be creative in developing new concepts

be capable of self-direction

possess integrity; be ethical

have a desire to excel

have previous sales experience

be reliable

be ambitious

Another list was prepared for a bank teller working in a drive-in booth that would serve automobile customers.

Job Responsibilities

make change accurately

keep accurate records

greet customers warmly

work adding machine

work alone

process transactions quickly

Qualities Needed

pay attention to details

be able to work alone

be honest

be punctual

possess mathematical accuracy

have good oral communication skills

be personable

Another case in point of how an interview can be tailored to the job and company circumstances involves the flight attendants for a major airline. For years, ambition had been a consideration in hiring attendants, and many people accepted the job with the hope that they could move into management positions. Turnover in the management positions of this company was not very great, however. Since there were few opportunities for promotion, the airline found itself with a number of dissatisfied flight attendants. Consequently, the airline now is searching for ways to choose people who will be satisfied to work as flight attendants for a number of years.

In analyzing any job, you should avoid taking too limited a view of the job. Coordination with other people, promotability, and growth toward a new position are often viable concerns in addition to the specific skills needed for an entry level job. For example, it may be anticipated that anyone who is selected for a managerial position ought to have the capacity to grow into more responsibilities than she or he will have at the entry level.

Making an appropriate list of specifications calls for skillful analysis and some very refined thinking about a position; it does not involve just making a casual list of the performance steps in a job. Walter Mahler describes the following steps in determining specifications for executive positions.[4]

1. Do not leave it up to the staff. (It is your responsibility.)
2. Use multiple inputs. (Check your list of specifications with others.)
3. Look at business or operating objectives.
4. Review the position description. (Keep it up-to-date.)
5. Consider present and past incumbents. (What personal factors contributed to their successes and failures?)
6. Analyze relevant competitors. (What personnel factors give them an advantage?)
7. Give attention to future changes. (Most job functions are not static; will the requirements for the job be changed?)
8. Separate critical from "nice to have."
9. Do not build in "crutches" in advance. (Do not cover up the candidate's inadequacy on a given specification by thinking you can change the candidate later.)

Identifying the Purposes

The purpose for a selection interview varies widely according to the type of job represented. It is important, however, that the interviewer always keep a clear idea of just what is to be accomplished. Discussed below are some of the purposes often ascribed to selection interviews.

1. *To initiate personal contact with the applicant.* For some unskilled jobs for which almost anyone will qualify, getting acquainted may be the only purpose for the interview. For more important positions, this purpose is often expanded to include a check of the personal chemistry with the candidate. It is particularly useful for supervisors who are hiring their own subordinates to be able to ascertain the degree of compatibility with the potential worker. It may also be a major consideration in hiring a member of a college faculty or a top executive.

2. *To give an orientation to the specific job and the company.* Maybe its useful to point out that one of the most frequent complaints about college recruiters is that they do not have enough information about specific jobs. Candidates who are selecting a job expect to receive information that will help them make a good decision. Consequently, interviewers need to state that the orientation is a major purpose of the interview and that one of the primary responsibilities, particularly in tight labor markets, is to sell the company.

---

[4]Walter Mahler, *How Effective Executives Interview* (Homewood, Ill.: Dow Jones-Richard D. Irwin, Inc., 1976), pp. 77–83.

3. *To maintain an adequate work force.* Interviews are conducted to keep a supply of workers who can do the work adequately. There may not be any attempt to discover and hire only the best.

4. *To suit the worker to the job.* Sometimes there is the notion that there is one best person for a given job, and the interviewer may exert considerable energy trying to make this determination. The higher one goes in an organization, the more important this purpose becomes. One implication of this purpose is that the interviewer knows the job requirements in detail.

5. *To gather information about the candidate that will enable the interviewer to predict successful performance.* This, of course, is the underlying function of the selection interview. In stating this purpose we have chosen to emphasize the predicting function more than the collecting of information, simply because the interviewer needs to be aware of the kinds of inferences needed in order to predict the future. It is often hard to judge the accuracy of such predictions, because there are so many external variables that affect an employee's success, like the economic and political environment, job offers from other organizations, or sudden changes in a candidate's personal life. Nevertheless, the predictions must be made. One representative of a major oil company reported to us that the company's records over 15 years showed that the best predictor of success in their company was the estimate made in the initial selection interview. That is quite a tribute to their skills.

6. *To find out what kind of person the candidate is.* People are not easily compartmentalized into the work self, the social self, the religious self, and so on. Consequently, in order to make a good decision there is a need for the interviewer to look at the candidate as a whole. A person's style is generally all pervasive. This is particularly true in the hiring of supervisors, professional staff, and managers. College recruiters, for example, have emphasized this purpose in two different surveys. In both surveys, they rated looking at the total person as being more important than just determining a candidate's nonpersonal work capabilities.[5]

Selecting Key Decisions

One important purpose is to discover what kind of person the candidate is, but you still need to find out other characteristics and qualifications of the person. One way of identifying these "decision points" is to phrase some general questions for your own evaluation:

1. Can the person do the job? Does the person have the requisite skill to be effective?

[5]Cal W. Downs, "Perceptions of the Selection Interview," *Personnel Administration* (May 1969): 11. The second survey was conducted in 1978 and has not yet been published.

2. Will the candidate do the job? Is the candidate motivated? Does this person possess skills that will be used energetically?
3. What will be the impact on others of adding this person to a given work unit? Will the person fit in or create disturbances?
4. Why does this person want this particular job? Will this person be willing to stay with it?

A second way of examining the key decisions to be made is to examine the characteristics listed on an evaluation form. (Figures 7.1 and 7.2 are two sample forms.) Periodically, these forms ought to be checked to determine whether or not they actually relate well to a given job. If they do not, perhaps you should refine them.

A third way of determining which key questions are important is to learn what others are doing. As an example, since we are interested in the recruiting that takes place on college campuses, we have asked recruiters to identify the kinds of judgments that they feel are most important. We also asked a large group of engineers who are middle-managers to rank in order of importance the same characteristics if they were hiring a direct subordinate. Table 7.1 contains the two lists so that comparisons can be made.

Keep in mind that the recruiters were conducting prescreening interviews, so some candidates will be invited back to the company for additional interviews. The engineers, on the other hand, were looking for direct subordinates. There are some differences in the rank orders, of course. The engineers, for example, placed a higher premium on loyalty and specialized courses. It is useful to point out that within each group, too, people placed different emphasis on the same factors. For example, in rating writing skills, 12 percent of the engineers said they were "essential," 43 percent said they were "very important," 43 percent rated them as "somewhat important," and 2 percent judged them to be "unimportant." These differences reflect the different demands of the different jobs.

What is important about these lists is that they reinforce the purpose of judging the kind of person the candidate is. General personal characteristics such as enthusiasm, motivation, and leadership ability are rated as much more important than specific training or experiences. The trick, of course, is to get the information that allows you to make judgments about the person's general personal characteristics.

Preparing an Agenda

Careful thought should be given to determining the kind of information that will let you make the kind of judgment that you want to make.

Several years ago we conducted an analysis of 20 actual recruiting interviews to determine what was actually discussed that enabled the

Applicant's Name _____ Code _____

CONFIDENTIAL
_____

I. **Job Preference.** List priorities identified by candidate. Translate the candidate's comments and goals into specific job openings.

II. **Geographical/Location Restrictions/Preferences.** List regions of preference or avoidance. Also try to list first, second, third choice of specific locations.

III. **Work Experience.** List any experience that qualifies candidate.

IV. **Academic Record/Campus Activities.** Include any insights on the candidate's academic education, record, experience, or interests beyond the information on the resume.

V. **Personal Characteristics.**

	+	Average	–	Comments
Technical Skills	____	____	____	_____
Communication Skills	____	____	____	_____
Intelligence	____	____	____	_____
Attitude	____	____	____	_____
Maturity	____	____	____	_____
Motivation	____	____	____	_____
Training	____	____	____	_____

VII. **Recommendation(s) on Job and Location.** Be specific on both job(s) and location(s).

A. (job) _____ (location/dept)
B. (job) _____ (location/dept)
C. (job) _____ (location/dept)

VIII. **Any Other Comments to Support Your Recommendations.**

_____ _____
Interviewer   Date

Figure 7.1   A sample: selection evaluation form.

5 = UNSATISFACTORY   4 = BELOW AVERAGE   3 = AVERAGE   2 = ABOVE AVERAGE   1 = OUTSTANDING   NR = NOT RATED

(Circle Appropriate Rating)

QUALITIES	DESCRIPTION	COMMENTS
Intelligence 1 2 3 4 5 NR	Academic performance: grades continuously high. Questions showed depth of purpose and were nonroutine.	
Responsibility 1 2 3 4 5 NR	College job experiences related to grade point average. Excelled at outside activities and has work goals.	
Appearance and Poise 1 2 3 4 5 NR	Physical appearance, grooming, manners, neat are appropriate for a professional person.	
Experience 1 2 3 4 5 NR	Business grades related to overall grade point average. Good business related work experience.	
Interpersonal Relations 1 2 3 4 5 NR	Activities and hobbies demonstrate ability to work with others; peers select candidate to lead.	
Integrity 1 2 3 4 5 NR	No unresolved inconsistencies in the interview.	
Self-confidence 1 2 3 4 5 NR	Poised and relaxed manner in the interview. Knows self. Desire for responsibility and opportunity versus concern over security.	
Maturity 1 2 3 4 5 NR	Evidence or logical thinking behind answers to questions. Knows priorities. Sets realistic goals.	
Communication Skills 1 2 3 4 5 NR	Responses were readily understood. Articulate; Used good grammar and expressed thoughts concisely; Listens well; Responsive.	

Interests

1 2 3 4 5 NR   Evidence of academic interests outside accounting. Hobbies indicate variety of interests with deep involvement.

Leadership Potential

1 2 3 4 5 NR   Held several elective offices; Recipient of leadership awards. Wants to exercise leadership.

Circle any adjectives which apply to this candidate.

Aggressive	Deliberate	Flexible	Introvert	Open-minded	Self-reliant
Casual	Discreet	Imaginative	Irresponsible	Overbearing	Shallow
Cautious	Dogmatic	Impulsive	Knowledgeable	Presumptuous	Tenacious
Closed	Dull	Indifferent	Lazy	Pushy	Vacillating
Cocky	Energetic	Industrious	Loud	Polished	Vigorous
Competent	Enthusiastic	Inflexible	Motivated	Reserved	Vulgar
Conceited	Erratic	Inquisitive	Naive	Resourceful	Warm
Cooperative	Extrovert	Insecure	Observant	Responsible	Witty

Overall evaluation and reasons for your decision _____

_____

_____

_____

_____

Candidate _____   Interviewed by _____

Office _____   Date _____

Figure 7.2 A sample: selection evaluation form.

117

Table 7.1 RANK ORDER OF DECISION FACTORS

RECRUITERS	ENGINEERS
1. Enthusiasm	1. Enthusiasm
2. Oral communication ability	2. Oral communication ability
3. Leadership potential	3. Confidence in self
4. Confidence in self	4. Emotional stability
5. Aggressiveness and initiative	5. Aggressiveness and initiative
6. Emotional stability	6. Loyalty
7. Writing skills	7. Efficient
8. Scholastic record	8. Pleasant personality
9. Pleasant personality	9. Leadership potential
10. Personal appearance	10. Writing skills
11. Moral standards	11. Compatibility with superior
12. Poise in interview	12. Work experience of particular type
13. Efficient	13. Moral standards
14. Interest in people	14. Interest in people
15. Extracurricular activities	15. Realistic salary expectations
16. Loyalty	16. Willingness to accept routine assignments
17. Preparation for interview	17. Poise in interview
18. Willingness to travel	18. Specialized courses
19. Formulated long-range goals and objectives	19. Good scholastic record
20. Realistic salary expectations	20. Good personal appearance
21. Humility	21. Willingness to travel
22. Work experience of particular type	22. Preparation for interview
23. Willingness to accept routine assignments	23. Formulated long-range goals and objectives
24. Compatibility with interviewer	24. Humility
25. Liberal arts courses	25. Extracurricular activities
26. Specialized courses	26. Liberal arts courses

recruiters to make their decisions. These topics are listed in rank order below. These topics were not necessarily initiated by the interviewer.[6]

1. Job expectations
2. Academic background
3. Preparation for the interview (How much is known about the company?)
4. Scholastic record
5. Work experience
6. Geographical preference
7. Interviewing for other jobs
8. Family background
9. Goals
10. Extracurricular activities
11. Strengths/weaknesses
12. Salary expectations

[6]Cal W. Downs, "A Content Analysis of Twenty Selection Interviews," *Personnel Administration and Public Personnel Review* (September 1972): 25.

Periodically, you ought to work out an agenda of relevant areas to be discussed. It might well look like this:

Work Experience
1. Current job
   a. Principal responsibilities
   b. Principal accomplishments
   c. Reason for wanting to leave
   d. Relations with others
   e. Leadership style
2. Previous jobs
   a. Principal responsibilities
   b. Principal accomplishments
   c. Reasons for changes

Education and Training
1. Kinds of education—high school, college, graduate school
2. Reason for choices
3. Specialized courses
4. Major accomplishments
5. Principal influences
6. Specific intellectual skills
7. Importance of education

Family Life
1. Discipline style
2. Basic values
3. Activities
4. Influence of family on job

Present Activities
1. Special interests
2. Energy level
3. Relation of job to social activities
4. Management of time
5. Extracurricular activities

Self-assessment
1. Strengths
2. Weaknesses
3. Self-image

Expectations/Goals
1. Present
2. Long-range

Management Style
1. Control

2. View of effectiveness
3. Kind of supervision preferred

This agenda is only a suggestion of what can be done. It would be possible to make it much more elaborate, but you would have to have a particular job in mind in order to do so.

So far the only content objectives we have discussed have been about the candidate, and we must not forget that a major purpose of the interview is to tell about the company and job. Consequently, a part of the agenda must focus on these areas. Topics that many have found to be useful include the following:

General Organizational Orientation
1. Organization
2. Company image
3. Advantages of working here
4. Management policies
5. Economic standing

Specific Job Requirements
1. Skills needed
2. Management development opportunities
3. Orientation to people on the job
4. Schedules
5. Salary

Framing Questions for Each Content Area

Several generalizations can be made about questions in the selection interview. The questions should reflect both careful planning of the agenda and the kinds of qualities you are trying to evaluate. Through experiences all interviewers develop particular questions that work well for them. Nevertheless, it is useful to reevaluate questions periodically in terms of the stated objectives. Listed below are some frequently used questions associated with the areas described earlier.

WORK EXPERIENCE

1. What jobs have you held?
   a. How were they obtained?
   b. Why did you leave?
2. What did you like most in your jobs? Least?
3. What were your primary accomplishments?
4. Do you prefer working with others or by yourself?
5. What were the most difficult problems you faced? How were they resolved?

6. What influences your productivity? Satisfaction?
7. What have you found that you do best?
8. What changes would you like to have made in your career?
9. How have you related to others at work?
10. What has been your level of earnings?
11. Why did you choose your particular jobs or field of work?
12. What have you done that shows initiative?
13. How much are you currently earning? What did you earn in your last job?
14. Did you ever work overtime? How did you feel about it?
15. How do you feel about routine work?
16. What has been your greatest frustration or disappointment in your current job?
17. Considering your accomplishments, what are some of the reasons for your successes?
18. What have been some of your disappointments? What things have you hoped to accomplish that you have not done? What has prevented you?
19. Describe your relationships with your last two supervisors?
20. What has been your experience in organizing a work unit?
21. Describe your supervisor.

Notice that these questions about work can be grouped under categories that deal with job histories and categories that deal with job conditions. A person's job history and reasons for leaving each job are very sensitive areas that should be probed thoroughly. These discussions can reveal the candidate's overall orientation toward work. Sometimes, the reasons behind job changes can tell you more about a candidate's suitability for a current job than anything else. Additionally, by identifying what kinds of experiences the candidate has had, you can assess whether preparation for this job and additional training are necessary.

Questions about work conditions should be straightforward. Items of routine work, relocation, overtime, travel, and all other job conditions of this type should be checked. Generally, it is wise to find out how the candidate feels about them before listing them as requirements for a position that is open.

EDUCATION AND TRAINING

Answers to the following questions give insights into a candidate's intellectual abilities, skills, personality, and motivation.

1. How did you choose_____ as a school? Would you make the same choice today?
2. Which of your college years was most difficult? Why?
3. What courses did you like best? Least? Why?

4. How did you select your major? Have you ever changed your major? Why?
5. How did you happen to go to college?
6. If you were starting college all over again, what would you do differently?
7. How do you rank scholastically in your class?
8. How did you rank in your graduating class?
9. What plans do you have for additional education?
10. Do you think grades should be considered by employers? Why?
11. What has influenced your performance in school the most?
12. Which were your best subjects? Your worst?
13. Exactly what did you study in your_____class?
14. How have you financed your education?
15. What have been your special achievements?
16. What have been your toughest problems?
17. How much effort was required for you to make your grades?
18. How well has your schooling prepared you for your career?
19. Describe your study habits.
20. What advice would you give an incoming freshman in your major?
21. Do you feel that your grades reflect the kind of work you are capable of doing?

Subject dislikes, for example, provide some clues about limitations. Discovering that a person hates mathematics might be of great concern if the person is applying for the job of bank teller. How well a person has applied himself or herself sometimes can be determined by grades or the candidate's view of grades. In all of these areas, however, watch for trends. Dropping out of a college, for example, may be viewed as a lack of motivation, a lack of ability, a rebellion against pressures, a reaction to a temporary conflict, or a very realistic assessment about what the person wants out of life. Consequently, you should look for trends or corroborating evidence to lead you in making your interpretation. Is there a pattern that a particular answer fits into?

SELF-ASSESSMENT

The following questions are designed to tap a person's modesty, realism, motivations, energies, flexibility, and communication abilities.

1. What are your strengths?
2. What are your weaknesses?
3. What are your special abilities?
4. You have 10 minutes; sell yourself to me.
5. How would you describe yourself?
6. How do you feel about your career to date?

7. What qualifications do you have that makes you feel that you will succeed in accomplishing your objectives?
8. How do you feel about your progress so far?
9. Some people like all instructions to be explicit; others like to do things on their own. How would you describe yourself?
10. How would you describe your standards of performance?
11. What has been your biggest mistake that you can recall?
12. What types of people irritate you?
13. How would your boss (subordinates or classmates) describe you?
14. Who are the most important people to you? Why?
15. In what areas do you need to improve?
16. What further training do you need?
17. What makes you a good investment for an employer?
18. What constructive criticism have you had from others?
19. Do you consider your progress so far representative of your ability?
20. Describe yourself.
21. Without naming him or her, describe your best friend. How are you alike? Different?

Talking about the self in this way is one of the most difficult chores interviewees face in an interview. Doing it articulately and objectively demonstrates some excellent communication skills.

ACTIVITIES AND INTERESTS

The next set of questions are not as directly job related as the others. Nevertheless, there is always the possibility that they will lead to great insights into a candidate. Therefore, they are worth the time.

1. In what school activities have you participated? Why?
2. What do you enjoy doing off the job? In your spare time?
3. What extracurricular offices have you held?
4. How did you become interested in_____(a special interest)?
5. What kind of health problems have you had?
6. How do your social interests relate to your job?
7. What requires most of your energies?
8. How do you manage your time off the job?
9. What do you read?

Participation in extracurricular activities, for example, may be quite revealing about a candidate's leadership abilities, management of time, and sense of competition or cooperation, as well as about the responses of other people to the candidate (as in election to offices). The activities themselves are not work related, but the qualities they reveal may have a very direct bearing on the way a candidate works. Even if they do not lead to great insights, they still are valuable in terms of building rapport with the candidate and letting the candidate talk about the things he or she really enjoys.

GOALS AND EXPECTATIONS

Most people cannot tell you where they would like to be ten years from now. In fact, you may not be able to answer this question yourself. Nevertheless, this line of questioning is valuable in assessing a candidate's thoughts about planning for a career. They also test a candidate's realistic expectations. Finally, they set the stage for a deeper analysis of this area. The following is a list of some sample questions.

1. Where would you like to be in five years? Ten years?
2. How much money would you like to earn by_____ (age)?
3. In what type of position are you most interested?
4. Why do you think you would like to work for us?
5. Do you prefer any geographical location? Are you free to relocate?
6. What job in our company do you want to work toward?
7. What is your idea of how our industry operates?
8. What do you think determines a person's progress?
9. What size city do you prefer?
10. Why do you think people succeed? Fail?
11. How long do you think it will take you to get where you want to go?
12. How have your aspirations changed in recent years?
13. Are there any conditions that limit your flexibility in taking on a new assignment?
14. If you could write your ideal job description, what would it be?
15. What are the most important things you do in a job?
16. Aside from money, what do you want most in a job?
17. What are you doing currently to achieve your career objectives?
18. What will happen if you do not meet your goals?

FAMILY BACKGROUND (OPTIONAL)

The following questions are an attempt to discover some of the early forces that are brought to bear on an individual.

1. What were the earliest influences on you?
2. How would you describe the discipline you received?
3. What kinds of expectations did your parents have of you? How did you react to them?
4. How are you different from the rest of your family?
5. How has your family affected your self-image?
6. Who are the most important people to you? Why?

7. What work do your parents do?
8. What have been the principal influences on your life?

Interpretation of such information is not always easy. Sometimes a question such as "What does your father do?" may seem irrelevant at first glance, and often it is. However, it may lead to other topics. For example, we have a transcript in which a youthful, inexperienced applicant was having difficulty talking about himself and his lack of work experience. When the interviewer suddenly focused on his father's occupation, the applicant suddenly became more articulate and began to talk readily about some of the travel experiences he had as a result of his father's occupation. Once again, it had some content relevance, but it also had a great deal of process relevance, since it was the key transition to a more pleasant communication between the interviewer and the interviewee.

Open questions dominate. While skillful interviewers use a mix of open and closed questions, the open ones are preferable here. The more the interviewee talks, the more data the interviewer will have to assess. Furthermore, open questions are preferable because answers to them generally tell the interviewer something about the interviewee's perspective. In terms of evaluation, a candidate's perspective of his or her life is often more important than the specific details.

Probe completely and frankly. Get complete details. The "why" about past behavior is just as important as the "what" or the "how." A useful, probing question for most areas is, "What are some of the reasons for this?"

Not all questions need to be phrased in the interrogative form. Directives such as "Describe your job," "Tell me about yourself," or "Summarize your accomplishments" are requests for information and are interesting variations.

Sometimes it is useful to give a preamble to a question to keep it from becoming a grilling, for example, "We sometimes compare our assets and limitations with our competitors. Let's do the same thing with your career? What are your principal assets?"

Ask about hypothetical problems. Since the interviewer wants to predict the extent of success a person will have in a job, it is suitable for an interviewer to ask an interviewee how he or she might perform in specific circumstances. These hypothetical situations need to be clearly described and fairly typical. For example, a person interviewing for an airline ticket agent's job might be asked:

Suppose you had been working several hours on Christmas Eve. The flights are crowded, and the ticket lines are longer than usual. All of a sudden, a woman with two bags and a little girl rushes to the front of the line and yells out frantically that she is going to miss her plane if she does not check in now. How would you handle this situation?

Ask questions about the candidate's meaning of terms like "success," "cooperation," or "management." They can reveal much about a candidate's perspective and how he or she thinks. A variation of this question is, "In your communication class, how was communication defined? What are the most important principles of communication?"

Structuring the Interview

Interviewers have many different reasons for choosing to structure their interviews in different ways, since structure is largely a matter of personal preference. The main point is that you should have some plan.

Reviewing the Information

You can not only tailor an interview to a job, but you can also tailor it to the individual. Therefore, the more that you know about the individual before the interview begins, the better off you are. Make it a standard rule that you will always consult the job application or resume before you begin.

Arranging the Setting

The timing and setting in a selection interview can have an important impact upon your relationship with the interviewee. Once again, you must decide what you want this impact to be. If you are interviewing someone to be your direct subordinate, you may wish to have your surroundings much as they will be in the work situation. If you have a formal relationship with your employees, by all means keep the interview formal. If you are a college recruiter, on the other hand, you may try for just the opposite effect. Many recruiters report that they try to avoid interviewing from behind a desk and that they also try to see that the chairs are fairly equal. The rationale behind these preferences is to try to avoid anything that might intimidate the interviewee or that might heighten anxiety.

If you have followed all of the guidelines mentioned, you will have arranged a very thorough interview schedule based on a thorough analysis of the job. When you put all of this information together, it might well look like the format of Figure 7.3. Remember that this is just the planning stage. Now it is time to interact with the interviewee.

MANAGING THE INTERVIEW

Detailed planning will help you to conduct a good interview, but there is still the challenge of implementing these plans when you meet the interviewee. Listed below are several considerations that should be helpful in making your interactions most effective.

INTRODUCTION		
Things to cover		**Things to look for**
greeting		appearance
orientation		poise
lead questions		manner

WORK EXPERIENCE		
Things to cover	**Questions to ask**	**Things to look for**
current job	What do you like best	motivation
other jobs	about work?	skill
	What have been your	relevance of work
	major accomplishments?	

EDUCATION AND TRAINING		
Things to cover	**Questions to ask**	**Things to look for**
college	What have been your	special interests
	best subjects?	intellectual ability
	What were your reasons	
	for choosing your major?	

SELF-ASSESSMENT		
Things to cover	**Questions to ask**	**Things to look for**
strengths	What are your strengths?	confidence
attitudes	What can you contribute	energy
	to our company	

ACTIVITIES		
Things to cover	**Questions to ask**	**Things to look for**
interpersonal	What are your off-the-job	amount of
relations	activities	interaction
activities	In what school activities	energy; breadth of
	In what school activities	activities
	did you participate?	

GOALS AND EXPECTATION		
Things to cover	**Questions to ask**	**Things to look for**
plans	Where would you like	ambition; realism
potential for	to be in five years?	adaptability
failure	What will happen if your	
	goals are not met?	

BACKGROUND		
Things to cover	**Questions to ask**	**Things to look for**
early influences	What are the earliest	priorities
self-assessment	influences on you?	objectivity;
	How are you different	independence
	from others in your	
	family?	

Figure 7.3   Interview guide.

1. *Introduce yourself and give an orientation to what is going to take place.* It is important to let the interviewee know what to call you—by your informal first name or formal last name. Also, find out how the interviewee would like to be addressed. The variety of forms of address for women, for example, make it particularly important that you address them exactly as they wish. This is merely an attempt to avoid any problems that could occur.

In the orientation it is customary for the interviewer to set the tone and the structure of the interaction. Suggest some guidelines for the interviewee's role. For example, if you say simply, "I have some questions to ask you and later I'll give you an opportunity to ask me some questions," the candidate knows that it is inappropriate to start off by asking you questions.

2. *Build rapport.* Normally, job applicants are interviewed in surroundings that are strange to them. This can make them nervous, particularly if they are in critical need of a job. A real challenge for the interviewer is to have a pleasant conversation that also yields sufficient data to arrive at a confident decision. This comes best when the candidate is somewhat at ease. How can this be done? The same thing will not work for all candidates, but listed below are suggestions we have compiled from professional interviewers.

> Give a warm, friendly greeting.
> Offer coffee or another drink.
> Conduct the interview in privacy and avoid interruptions or distractions.
> Talk about the weather, ball teams, and so on, before moving on to the interview topics.
> Let the interviewee observe possible peer workers in order to get him or her to relax.
> Start off with topics that are very familiar to the interviewee.
> Arrange a relatively informal setting.

Finally, in a very conversational manner, give the candidate a thorough orientation as to what is going to happen in the interview. People tend to relax when uncertainty or ambiguity is reduced. Make the interview a pleasant experience for both of you.

3. *Structure the interview.* Research shows that generally structured interviews are more reliable and cover information more consistently than do unstructured ones. There is also some legal pressure to cover the same topics with everyone. We do not advise anyone to devise a strict, rigid structure, however. After all, this would eliminate any adaptation to the communication needs of the candidate. Furthermore, good, pleasant communication does not take place when people act only out of habit, but we do advocate that you use the same general format for most people.

The most common procedure is to spend the first 60−70 percent of the interview discussing the candidate and the last 30−40 percent discussing the company and the job. Occasionally, people like to start off with a discussion of the job requirements. However, this procedure has the distinct disadvantage of letting the candidate know exactly how to shape answers to fit the job description, and we recommend against it. Even some interviewees have discussed how easy it is to second-guess the interviewers under these conditions.

Even though you may have a fairly comprehensive interview guide or schedule, it is often wise to give the candidate a fairly free rein in determining what to discuss first. For example, if you open with "Tell me about yourself," you not only get some factual information, but you also get some information about the candidate's priorities and what she or he thinks is really important. A candidate's perspective about himself or herself may be more important in making a good assessment than the specific details.

4. *Probe analytically and thoroughly.* Our research shows that most interviewers believe what they are told, and a look at transcripts shows that many of them are also manipulated by the candidate. For example, we recently recorded an interview with a candidate applying for a job. He had a current job in which he was very unhappy. However, the interviewer never discovered this. Every time the interviewer asked about the current job, the candidate talked at length about how much he enjoyed "working with people." When we had a chance to discuss this with the candidate later, he admitted that this was a deliberate tactic on his part to avoid telling the interviewer about his unhappiness. He was afraid that his admitting that he had problems would be judged negatively by the interviewer.

This example demonstrates the need for you to analyze carefully the answers that you receive and for you to be business-like and assertive about pursuing needed information. Occasionally it may be useful for you to write down some directions for yourself, such as "Explore this in detail" or "Get at least three assets and three limitations," to remind yourself that a verbal response is not necessarily a complete answer. Finally, be particularly cautious about accepting ambiguous phrases such as "loves to work with people." Ask exactly what this means. Remember that people often give such answers because they are socially acceptable ones and not necessarily because they are true. Probe and test for inconsistencies.

5. *Avoid errors in asking questions.* First, avoid asking many questions that can be answered by a "yes" or a "no." Use a more open or journalistic style. Second, keep your questions as clear as possible and be sensitive to indications that the candidate has not understood. If there is a misunderstanding, avoid making the candidate feel that he or she has done something wrong or is somehow at fault. Third, avoid cutting off the

candidate too soon or interrupting the candidate if he or she is thinking about an answer. Silence is not wasted time.

Avoid coaching the interviewee through obvious argument or agreement with the answer. Comments like "That was a wise choice," "I agree," or "That was a good reason to. . . ." can have a profound influence on how the person answers future questions.

6. *Make notations of key information.* Taking notes was discussed in Chapter 3. Whatever your preferred method is of aiding your memory, be certain that you have specific data to use as a rationale for your conclusion.

7. *Pace the interview.* Most interviews have some time limits, and it is important that you do not wander aimlessly or get bogged down in one area. Consequently, you must control the timing within the interview. Our research indicates that feeling rushed or not having enough time is one of the most frequent complaints heard about selection interviews. A well-paced interview is probably more satisfying communicatively to the candidate as well as to the interviewer. Everybody appreciates a feeling of progress.

8. *Allow the candidate time to ask questions.* You may be shopping for an employee, but the candidate is shopping, too, and there are things that he or she will want to know. Furthermore, you can get an idea of the candidate's qualifications and interests by examining the nature of the questions that he or she asks.

9. *Conclude the interview.* The conclusion should be pleasant and instructive. A summary of what has been discussed is always useful. Additionally, the candidates should be thanked for their time and told what to expect in terms of a follow-up. It is not uncommon to promise to contact them by mail within a certain time frame. If you make the promise, keep it.

In the conclusion, special care must be made to keep from giving misleading cues to the candidate. For example, one interviewer ended an interview with the statement "We had a good interview." The interviewer meant that it was a pleasant communication; the candidate interpreted this, however, as meaning that her qualifications were good and that she could expect an offer.

Should you offer a job at the end of the interview? Yes, if you are in a position to do so, and if you are certain of your decision. Should you reject someone outright? Normally, less emotion and embarrassment is created if this is done by mail.

INTERPRETING THE DATA

Our surveys on selection decisions have shown that most professional recruiters make their decisions in the first half of an interview and that they are quite confident of their decisions. Apparently, the most desirable and undesirable candidates are easily identified. Nevertheless, the following guidelines will be useful in interpreting whether a candidate should be hired.

1. *Review the job specifications made in your planning and make the kind of judgments that are consistent with them.* For example, a qualification for a managerial position may be the ability to communicate orally. In this case, performance in the interview rather than answers to specific questions would be the data you would use to make your decision. How articulate is the interviewee in answering questions? Can the interviewee express ideas well? How well does the interviewee listen? How well can the interviewee organize thoughts? Is the interviewee able to give precise, coherent answers? Keep these specifications in mind in order of their priority.

2. *Be aware of potential biases and try to counteract them.* It should be noted that not all interviewers feel that biases are undesirable. For example, one interviewer suggested that his biases were those of his organization and that he let them have full sway. If bias is defined as *unwanted* influence, however, then most people will try to counteract them, and awareness of them is the first step in overcoming a problem.

3. *Differentiate between inferences and observations about the interviewee.* The material in Chapter 2 demonstrates how frequently people insert information that is not there because they make unwarranted assumptions. Mahler, for example, makes the following point about inferences: "There are many instances during an interview in which judgment shows up. The most important place is the inference one has to make as to the extent to which judgment accounts for accomplishments, and the extent to which poor judgment accounts for failure to accomplish results."[7] It is not undesirable to make inferences. You just have to realize that you are doing so and collect as much supporting evidence as possible.

4. *Use multiple interviews as an option.* These are standard practices that exist in the higher levels of an organization, but they may be useful at any level when there is some uncertainty about a candidate. They take two forms. You may interview an interviewee more than once, or you may elect to have another interviewer do the interviewing so they can compare their assessments.

5. *Interviewers tend to be influenced more by unfavorable than favorable information.*[8] Since you know that the interviewee will be stressing his or her positive and covering up his or her negative qualities, pay particular attention to the negative. Distinguish between items that cause an immediate rejection of the candidate and those which merely raise your caution. Uncovering such information helps make it easier to distin-

[7]Mahler, *Executives Interview*, p. 101.
[8]Mayfield, "Selection Interview," p. 253.

guish among candidates. The only caution you should observe is that the negative characteristic not actually interfere with the person's ability to do the job. Probe deeply and always look for corroborating data. The more often negative or positive information shows up, the more positive you can be in your decisions.

6. *Judgments about one applicant are often influenced by the characteristics of and judgment about the previous candidates.* Naturally, comparisons are going to be made; that is the purpose of the interviews. However, it is possible for the evaluation to be exaggerated. A good prospect may sometimes be rated excellent because the interviewer happened to see three very poor candidates just prior to the interview. An awareness of this possibility will help you maintain a more consistent form of assessment.

7. *Evaluate the relationship between questions, the data you receive, and the judgments you make.* The point is that the specific data are frequently important only in terms of what they indicate about the candidate's motivations, leadership potential, enthusiasm, and so forth.

8. *Finally a decision must be made to hire or reject a candidate.* You should be able to give the rationale supporting your decision. The candidate does or does not meet the specifications for the job for specific reasons.

LEGAL CONSIDERATIONS

Governmental regulations concerning selecting employees is a fact of life, and there are indications that the government's role may increase. It is not the purpose of this section to try to explain what you can and cannot do in the selection interview. It is, however, our purpose to indicate an approach that might be helpful in dealing with an ever-changing aspect of your work.

1. There are *no universal* legal restraints imposed on the selection activity. Restraints include court decisions, federal laws, state laws, local laws, and the organization's own affirmative action plans. This means, of course, that there may be some differences as one goes from state to state or from organization to organization. Furthermore, most laws have exceptions to them, so they may not apply to every organization. Congress, for example, has exempted itself from such legislation. Executive Order 11246 applies to organizations with (a) a total of 50 employees and (b) government contracts worth more than $50,000. The Age Discrimination Act covers the ages of 40–65 in organizations of more than 20 employees. Therefore, it is up to interviewers to know the rules that apply in their particular circumstances.

2. Review the major federal laws that apply. The following are some that you should remember. They are described in Figure 7.4.

1866—*Civil Rights Act*
This was the first law that prohibited discrimination against minorities. It was amended in 1972.

1963—*Equal Pay Act*
This act amended the Fair Labor Standards Act to prohibit employers from paying members of one sex a lower salary than members of the other sex for equal work. It exempts academic, administrative, and professional employees. The Department of Labor administers it.

1964—*Civil Rights Act*
This is by far the most comprehensive act that has been designed to prohibit discrimination on the basis of race, color, or national origin. Its provisions are that: the lack of an intent to discriminate is no defense; customer preference is not a legitimate consideration; employee testing and selection procedures must follow rigorous guidelines to make certain that all potential employees receive equal treatment; the Equal Employment Opportunities Commission (EEOC) may examine the personnel records of an employer without limitation in an attempt to discover systematic patterns of discrimination; suits in federal court may obtain relief for promotion or pay discrimination for up to two years prior to the filing of a discrimination charge with the EEOC.

Provisions of this act are administered both by the Office of Civil Rights of the Department of Health, Education and Welfare (HEW) and by the EEOC. Thousands of lawsuits already have been filed under this act. Some of the important ones are *Diaz vs. Pan American Airways* in 1971, *Franks vs. Bowman Transportation Company* in 1975; *Albemarle Paper Co. vs. Moody* in 1975, and *McDonald vs. Sante Fe Trail Transportation* in 1976. It was in the latter that "reverse discrimination" surfaced.

1967—*Age Discrimination in Employment Act*
Discrimination is prohibited against any applicant between the ages of 40–65, if the employer has more than 20 employees. The act does provide for exemptions where bona fide occupational qualifications are concerned. It is administered by the Department of Labor.

1972—*Equal Employment Opportunity Act*
The Civil Rights Act of 1964 exempted educational institutions from its Title VII. This act removes the exemption. EEOC administers it.

1972—*Education Amendments to Higher Education Act of 1965.*
These amendments prohibit sexual discrimination in all federal assisted educational programs and amend the Equal Pay Amendment to remove the exemption of academic, administrative, and professional employees. The former is administered by HEW and the latter by the Department of Labor.

1973—*Rehabilitation Act*
Federal government contractors who have more than 50 employees and have contracts in excess of $50,000 must develop affirmative-action programs for disabled employees; a person may be "handicapped" but still have the mental and physical qualifications for a job. Compliance is administered by the Department of Labor and HEW.

1974—*Veterans Readjustment Act*
Affirmative-action programs to find jobs for Vietnam veterans are required of all federal government contractors who have contracts of more than $10,000. This applies to any Vietnam veteran, whether or not the person is disabled. The Department of Labor handles complaints.

Figure 7.4   Laws that apply to selection interviews.

Civil Rights Act of 1866
Equal Pay Act of 1963
Labor-Management Reporting & Disclosure Act, 1959
Civil Rights Act of 1964
Fair Labor Standards Act, 1966
Age Discrimination in Employment Act, 1967, 1974
Title IX of the Education Amendments of 1972 to the Higher Education Act of 1965
Rehabilitation Act of 1973
Vietnam Era Veteran's Readjustment Assistance Act of 1972
Executive Order 11246 pertaining to federal contractors

3. Keep up-to-date. There are 25 different governmental agencies that share control over discrimination, and their efforts are not coordinated. Daniel Leech, an Equal Employment Opportunity Commission member, described it this way: "Some employers have gotten bouquets from the Labor Department and then we've come in and said, 'you're the worst in the world.' "[9] Furthermore, new precedents are being set all the time. The principal enforcing agencies are the Equal Employment Opportunity Commission and the Department of Labor. At this writing, there are approximately 8000 new job discrimination cases filed before governmental agencies each month, and it takes an average of two years to settle a complaint. New guidelines will probably come from these settlements.

This fluctuation indicates that as an interviewer you need some help in interpreting the laws and keeping abreast of the latest guidelines. Our surveys indicate that many interviewers do this by (a) contact with their own Equal Employment Opportunity Commission officer, industrial relations or legal departments, and employee relations (b) attending special seminars, and (c) reading the *Federal Register, Recruiting Trends, Wall Street Journal,* and certain personnel journals. We also recommend that you subscribe to a service such as the Fair Employer Practice Guidelines of the Bureau of Business Practices.

3. It is instructive to know that according to our surveys, many interviewers do not feel hampered at all by the legal guidelines. The one-third who do consider them somewhat of a nuisance just have to live with them.

4. When the current number of lawsuits concerning discrimination and reverse discrimination are considered, there may be no such thing as a completely "safe" decision. Our sources indicate that the best policies to follow in the case of a lawsuit is to (a) cooperate with the investigating agency and (b) refuse to take the suit personally. One personnel manager

[9]Walter S. Mossberg, "Besieged by Criticism, Job-Bias Agencies Seek to Bolster Programs," *Wall Street Journal* (August 26, 1977), p. 1.

revealed to us that this has been his strategy in 40 suits, all of which he has won.

5. Keep refining your interviewing techniques.

6. The biggest deterrent to a lawsuit is exhaustive *documentation,* which describes exactly what happened in an interview and why the decisions were made. The director of personnel for a hospital designed a system which has been fairly successful. First, there is an Applicant Interview History, which records all of the topics covered in the interview, comments from each interviewer, and any other information collected from the interviewee. Second, there is a Position Interview History, which records each person who was interviewed, who conducted each interview, and the disposition of the interview.

OVERCOMING PROBLEMS

Now that the planning, managing, and interpreting roles of the interviewer have been sketched, it is useful to consider some of the problems that occur in an interview. Some of these already have been mentioned, but repeating them will help you become even more aware of them. The problems can be grouped in terms of those that stem from the interviewee and those that stem from the interviewer.

Problems Stemming from the Interviewee

Nervousness is the most common problem. You have something that the interviewee wants—a job. In a sense, you may be in control of the person's destiny. Frequently, the interview takes place in strange surroundings. Therefore, you can expect many interviewees to experience some anxiety. You can alleviate nervousness, if you choose to do so, by building rapport, arranging an informal setting, talking about things that you and the interviewee have in common, and having a friendly manner.

Vague answers are also characteristic of many interviews. Some people are uncertain as to what you want or what is the best way of answering your questions. Therefore, they may try to hedge or remain noncommittal. Vagueness is particularly acute in questions dealing with self-assessment and long-term goals. It is your responsibility as the interviewer to move beyond the vague and superficial answers that are given, and you can do this only through very skillful and very determined probing.

Defensiveness is characteristic of many interviewees. It occurs when your purposes and those of the interviewee are not entirely consistent in the interview. You are determined to discover both the strengths and the weaknesses of the interviewee, whereas most interviewees are determined to expose their strengths and to hide their weaknesses. They have a perfectly good rationale for doing so: They know that interviewers are more influenced by unfavorable than favorable information. Recognizing this tendency to hide weaknesses will help you to plan your questions.

Interviewing persons who are almost too well rehearsed and too polished creates a different kind of problem for you. In recent years, a number of books and training programs have been designed to tell interviewees how to present themselves well in an interview. The result is that they know the questions and prepare good answers for them. No one blames them for doing this; in fact, it is very wise on their part. Nevertheless, their skills do make it a bit more difficult for you as the interviewer to discriminate among the various candidates for a job. This was graphically described to us by a recruiter who identified a certain university that apparently has trained all of its M.B.A. students so well in interviewing techniques that discrimination there is very difficult.

Problems Stemming from the Interviewer

The following list of problems was compiled from a survey of college recruiters and students being interviewed. They are listed in rank order. Although they originated from just one context, a number of them can be applied to selection interviews in general.

Inadequate information about a job. Candidates often want more specific information than the recruiter or personnel representative is prepared to give them.

Failure to listen.

Lack of time. Many interviews become rushed because of the interviewer's schedule. The result is an unfulfilling communication experience.

Failure to probe.

Failure to recognize own biases.

Interviewer fatigue after many interviews. Fatigue is a natural phenomenon, and only wise planning of your schedule can overcome this. Interviewing while you are tired is not fair to you or the interviewee.

THIS CHAPTER IN PERSPECTIVE

This chapter focused on the planning, managing, and interpreting roles of the interviewer. There was a heavy emphasis upon techniques, which, of course, are important. In most instances, however, you were presented with alternatives so that you can make your own decisions about what will work for you. You may need to test several techniques out before you can determine which ones work best.

The very fact that you have alternatives, however, means that you must have a basis for making choices. The reasons behind those decisions are very important because they are the factors that reveal your understanding of the selection process. Keep in mind that you have a great deal of power as the selector and that your control of the interview can be almost absolute. Nevertheless, for an interview to be a truly beneficial experience in the long run, it must be a genuine joint interaction. Evaluate your behaviors, not only in terms of what they achieve for you, but also in terms of the kind of impact they have upon the interviewee. Whenever possible, make it a win-win situation.

PROJECTS

1. Interview several professional recruiters to learn about their interviewing methods. Identify any common trends as well as any great differences among them.

2. Analyze the partial transcript on pp. 140–143. It is taken from an actual interview. Notice particularly the interviewer's probing techniques. What impressions do you get of the interviewee? See what impressions other people have after reading the same transcript and discuss your differences.

3. Prepare an interview guide for the position of a bank teller, as described in Figure 7.5, or prepare the most thorough interview guide for your next selection interview.

4. Identify the problems that personnel specialists most often have in making decisions about candidates. In order to do this, plot the entire selection process for a company.

5. Choose a particular job—perhaps your own. Then try to discover all of the legal laws and court decisions that pertain to selecting someone for that job. What sources for these legal decisions might be profitable for people to review who are personnel specialists?

6. Plan an interview for the position of an airline ticket agent. The resume and a description of the person, as given in the case on pages 144–145 will help you. Then role-play the interview with someone acting as the interviewee, using the following instructions. Tape-record the interview and then analyze it together.

   a. Read the information provided in the case at the end of this chapter and try to become that person. The overall interpretation is more important than the details; just be certain that you keep the character consistent. There is not enough information given, so you may need to invent some details as you go along.

   b. Once you have read the information, lay it aside. It is better to invent details than to keep looking back at the information during your role playing.

   c. Remember that there is no right or wrong way to interpret a role. People do interpret the same roles differently because they themselves are different. It is likely that you will place a lot of yourself and the way that you relate to people in your role playing.

Grade _____

General Responsibilities

This is responsible work, which involves servicing the needs of commercial, individual, and savings account customers. It follows prescribed policies and procedures that require some bank operations knowledge and experience.

The job requires accuracy, alertness, and good judgment under a variety of situations, concerning correct handling of various instruments and a proficiency in handling large amounts of currency and coin. Errors in handling transactions could cause embarrassment and loss to the bank.

Frequent customer contact requires patience, courtesy, and tact, and a thorough knowledge of certain policies and practices and other bank services.

Function	Description of Function	Reference
accept deposits	accept deposits on commercial, individual, and/or savings according to standard operating procedures	B.I.A. teller training film and on-the-job training
cash various checks	cash various checks, observing check cashing rules and cash savings withdrawals	same as above and check cashing policy sheet
package currency and coin	count, sort, and package currency and coins; accept currency on deposit and follow procedure for accepting and wrapping; get currency ready for sale to head teller	same as above
fill cash orders	make change and fill cash orders as requested according to set procedures	same as above
balance day's transactions	count cash and balance a daily blotter according to standard procedures	same as above
accept installment loan payments	handle miscellaneous transactions according to standard procedures	same as above

Figure 7.5   Position description of bank teller.

d. You can, of course, learn a lot from the interaction. For best results, you may choose to record the role playing and then listen to it with your interviewee. The two of you can then share information about why you did certain things.

7. Collect several review forms that interviewers have filled out after an interview. Contrast the items on which they are to make decisions about candidates.

PARTIAL TRANSCRIPT OF AN ACTUAL INTERVIEW

Interviewer: You indicate that you have an interest in marketing. As I see it, this is fairly broad—at least as far as B & G practices it we don't have such a thing as a marketing department. We have a sales department, we have an advertising department, we have a market research department all performing together the marketing function, you might say. Well, I'm wondering if you feel your interest is in one of these fields more than another.

Interviewee: Well, I'd say to a large degree it wouldn't be in marketing research—predominantly sales, possibly advertising. And on that note, I notice that in your brochures there was sort of an overlap, whereas the advertising trainee did go into sales for a while. I'd say probably less interested in marketing research.

Interviewer: Okay, we'll strike that. So, primarily sales, secondarily advertising of brand management. But, why sales, Andy?

Interviewee: Well, I'm under the impression—I don't know how your company works on the incentive system—but I'm under the impression that there is a chance to earn money in sales. And naturally your're meeting people all the time. I like this, I think I'd enjoy it. So, primarily for that reason. I like to travel, I like to get around and do different things, and it was my impression that there would be a little more leeway in sales, whereas [with] something like accounting, there might be a certain routine or coming in and sitting down at a desk and the same problems. I don't think that would be my cup of tea.

Interviewer: Well, you're not far wrong. Let me get back a little more deeper in sales. Is there some time or some place in your background, Andy, where you've demonstrated an ability that you think is transferable to a sales career in the future?

Interviewee: Well, I think as a general question, in a way I think everything I've done in the past has contributed to this or confidence that I think I can sell. Although, I've had specific jobs in the past, I've worked a New England Ski Show for two years and I had a booth there up in Boston, and I sold them.

Interviewer: This is a Ski Show?

Interviewee: Yes, I toured the country, and when I was a junior in school I needed a little money and I went down there. This was while I was in college in Boston.

Interviewer: Okay, I'm sorry to interrupt. What happened then? You were touring the country?

Interviewee: No, I wasn't touring the country; the show was. And I went down there—there was an ad, when I was a junior, in the paper for people that might want to work and I went down there. I sold for about three or four days; it was programs this time and the following year came around and I got another job where I got my own booth down there and I worked for the show selling records. And I figure if I could sell those records, I could sell anything.

Interviewer: What were the records?

Interviewee: It was, "Let's Go Skiing," and originally they were tempted to give it away.

Interviewer: What were these—lessons or something?

Interviewee: Well, the ski song by some obscure artist, sang this and I guess you were just supposed to buy it on emotion, because they would play the record and I would say "Well, here it is, and it is $2" and I'd give them something free with it and finally they wound up, they had to give a lot of these away because it was just that nobody wanted them.

Interviewer: Well, I haven't heard of the Ski Show. Is this a pretty big thing in Boston?

Interviewee: I think it is in the large cities. I know it was in Chicago earlier this year and it hits five or six cities—I would say New York, Detroit, and Chicago.

Interviewer: This is a group of people that tour the country, and what do they do with the show?

Interviewee: Well, mainly they are promoting skiing. You'll find that at each ski show a lot of the area lodges and resort areas will be represented with different booths along with the ski manufacturers, different equipment manufacturers, and it's quite a thing. I know in Boston for three or four days when I was there, I think they had about 60,000 or 70,000 people coming through, and of course you're only going to find it in the areas where skiing is a major interest.

Interviewer: Where do they hold it in Boston?

Interviewee: It's in the Hotel Bradford down there. They had three floors in that and three rooms. And also they have exhibiting there. They have these carpets that move—I don't know if you've ever seen them—which enable a person to ski and remain safe and never even go back and forth and demonstrate. And they had a few people who were on the Olympic team, and there were also fashion shows—a sporting goods' manufacturer put on fashion shows— plus entertainment by various singing groups.

Interviewer: And this was how long, about a week?

Interviewee: This was four days.

Interviewer: And you sold programs?

Interviewee: Yes.

Interviewer: What did you do, stand by the entrance as people came in?

Interviewee: Well, more or less you had a table and you had to dress up, and you had to talk to them and the whole thing was how many you sold. And so I've had some selling experience there; I've sold. I worked in a liquor store for about six months, my last six months in college.

Interviewer: Before you worked for the ski show, you sold records; that was another year, wasn't it?

Interviewee: Yes, that was the second year.

Interviewer: Then you gave up the ski show business?

Interviewee: Well, it's a once-a-year thing, and I wasn't in the city anymore.

Interviewer: Was this on a commission that you were selling? Did you get a certain percent of [the profits from] the records and programs you sold?

Interviewee: The programs were on a commission; the records weren't.

Interviewer: So you did this and you felt you did reasonably well and you liked it. You would like this for a foundation and would like to try this out for a career.

Interviewee: Well, I'd like to try it and find out. Also, last year I said I worked in a liquor store, and there was quite a bit there of contact with people and being a neighborhood store and living in a neighborhood around the school.

Interviewer: Were you doing this part-time while you were going to school?

Interviewee: Yes, it was more like going to work full-time and going to school part-time.

Interviewer: Okay, clerk and delivery work—I'm not familiar with the liquor distribution in Boston or in Massachusetts. I know in Ohio where I'm from, it's all state stores, but apparently it's not that way.

Interviewee: Well, it's not that way in Massachusetts. And another thing that distinguishes especially the Boston area is price-cutting up there, and you have big retail outlets and, of course, the prices have to be posted on the shelf with what is set by the state, but your big retailers will undercut and they'll have two sets of prices. It's an action when your working in a store, somebody wants to buy something and you more or less have to bargain with them. I mean you have a price on the shelf, but the guy can say, "Oh, I can get it for $2 down the street," and you know he can't, so it was interesting in that respect because you know how much profit there was on the item and you, of course, had to figure out who the regular customers were, who you'd give it to, who you wouldn't. And also who worked for the Alcoholic Beverage Commission.

Interviewer: This was not completely legal was it?

Interviewee: No, this was definitely not legal, but it was going on though, and at that time last year, it was pending in court, so I don't know how this came out. But it was interesting in that respect, plus this was a small store and myself and the two kids I live with—we all worked there—and the gentleman who owned the store, I guess, was about two or three years older than us and he more or less gave us a free hand around the place and we all wound up, I guess, working about 30 hours a week, and there was some responsibility I think in taking orders.

Interviewer: How did you get that job, Andy?

Interviewee: Well, we had stopped by there to purchase our liquor—it was about two or three blocks away—and at this time we all needed some extra spending money, and I had another job, and one of my roommates went over there, and his father had owned the liquor store, and he asked him if he could get part-time work, and the guy said fine. I need someone and then he had it, and I told him that if an opening came along I'd sure be interested in it 'cause this other thing I had was just working weekends.

Interviewer: What kind of work was that?

Interviewee: This was just handy work for the Massachusetts Unemployment Agency. At that time a company was renovating a factory, and they had work every weekend.

Interviewer: Did you start here at Northwestern in June?

Interviewee: Yes, I did.

Interviewer: And you've been going on a full-time basis straight through?

Interviewee: That's right, a four-quarter program.

Interviewer: What have you been doing here other than your actual academic endeavors—going to class, studying, library, research and so on? What do you do with all that free time you've got?

Interviewee: I go to football games. . . .

CASE FOR ROLE-PLAY

Selection Interviewee
Pat Bronson

You are a high school graduate from Kansas City. As a student you were average. Nevertheless, you felt that you should go to college, so you enrolled at Washburn in Topeka for a year. After that year, however, you realized that you probably could enjoy life doing something else and still live a worthwhile life. Consequently, eight months ago you applied for a job with the Bigdome Company, and you wanted to work desperately. Even during high school you had worked part-time as a salesperson.

During the time you applied for your job, you thought your chances of being hired were good because you had gotten along well with previous employers. The general employment office of the Bigdome Company gave you several tests, indicated that you passed them with an average score, and hired you.

You worked first as an assistant in the mailroom. After three months you were moved to the personnel office where you were involved in making a telephone directory for the company. At this time you received a raise. After the directory was finished, you were given a clerical inventory job in the office supplies room. This last assignment required you to work alone in keeping records of all office supplies used in the home office.

You have been working at this job for six months, and you have not liked it particularly. Furthermore, your supervisor has complained twice about your work. When you recently ran out of some supplies, he really let you have it, threatening to fire you if you did not improve.

Things have gotten so bad that you just do not feel that you can continue working there. Since you like working with people and also like traveling, you have decided to apply for a job with Best Airlines as a ticket agent at its Los Angeles International Airport. On a recent trip to L.A., you met some people who worked at this, and you were impressed with their opportunities for free travel.

You are one of three children. Your older brother and sister went to Kansas University. Your brother finished school and is now teaching; your sister is a senior majoring in social welfare. You have resisted any pressures to be like them and are determined to make it on your own. Your dad is a police officer.

You think this new job will be easy for you because people have always told you that you have a great personality. Furthermore, you are attractive, out-going, and have the ability to make the most of situations. Someday, you may go back to college if you feel it is ever necessary. You realize that you have not been terribly anxious about the future; you want to enjoy the present. You feel that you can make plans for the future later.

Best Airlines, Inc.
Los Angeles International Airport

Applicant Data for Airline Ticket Agent

Requirements
    Age: 18–35
    Physical: Neat, attractive and well-groomed appearance, pleasant

personality and courteous manner.

Education: High school graduate; some college preferred.

Preparation

Courses recommended in preparation for this position would include social studies and general business courses in high school and/or college such as grammar, public speaking, voice training, geography, mathematics, and psychology.

General Information

Since this position constantly calls for direct and personal dealing with the public, a sincere enthusiasm and desire to be of willing assistance is essential. Other qualities necessary to be a successful counter sales agent are stability when working under pressure, ability to converse well on subjects of interest to all types of people, understanding, and patience.

General competency in clerical and arithmetic skills is essential due to the necessity of computing fares accurately.

Female counter sales agents are required to wear uniforms; men are to wear airline blazers.

Saturday work is involved periodically in this type of position, since most of our city ticket offices are open Monday through Saturday. However, employees work only 40 hours a week, 5 days a week, and substitute another day off when scheduled to work Saturday.

Duties

Make reservations for travelers over our own or the systems of other airlines; confirm or check reservations and issue tickets or make arrangements for passengers to pick up ticket at airport ticket counter. Assist travelers by providing complete information service, advising and recommending best routes, connections, lowest fares, and fastest schedules.

Must have basic knowledge of all passenger and cargo tariffs and allied publications to answer all inquiries from prospective customers.

Tactfully and willingly handle complaints of service or baggage handling, referring such problems to the proper department for final disposition.

Must neatly and accurately prepare various reports, such as daily ticket agent's report of sales; must balance cash receipts, change fund, and make bank deposits or secure valuable items in company safe as directed.

Chapter 8
Selection Interviews

THE INTERVIEWEE'S PERSPECTIVE

The selection interview is a joint process in which all participants have their own purposes. In a sense, it is a sales interview, with the interviewer trying to sell a company to a candidate and the interviewee attempting to sell himself or herself. In a somewhat different sense, it is an information getting interview for each of them. The interviewer tries to measure as many of the candidate's strengths and weaknesses as possible, while the interviewee tries to ascertain the strengths and weaknesses of the job with the company. The interviewer is shopping for good employees, and the interviewee is shopping for a company that suits his or her needs. Finally, both individuals try to test the personal chemistry of their interactions.

It is appropriate to begin this chapter by contrasting the different purposes that interviewers and interviewees have in selection interviews because too frequently "purpose" is defined only in terms of the interviewer. If you are going to be a successful interviewee, you must be aware that you are not just a passive element in the interview; you are an active agent with some very specific goals. Like any good communicator, you can identify these goals and plan the means by which you can achieve them. Remember that your chief goals should be: (1) to sell yourself and (2) to find out how well the job and the company suit your needs.

As was done in the previous chapter, which focused on the interviewer, this chapter will emphasize the kind of planning that you can do and then set guidelines that you should follow in interacting in the interview itself.

PREPARING FOR THE INTERVIEW

Familiarity with the Interview Process

You will be more confident in the interview if you know what to expect than if you do not know what to expect. You can make the situation less ambiguous by doing some research. First, learn what the interviewer is trying to accomplish. Read the previous chapter, which even though it is aimed at interviewers, can be read also from the standpoint of the interviewee. You will gain some very useful insights into how to become a more effective interviewee. If you are aware of what the interviewer is trying to do, you can adjust your own reactions.

Second, there are now in print a number of books aimed at helping the interviewee. These include the following books: Jason Robertson's *How to Win in a Job Interview*, Tom Jackson's *28 Days to a Better Job*, and Ross Figgins's *Techniques of Job Search*. In addition to books like these, there are a number of training programs held by placement centers and professional recruiting firms.

Once you have familiarized yourself with the overall process, you can turn your attention to some very specific kinds of preparation for the interview. Table 8.1 will provide you with some direction, since it lists

Table 8.1 MOST FREQUENT COMPLAINTS ABOUT INTERVIEWEES

RANK	ITEM
1	*Poor communication* Lack communication skills; are evasive; do not answer questions directly; give rambling responses; talk too little; talk too much; are nervous
2	*Ill-prepared for the interview* Have no information about the company or the job; have no good questions to ask; have no interview training
3	*Vague interests* Lack career goals; do not know what job they want
4	*Lack of motivation* Lack enthusiasm; are apathetic; lack interest; do not sell self; are too agreeable
5	*Unrealistic expectations* Lack flexibility; are too concerned with salary; possess attitude of "What can you do for me?"; are immature

five of the most frequent complaints made about interviewees. Once again, these complaints were made by recruiters who primarily interview college students, but the specific items do pin-point important mistakes that you should avoid in all kinds of selection interviews. The rest of this chapter is designed to help you avoid them.

Self-analysis

The first preparation that you can make for an employment interview is to give some very serious thought to your needs, interests, skills, and goals. You can be assured that self-assessment will be one of the targets investigated in the most depth by the interview. Be prepared. Forrest Amesden and Noel White contrast what happens in an interview with what happens in other important communication situations: "Very few people are experienced enough, or stupid enough, to give a major speech 'impromptu' style (off the top of their heads); yet this is the case, day after day, in employment interviewing."[1]

Where should you begin? A good place for you to start is to prepare a resume, which is merely a brief, well-organized record of your accomplishments. As you prepare it, you will have to review your knowledge, skills, experiences, and special qualifications. On the rough draft list everything that you can think of that might be of value. Probably you will suddenly remember some things that you had forgotten. If you do list everything, then you will have to begin to sort out the things that are of most value and leave everything else out. Making these kinds of decisions is quite a useful process because it will force you to think about yourself and your own value as a potential employee.

Keep in mind that *the resume is an advertisement*, designed specifically to communicate your value as an employee. Therefore, it should look very professional, since it will be a reflection of your abilities. Generally, it should be designed to call attention to your major advantages with the least amount of reading effort. There are companies that specialize in preparing resumes but you should always guide them in terms of your own preferences. Listed below are some guidelines for preparing a good resume.

Use a lot of white space; it will be easier for the interviewer to read and will also look more attractive.

Prepare blocks of information and use headings to designate them. Some of the most common headings include "Personal Data" (address, telephone number, etc.), "Education," "Work Experience," "Honors," and "References." There is no set way of arranging these; start with the things that will grab the most attention.

[1]Forrest M. Amesden and Noel D. White, *How to Be Successful in the Employment Interview* (self-published, 1974), p. 13.

List items under each heading in reverse chronological order. You are out to make an impression, and probably the most impressive things about you are the ones that have occurred most recently. For example, your highest educational degree is the one that most interviewers will be interested in; list it first. Similarly, your latest or current job probably says more about your abilities than your first job, so begin with the latest one.

Keep the resume brief. It is a summary designed to whet the appetite for more information about you; it should not be a complete biography. It should rarely be more than two pages long.

Cover all time periods.

Retain the option of having more than one resume. You may tailor one resume to one kind of job and another for a different kind of job.

It is common to list references on many resumes. However, if you are going to be applying for more than one kind of job, you may wish to use different references for different kinds of jobs. In such a case, it might be advisable for you to specify on the resume that references will be supplied on request. This gives you the option of varying the references without changing the resume.

In some cases, candidates are advised to state their job objective on the resume. This is a common practice. Nevertheless, the same thing could be stated in a covering letter more effectively in terms of adapting it to a specific job possibility.

Figures 8.1 and 8.2 display two different resumes. Examine them for their relative advantages and disadvantages.

After you have prepared a resume, then write down answers to the questions that you can certainly expect. Review the questions about your self-assessment, education, work experience, family background, goals, and activities listed in the previous chapter, since they represent standard ones asked by interviewers. Determine how you would answer them. This is a very important aspect of your preparation because it can make you more articulate in describing yourself. Remember that "poor communication" and "vague answers" were high on the list of complaints that recruiters made about interviewees. A little preparation can give you a great advantage.

Take a few of the questions and try to write out what you might say in answer to them. For example,

What are your greatest strengths?

_____

_____

WILLIAM MEANS

77 Caption Drive
Evanston, Illinois 60621

Height: 5'11"
Weight: 160
Marital Status: Married
Birthdate: November 22, 1954

Career
Objective

To pursue a career within a consumer goods industry, leading into fields such as advertising, brand/product management, and market research and development. Ideally this would integrate a degree of creativity and ingenuity with the structure of problem identification, analysis, and decision making.

Education MIDWESTERN UNIVERSITY, GRADUATE SCHOOL OF MANAGEMENT

1975–1977 Major: Marketing/Finance G.P.A. – 3.5/4.0.
Candidate for M.A. Degree in June on 1977.
MIDWESTERN UNIVERSITY, SCHOOL OF SPEECH

1972–1975 Major: Radio/TV Production, Communication Theory
Minor Interests: Mathematics, Architecture
Graduate of a 3–year B.S. program G.P.A. – 3.3/4.0.

Work
Experience Summer

1976 MOTOROLA, INC. – Schaumburg, Illinois

Research analysist and co–project director. The assignment was to design and implement an exploratory market research program which would:
(1) Indicate the existence of a mass consumer market for radio paging produces, and
(2) Describe the market and determine appropriate channels of distribution, price elasticities, and product form characteristics.
Also assisted on the design of a CB radio product trade–up research program.

1975 MARSHALL FIELDS – Evanston, Illinois

Assistant manager of a textbook warehouse dealing primarily with inventory levels and order processing.

1973–1974 AMERICAN AIRLINES – Chicago, Illinois

Ticket agent and Public Service Representative at O'Hare Field, Chicago.

Outside
Activities

D.J. on campus radio station WNUR, intramural sports superstar, N.U. Sailing Club co–chairman 1975 Homecoming activities, Young Alumni Council, member of Psi Upsilon fraternity, host of employment program – Careers '77

Other
Interests

Photography, golf, hand–gliding, surfing

References Furnished upon request.

Figure 8.1

TRACY DEWS

Address	**Current:**
	122 Place Avenue
	Apartment 1–A
	Evanston, Illinois 60202
	Telephone: 312–411–3111

Permanent:
221 Pine Rd.
Peale, California 94608
Telephone: 415–622–2132

Job Objective

Management position in marketing research or analysis, utilizing management information systems.

Education 1978–79

UNIVERSITY OF CHICAGO   Chicago, Illinois
Candidate for Master of Management Degree in June, 1978.
Specializations: Marketing and Quantitative Methods. Recipient of Exxon Corporation Fellowship and Sachs Foundation Scholarship, 1976–78. Black Management and Graduate Management Associations of Northwestern University.

June 1977

BROWN UNIVERSITY   Providence, Rhode Island
B.A., Mathematical Economics and Applied Music. Recipient of Brown University and Sachs Foundation Scholarships. Chorus of Brown University, 1974–77 (Co–Director for a brief duration); Brown University Freshman Week Committee, 1976–78 (Welcoming Committee Chairman, 1977–78). Gave Senior Recital in completion of Music Degree.

Employment 1979 Summer

EXXON CORPORATION   New York, New York
Marketing Planning Analyst, Cargo Trading Department, Exxon International. Computed discounts, subtotals, and summary tables for quarterly performance reports; researched North Slope oil legislation; performed weekly netback calculations; organized cable project to notify third–party and affiliate customers of Saudi Arabian Government Certification Directive.

1977 & 1978 Summer

DEPARTMENT OF PARKS AND RECREATION   Denver, Colorado
Swimming Pool Manager, Congress Swimming Pool. Manager of pool facilities and maintenance; responsible for the interviewing, hiring, and supervision of pool staff; worked with the Congress Park community organization to insure staff responsiveness to community needs.

1976 Summer

Lifeguard, Congress Swimming Pool. Taught swimming and enforced water safety programs.

Personal

Birth Date: 5–10–54
Marital Status: Single
Hobbies: Horticulture, piano, reading, sewing, swimming, & tennis.
Languages: Knowledge of Spanish and French.
Travel: Toured parts of East and West Africa; brief duration in Athens, Greece and Bermuda; extensively across the United States

References

References will be furnished upon request to:
Career Development, Brown University
P.O. Box 1907, Providence, Rhode Island   02912

Figure 8.2

What type of boss do you like?

_____

_____

If you could change your life in any way, what would you change?

_____

_____

An alternative to writing out the answers to these questions would be to tape-record them. Have a friend ask you some questions, tape them, and then listen to your answers. Try to talk comfortably about each question for one minute. After listening to your answers, be analytical and ask, "Would I hire me?"

At this point, you should be confronted with a strong word of caution. "Canned" answers are taboo. You actually weaken your image if the interviewer has the feeling that you are just spouting out some rehearsed speech. Therefore, do not try to memorize answers to these questions. The reason we advocate that you familiarize yourself with the questions is so you can avoid being surprised by them and also certain that you can talk about these areas naturally and comfortably.

Still another aspect of your self-analysis is to do some serious thinking about what you really want in a job and what you are most qualified to do. A good way to do this is by *brainstorming*: making lists of things without evaluation them immediately. First, list those work activities that you really enjoy. Do not try to organize the list at first, but it is important that you try to get a list of 15–20 items if you can. Once the list is made, look at the items and try to select the four or five that have the highest priority for you.

Second, do some brainstorming about your skills that might be relevant to a job and make the lists as long as you can. Try to make the list as broad as you can, too. Once it is complete, select the four or five items that again have the highest priority for you.

Having done this, you are now ready to think seriously about some specific job targets. What are the kinds of jobs that will allow you to use your best skills and fulfill your main interests at the same time? As you think about this question, think in terms of a long-range career. There are a lot of jobs that might have some immediate interest for you but that may not let you be where you would like to be in the future.

Research About the Organization

Before the interview it is absolutely necessary that you learn something about the company. Remember that the failure to do this kind of research was the second most frequent complaint listed in Table 8.1. You need to have some idea of how big the company is, what it produces, what its reputation is, and its financial standing. One of the best places to obtain this information is from the company itself. Write for some of its publications, including an annual report, or pay a visit before your interview to its personnel or public relations departments. Most organizations are so concerned about their public image that they provide this information on request. You can also gather some of this information from publications such as the *College Placement Annual, Thomas' Register of American Manufacturers, Moody's Industrial Manual, Standard and Poor's Register,* and *Dun and Bradstreet's Reference Book.* If you cannot find these in a library, you may be able to locate them at a stock brokerage firm. College students can obtain a lot of information from their placement centers. The better you understand an organization, the better you will be able to participate in the interview. Furthermore, being knowledgeable about the organization is one of the best ways of impressing the interviewer, because it shows that you are indeed interested.

In addition to knowing general information about the company, you ought to be well equipped with (1) general information about the nature of the job for which you are interviewing, (2) a realistic salary range for the job, and (3) the kinds of growth that you might anticipate in the company using the initial job as a stepping-stone.

The culmination of all this research is that not only will it give you some needed information about the company, but it should also bring to mind questions that you will want to raise in the interview. In fact, you ought to prepare a list of questions that you can take to the interview. If they are incisive questions, they will be a demonstration of your knowledgeability and experience.

Taking Important Materials to the Interview

A final aspect of preparation is to make certain that you carry with you all the things that you might need in the interview itself.

1. Always carry some extra resumes. You may have already sent one to the interviewer, but it is useful to be prepared; your resume may have been misplaced.
2. For certain kinds of jobs, it might be helpful to have samples of your work to show. If you were interviewing for a job as a photographer or a layout editor, for example, it would be to your advantage to have some of the best examples of your work with you.

3. Take along a list of questions that you might want to ask or the background notes on the company that you have made for reference.

4. Be certain that you go equipped with pen and paper so that you can make more notes during the interview if you desire.

PARTICIPATING IN THE INTERVIEW

Thorough preparation will enable you to approach the actual interview with confidence, and letting that confidence show is important because recruiters will make a number of estimates about you that are related to the amount of confidence you have.

Remember that each interviewer is different from others in important ways, and look for ways to adapt to each one as a unique individual. Despite such differences in personality, you can use the following suggestions as a guide for most job interviews.

1. *Be prompt.* During the first few minutes, you can strongly influence the interviewer's assessment of you. Promptness alone will not get you a job, but keeping the interviewer waiting can cause him or her to have reservations about you.

2. *Be dressed for success.* In recent years people have become more aware of how their clothes influence the impressions they make on others. One of the best-selling books on this topic has been John Malloy's *Dress for Success.*[2] Some of his prescriptions are controversial, but you may wish to examine them so that you can evaluate their merit for yourself. Choice of any particular ensemble will violate some people's taste, but generally you can be assured that there is a range associated with any job level as to what is acceptable. Stay within that range.

3. *Be warm and responsive.* Your greeting should be warm, friendly, and confident. Give a firm handshake and make immediate eye contact with the interviewer. You may feel anxious, but it may be helpful to tell yourself that the interview is an opportunity to meet a new individual and to get some new information. In other words, it offers a challenge to communicate, and you can be enthusiastic about the challenge.

4. *Follow the interviewer's lead.* Interviewers differ widely in their manner of operating. Do not feel that one interviewer is going to be like all the previous ones that you have met. Most interviewers expect to control the interview, and you will only make a bad impression if you try to take over.

Specifically, follow the interviewer's lead about the formality of address. It is popular in some quarters to use first names, for example, but it is always preferable to err on the formal side. Use the Mr., Ms., or Mrs.

[2]John T. Molloy, *Dress for Success* (New York: Warner Books, 1975).

designation first. If the interviewer wants to make it less formal, he or she can request it. If you err by using the first name when the interviewer prefers the more formal form of address, you have inadvertently created an overly aggressive image right from the start. When the interviewer is female, listen carefully to see whether she uses Mrs., Miss, or Ms. when she introduces herself.

Generally, the interviewer will indicate when it is appropriate for you to ask questions. Follow this lead also. You will then conform to the role expected of you.

5. *Be a good listener.* Watch for the verbal and nonverbal cues that come your way. Concentrate on what the interviewer is saying, and train yourself to remember details about the company and the job.

6. *Sell yourself.* There is no more important bit of advice that we can give you than this one. You already know that the interviewer wants to make a judgment of what kind of person you are. Help him or her do so in a positive way.

7. *Answer questions positively.* If you have reviewed the questions listed earlier that interviewers generally ask, you should be able to give articulate answers. Also, the answers should accentuate the positive. Like any good salesperson, stress your positive features and downplay your negative features. The objective even when discussing weaknesses is to minimize them or to turn them into advantages. For example, contrast these answers to a question posed about an interviewee's weakness.

1. I have trouble working with some people and would rather work alone than have to work with them.
2. In some cases when I am assigned to work with new people, it takes me a while to be comfortable. After a few days, everything is all right. I've been working on this, though.
3. I have trouble working with people who are lazy or won't do their share. I like to do a good job, and I'm afraid that I'm a little impatient with people who don't.

Notice that the first answer is overwhelmingly negative and ends on a negative level. The respondent should have done something to bring the discussion back up to a more positive level. The second response admits a weakness, but the weakness is described in tentative terms and the interviewee also makes a positive statement about doing something to correct it. The third response employs another useful technique: the interviewee has selected something identified as a weakness, that is, impatience, that could easily be turned into a strength. After all, a mark of one's own enthusiasm and dedication is impatience with people who do not do a good job. Few interviewers would consider this a fault.

8. *Volunteer information.* Fill in any gaps that may be left in an application form or on your resume. Facts are not enough, interviewers

will be impressed by any information that demonstrates your mental effectiveness, enthusiasm, motivation, and dedication. They get this information from the way you talk about things as much as from the specific details you discuss. As you volunteer information, try to make certain that the interviewer understands how it makes you qualified for the job. In other words, be rather pointed in your explanations of how you are exceptional in some important ways. If you have something unique to offer, sell it. Remember that the "Interview is not a confessional."[3]

9. *Be assertive.*[4] Assertiveness is the ability to express your feelings honestly and to take charge of your rights responsibly. It is typified by a healthy self-respect, confidence, and a general good feeling about yourself. Perhaps one way of describing assertiveness is to contrast it with nonassertive and aggressive behaviors. Nonassertive behavior is characterized by self-denial, inhibition, and anxiousness. The nonassertive person sublimates his or her own goals to those of others so that he or she rarely achieves desired goals. This sometimes results in unexpressed feelings of guilt or anger. In an interview, the nonassertive person becomes a passive participant, and as such, the interviewer will probably pick up the negative self-assessment. Aggressive behavior, on the other hand, is characterized as being very expressive and self-enhancing at the expense of others. The aggressor tears down others and makes choices for others in order to achieve his or her own goals. It is displayed in the interview by putting down others, character assassination, and trying to wrest control from the interviewer. Most interviewers will be "turned off" by such behavior.

Finally, the reason for pointing to assertive behavior as a way of selling yourself is that it strives for self-enhancement on a person's own merits. It does not need to defer always to someone else; neither does it attack others. In other words, assertiveness displays a good self-assessment and a respect for the rights of others—two things that are highly valued in interpersonal relations.

10. *Be frank and honest in your answers.* In order to sell yourself, you should not lie or distort your answers. If you must recast yourself in order to get a job, you may not like it once you get it. Consequently, the answers to questions need to reflect the real you in its most positive aspects. It is just a matter of what gets emphasized. Furthermore, you will often find yourself being interviewed by several individuals within the same organization. Keep your answers consistent. Comparisons will

[3]Jason Robertson, *How to Win in an Interview* (Englewood Cliffs, N.J.: Prentice-Hall, Inc., 1978), p. 115.
[4]Robert E. Alberti and Michael L. Emmons, *Your Perfect Right* (San Luis Obispo, Calif.: Impact, 1974), p. 11.

inevitably be made, and inconsistencies that are discovered will not work to your advantage.

11. *Ask good questions.* If you listen well to the interviewer, you can pick up information that needs developing further, so ask questions. Your questions will demonstrate how conversant and knowledgeable you are. As we stated earlier, go to the interview with good questions about the company and the job. It is up to you to determine whether you *fit* the job and whether you *want* it.

12. *Control your own behavior.* Suppose an interviewer asks you a question that you consider inappropriate. How should you respond? Of course, no one can force you to answer any question, and you can evade it or refuse to answer it. However, this is not likely to make a favorable impression on most interviewers. Neither is it wise to correct or to coach the interviewer so that he or she becomes hostile. It is easy for these situations to become win-lose situations. The interview is no longer a pleasant communication experience, and the interviewee often loses the possibility of being offered the job. There is a third alternative. Answer an inappropriate question carefully, unemotionally, and in a straightforward manner. This will demonstrate your ability to control yourself. If you feel that you can prove illegal discrimination, a complaint may be appropriate, but not in the interview. Laws generally regulate decisions, not questions, and it is inappropriate to process prior to the decision.

13. *Do not break confidences or deal in character assassinations.*[5] In either case you will be demonstrating a lack of personal integrity that might lose you the respect of the interviewer. If you will do it to others, there is a risk that you might do it in your new job, too. You will be viewed as having a more professional and healthy outlook if you avoid these two errors.

14. *Know your worth.* The topic of money eventually comes up in all but prescreening interviews, and you ought to be prepared to discuss it. A little prior research will tell you what the average salaries are for particular jobs. Frequently, job descriptions list ranges of pay. If they do, you will want to bargain for as much as you can. If they do not, consult a counselor, placement officer, or a friend to determine what the scale is. If you bargain, you run two risks: if you ask too much, you may appear to be unrealistic; if you ask too little, you may appear naive or lacking in confidence. Therefore, it is important for you to know the acceptable ranges and to justify your demands.

15. *Do not press the interviewer in the conclusion.* You might like immediate feedback, but resist the temptation to ask "How did I do?" or "How does it look?" Many people will coach you against emphasizing that

[5]Robertson, *How to Win in an Interview,* and Alberti and Emmons, *Your Perfect Right.*

you really need the job. People like to play from the strength of having several options. This helps, and perhaps the generalization against the plea is a good one, but there are exceptions (one of us once got a job just that way).

ISSUES OFTEN RAISED BY INTERVIEWEES

There are a number of common issues that interviewees often raise about what is appropriate behavior for them. The following discussion concentrates on some of the most common ones.

1. *What kind of follow-up should you make to an interview?* Most of the time the interviewer is expected to make the first move after the interview. However, some people do try to reinforce their interest by writing a letter thanking the interviewer for the interview.

2. *What should you do if several weeks go by and you have not heard from the interviewer?* If a long period goes by, you probably can assume that you are not being considered for the job. A poll of some recruiters revealed that they appreciated letters of inquiry; in fact, they tended to be impressed by someone who would show that kind of incentive, but they also advised, "Write; don't call."

3. *When should you talk about money?* Generally, it is not advisable to bring up the subject in a prescreening interview unless the interviewer mentions it. Your mentioning salary and fringe benefits too soon will create a negative impression about your motivation for working. However, it is a very necessary issue in any final, in-depth interview, and the interviewer probably would be surprised if you did not want to discuss it.

4. *What should you do if you suddenly realize that you are not interested in the job during the interview?* Indicate this to the interviewer. Be cordial, however, rather than blunt or abrasive. Actually, most interviewers probably would appreciate your admission since it will save them time and energy.

5. *What should you do if the interviewer does not seem very interested.* Keep trying to sell yourself. Something you say may suddenly strike a spark of interest. It is a mistake to feel defeated by an apparent lack of interest. You may also be making an incorrect inference. Interviewer fatigue is a common occurrence, and a tired person may not make all of the outward signs of interest that he or she normally would.

6. *What should you say if you do not see how some of the interviewer's questions relate to the job?* No one can force you to answer a question, and it is always your prerogative to ask why a question is being asked. It is possible, however, that you are overly sensitive. Keep in mind that an interview can be analyzed in terms of the relationship as well as the content. Whatever you talk about, you are going to be revealing some-

thing about your communication skills, the way you think, and the kind of person you are. These qualitative dimensions are usually of more immediate interest than the surface content of the answers.

THIS CHAPTER IN PERSPECTIVE

Your primary role in the selection interview is to sell yourself, and the objective of this chapter has been to help you put together an effective delivery system in order to sell yourself. Too much of a "hard-sell" will make you seem pushy, but a "soft-sell" may make you seem unconfident and uninterested in the job.

In addition to your past work experience and training, the things that influence an interviewer most in assessing you are your communication skills, the way you present yourself in terms of attitude and maturity, your physical appearance, and your preparation for the interview. With a little effort and work, you can enhance your proficiency in each one of these areas, and the estimates of your competence will then increase.

PROJECTS

1. Prepare several versions of your resume and ask people to critique them for you.

2. Make a collection of as many types of resumes as you can find. What are their important differences? What features do they have in common?

3. Role-play a situation in which you are applying for a job. Get an actual job description in which you might be interested; then team up with someone who will play the role of the interviewer.

4. Review the questions generally asked of interviewees in Chapter 7. Determine those that you like least. Then analyze why you do not like them and begin to prepare answers for them. It is these questions that will probably give you the most trouble in an actual interview.

5. Discuss the extent to which you would be willing to reveal negative information about yourself to an interviewer. Make a list of those items that you feel are negative.

6. Invite a counselor from the placement center to talk about the total process of finding a job. Cover the general area of job search.

7. Discuss the extent to which what you have done in the past is the best predictor of what you will do in the future.

8. Make a list of the kinds of jobs for which you might be eligible. Try to secure a complete description of each one of these.

Chapter 9
Appraisal Interviews

When a company has selected a new employee, a new type of relationship has been established. In this chapter we will focus on a new type of interview as the manager monitors and appraises the subordinate's performance. This interview occurs in a context different from the selection interview. Whereas the selection interview often takes place between two strangers for the purpose of exchanging information, the appraisal interview takes place in an organizational context and is very much influenced by the formal superior-subordinate role. Differences in organizations and in management styles will create differences in the role relationships and in the kinds of appraisals that are given. Nevertheless, we will outline some of the major considerations for giving an effective appraisal.

HISTORY OF APPRAISALS

Managerial appraisal has sometimes been referred to as the Achilles heel of management development. But one can say more. It is probably the key to managing itself. . . . Appraisal is, or should be, an integral part of managing itself. . . .

It is commonplace to say that the task of the manager is to set goals and methods of their attainment, and to enlist the support of people for whom he [or she] is responsible in working toward making plans. Therefore, if a company, a government agency, a charitable organization, or even a university is to reach its goals effectively and efficiently, ways of accurately measuring management performance must be found and implemented.[1]

As Koontz suggests, appraisal processes have become an established management tool; however, they are not just a recent creation. There has always been a need for a manager to evaluate the work of subordinates, either formally or informally. Formal systems of evaluation began to surface in the 1920s as industrial growth created a need for equitable salary administration. After World War II the need for qualified management personnel spurred renewed interest in developing ways of assessing how well workers and managers did their jobs. In the 1960s appraisals began to be used as a means of management development as well as for performance evaluation. The experience of IBM offers a good example of how appraisal systems have grown. Before 1958 many units of the company held individual appraisal interviews. In 1959 the company initiated a formal appraisal system, and in 1969 it refined the system to include performance planning.

During the 1970s the practice of giving some form of appraisal to employees has become almost universal. First, it has been demonstrated to be a beneficial process. Workers want to know how they are being evaluated, so the practice is a satisfying one to them. Furthermore, discussing performance is a good way to achieve improved performance. In fact, some managers now feel that the giving of effective appraisals is one of the features that distinguishes the most productive supervisors from the less productive ones. Second, the 1970s have seen a great increase in litigation about merit evaluations, pay, and promotions. The appraisal process is one means of *documenting* the reasons behind decisions. In this sense, the personal appraisal has become one of the most important management strategies in most organizations.

Definition of Appraisals

Appraisals come in many variations, but they nearly always include two things: (1) a formal evaluation of a subordinate and (2) a feedback interview in which the evaluation is communicated to the subordinate.

Stripped of all jargon it is simply an attempt to think clearly about each person's performance and future prospects against the background of his [or her] total work situation. Performance can be appraised succinctly by de-

[1]Harold Koontz, *Appraising Managers as Managers* (New York: McGraw-Hill Book Co., 1971), pp. 1–2.

scribing the best aspects of the individual's work and suggesting possible areas for improvement. Future prospects can be reviewed constructively. . . .[2]

The formal appraisal, or job performance review, as it is often called, must be differentiated from the day-to-day correction and praise that a supervisor gives an employee. This appraisal is generally given once or twice a year and is the time when both people look at the overall picture of the employee's performance. It is this very *general perspective* that makes it such a valuable addition to the normal day-to-day exchanges. In this sense, it is a *very special event*. Perhaps the best way to examine the concept of appraisal is to review several operational definitions, that is, actual systems that are employed by organizations.

The first system is used in a large chemical company. It involves three steps:

1. The manager and employee independently fill out a goal evaluation worksheet and results review form. They discuss conclusions and try to reconcile any differences.
2. The manager discusses the results review form with his or her immediate superior for agreement and signature. A copy is given to the employee for comment and signature.
3. The manager then sends three typed copies to the personnel manager for distribution. This system is designed to be used quarterly.

The results review form used by this company is one of the least structured forms in use. The manager is asked to rate the employee as exceptional, good, satisfactory, or unsatisfactory. Then the manager writes an essay about the employee describing the employee's overall performance in accomplishing goals and responsibilities. Since the form is also used for career development, the manager is asked to write a brief summary about four areas: (1) strengths and significant areas for improvement, (2) career interests, (3) possible future assignments, and (4) a personal development plan for the next 12 months.

The second system is one that a large food processing company uses. The appraisal is made by the subordinate's immediate supervisor, who then forwards the review to his or her superior for approval. It also comes in two parts.

The first part involves filling out a standard form listing 26 performance review factors, which are rated on a $1-7$ scale with a place provided for "any obvious strengths and/or areas for improvement." An example of one of these performance review factors is shown in Figure 9.1. The 26 performance review factors are

[2]Harold Mayfield, "In Defense of Performance Appraisal," *Harvard Business Review* 37 (1960); 82.

Communication	clear, timely, and precise oral and written communication to all necessary people on all subjects	Score	Weight	Points
1 2 3 4 5 6 7 rarely average always				

Figure 9.1   One performance review factor from an evaluation form.

accuracy
analytical skill
attendance and promptness
attitude
communcation
concern for costs and profits
control
cooperation
decisiveness and judgment

delegation
dependability
development of self
development of others
human relations
initiative
job knowledge
leadership management
   ability
organizing

planning
productivity
quality of work
quantity of work
resourcefulness
creativity
responsibility
versatility
adaptability

There are two important observations that we need to emphasize about this system. First, a person is not judged on all these factors; he or she is rated on only those that apply to a particular job. The personnel department prepares a list indicating which ones are applicable. Second, the items are weighted so that they are not all equal. Again, the company has designed this weighting system. The manager, for example, multiplies the number that he or she gives on the rating scale $(1-7)$ times the weight of that item in order to come up with a certain number of points. For example, let us assume that the manager rates an employee a 5 on communication on the review form. If the weight of the communication item is 60, then the points that the employee would receive would be 300. The total of points across all items is the employee's merit review rating.

In the second part of the system, the rating form is then mailed to the manager's own supervisor for approval. Before mailing it, however, the manager uses this form to write a summary sheet, which will be used in a face-to-face interview with the employee. It is the only form that remains with the manager for the interview and thereafter. It has four broad sections for evaluation: (1) Is the employee performing to full potential? (2) Is the employee's performance improving, constant, or deteriorating? (3) Should the employee be promoted or transferred? (4) What are some overall comments on the employee's performance and promotability? Copies of this form are sent to the wage and salary administration officer, the corporate functional manager, and the employee's personnel file.

Finally, after the interview there is an interview summary form on which the manager summarizes achievement or progress toward previous set goals and plans, new or revised plans for achievement of goals (with target dates), and anything else that was discussed. The subordinate is asked to sign the summary and is given a copy of it.

The third system is used by an international conglomerate that specializes in packaging and equipment. It is a voluntary system, since managers are encouraged to give yearly appraisals, but this rule is not enforced by corporate management. The system is designed to appraise managers in terms of their job performance in achieving targets and in terms of their management skills. The form for evaluating job performance is very open; no particular elements of the job are listed on the form. The supervisor lists the responsibilities individually, makes comments about each one, and rates the person on a 1–5 scale from marginal to superior. The form for rating management skill performance lists nine areas to be rated:

planning	leading	team member
problem solving	decision making	innovating
communicating	training	job expertise

In this form, the rating is done by placing a checkmark somewhere on a continuum, and no numbers are used. (See Figure 9.2.) Both the manager and the subordinate fill out these forms prior to their meeting. During the interview they try to come to a joint evaluation.

The fourth system is used by an airline to evaluate its managers; a different system is used to evaluate nonmanagerial personnel. The evaluation of managers is done with two forms: The superior completes a workbook, and the subordinate (manager) completes a self-review form. They are alike, but the evaluation is done by the superior and manager individually, prior to an interview. These forms provide for rating on a 1–6 scale of eight factors:

unit achievement	organization and planning
subordinate coaching	flexibility and innovation
teamwork	leadership and motivation
job knowledge	interpersonal skills

In addition to the ratings, space is provided so that the superior can write out the rationale or reasons for the ratings. This form also provides a brief explanation of what the eight factors are. For example, the explanation of flexibility and innovation is "the ability of the manager to tailor and approach problems and plans in accordance with the needs of the situation; and, where required, move outside the boundaries of tradition to establish new approaches to problem solving." Interpersonal skills are defined

Decision–maker	Extent required	Weak	Reliable	Decisive
	not applicable light medium heavy			

Figure 9.2   Sample evaluation form.

as "the ability of the manager to work with and through people at various levels in meeting objectives, formulating solutions to problems and getting things done. Included is the ability to understand and respond to another person's point of view and concern while working with that individual to solve problems and resolve conflict."

After the ratings are prepared, the forms are brought to an interview where they are discussed. During the interview, a heavy emphasis is placed on setting goals for the future. At the close of the interview a summary form is prepared and signed by both individuals.

Finally, the fifth system is an evaluation system that is used by a much smaller organization of engineers and architects. Each supervisor is asked to fill out an employee evaluation report. This form lists ten categories:

quality of work	organization of work
quantity of work	judgment
cooperativeness	leadership
dependability	utilizing personnel
initiative	training and developing others

Evaluators are urged to rate only five to eight factors that apply to the position and then to select the four most important ones for special emphasis. On each of the ten items there are some forced choice statements from which the evaluator might choose. After making these evaluations, the reviewer assigns a general rating to the employee and arranges to meet in an interview. After the interview, the evaluator writes comments in essay form and signs the evaluation; then the employee writes reactions to the form and signs it. Finally, the form is sent to the partner in the firm.

OBJECTIONS TO APPRAISALS

Despite the fact—or perhaps because of the fact—that they are so commonplace, there are still occasional objections raised about formal appraisals. Perhaps a knowledge of these objections will spur a constant improvement of the process. Some of the most frequent objections include the following:

1. Some review practices are unethical.
2. The interviewer wears a judicial hat and plays God.
3. Subordinates resist them.
4. Evaluations are too subjective.
5. A worker's performance may be influenced by things other than self.
6. Management's idea of fairness often leads to discouragement and alienation.
7. Evaluation creates a defensive climate.

Such objections are often echoed by some managers and consultants. Rensis Likert, for example, comments:

> The fundamental flaw in current review procedures is that they compel the supervisors to behave in a threatening, rejecting, and ego-deflating manner with a sizable portion of his [or her] staff. This pattern of relationship . . . not only affects the subordinate but also seriously impairs the capacity of the superior to function effectively.[3]

It is not our purpose here to deny that some appraisal systems do create problems. In fact, a manager recently complained to us that he was required by his company to distribute the ratings of his subordinates according to a bell-shaped curve with 50 percent being rated less than average. The evaluation system did not take into account that the company ought to be choosing capable people through its selection procedures and, therefore, the normal bell-shaped curve should not apply. This manager did have problems and hated the system. Nevertheless, an examination of the objections leads us to the conclusion that they indict only specific procedures, not the general idea of evaluation. Consequently, these objections only challenge us to refine our procedures. In other words, if appraisals are here to stay, as they appear to be, the essential question is: How can we make them better?

RATIONALE FOR APPRAISALS

Perhaps we should not take appraisals for granted. Even though most organizations have some kind of system for appraisal, the fact is that they are often voluntary. Even when there is a rule that all subordinates must have a yearly appraisal, it often goes unheeded or the appraisal is not very effective. Walter Mahler conducted a survey among some organizations that have a policy of formal appraisals. He asked, "In the last year has your

[3]Rensis Likert, "Motivational Approach to Management Development," *Harvard Business Review* 36 (1959): 75.

superior talked with you about your evaluation of your formal performance of your major responsibilities?" Eighteen percent said that they had not, 32 percent said that it had been done in very general terms, 29 percent said that they had had one in some detail, and 21 percent reported that their superiors had held them quite specifically.[4] Perhaps, some managers still need to be sold on the idea of having an appraisal.

First, contrary to the objections above, appraisals have been widely accepted by managers and employees. Our research shows that employees at every level like to know where they stand. Harold Mayfield found that "90% of the people who have been interviewed express satisfaction with the procedures."[5] A case study by Cal Downs and David Spohn found that 87 percent of the interviewers regarded the appraisal favorably, as did 71 percent of the interviewees.[6]

Second, personal feedback has a strong relationship to a person's job satisfaction and productivity. A form called the "Communication Satisfaction Questionnaire" has been used to measure satisfaction in a number of organizations. In most of these, a factor called "personal feedback" has consistently had a significant correlation with job satisfaction. In these studies, employees were asked to identify which of the eight factors being studied affected their productivity most. Personal feedback ranked second.

Third, appraisals offer one of the best means of documenting why organizational decisions have been made. They become a form of management protection. At the same time, they probably have forced managers to refine their decision making, so that more equitable decisions are now being made than were made in the past.

Fourth, the job performance review provides a unique opportunity for two-way communication, and there are distinct advantages to communication flowing in both directions. Both individuals exchange information, but the feedback interview allows the subordinate to express ideas and provide input in ways that are usually not allowable. In this sense, the communication exchange fills an integrative function, making the individual feel a part of a relationship.

Fifth, some managers, as we have pointed out, seem to avoid having reviews. We do not judge their reasons for doing so, but a system that forces them into some interaction is probably beneficial. Because of the other considerations just discussed, perhaps even forced communication about performance is better than no communication at all.

In summary, implementing a job performance review system meets

[4]Walter Mahler, *How Effective Executives Interview* (Homewood, Ill.: Dow Jones-Richard D. Irwin, Inc., 1976), p. 105.
[5]Mayfield, "Performance Appraisal," p. 82.
[6]Cal W. Downs and David Spohn, "A Case Study of an Appraisal System," paper presented to the Academy of Management, Kansas City, Missouri, 1976.

needs of the individual as well as needs of the organization, and the remainder of this chapter is designed to set guidelines for making the appraisal as productive as possible.

PREPARATION FOR THE EVALUATION

Since the evaluation is a major opportunity to examine a person's performance in a long-range perspective, thorough preparation is absolutely critical. For one thing, the degree of preparation is one of the signs that employees use to determine how much importance you are placing upon the interview and perhaps upon them.

To give an appraisal to every subordinate takes a great deal of time. If you are like most managers, you feel rushed in just getting your job done. Nevertheless, you must avoid the inclination to put it off indefinitely or make very little preparation. As a supervisor, you are the chief communicative link between your subordinate and the organization. Therefore, what you do influences greatly the subordinate's view of the organization and of his or her job. Viewed from this perspective, the time spent in preparation can produce very beneficial results.

Start with the Job: Review Job Responsibilities

Managers often take job descriptions for granted, feeling that they know what a given job entails. It has been documented, however, in a variety of studies that superiors and subordinates often have quite different perceptions about their respective jobs. Frequently they disagree as much as 25 percent in listing the functions associated with the subordinate's job. No job remains completely static; they contract or expand as the work environment undergoes constant changes. Consequently, it is well to begin your preparation by identifying your perceptions of the job.

As you enumerate the responsibilities of a particular job, weigh them for their relative importance. Forms similar to the one shown in Figure 9.3 are widely used because they force the manager to make these kinds of evaluations. In some cases, you may want to distinguish between continuing responsibilities and special or optional responsibilities. Note that such a system as this not only tailors the evaluation to the specific job but also tailors it to the specific individual in the job.

Types of Performance Evaluations

You have several options as to the form your actual evaluation can take, and people in different organizations have used each of them successfully. By enumerating them here, you may become aware of new alternatives.

Job Assignments and Responsibilities	Relative Importance	Comments	Rating

Figure 9.3   Sample appraisal form.

By all means, choose the one or two that will work best for you in your situation.[7]

ESSAY

An *essay* appraisal is one in which the manager describes in narrative form the strengths and weaknesses of the subordinate. No set form is used, and no particular items are prescribed. It has the advantage of flexibility and the disadvantage that the essays for several different subordinates may be very hard to compare.

GRAPHIC RATING SCALE

A *graphic rating scale* lists a number of items on which the superior will rate the subordinate as outstanding, above average, average, or unsatisfactory. Instead of phrases, the ratings are given on a numerical 1–7 scale. Such classifications are widespread; however, one of the problems associated with them is that a rating of 7 from one manager may be viewed quite differently by another. The numbers appear to make comparisons easy, but in fact they may not be comparable across supervisors.

FORCED-CHOICE RATINGS

Forced-choice ratings require the superior to choose among groups of statements that describe the subordinate. For example, one form makes the following statements about degree of cooperation, and the superior would be required to select the one that best describes the subordinate. An example follows.

> *Cooperation*
> 1. refuses to cooperate

[7]Winston Oberg, "Make Performance Appraisal Relevant," *Harvard Business Review,* **49** (1972): 61.

2. frequently not cooperative
3. generally works with others
4. willing teamworker
5. exceptionally good teamworker

RANKING METHOD

A *ranking method* requires that each employee be compared with every other employee in the work unit. It forces the supervisor to choose one employee as better than the others until all the employees in the unit are ranked. In a strict merit sense, this may sometimes be useful, but many supervisors object to it because someone has to be ranked last even though the entire unit may be competent. This is not likely to help morale. Furthermore, in some cases it may foster competition instead of the cooperation needed to work as a unit.

FIELD REVIEW

The *field review* is a technique designed to reduce supervisory bias in the ratings. The supervisor describes the subordinate's performance; then teams from personnel read the descriptions, compare the ratings for all people in a given work unit, and make final assessments of the employees. Whether or not this works well depends on the purpose of the evaluation. If the emphasis is upon fostering supervisory-subordinate interactions, it is deficient.

MANAGEMENT BY OBJECTIVES

The *management by objectives* technique has produced a format in which the manager and the subordinate interact to set goals for the subordinate. These goals then become the criteria by which the subordinate is judged in the future. It is a widely used technique that is quite consistent with the guidelines that we describe for effective appraisals.

All of the methods just described involve some degree of formal planning. We would be remiss if we did not point out that some supervisors hold their appraisals in a very unstructured, often indirect way. We do not advise this, however, because we feel that the best examination of performance from a very broad perspective requires thought and planning.

In order to formalize appraisals, most organizations now adopt a form to guide the supervisor. It is sometimes possible to include several of the methods just described on the same form. There is often a section like that in Figure 9.1 that offers great flexibility in what is evaluated. There may also be a section in which the various categories to be evaluated are clearly spelled out, as in Figure 9.2. These categories will vary with the nature and the level of the job, but we have tried here to summarize some of the categories that appear most often for managers, supervisors, and exempt employees.

Personal Traits and Skills

1. cooperativeness
2. leadership
3. judgment
4. dependability
5. level of motivation
6. flexibility
7. organization/planning
8. coordination
9. appearance/grooming
10. problem solving
11. use of time
12. communication skills
13. initiative
14. creativity
15. objectivity
16. analytic ability
17. decisiveness
18. self-control
19. ambition

Responsibilities and Relationships

1. unit performance/quantity of work
2. quality of work
3. teamwork
4. interpersonal relations
5. self-development
6. utilizing subordinates/ delegation
7. developing others
8. job knowledge
9. innovation
10. relation with supervisor
11. equal employment opportunity (EEO) goals
12. attendance
13. loyalty
14. consistency of achievement

Environmental Factors

1. pay
2. nature of problems
3. causes of problems

Each one of these categories may be further broken down into subcategories. For example, "use of time" may be subdivided on one form to include three statements on which the subordinate is rated, for example,

1. completes assignments and projects accurately and on time
2. recognizes work priorities and devotes appropriate time and resources to each
3. delegates work effectively and provides appropriate follow-up to insure proper completion

The difficulty with adopting any form for a complete organization is that frequently it is superimposed on people that it does not fit exactly. This happened in one company, for example, that used the same form for all managers. Certain professional and technical people were listed as managers even though they had no direct subordinates, and they were frustrated by the form. If this happens, appropriate individuals should be contacted immediately about designing a new form.

Performance Evaluation

As we have implied throughout this chapter, not all evaluations are valid, productive, or acceptable to employees. Consequently, we offer several guidelines that should make your evaluations as productive as possible.

1. *Keep the proper time frame in mind.* Ideally, you will keep a file for each subordinate over the complete time period covered by the appraisal, and in this file you will have recorded specific incidents, letters, reports, and any other information that will help in the evaluation. In terms of the time period to be evaluated, it is possible to make two drastic errors. First, managers who do not keep a file on the employee are likely to emphasize just the performance record for the most recent five to six weeks before the evaluation, and this defeats the purpose of having a long-range perspective. Second, some managers keep their files so long that they "freeze" the evaluation of the employee. For example, sometimes employees have found themselves downgraded because of something they did several years ago. It is unfair to the employee to be judged in this manner.

2. *Base the evaluation on known criteria.* With each new appraisal the criteria needs to be explained thoroughly. No one likes surprises.

3. *Be specific; get down to details.* Subordinates often complain about generalized criticism because it only suggests a problem area without being explicit about changes that are needed. The more specific the evaluation is, the clearer it is, and the greater is the change that it is likely to produce. If a subordinate has been "uncooperative," for example, he or she will better understand what is meant if you can cite specific examples or describe critical incidents. Figure 9.4 is a form designed to assist in such record keeping. Talking about the specific behavior will let the subordinate know exactly what you are concerned about and will also let the subordinate know what can be done to correct it.

4. *Limit the problem areas to those that are most important.* The idea of setting limits is a useful one. Frequently managers forget that they can choose what to talk about, and they try to cover everything, but everything is not of equal importance. The "20/80 rule" specifies that you should concentrate on those 20 percent of the problems that will yield an 80 percent improvement in performance. The key idea is progress, not perfection. In the survey by Downs and Spohn, the average number of problems discussed in appraisal was 3.[8]

5. *Base the evaluation on job related matters.* This is why analyzing the job responsibilities is an important prerequisite to evaluation. Appearance, for example, may be very important for a salesperson but not at all applicable to a person on an assembly line. Figure 9.5 is given to stimulate some thought as to what areas ought to be evaluated.

[8]Downs and Spohn, "A Case Study," p. 15.

Effective Examples		Examples That Show Need for Improvement	
Date	Incident	Date	Incident

Figure 9.4   Critical-incident file.

	Job Related Items	Nonjob Related Items
Objective Measures	A	B
Subjective Measures	C	D

Figure 9.5   Areas of evaluation.

Some people would like to limit evaluations to Box A, but Box C in Figure 9.5 may involve some of the most important aspects of the job. For managers, the ability to coordinate is terribly important, but also it is difficult to measure. Measurement, in this case, is not done necessarily in terms of numbers but in terms of important examples. In addressing the question of what is appropriate to evaluate, we asked 200 managers what should be used in judging the effectiveness of subordinates, and their answers (see Figure 9.6) indicate that some combination of personality and behavior is inevitable.[9]

6. *Separate actual performance from your estimate of the person's potential.* There is always a possibility of being influenced by predictions of what the person may be able to achieve in the future. It is useful to recognize and develop potential, but current performance should be viewed realistically.

7. *Balance the favorable and the unfavorable.* In an assessment of one review system, this was one of the most frequent objections that we received about the malfunctioning of the system. Some supervisors apparently tended to emphasize the negative evaluations of the appraisal; this left the persons being reviewed with the feelings that they were not appreciated or were not getting the fair amount of recognition for their efforts. On the other hand, there were also those supervisors who tended to talk about positive items only. The persons interviewed in such cases felt that their interviews were not as productive as they might be. Furthermore, they felt that they really did not understand what their supervisor wanted from them because they were given little direction.

8. *Set priorities.* Not all points are equally important. Therefore, a way of differentiating the most important from the least important is necessary to the person being reviewed. This is why some kind of weighting system, described earlier in the chapter, can be very important.

9. *Keep your evaluation tentative.* Some systems even encourage their managers to write the first evaluation in pencil. The reason for this is that a manager often learns things in a feedback interview that may modify or change the evaluation.

10. *Assess your own impact on the subordinate.* People do not work in a vacuum, and they are influenced by circumstances and by supervision. In fact, subordinates often feel that a manager cannot appraise a subordinate without appraising himself or herself.

	Manager	Subordinate
Personality traits alone	0%	0%
Behavior on the job alone	23%	19%
Both of the above together	37%	46%
Impossible to separate the two	40%	32%

Figure 9.6   Bases for evaluation.

[9]Ibid.

THE FEEDBACK INTERVIEW

Thorough preparation is absolutely critical to the success of a job performance review. In fact, the time and energy necessary to prepare well may be one of the greatest blocks to having frequent performance reviews. To do it for every subordinate can take a great deal of time, and most managers already feel rushed to get their jobs done. Nevertheless, the results can be worth the expenditure.

If you have made an evaluation just described, you are now in a position to make concrete plans for your interview. At this point, you are keenly aware of the strengths and weaknesses of your subordinates, and you can plan accordingly.

Preparing for the Feedback Interview

1. *Set a specific time for the appointment.* This is the kind of interview in which you will need a block of time from one to two hours long so that you can explore points comprehensively. Both you and the subordinate ought to make provisions so that you will be uninterrupted and also free from the pressures of competing demands on your time. The importance of time is suggested by the fact that in one case study, 60 percent of those who felt negatively about their review indicated that it had lasted less than 45 minutes.[10]

2. *Assign the interviewee some means of preparation.* This can be done in a number of ways. Some systems require the subordinate to fill out a form prior to the interview. Others require that the manager give the subordinate an opportunity to see the manager's completed form prior to the interview so he or she can study it and shape a response. You may not choose either of these systems, but it is important that you require the subordinate to do something in terms of preparation so that he or she comes to the feedback meeting with an overall view of his or her performance. If there is no official form, have the subordinate write an outline of important points that he or she wishes to discuss.

3. *Assess your purpose for this particular interview.* Since most organizations require some kind of periodic review, it is important that you break the temptation to treat all the interviews across subordinates or even with a given subordinate in the same way. Different interviews may require that you accomplish different things because the circumstances are different. Therefore, there is some value in our listing some of the most frequently stated purposes given for appraisal interviews.

To Give Feedback That Lets an Employee Know Where He or She Stands
1. to praise good work

[10]Ibid.

2. to warn or threaten
3. to communicate the need for improvement
4. to let the person know what is expected
5. to recognize and reward contributions
6. to get things "off one's chest"
7. to determine salary standards and award merit increases

To Analyze Problem Areas
1. to determine the training and development needs
2. to establish standards of supervision
3. to make inventories of talent
4. to improve superior-subordinate relations

To Set Objectives for Future Performance
1. to assess the employee's future in the organization
2. to discover an employee's aspirations
3. to persuade employees to work in certain directions
4. to serve as a record of career development
5. to select qualified individuals for promotion and transfer

To Give the Employee a Sense of Participation in the Job
1. to listen
2. to discover what employees are thinking

To Serve as a Record for an Individual
1. to document an individual's progress or lack of it
2. to clarify decisions that are made
3. to make inventories of talent

Not all of these purposes are going to characterize any one interview, but several of them might. Furthermore, not all of them will be of equal weight, so listing them in rank order might be helpful. After identifying the purposes, state them as well as you can. Note that the way they are stated above is not very concrete. As you analyze a particular person's performance, you can state the purposes more specifically. The more concretely you state them, the easier it will be for you to devise strategies to attain them.

4. *Plan a general agenda.* Four topic areas need to be covered in most appraisals. A discussion of the *job definition* and requirements should give the subordinate a firm understanding of how his or her job fits into the overall context of the organization. This discussion also should explore what changes are taking place that affect the job. *Past performance* should be discussed in a straightforward manner with both manager and subordinate sharing their insights. A general idea of *goals* or targets for future performance should be planned. Finally, more and more appraisals are being related to the overall *career* opportunities and limitations of the particular individual. This discussion should be very realistic.

5. *Choose a structural approach.* Planning a structure to your interview is very important, because it determines how you are going to relate to the subordinate. We shall discuss three basic structural strategies: (1) tell and sell, (2) tell and listen, and (3) listen and tell.

In the tell-and-sell approach,[11] the manager communicates the evaluation to the subordinate at the beginning of the interview. The manager assumes the evaluation is accurate and fair and tries to persuade the subordinate that the appraisal is correct and that the steps outlined for improvement should be followed. The role of the manager in this kind of interview can range from being a dictator to being a salesperson, if the manager chooses to be less heavy handed. The skill needed to conduct this kind of interview is the ability to persuade and to use the promise of reward or the threat of punishment effectively. In such cases, the interviewer tends to monopolize most of the conversation.

For some people who stress the value of human relations, this telling and selling seems to be lacking in merit. Nevertheless, it works well for some interviewers who are very conscious of their authority and power. Note the following actual case.

> Mary Smith was my subordinate, and she was a very poor performer in her job. Every time that I talked with her about her need for improvement, she said that she understood and would improve. But her performance did not seem to get any better.
>
> Additional discussions became very heated and brought on a defensive attitude, and she tried to assign the blame for her poor performance to everything but herself. Primarily, she felt that it was others that caused her to look bad. After these discussions, there was still no improvement in her work.
>
> Finally, out of desperation I decided on a last round of talks with her. In preparation, I wrote down exactly what I wanted to say.
>
> 1. I as your boss want to help you.
> 2. I don't feel we have communicated very effectively in the past and we may not in the future.
> 3. You can accept or reject what I say—as you wish.
> 4. I have 20 minutes of talking; you have 20 minutes of listening. I will not accept rebuttal. I will only accept questions that help to clarify my position.
>
> This was a different approach for me, and I wasn't certain that it was the best approach, but it worked. She accepted the input and thanked me for it. Today, her attitude seems to have turned around, and she is a much improved performer.

In this case, the interviewer did not pick the tell-and-sell method as a first option, but it was the one that finally worked. Apparently, there are certain types of individuals for whom this method works best: (1) very

---

[11]Norman Maier, *The Appraisal Interview* (New York: John Wiley & Sons, Inc., 1958).

young employees who often are naive and lack the experience necessary to evaluate themselves; (2) employees who have much less status than their bosses, and who, therefore, are likely to be aware of the difference and accept the evaluation because of this difference in status or expertise; (3) employees who are very loyal to the organization or who have a strong identification with a particular supervisor; (4) employees who do not want to determine what their jobs entail and, therefore, need and appreciate direction. It is a mistake to think that everyone wants to have a say in their job and perhaps most do, but there are those who would make the remark, "Just tell me what you want done, and I'll do it."

While the tell-and-sell method may be quite effective with these kinds of individuals, there are also some situations in which it may not work. In these situations, there are two potential pitfalls the interviewer should avoid. First, if only one side is explored in any depth, it may lead to an incorrect assessment. Second, defensive or hostile feelings may be aroused that eventually may impair the superior's relationship with the subordinate. Third—and this is very important—an interviewer may attempt to persuade the interviewee as long as he or she thinks there is a chance of success. If the interviewer ever becomes convinced, however, that he or she cannot be successful in these persuasive attempts, then he or she is likely to appraise the subordinate as "stubborn" or "illogical." We have seen occasions where employees who perform well on their jobs were penalized in the interview—in some cases, fired—because they did not agree with their superiors' evaluations or recommendations.

The objectives of the tell-and-listen approach are to communicate an evaluation and to get the interviewee's reactions to the evaluation.[12] This is the method, for example, that is built into the system in which the manager is required to show the subordinate the completed evaluation forms in advance of the meeting. In this type of interview, the superior assumes that there are going to be differences in perception and wants to draw them out. This requires great skill in active listening and probing. The normal pattern for the tell-and-listen approach is for the superior to give the evaluation and control the early parts of the interview; the subordinate will then do most of the talking as the interviewer attempts to draw out reactions to the evaluation. After this the superior again takes control at the close of the interview.

The tell-and-listen approach tends to work best for people who have a high need to participate in their jobs, who feel that their superiors do not understand their jobs, who are close to their superiors on the status hierarchy, and who are recognized as professionals with a great deal of expertise on their own. The obvious advantage of the tell-and-listen approach is that the interviewer may learn things about the interviewee and

---

[12]Ibid.

the interviewee's job that broadens his or her own understanding of why the interviewee performs as he or she does.

Like the tell-and-sell approach, however, it does not work well with all people. Furthermore, listening does not necessarily lead to agreement. Frequently, a supervisor may listen to a subordinate's explanations and still have to consider them unimportant or invalid. The listening role still does not take the supervisor out of the evaluator's role.

A variation of the tell-and-listen approach is the listen-and-tell approach. In this approach the manager does not start off the interview with an evaluation but instead may have the subordinate begin. This is particularly common in organizations that have both the manager and the subordinate prepare evaluation forms prior to the interview. In one system the manager is instructed to have the interviewee present his or her evaluations, then the interviewer presents his or her own and work toward agreement on the need areas. This structure is designed to (1) have the subordinate introduce problems that are important to him or her and (2) to avoid having the subordinate's participation be just a defensive reaction to the interviewer's evaluation. We think that these are very worthwhile purposes.

The skills required in this kind of interview are active listening, skillful probing, and maybe some persuasion. There is another crucial variable that affects this kind of interview, too, which is the trusting relationship between manager and subordinate. Research on upward communication indicates that subordinates are reluctant to expose their major weaknesses or problems to people higher in the organization because they want to create or to maintain a positive image. Additionally, they want to protect themselves from any potential danger to either their salary or promotion potential. Consequently, the extent to which they will introduce major problems may depend upon their level of trust in the interviewer. So far we have concentrated on people's willingness to participate in this way, but we should also point out that there are those people who probably are unaware of certain kinds of problems until the problems are pointed out to them.

We conclude this section by pointing out one other misuse of this approach. A manager recently had an appraisal meeting with his subordinate, and he started off by using the listen-and-tell approach. The subordinate was a dedicated worker who had prepared thoroughly, and she began to identify some of her thinking. Finally, she stopped and became incensed when she noticed that her supervisor had not filled out his form at all. In other words, he was relying on her evaluation to be the basic framework for the discussion. He was not prepared. The point that we want to stress is that regardless of the structures that you choose, you must be prepared to give an evaluation to the subordinate.

6. *Prepare an interview schedule.* As the example above illustrates,

the interviewer should have a schedule, even if it is a modified one. Structuring is easiest when it is done from a schedule. As you plan, decide whether the points are going to be introduced one by one, with each point being developed individually, or whether several main points will be presented together. Whenever you start off with your evaluation, cover the main areas in a summary preview and then go back over the points individually.

7. *Select the setting.* Select a place for the interview that is going to reinforce your purposes, most of which were covered in Chapter 4. The options most often cited are superior's office, a conference room, or a lounge. The superior's office will reinforce the status difference and make the tone very business-like. It would be very useful in the tell-and-sell approach. A conference room or a lounge, on the other hand, may play down the status differences, and this environment may make it easier for the subordinate to feel free to participate. Whatever the choice is, however, the essential criterion is that the place be private and free from interruptions.

CONDUCTING THE INTERVIEW

As a manager, you have the primary responsibility for making the interview a success. Let us assume that you have made as thorough plans for this interview as possible. You must remember that the planning just represents your best thinking *to this point.* It should not become a straightjacket for you, because you will need considerable skill in adapting your plans to the subordinate in the context of the interview. Consequently, be flexible as you try to manage the interview.

1. *Communicate the seriousness and importance of the meeting right from the start.* Start the meeting on time. Do not postpone or delay it unless there is some emergency. Give the subordinate a thorough orientation as to what you are trying to accomplish and how this meeting fits into the overall appraisal system. Avoid treating the interview lightly by making statements such as "Well, it's that time again." If the subordinate gets the slightest hint that you think the meeting is not important, it will be a dissatisfying experience.

2. *Seek subordinate participation.* Subordinate participation lets the interview become a channel of upward and downward communication so that differences of perception are uncovered and the manager becomes "educated" about the subordinate. It can breed mutual understanding— sometimes even agreement—which also can lead to a better working relationship. Finally, the fact of participation is satisfying in itself for many subordinates.

The more subordinates feel they are participating in the interview by contributing their ideas and feelings, the more likely they are (1) to feel that their superior is helpful, (2) to feel that their current problems are cleared up, and (3) to report that future targets or goals were set.[13] In another study, E. B. Kirk and associates found the following advantages for a high amount of appraisee participation. Such participation increased the likelihood that the subordinates:

> know what is expected of them.
> understand the results to be achieved.
> think they are supervised "about right."
> know what the supervisor thinks of their work.
> get frank discussions of their performance.
> discuss specific ways of doing a better job.
> get full discussion of their future.
> see their superiors as helping them.
> get recognition and encouragement.
> are motivated to do the best job.[14]

There are several ways in which participation can be maximized.

a. Make an effort to set the subordinate at ease.
b. Have the subordinate prepare for the interview. If no form is available, have the subordinate bring a written outline of points that he or she wishes to cover.
c. Ask questions and offer time to the subordinate. The questions should usually be open to facilitate the greatest discussion. Sample questions that might prove useful are listed below.
   1. "Generally, there are some things that people like about their jobs and some things that they do not like. What are some of the things that you like best?" "Least?"
   2. "In terms of the last year as a whole, what are some of the things that you have learned in your job?"
   3. "What would you say has been your chief accomplishment in your job in the last year?"
   4. "Are there any parts of your job for which you would like more experience or training?"
   5. "How do you feel about your career progress to date?"
   6. "What do you see as your competitive advantages for promotion? Your disadvantages?" "What can be done to overcome the disadvantages?"
   7. "Are there any considerations, such as location, change in location, amount of traveling, family situation, which need to be taken into consideration over the next few years?"

[13]Ronald J. Burke, Tamara Weir, and William Weitzel, "Characteristics of Effective Employee Performance Review and Development Reviews," an unpublished paper, 1978, p. 8.
[14]E. B. Kirk et al., "Appraisee Participation in Performance Review," *Personnel Journal* 44 (1965): 23.

    d. Listen to the subordinate. This is one of the best ways of encouraging participation. However, we should point out that there are varying degrees of listening. One of the most telling comments that we have heard came from a manager who said, "My participation is allowed to be high, which cuts down my nervousness; however, I don't feel that anything I say would make a difference."

    3. *Allow time for the development of main points.* There is a great difference between talking about subjects and actually covering them. In the case of the appraisal interview, the most important areas need to be well developed and firm decisions must be made about them. This is another reason for not trying to cover too much in the interview.

    4. *Discuss; do not make the interview a presentation.* Your own participation in the interview should be aimed at facilitating discussion. This point obviously applies less to tell-and-sell situations than to others; nevertheless, even the selling supervisor should try to secure some reaction from the subordinate.

    The main reason for this is that you can expect differences in perception about the job and evaluation. As these differences come up, it is particularly useful to analyze mentally what they are and what can be done about them. For example, if there are different assessments about the amount of turnover in a subordinate manager's unit, this is a question of fact and can be researched in order to determine if it is correct. On the other hand, if there are differences about whether a good subordinate should be given the most interesting job assignments as a reward, while lesser employees are left with routine assignments, this is a question of values, and the solution is simply to make a persuasive case for the manager's value system.

    5. *Keep a sense of priorities about the discussion.* It is easy to get side-tracked sometimes by discussing things that are not really as important as others. Avoid discussing other people in the interview. Sometimes, subordinates try to lead the discussion away from themselves and toward others. They may even ask questions about other individuals in the work unit. It is best not to let yourself be led into this kind of digression.

    Balance the good with the bad. It is not necessary to balance each negative point with a corresponding good one, but it is useful to make certain that strong points are clearly appreciated. One of the most common deficiencies in the appraisal process is what we call the "yes-but" syndrome. It is easy to compliment an employee in one sentence and then spend the rest of the interview talking about weaknesses. Watch the tendency to say, "You really are one of our most valued workers, but there are some points on which you need to improve." It is likely that the good points will not get covered very specifically, but the bad ones will. This leaves a bad impression on the part of the subordinate.

6. *Make the evaluation specific.* Let us emphasize the need for you to communicate your evaluation. It is possible to discuss things without the subordinate receiving a clear idea of your evaluation. Theoretically, you were quite specific as you made your evaluation. Now it is time to communicate some of those specific items to the subordinate. The specifics will provide the rationale for your general evaluation.

7. *Be problem oriented in guiding the discussion.* A good assessment not only covers what has occurred but also why things have happened as they have. To keep the interview focused in this direction is often difficult, because many subordinates would rather focus on future actions (goals) than on their past performances. Once the performance has been covered, however, it is time to focus on goals.

8. *Separate salary from the performance review.* Obviously, a performance review generally is related to merit increases, and different organizations have different ways of connecting the two. In general, however, introducing the subject of money into the appraisal interview raises an emotional roadblock to a conscientious analysis of strengths and weaknesses.

9. *Set goals.* The subordinate should not leave the interview without identifying some targets for future performance. Some general goals may even have been set out in your planning. However, there is a real advantage in having a mutual agreement about them set during the interview. Often the goals will be evident as you analyze past performance. In general, setting goals can be done best if it follows these guidelines.

1. Set priorities. Any aspect of a job can be explored in terms of potential goals, but they should be limited to the ones that are going to be most important.
2. Limit the number of goals so that the subordinate has a definite focus. It is easy to spread the person too thin.
3. Tailor the goals to the individual. The ultimate goal for one subordinate to make progress in the job; others may need a different set of goals.
4. Make the goals specific and set criteria so that both you and the subordinate know when they have been achieved.
5. Set a definite time frame. Identify the date by which achievement of a given goal should be evaluated.
6. Set obtainable goals that offer challenge and growth. The objective is to stretch the employee but also to make certain that the goal is within reach. Setting impossible goals has a demoralizing impact on the subordinate's work.
7. Write out the performance plan. Written goals tend to force people to be more exact and to clarify what they mean. It also gives the documentation necessary for comparing later achievement with the goals set.

10. *Give the interview a definite conclusion.* Too often interactions like appraisals just end with a statement such as "Well, maybe we've covered most of the important points." This is weak and does not really accomplish what the interviewer should in ending the interview.

First, there should be another orientation so that each individual knows exactly what to expect as a result of the interview: The things that have been covered; the goals that have been set; and what is going to happen with the information and what is expected in terms of follow-up.

Second, most organizations now request that the subordinate sign something to show that the interview did in fact take place and that the subordinate has seen the ratings. Some interviews conclude with the manager and the subordinate working together to fill out a summary report.

Third, a follow-up should be provided for. The time spent in appraisal can only be useful if there is some follow-up. This means that periodic checks need to be made to determine how well a subordinate is accomplishing the goals set up, the difficulties, if any, that are being encountered, and whether the goals need to be restated.

FINAL CONSIDERATIONS

We conclude this chapter by emphasizing that there are some major differences between "good" and "bad" appraisals and between effective and less effective supervisors. Research demonstrates that the more effective supervisors do some things differently, which makes their relationships with their subordinates much more effective:

1. Better supervisors check "more least strengths and fewer strengths over-all, which suggests that they tend to be somewhat tougher raters."[15]
2. Effective supervisors "also show more 'spread' or variation in their ratings between high and low-rated subordinates than do less-effective supervisors."[16]

As these findings suggest, making the final evaluation of a subordinate often creates a problem for the manager, and the tendency in recent years has been to inflate the ratings, that is, to give everybody good ratings. It is difficult for many people to confront the unpleasant task of having to be critical of another person in a face-to-face situation. There is also the possibility of having to justify any low ratings, which takes more time and effort. So for many managers, the easy way out is to give high

[15]Wayne Kirchner and Donald Reisberg, "Differences Between Better and Less Effective Supervisors in Appraisal of Subordinates," *Personnel Psychology* 15 (1962): 295.
[16]Ibid.

ratings. This makes it easy for the manager, but it makes it difficult for the system to discriminate among individuals if everyone is rated high.

There is also another related problem. In order to compare people, it is necessary to know what the ratings mean. It is common knowledge that supervisors do not all agree as to what a "3" means, or even what a "good" means as opposed to an "excellent." The result is that one manager may use a "2" to designate what another manager would designate as a "3." Is there any way out? Not conclusively. The fact that meanings differ among people is a fact of life. Nevertheless, there are two things that we would advocate to minimize this problem.

First, be consistent in your own ratings. Develop your yardstick and keep to it. Base your conclusions on facts and try to overcome any halo effects from other evaluations. The following suggestions come from an evaluation system used by a bank.

1. Do not overrate employees on difficult jobs or underrate employees on simple jobs. The difficulty of the job is measured in establishing job grade and should not be duplicated in performance appraisal.
2. Do not rate employees by working backwards from employees' salary positions.
3. Do not overrate older employees or underrate new employees, or vice versa.
4. Do not overrate employees that you have personally trained.
5. Do not overrate an employee because of anticipated future development.[17]

Second, some organizations are now trying to train supervisors in rating personnel. For example, one organization that uses a 1–6 rating scale also has a verbal definition of what each factor means. This is included in Figure 9.7. Of greater utility, however, is the training that is now being done to examine profiles of employees, so that each manager can be coached in how to rate a particular profile. Standardization is probably unreachable—and we are not too certain that it would be desirable either—but there can be no question that there ought to be some general agreement as to what the factors on a rating scale mean.

Other things that more effective supervisors do differently are:

1. More effective supervisors are more "communication-minded." They enjoy talking and speak up; they enjoy conversations with subordinates; and they are able to give instructions well.[18]

[17]Federal Reserve Bank of Kansas City, Missouri, "Guide for Supervisors," an unpublished paper, 1978.
[18]Fredric Jablin, "Superior-Subordinate Communication: The State of the Art," unpublished paper given to the International Communication Association, Chicago, 1978, pp. 9–10.

	Scale for Evaluation
Unsatisfactory	1 Presently not acceptable. Requires continual close supervision and direction. Substantial and immediate improvement required.
Satisfactory	2 Normally meets minimum job requirements but requires above normal supervision and direction. Manager meets minimum standards but requires improvement for the long term.
	3 Manager meets reasonable and realistic standards. Results represent more than a minimum effort. Manager requires some periodic supervision and direction.
	4 Meets reasonable and realistic job requirements and often exceeds them. Manager is effective with only occasional guidance and supervision.
	5 Consistently exceeds requirements and standards. Highly effective with only general guidance required. Manager substantially above expected standards.
Exceptional	6 Outstanding performance on a level rarely achieved. Requirements and standards being accomplished at the highest possible level. Manager has been unique and outstanding over the last 12 months.

Figure 9.7   Verbal definitions of factors on a rating scale. (Source: Al Cross, "Scale for Evaluation," *Reviewer's Notebook for the Job Performance Review,* p. 3.)

2. They tend to be willing to listen and to respond with empathy and understanding to employees' questions. In other words, they are approachable.[19]

3. They tend to be sensitive to the feelings and ego-defense needs of subordinates. These defensive needs are especially likely to occur

[19]Ibid.

in any kind of evaluative situation, and the effective supervisor handles them carefully.[20]

4. They tend to be more open to passing information to subordinates. They give notice of impending changes and explain the reasons behind their actions and regulations.[21]

5. They are more adept at setting realistic goals with subordinates.

6. They see the appraisal as not just an isolated event but rather as part of an integrated personnel system that is related to recruitment, placement, and development of employees.

PROJECTS

1. Collect as many appraisal systems as you can and compare them in terms of procedures. If you cannot obtain these from interviews, examine the forms listed in *Appraising Managerial Performance,* published by the Conference Board, Inc., 845 Third Avenue, New York, New York 10022.

2. Discuss the ethical considerations that should guide you in appraising someone's performance.

3. Interview several people who have been appraised recently in order to get their reactions to the process.

4. List the assumptions on which a good appraisal system should be based.

5. Select a job, get a description of the job, and try to identify the *behavioral* categories that most apply to it that can be evaluated.

6. How many supervisors should make an input to a person's appraisal?

7. What are the characteristics of goals that should be set in an appraisal?

8. What should be the optimum amount of participation by the interviewee? How can you generate this participation?

9. What lessons can be gained from the following reported experience?

The Case of John Jones

In an annual performance interview with my supervisor he rated me "superior." Less than one month after the interview, he rated me "satisfactory" in preparing a written evaluation of my work for use by a promotion committee. Apparently, he did not expect that I would see the evaluation.

I decided to find out why he had done this. When I confronted him, he at first denied that he had rated me lower. But when I finally convinced him that I had actually seen the report, he said simply that his "standards had changed." Face to face, he never did tell me why he had given a lower rating on the written confidential form.

This experience destroyed my relationship with my supervisor, and I transferred to another department a few weeks later—at my request.

[20]Ibid.
[21]Ibid.

Chapter 10
Counseling Interviews

There are numerous synonyms for the word "counsel": "advise," "consult," "exhort," "warn," "inform," and so forth. When you begin to examine the synonyms, you will realize that there are many different contexts in which people counsel one another. Sometimes this activity is very formal; at other times, it just seems to happen informally or almost imperceptibly. Sometimes it is sought; at other times people seem to volunteer their services. In a sense, therefore, a form of counseling may take place in interviews such as the job performance review, discipline interview, or information giving interview.

This chapter, however, focuses on those situations—defined formally as counseling—in which the primary aim is to "help" another individual (1) understand, (2) adapt to, or (3) solve a problem. This problem may be about anything involving the person—attitudes, behaviors, or relationships with other people. Furthermore, the problem may be personal or work oriented. The interview may be initiated by either the counselor or the client. The principle objectives of this chapter are (1) to suggest a personal philosophy toward counseling and (2) to set guidelines for effective communication in counseling situations.

DIFFERENCES AMONG COUNSELORS

Any discussion of counseling must take into account the variety of actions and professions that are subsumed under the term "counseling." A list of these is given below.

academic counselors
career counselors
financial counselors
legal counselors
mental-health counselors
psychologists
psychiatrists
medical counselors

marriage counselors
family counselors
drug counselors
sex counselors
social workers
placement counselors
religious counselors
managers

This is only a partial list of professions that involve counseling in some way. As you examine the list, you will become aware of great differences in what these people do. Yet they have something in common that is called counseling, advising, or informing. In order to make our discussion more beneficial, perhaps we should point out some major differences among the counseling situations suggested by this list.

First, there are the people for whom counseling is the *primary activity*. These are the professional therapists who are trained and licensed to work as psychiatrists, psychologists, social workers, school counselors, doctors, and mental-health workers. In almost all cases the clients interviewed by these professionals have gone to the counselor voluntarily or by referral to get help with a physical or a psychological problem. In other words, the clients generally initiate the interaction to be "worked on" by the person who is supposed to have the answers. The goal may be a helping relationship, but the client generally pays for the services, and it is important that we recognize that it is a business transaction.

Second, there are people for whom counseling is a *secondary activity*, and clients go to them because of their recognized expertise in certain specialized fields. Included in this group would be lawyers, police, judges, ministers, teachers, financial consultants, nurses, and representatives of numerous volunteer aid agencies. This group differs from the first in several ways. As a group, they, too, are professionals, but they deal with very specialized areas and generally do not use therapy for physical or psychological problems. The counseling that they do is somewhat incidental to their work. With the exception of lawyers and financial consultants, these people may not receive direct payment for their advice. Furthermore, the interaction may be initiated by either the counselor or the client.

Third, there are those superiors or managers who often *find it necessary* to counsel their direct subordinates. There are also personnel representatives who are called upon to give advice about all kinds of company matters. These counseling situations, too, may be initiated by either person—the manager or the subordinate. The supervisor may detect an attitude, a behavior, or a relationship that is affecting the subordinate adversely, or the employee may respect the manager enough to go seek advice about a personal or a work related matter. For this group the counseling occurs in an overall working relationship that shapes the nature of the interaction. In addition to the empathy that the manager may have for the subordinate, there is often a sense of responsibility to the organization that guides the manager a great deal.

One reason for giving these classifications is to suggest that there can be no formula that is going to apply equally to all situations. Each case is a unique encounter. The minister, for example, may have some options or latitude that the manager may not have because the environments and roles are different. Different situations may call for different approaches to counseling. Nevertheless, there are some basic principles that can be applied to most counseling situations. Our emphasis in this chapter is toward the last two groups—those for whom counseling is a secondary activity and managers. Therefore, the word "counselors" refers to managers, teachers, and the like and not necessarily to professional counselors.

A BASIC ORIENTATION TO COUNSELING

Counseling is essentially a *helping* relationship. The help takes the form of assisting someone to change attitudes or behaviors in a corrective way. Both discipline and counseling are attempts to correct behavior, but the essential difference is that counseling provides the client with a positive motivational approach to his or her problem, whereas discipline involves a more negative, punishing approach. For counseling to be effective, there must be a meaningful relationship between the two people, and this relationship takes place by the mutual consent of the people involved.

As we suggested above, counseling is unique activity in some important ways. Whatever approach you use in helping people deal with their problems, the following principles should be helpful in developing a basic orientation toward your counseling activity. All are positive statements, designed to construct a healthy foundation for effective counseling.

1. *People can grow; they can improve.* An effective counselor is going to be optimistic about people's abilities to change and to grow. This, perhaps, is the most fundamental principle of any form of counseling. To believe otherwise is to accept defeat too easily, and it is likely that the counselor will not try hard enough to help. We emphasize this point because a common communication problem is a *frozen evaluation*, which is a tendency to see a person (or a situation) always in the same way and to forget that people (and situations) are constantly changing.

It is evident that not everybody will want to change in ways that a counselor might suggest. However, any person can have his or her perspective modified in important ways. Untapped potential is a resource in every individual, and good counseling may be needed to challenge the person to use it.

2. *Counseling is an investment in the individual.* You decide to invest your time and energy in the other person because you are reasonably sure that this person has the potential to improve. Like other investments, you sometimes win; you sometimes lose. But you always *expect* to win.

3. *Counseling is a learning process.*[1] Growth comes by learning, and maybe herein lies a distinction between counseling and persuasion or regulation. A person may change behavior because he or she has been persuaded or commanded to do so and yet not change or grow personally. Therefore, counseling is more than just giving a little friendly advice, having a heart-to-heart talk, or even helping someone make up his or her mind. Walter Mahler writes about the executive as a counselor, but his description of this principle can apply to all types of counseling.

> The object of counseling is to change the attitude and behavior of counselees by changing the thinking which has led to these attitudes and behaviors. The counseling session must be largely devoted to the counselees and an exploration of their present thinking. The counselees do not need advice and criticism, rather they need help in looking at the situation realistically. The counseling process should aim at bringing clarity and objectivity to an analysis of the inappropriate behavior or faulty attitude. It is the function of the counselor to help counselees to see what the facts are—and the ultimate price which must be paid if a behavior change does not occur.[2]

The counselor, therefore, does not just address a solution to an immediate problem but rather looks for a change in the individual.

4. *Counseling can involve confrontation.* Earlier in this book we stressed that people like to avoid confrontation because it is often unpleasant, but a person will not learn and will not change until he or she has been made to confront the differences between where he or she is and where he or she ought to be or wants to be. Herein lies a major difference between those who counsel as a business and those who counsel as part of a working relationship. In fact, some of our most teachable moments come during periods of crisis. Confrontation in a clinical environment may be relatively impersonal and may stay on a fairly objective level; furthermore, the counselor may assume no responsibility for the client's ultimate choices. The manager who tries counseling, however, is locked into an organization with the counselee, has responsibility for the indi-

---

[1]Walter R. Mahler, *How Effective Executives Interview* (Homewood, Ill., Dow Jones-Richard D. Irwin, Inc., 1976), p. 133.
[2]Ibid.

vidual, and is not likely to have the same kind of detachment permitted the clinician or the professional.

Not all confrontation is stressful or negative; there are many times when people welcome insights into themselves or information that is going to improve themselves in some way. However, there is a need to emphasize that counseling asks a person to change, and change often produces some degree of stress, and under stress people often "react negatively before they react positively."[3] Therefore, the counselor must be prepared to cope with a certain amount of negativism. The counselor's reaction is a fundamental determinant of the success of the counseling. If the counselee reacts defensively, then the interview may evolve into a win-lose or me-you situation. By all means, avoid resonating the negative while respecting the defense mechanisms that are naturally brought into operation to protect the self from danger, attack, or change.

5. *Acceptance of an individual as he or she is is a good beginning for counseling.* We can look at two important aspects of this statement. First, it is crucial to find out the individual's perceptions of the situation. This involves listening for the client's motivations, emotional involvements, and self-image, as well as listening for the objective facts that he or she might describe.

Second, "acceptance" is a term difficult to describe. It does not mean that you agree with the counselee necessarily or that there will be no negative consequences to what you say. It does imply that you accept a view of human dignity—a person's right to make his or her own mistakes and to pay the consequences. In other words, you tend to be non-judgmental and leave your own personal values out of the decision. Such acceptance is not to be regarded as a panacea or a key that is automatically going to get people to change, but behavioral science has demonstrated that it does tend to reduce a person's defensiveness, which is a precondition for change.

6. *Counseling is a continuous process that is likely to take more than one session.* Change takes time; few people can redirect themselves suddenly. It is unrealistic to expect one interview to facilitate major changes. Clinicians recognize this better than managers do, which is why they provide for many counseling interactions with the same person.

7. *The effectiveness of counseling varies with goals, but it generally is determined by some kind of change taking place.*

Golda Edinburg and her associates describe success in therapeutic counseling as assisting

> the client in discovering how he as an individual works. . . . He becomes increasingly able to accept himself and to change within limits, parts of his

[3]Ibid., p. 131.

thinking that are impeding his functioning. With greater objectivity and perspective the client can better handle this problem.[4]

Mahler gives some conditions under which counseling between manager and subordinate can be considered effective.

1. The subordinate recognizes that a behavioral change is needed.
2. Both the executive and the subordinate share in a deliberate effort to get a behavior change.
3. The deliberate effort results in a resolution of the problem. The resolution may be a behavior change, or it may be resolved by the subordinate leaving his [or her] position.
4. The subordinate respects the supervisor for imposing standards and for endeavoring to be helpful.[5]

With these principles in mind, you are ready to examine some basic guidelines for conducting a counseling interview.

TWO BASIC APPROACHES TO COUNSELING INTERVIEWS

There are two basic schools of thought about counseling: the *directive* and the *nondirective*. The choice between the two is probably the greatest decision that any counselor makes, because it influences every other behavior in the interaction. We shall describe them in their extreme forms, but we feel that it is necessary to emphasize that the two schools exist on a continuum, which means that there are degrees of being directive or nondirective, as the diagram below shows.

Directive __/__/__/__/__/__/__ Nondirective

Rarely will you have an interview that is completely directive or completely nondirective. Yet, these different orientations affect the structure of the interview, the amount of participation, and the role that the counselor plays.

Directive Counseling

Directive counseling is characterized by a very direct assault on the problem by the interviewer. The interviewer will collect information, define and analyze the problem, give opinions and information, suggest solutions, and give quite specific directions to the interviewee or client. In its purest form, the interviewer becomes a persuader or a regulator of how the client should behave by trying to get the person to change a particular

[4]Golda Edinburg, Norman Zinberg, and Wendy Kelman, *Clinical Interviewing and Counseling* (Englewood Cliffs, N.J.: Prentice-Hall, Inc., 1975), p. 3.
[5]Mahler, *Executive Interview*, p. 4.

attitude or a behavior that is inappropriate. In a sense, directive counseling may be similar to the tell-and-sell approach, which was described in Chapter 9.

The directive approach is based on an assumption that the interviewer is more capable than the client in analyzing and solving a particular problem. There are, of course, many circumstances when this assumption is warranted. A supervisor may have more expertise and more experience than a subordinate; a financial counselor may have more insights into the complexities of a situation than someone who has just inherited some money and wants to invest it; and a teacher may be able to offer good advice to a student about ways of improving a term paper. The situations described below are ones in which managers have been called upon to give some counsel and have elected to give some rather direct advice.

CASE 1

A female manager had a very plump woman working for her, whose personal grooming was very sloppy and in poor taste. This woman's appearance was accentuated by baggy clothes made of extremely colorful prints. The manager felt that the woman could be promoted in terms of her skills if she would only make some changes in her grooming. The job that might open, however, was one that called for a lot of interfacing with other units, and the manager knew that the woman's current grooming patterns would cause her department to have a very unprofessional image. What could she do? One option was to do nothing and not even mention the possibility of promotion, but somehow she felt guilty about doing this—as if she were making the subordinate's decision for her. Another option was to be rather nondirective and try to make some hints, but taste in clothes is a hard thing to be nondirective about. Finally, she decided to counsel the employee in a very straightforward manner. She told her of the job potential and also about the problem of her grooming. In this respect, she felt that she had done her part. Now the woman could elect either to make some changes in order to win the promotion or to stay as she was in her present job.

CASE 2

A male manager in a shoe store had complaints from several salespeople about the body odor and lack of personal hygiene of a particular salesman. At first, they tried to make indirect suggestions tactfully, but the man always interpreted the messages as being about somebody else. Finally, the manager decided to be very direct because the problem was causing some disruptions among the salespersons and had potential for ruining some business.

CASE 3

A first-line supervisor was having a problem with a minority worker who often came to work late and who also socialized a lot on the job. This supervisor was worried about running afoul of some legal restriction. Therefore, he went to his own manager to ask how to handle this problem.

CASE 4

A sales trainee was making the rounds with her supervisor. Finally, the supervisor told her to handle the situation with a couple of clients. The trainee conducted the interaction with two clients. Then she met with her supervisor to identify the problems that she had and to ask for ways that she might have handled them differently. The counseling in this instance was a form of instruction.

In each of these situations, the counseling supervisor did have information that was useful to the subordinate. These were instances when the assumption that the counseling supervisor had greater knowledge or expertise was warranted. There may be times when this is not so. It is very difficult, for example, to make decisions for people about career choices, promotions, marriage, or any other major event in their lives. The counselor may know about the problem area but may not be an expert about the feelings and preferences of the client. In such cases an attempt at being highly directive may be resented, and the client may disagree with the counselor's interpretation or may feel that the counselor has not really listened.

The real liability of the directive approach, therefore, lies in the fact that there is a potential risk involved for the counselor—the risk of being wrong or of giving what may turn out to be bad advice. A healthy respect for, or a desire to avoid, this risk has caused many counselors, particularly clinicians, to emphasize the nondirective counseling approach.

Nondirective Counseling

Nondirective counseling casts the counselor in the role more of a facilitator than an adviser. The counselor may be more involved in the *process* of reaching a solution than in the actual *content* of the decision itself. In other words, most trained counselors use a form of direction even when they are using indirect methods, but their direction involves probing and asking questions rather than making content suggestions.

Nondirective counseling has grown out of clinical psychology and is frequently identified as the client centered approach associated with Carl Rogers. It is used widely by clinicians and by people dealing with mental and emotional problems. It is based on the assumptions that (1) each person has the capacity to reach his or her own best solutions, (2) no other person should, or is capable of, telling another person what he or she should do, (3) only the client can decide what is truly better for him or her, and (4) listening is the best avenue for counseling.[6] Therefore, the nondirective counselor helps the client probe his or her own problems, refine his or her own thinking, and solve his or her own problems.

Like the assumptions of the directive approach, these assumptions are helpful in many cases, but in some cases they are not. When they are helpful, they do much to help the individual grow; when they are not helpful (when the client cannot analyze a problem or refuses to admit that there is a problem), little progress can be made using the nondirective approach. For example, the offender in Case Number 2 would never have known about his problem if the nondirective approach had been used.

Which approach is better? Neither one is. They are simply two basic alternatives that are available to the counselor, and, of course, as we showed in the diagram of the continuum, there are an infinite number of gradations between the two basic forms. It is unfortunate perhaps that the "helping" relationship has become associated only with the nondirective type of counseling, because help may be appreciated in both direct or nondirect forms, depending on the manner in which it is given. We advocate that the best general counselor will not get locked into either of the two styles but will develop the ability to determine when each is needed and the necessary skills to conduct each type well. The techniques can be quite complementary. The manager, for example, may use the nondirective approach in dealing with a relational problem but a highly directive approach in dealing with a technical operational problem. There are a number of authors who advocate—unrealistically—that the nondirective approach is preferable in business, education, and government. The ultimate choice of which approach to use must rest with your own personality, your objectives, your relationship with the counselee, the amount of time and energy you can spend, and most importantly, the counselee's expectations of you.

PLANNING THE INTERVIEW

We recognize that much counseling is done with people who initiate counseling on their own. In these situations, the counselor may not have the opportunity to make elaborate plans. The particular skills called for in these circumstances include patience, probing, and listening in order to discover exactly what the client wants from you. Frequently, it is useful to use this period to lay some groundwork for a more in-depth meeting later.

On the other hand, there will be many opportunities when you will know about counseling sessions well ahead of time. It is for these sessions that we have set out the following suggestions for planning your best interview strategies.

[6]Edinburg, Zinberg, and Kelman, *Clinical Interviewing*, p. 2.

1. *Make the decision to counsel or to refer*. Actually, there is a third option, as we pointed out in Case Number 1 (the woman with poor grooming habits): sometimes a counselor or manager may choose to leave a person just as he or she is. If there is the possibility, however, that someone can profit from counseling, most counselors will give it. Therefore, there is the decision to be made as to who will do the counseling.

Counseling is an investment of time, energy, and money for both individuals; therefore, it should be worth the investment. Every counselor, professional or not, has certain areas of expertise but also certain areas of deficiency. Even when therapists, ministers, or lawyers have specialties that attract only certain kinds of clients, there may be times when they need to refer a client elsewhere. In an organizational setting, every manager needs to recognize limits imposed by time, energy, and training. The desire to help, for all its altruistic motives, may not be enough. For example, whenever problems with drugs, alcohol, debts, or personality disorders are encountered, the best help you can give a person is to refer the person elsewhere.

Suppose a subordinate comes to you and asks for help with a personal problem. What should you do? Your first inclination probably would be to try to help, but you ought to listen a while and then make a very objective decision as to (1) *whether or not you can actually be of help to the individual* and (2) *what the consequences would be to the relationship if you try*. If it is a problem with another worker, you may decide to help, but if it is a drinking problem or a financial problem, you may send the person elsewhere. A case study may help to demonstrate this suggestion further:

> A teacher noticed a student over several class periods who was obviously distraught to the point of shaking. The teacher went to the student and offered, "If you ever need to talk, I'm available." Several days later the student came by and said that he "just had to talk to someone." So the teacher listened to a tale about his wife's having gotten pregnant by someone else, although they had been married less than a year. What should he do? Well, a lot of people had counseled him—the families, a doctor, and some friends. You can imagine that a lot of it was very directive. This teacher chose to listen and to help sort out several alternatives available to him. There was no attempt to reach a decision, which came in the months ahead. This process seemed to be helpful to the student. Later on, however, the teacher noticed that this student avoided him whenever possible, and he became convinced that perhaps the relationship had been destroyed because the student confessed too much. Perhaps there is a lesson in this, which suggests that you should not be too eager to give counsel to those with whom you work. A stranger may be less threatening.

2. *Collect the facts; do your homework*. Counseling needs to be specific, not ambiguous. Like a good detective, a good counselor starts with the facts. The supervisor who is going to counsel an employee about

verbosity is going to need some good specific examples to show what he or she means; the social worker who is going to counsel a client about spending habits may need to interview other members of the family first; or the therapist's homework may be a review of what has been covered in prior interviews.

In collecting the facts, it will be useful for you to determine which of two paradigms is most relevant to the situation. One paradigm suggests that the person is responsible for the problem, and, therefore, the solution to the problem lies in changing the person. The second paradigm suggests that the problem is caused by the environment or work situation and not by the individual's characteristics or behavior. Either one may apply. The best counselor will not always look to either of these paradigms for the answer but instead force himself or herself to investigate both.

3. *Review your purpose.* Even though counseling is a helping activity, avoid stating your purpose in such an abstract way as helping. Rather, state it in terms of the exact changes in attitude or behavior that need to take place in the client. Sometimes, you may want the person to change, but at other times you may expect the person only to understand a situation better. Counseling often involves helping people cope with situations that are unlikely to change.

In reviewing your purpose, you ought to investigate whether or not it is congruent with the client's purposes. This involves distinguishing between a request for information, a request for action, or an effective request for understanding and involvement.

4. *Limit your objectives for each interview.* As you plan the content areas to be discussed in the interview, you may wish to break them into several general categories, such as

1. problem areas
2. reasons for changes
3. alternative changes
4. benefits of change

The mental-health therapist, for example, may focus primarily on the causes of a given behavior. The manager, on the other hand, may be reluctant to work on causes, preferring instead to refer a subordinate to someone else for such counseling. The manager may focus on the aspect of behavior that is going to have to change, regardless of the cause. For example, you may insist that absences due to alcoholism are jeopardizing a subordinate's job without trying to work directly on the alcoholism itself. If the subordinate is willing to work on the root of the problem, a professional counselor may be secured.

Additionally, you may wisely restrict the number of problems that you talk about in the session. In the transcript at the end of this chapter, for example, there are two areas in which the manager would like the subordinate to change. If you were the manager in this case, you would face a strategic question: Should you attempt to work on both of these areas in the same interview? Whether or not you do may depend upon how the subordinate reacts to your counseling or how much progress you make on the first problem. In other words, you would be wise as the manager to approach the session with some contingencies. Approach both problems only if the subordinate is receptive and progress is made quickly. Otherwise, you may wish to separate the two. Keep in mind that it is possible for the subordinate to become suddenly overwhelmed if you try to cover everything in one interview.

5. *Choose a structure for the counseling.* You may choose to be directive or nondirective, but do not go into the counseling situation ambivalent about what is going to happen.

6. *Plan the kind of climate that you want to develop.* Far too often we expect certain conditions to occur without really planning for them. Perhaps this is one of the major differences between a professional and a novice. The professional sees the need for explicit planning, and nowhere is this more important than in building a climate.

Normally, the climate most beneficial for counseling is described as "open," "interactive," and "objective." Openness is characterized by self-disclosure. It is particularly difficult to achieve because people want to protect themselves, and they often feel that being open may make them vulnerable. Therefore, when an interviewee is eager to please, eager to avoid criticism, or particularly distrustful of you, he or she may restrict his or her responses. Therefore, counseling may require a degree of trust between the two of you so that you can be honest with one another. This is particularly true in work situations where there will be a continued relationship. Most of the time absolute confidentiality is a prerequisite to openness.

Objectivity is another important aspect of climate. Sometimes we think of it as being nonjudgmental or as not trying to impose our own values on another. Stressing the facts rather than values and opinions contributes a high degree of objectivity. There must be a balance between adequate role distance and attempts to reflect understanding. In terms of role, for example, some professional counselors try to maintain objectivity by maintaining a social distance from the client. They prefer formal forms of address such as Mrs., Mr., or Ms. Some prefer to sit behind a desk in order to preserve distance and enhance their objective counseling role. Personal appearance is of great concern to them because it affects the client's image of them. We are not trying to tell you to use particular forms of address, arrange the seating in certain ways, or dress in particular ways but to say that all of these things are important in establishing a particular relationship with the interviewee.

Finally, the greatest contributor to an open, objective, interactive climate comes when interviewees are convinced that "you have a genuine interest in them as a person, if they sense you understand them, even when you are expressing dislike for an idea of their behavior. . . ."[7]

7. *Arrange the setting so maximum interaction will take place.* The setting is also an important determinant of the kind of interaction that will take place. Listed below are several major considerations.

Make an appointment with the client and specify how much time the meeting is likely to take. The appointment permits each person to prepare psychologically and reduces competing time pressures.

Select a private, comfortable area that will be free from interruptions. Privacy is essential. By no means should you try to counsel in a shared office or in a lounge with someone else present.

Arrange the furniture to assist you. It is a mistake to think that all counseling must be informal or that it all must be formal. Decide what degree of formality you want and make your arrangement work for you.

Sitting behind a desk will tend to stress formality and authority. This may be exactly what you want, if you are a manager. On the other hand, students in meetings with teachers sometimes complain that this makes them uncomfortable. They seem to prefer that there be a chair at the end of the desk or two chairs facing one another. It should be apparent by now that such arrangements do influence the interaction between two people.

Alfred Benjamin, a professional counselor, describes what works best for him in using the room to set a professional atmosphere. He uses

> two equally comfortable chairs placed close to each other at a 90 degree angle with a small table nearby. . . . The counselee can face me when he [or she] wishes to do so and at other times he [or she] can look straight ahead without my getting in his [or her] way. I am equally unhampered. The table close by fulfills its normal function. . . .[8]

Even lighting is thought to influence the counseling. It is a common technique for therapists to use a low amount of light in their sessions because it seems to reduce the client's defensiveness. Some managers also have told us that they, too, have seen that subdued lighting often gets people to open up more.

CONDUCTING THE INTERVIEW

The introduction of a counseling interview should accomplish four things. It should (1) establish rapport, (2) establish the working agreement, (3) lead to a discussion of the problem areas, and (4) assure confidentiality.

1. *Establish rapport.* Rapport is necessary to win confidence and to make the client comfortable with the interview situation. Building rap-

---

[7]Mahler, *Executive Interview,* p. 136.
[8]Alfred Benjamin, *The Helping Interview* (Boston: Houghton Mifflin Company, 1969), p. 3.

port starts with the very first comments. If the client initiates the interaction, this may not be a problem.

> When someone comes to see us because he [or she] genuinely wants to, and because he [or she] initiated the contact for this purpose, almost whatever we say will go unnoticed for he [or she] is anxious to get started. As long as we do not get in his [or her] way too much, he [or she] will begin to talk.[9]

However, if you initiate the interaction, then you can build rapport through small talk, a good orientation, and a very warm, friendly manner. Actions that tend to curtail rapport are negative comments, a monologue by the counselor, second-guessing of the client, a condescending attitude, and a hurried approach to the interview.

When some degree of rapport is established, the counselor must then establish the working agreement. A professional counselor would use this period to discuss fees and frequency of counseling sessions, but a manager would move directly to a statement of goals or purposes by asking the subordinate why he or she has come or by stating his or her own purpose if he or she has called the subordinate in. In stating the purpose, the counselor should be certain to demonstrate a concern for the individual as well as a concern about the individual's specific behavior and its ramifications for the company, society, or other people.

It is not uncommon, for example, for a manager to see a sudden change in an employee's productivity or performance. Such changes may be red flags that signal a need for counseling. When you call the interviewee in for the interview, you might state the purpose like this: "John, you've always been a very good worker for us; the company has benefited a great deal from your service, and I've always thought that you had a good future with us. Something has happened though to cause your performance level to go down, and I called you in to see if I can't help you get back to normal again. You're much too valuable a person for us to let this happen. If I can help, I want to. If it's something that I can't help with, perhaps we can find someone who can." In this case, the manager tried to show a concern for the person while also identifying the reduced productivity as a problem that needs to be resolved. The manager also recognized that the productivity level may actually be a symptom of something about which he may or may not be able to counsel John.

The nature of effective counseling demands openness on the part of both the client and the counselor. You cannot get at the root of a problem if the person avoids discussing it. Consequently, there are several things that you can do to draw out the client.

1. Assure him of confidentiality.
2. Demonstrate your commitment to be helpful.
3. Be honest.

[9]Ibid., p. 13.

4. Listen from the start.

5. Show your acceptance.

2. *Be specific in identifying and defining the problem, behavior, attitude, or relationship.* Suppose, for example, that you want to counsel an employee who has been clowning around the office. "Clowning" is too abstract a word to be helpful in telling the employee exactly what is disruptive, why it is disruptive, and what needs to be done about it. You would need to describe some of the actual activities of the subordinate before real progress can be made.

If the client initiates the interaction, there is still a need to be specific. You will have to probe and question in order to draw out of the client the problem areas. In this connection, we should stress that first impressions are not always acceptable. Even when a client comes to you with a fairly well-defined purpose, you may need to double-check through probing to determine whether or not the stated problem is the actual problem bothering the person. Frequently, it is not. We are all prone to avoid unpleasant matters by stating them in more socially acceptable ways.

Finally, being specific is helpful in another way. Several managers have reported that three-quarters of their time and effort is spent convincing a subordinate that there is a problem. After the subordinate is willing to admit the problem, progress may come rapidly.

3. *Explore the client's perceptions.* Ask evocative questions and refuse to let the client avoid potentially embarrasing topics. It is particularly important that you avoid second-guessing the client. If you feel that the client has a certain perception, test it out. Ask the client to endorse or to deny it specifically. If it is done in a straightforward, unindicting, and unemotional manner, this can be very effective in exploring perceptions. By doing this consistently, you can ensure that you are always where the client is.

4. *Listen and absorb.* Asking questions is important, but you can only do this well if you are a good listener who absorbs not only what is being said but also what is being left out. Of particular importance is your ability to detect (1) subtle shifts in conversations and (2) inconsistencies. These behaviors generate additional questions that may be absolutely essential for clarifying the client's feelings and impressions. Finally, attend to all the messages being sent by the client. Nonverbal behaviors are often more revealing than certain camouflaged verbal ones.

5. *Probe the reactions fully.* In a nondirective interview, you will receive much feedback about the client's reactions, but even in a very directive interview, you will benefit from taking the time to secure feedback. Only then can you determine the degree of acceptance of your direction.

In probing reactions, confrontation may be necessary. An interviewee should not be allowed to avoid topics just because they are unpleasant, since often people want to "whitewash" those things that make them uncomfortable. Indeed, the fact that a topic is unpleasant may indicate the importance of it to the general problem area.

6. *Be problem oriented.* Frequently, a counselor starts talking about solutions before he or she even knows what the problems really are. The very word "counseling" carries with it the connotation that decisions will be reached. For this reason, it is particularly important that you *be problem oriented* before becoming solution oriented. This reinforces the idea that the time spent by a counselor in probing the nature of a problem is not wasted. You need particularly to watch out for the inclination to define problems in terms of solutions that the counselee already has available.

7. *Explain the ramifications of the problem and explore the reasons why a change is necessary.*[10] We deliberately use the word "explore" in order to stress the desirability of contrasting the client's perceptions with your own. This allows you to account for the client who initiates the counseling as well as the client whom you call in for some counseling. In a work situation, it is wise to avoid getting to the point too quickly. The negative impact of a loss of job is always there for a manager to use as a motivating factor, but you should not be too quick to call on it. In such cases, counseling turns into discipline. Try to motivate by showing that an improved self-image, pride, better relationships, and other positive rewards will be a result of change before resorting to removal from the job.

8. *React to the client.* "Give information rather than advice" is an often stated maxim.[11] Perhaps it is useful in helping us state some priorities. Research suggests that people respond better to a decision that they have participated in making than they do to one that is superimposed upon them. Consequently, if you can give a counselee information that will help him or her make a good decision, it is better than giving the counselee a decision. When advice is given, you need not give it in an omniscient, paternalistic, sermonizing way. It is possible to give advice in a business-like, sometimes impersonal way by directly relating it to the goals already determined.

Frequently in counseling sessions, clients ask for personal information about the counselor or comparisons with other people. It is generally wise to dodge such questions, because they can focus attention away from the client and onto others. This may not be what the client is consciously trying to do, but it often turns out this way. Furthermore, information

[10]Mahler, *Executives Interview*, p. 143.
[11]Charles Stewart and William B. Cash, *Interviewing* (Dubuque, Iowa: William C. Brown, Company, Publishers, 1978), p. 196.

about others may violate confidences and giving information about yourself may inadvertently put you in the position of defending some of your own values.

9. *Develop a plan of action.* As we have emphasized before, talking about a problem is not equivalent to solving it. Far too frequently counseling interviews end without either person knowing what the client is going to do about the problem. Depending upon the nature of the interview approach, you have two options in developing such a plan. Using the more nondirective approach, you would ask the client to identify some plan of action. Not only would this emphasize the fact that it is ultimately the client's responsibility to implement a solution to the problem, but also it would be a good way for you to test whether or not the client has accepted the counseling. In a more directive approach, you would suggest the plan of action. Keep in mind that people need some degree of success to reinforce them. Therefore, even for very complex problems your plan ought to (1) be specific enough so that you both know when it is completed, (2) be small enough so that the client is likely to be successful, and (3) involve something that the client can begin immediately. Finally, even in directing the client toward solutions it is useful to get some measure of the client's reaction to the solutions.

10. *Close the interview with some provision for follow-up.* You normally have the responsibility for closing an interview, and the way you close it is just as important as the way you begin it. Since most counseling involves a continued relationship, the climate at the end will set the stage for future encounters. There are two main considerations that should guide you in closing the interview.

First, when you recognize that a psychological close is evident, terminate the interview, regardless of the amount of time spent. There may be times when you have not accomplished all that you wanted to accomplish, but something happened in the interaction to make it unlikely that much more would be accomplished. Alfred Benjamin made this point very well with his statement: "When we have nothing else to add, the more we say, the less meaningful it becomes, and the more drawn out and painful the closing is."[12] There is a caution here for those who want to give directive counseling, for they may not recognize the inevitability of having some occasional resistance. However, if they review the basic principles with which we started this chapter, they will recognize that immediate resistance is not final and additional periods of counseling may be very effective.

Second, provide for follow-up. Make some arrangements with the client concerning when the client will report back or schedule another session. Such follow-up has the inherent value of setting goals to be

[12]Benjamin, *Helping Interview,* p. 31.

achieved in a definite time frame. In this way, successful behavior can be reinforced.

11. *Keep your voice and your body under control.* Questions must be asked and comments should be made in an even, business-like tone. You can be empathic and accepting without getting too emotionally involved with the client. By all means, exercise enough control to avoid registering shock, even if you are. There can be few more curtailing influences on the openness of an interaction than the demonstration of disapproval or shock.

12. *Make comprehensive notes.* No interviewer can take everything in, nor can anyone remember all details of a given session. Consequently, note-taking is advisable. Special care, however, should be taken to write them unobtrusively and to keep them confidential. Furthermore, due to the nature of counseling, the counselor frequently can review these notes after the interview in order to gain greater insights into the client's problems.

CONFRONTING SPECIAL PROBLEMS

Hidden Meanings

Be sensitive to hidden meanings. Frequently, people prefer to state their feelings and ideas indirectly. Consequently, a statement such as "My supervisor is always picking on me" may cover up the fact that the person's work is substandard. The supervisor may be a scapegoat.

Inarticulate Clients

Help clients to refine their ideas and expressions. Many people are not very articulate when it comes to analyzing their own problems, because they are just too close to the problems. Consequently, they may need time and lots of probing to help them sort out their reactions. This is why probing is so important. Furthermore, counseling cannot be rushed; it simply takes time to think through a problem and assimilate new information. Some counselors deal with this challenge by trying to reduce threat by getting clients to talk first about things other than their problems.

Wanting to Leave

In the emotional tension of counseling, many interviewees want to leave and to get out of the situation. Should you let them go? If you do, then it is sometimes unlikely that renewed meetings will ever take place. Therefore, the alternatives are for the interviewer to reduce the tension or to point out the value of continuing the relationship.

Dependency

Dependency occurs when the client expects the counselor to be able to solve the problem for him or her. Counselors who use a directive approach will not be bothered by it; they may even foster it. On the other hand, it is a great problem for those who wish to be nondirective and force the client to generate his or her own solutions.

Denial

One of the most common obstacles to counseling is the client's denial that a problem exists, denial of certain feelings, or denial of the need for help. This must be overcome in order for progress to be made. You may respect the client's denial as a common psychological defense mechanism, but you may also be determined to overcome it by proving it with perseverance, by confronting it with facts, and even sometimes by *leading* the client into an admission. We remind you of the manager who stated that he spends three-quarters of his time in counseling in order to get employees to face a problem. Overcoming denials is difficult, but it must be done.

THIS CHAPTER IN PERSPECTIVE

In this chapter, we have set out the most basic approaches to counseling, identified a basic orientation to the nature of counseling, and established some communicative guidelines for conducting an effective counseling session. There are two thoughts that need heavy emphasis as we conclude this chapter.

1. *As a counselor*, you have a great responsibility to be ethical and nonmanipulative in your interactions with your clients. There is power associated with your role that gives you great advantage over most clients. Use it wisely.
2. Counseling involves corrective behavior, and so does discipline. Yet there is a great difference between the two. It is in your power as a manager to define the situation. Some managers will look at a situation and define it in terms of a need for discipline; others will look at the same situation and define it in terms of counseling. Be sensitive to the different ramifications of these two, and give counseling a try first.

PROJECTS

1. Analyze the transcript on pages 208−212 in terms of the counseling techniques that were used. Would you judge it to be effective? What criteria would you use to judge it?

2. Interview several different types of counselors to discover differences in their approaches. For example, you might select a guidance counselor, a manager, a psychologist in a mental-health clinic, and a teacher. Keep in mind that people within each of these jobs will vary in using their techniques.

3. Which of the two basic counseling approaches seems most suitable to you?

4. Contrast the expectations of a manager with those of a clinician?

5. If you were a manager who had to counsel a problem subordinate, what general guidelines would you set?

6. Role-play the case on page 213 and critique the interaction in terms of strategies and tactics. Have the interviewers plan exhaustive strategies before the role-playing.

Craig: Good morning Dick, have a seat.

Dick: Thank you, thank you.

Craig: Like some coffee?

Dick: Yeah, think I will.

Craig: Or you want some coke?

Dick: I think I'll have a coke.

Craig: All right. A little late in the afternoon for coffee. Well, I wanted to have this meeting with you. You know I scheduled it quite a while ago.

Dick: Right, right. I've been expecting it.

Craig: But I just want you to relax and have a general discussion with you. I've been wanting to do it with you and many other people so I thought we would get right to it.

Dick: Sure.

Craig: What I want to talk about is developing you.

Dick: I'm particularly interested in that because I do want to move up in the company. Well, I am really interested in what I can do to develop myself and move up because I do want to succeed.

Craig: Well, I checked your record out and of course it is well known. But I wanted to make sure so I checked it out thoroughly. You have been with us two years now; constantly got good ratings. I think your raises have been substantial so I think we have rewarded you that way, so I think it's no surprise I'm telling you this. You are one of our more competent people, that is sure, especially at your level. You are quite a bit higher at your level than most people but that wouldn't be development if we talked about all the good points. What we like to do is try to develop potential, and we are talking about management. Now you have been working for me for two years now, indirectly, of course, but we are looking for new supervisors. To be a good supervisor I believe that you have to qualify technically. That you are. You have to get yourself motivated, etc., etc. You're that, too. Particularly fast in getting your assignments done, but one thing I have noticed when you do get them done, you tend to socialize. Now that in itself. . . .

Dick: You mean socializing on the job?

Craig: Oh, yes.

Dick: More than I should be?

Craig: Well, I wouldn't put it exactly that way, that's turning the words around. What I'm saying is that you do tend to socialize, which is good because that is a good quality in a supervisor, too. They have to be able to get along with people, relax with people, and motivate them. That you do, but I think you're choosing the wrong time to socialize with people. Like I said, you get your projects done first;

you're the fastest one around, but what you tend to do is talk to people who haven't got their projects done. Now that's not quite fair to them because they can't get their work done. So I think you should concentrate on that a little bit. I don't see it as a serious problem, otherwise this wouldn't be a relaxed meeting we are having right now. But I think. . . .

Dick: Well, I'll admit I might be socializing a little more than necessary, but I do feel like you said, and I thank you for it, I do get my work done well, on time or before. The socializing I think is to help the morale out. The morale in any workplace I feel is as important as getting the job done, and as long as the work gets done—gets done well—I don't think there is much to say against it. There can be a problem and I've noticed it. And I'm down here in the trenches with the troops. Lately I've noticed the morale seems to be dropping. Everybody seems to be tense. That's what I'm trying to do; I'm trying to keep the morale up, keep everybody a little loose so that they can work together. By keeping the morale up we avoid interpersonal conflict between guys, because that doesn't help you on the job at all.

Craig: Well, what do you think causes this morale problem?

Dick: Well, in talking with some of the people I see myself as one of the leaders down there in the office. We would like to see you come down and see us more often. It's been three weeks since you have even been down to the office. Some of the guys really seem to think that you don't care about us. You just sit up in your grand office. We would like to see you down there just to talk, come to the coffeepot one day.

Craig: I didn't realize that.

Dick: Five minutes, just to let the guys know that you're a good fellow.

Craig: Well, I want you to pass on to the guys the reason I may not have been down there. I'm not going to use the excuse that I'm overworked; that's not the reason, even though it may be part of the truth. But what I'm saying is that I'm working on things like getting your substantial raises.

Dick: I think we all realize that everybody has his or her own job to do and that you are probably busy doing many things that we don't know about, but I think it would still be good. It keeps tension in the office down and really doesn't take much time. Five minutes a day, five or ten minutes just to walk through to get a cup of coffee.

Craig: I agree with you. I have no problem with that.

Dick: We would like to see you down there.

Craig: I'll sure do that. I can't say ten minutes is going to hurt me. I just didn't realize it. What are some other reasons you think there is a morale problem down there.

Dick: Well.

Craig: It sure isn't money, right?

Dick: No, everybody is pleased about money.

Craig: OK, so we can get that big one out of the way.

Dick: One of the things might be that—this again this might be a personal type of problem, possibly mine—I wanted to talk to you about this too; the communication in our department is not good now. It seems to be declining.

Craig: On what level? On the peer level?

Dick: Yes, down in the offices there. All the communication seems to be vague, which is not good.

Craig: Directly related to work?

Dick: Yeah, the letters we write. I think I try to take time to do my job the best I can and do all the written reports and letters and clear and concise wording as possible so there won't be any misinformation passed. I think some of the other guys could benefit too. I try to help them out.

Craig: Well, let's just hang with that for a minute now. As I said, it's just repeating, but I think it needs repeating; you're fast, you do your job well, OK. Now that's good for you. Now what would you think about this if other people in the area aren't as fast? Other people aren't as fast as you, you know this. You're a happy-go-lucky guy and you have every reason to be. You get your job done and then what do you do? You go socialize. Very nice life. But what do you think that looks like to other people in the department or to the ones you are talking to who are trying to get their projects done? What do you think that does to them? What is your opinion on that? They are trying to concentrate on their project, to get it done. They see you getting yours done fast and you are over here socializing. Now what do you think that does to their morale?

Dick: Probably doesn't help morale at all.

Craig: Let's turn it around. Let me make it a little easier for you. You're striving to do your project. You're not incompetent. You just have a little more trouble than Dick over here, OK?

Dick: Yeah.

Craig: Now Dick whips his project out fast as hell—accurate, more accurate than most people. He comes over smiling all the time, feeling good and socializes. Nothing gets said to him, his work is done. Right? Now how would you feel about that? Here you are having a hard time.

Dick: Well, I would feel that I was being intruded upon. Not being able to get my work done as much as I would want to.

Craig: What do you think would bother them most? The socializing? Or the timing?

Dick: The time of it. Because I still say that the socializing that we do at work, not being excessive, is good for morale. There is nothing wrong with that that I can see.

Craig: But the timing.

Dick: The timing could be better, I'll have to admit. I'll work on that. Since I do get my work done, I would be more than pleased to have more work, 'cause like you I feel I have potential to move up in this company and whatever I can do, such as take on extra tasks, since I have the time, and I'll do that because I want to improve; I want to be noticed. Just continuing to get good raises in one job is not what I want. I want to move up.

Craig: OK, I would like to stop it right there because what we are talking about here—why I called you in originally—is to talk to you about developing you and your potential. Since you do finish your task and have the excess time and since part of the job of supervising is essentially in this particular job, you would still stay semitechnical but you would have more paper work. What would you think about absorbing some of the administrative duties for these people?

Dick: I'm willing to, because I think I'm capable of doing that. I think it would help me because I would see more about what a supervisor or manager does and I need that training in order to move up.

Craig: OK, now at a supervisor's level, do you think . . . let's take the reporting . . . , if you had to do the reporting for all the people. OK, that means that you would have to do all the reports and all their work. At that level would you think that the reports would be more detailed or concise and to the point?

Dick: Now, I can't do all their work but . . .

Craig: But if you were asked to do their reports, would they be? Detailed reports? Or do you think they would be a little more general?

Dick: I think I am fully capable of making reports in detail and clear as I do my work now because that is my style.

Craig: Well, detail on your own, fine. But what I am asking is, do you think it would be advisable to have these reports as detailed if you did them for everybody else? Would it be practical that way? Or would you want to write to a different level? See different people would read these now. You would be writing for your peers *and* your superiors. Would you write in such a detailed nature if you took that job?

Dick: It's hard to say.

Craig: Do you think your supervisors would understand the detail of them? Do you think they need to know all that detail?

Dick: They don't need to know everything . . . every little thing, every little detail.

Craig: So would you summarize more?

Dick: I think you know my ability. Writing ability will lend itself to making anything as detailed or nondetailed as the situation demands. So I can still take the small details out with no problem at all and still have a thorough report. And I think it would be readable to all supervisors up the line without any trouble.

Craig: Let me ask you this then. If you wrote a report to me . . . OK, now I don't know the technical end of your job. I'm not supposed to know, I don't have to know, OK? Do you think I would be interested in knowing that detail? Would you—knowing who you are writing to—would you put that much detail in?

Dick: No, I would leave some of that out.

Craig: So you are saying you would put detail in only if it were necessary.

Dick: I would still put detail in only as necessary?

Craig: Un huh. Let me get a little more direct. You sometimes write up the complete details on any project that is completed in this department. For instance, when you turn in some that are more pages, you just use the second to fourth pages to continue what should be on the first. I think that may suggest that some summarization is necessary, don't you?

Dick: It's possible, but the type of training in writing reports to different people is something that I need and unless I'm given the chance to take on these extra duties to begin writing reports in different styles to different people I'll never learn. So I need to take on these new responsibilities so that I can learn. I'm not saying that I will be perfect on the first report, but unless I get the chance to start, I'll never learn so that is why I'm asking for the chance.

Craig: Well, why don't we then do two things. First, we can—as you already said—you will work on timing your socialization. We don't want that cut out, just retimed because it would be even more important if that is kept. Second, we will give you some experience plus some training. Some communication training courses taught well, why don't. . . .

Dick: I would be more than glad to attend some of these courses on it.

Craig: OK, we will send you to one of them plus we will give you some practical experience writing to a different level—meaning summarizing your reports.

Dick: I would be more than glad to have that opportunity.

Craig: And I am sure that you will write the reports so that they will be general enough so that most supervisors will understand, but not so detailed that you will lose them. Well. . . .

Dick: I agree.

Craig: Well, I guess that is about it for today. We will work on those two things, and I will get back to you as soon as I get them set up.

Dick: All right. Thank you very much.

COUNSELING ROLE-PLAY

PREPARATION

1. Assume your own position. Identify the organization and assign a position title to your subordinate. You may even brief the EE on the job duties.
2. Assume that an appointment has been scheduled for this interview well in advance.
3. Read only the role that you are playing.

SUPERIOR

This subordinate is a very competent worker who has been in your work group for the last two years. The subordinate's work, in general, is better than most other workers at that level, and appropriate raises have reinforced this good work.

In spite of his good work record, however, the subordinate has two undesirable characteristics. You have not said anything about them because you thought that they might be corrected naturally and that you could live with them. Now they seem to be getting worse. Consequently, you have made an appointment to talk to the subordinate about them.

First, the subordinate is terribly verbose, both in talking and writing. It takes twice as much time or space as it should to say things. This is aggravating, because it takes more of your time than it should and it is also a reflection on you when your superiors see his or her work. Even co-workers have now begun to joke about his verbosity behind his or her back.

Second, the subordinate is quick and finishes work before a lot of others. When he or she finishes a project, the normal pattern is to visit with fellow employees. Frequently, these visits take the form of clowning or telling jokes, and sometimes the jokes are not appreciated. You have tolerated this because of his or her work record, but recently in a conversation one of your superiors remarked rather curtly, "Can't you keep that clown busy?" Again, his or her image is getting in the way of any appreciation for his or her work. It is now apparent that it is hurting your image, too.

SUBORDINATE

You have worked for the manager for two years (in the job described). You like the work and have performed well. The supervisor seems to appreciate your work because you have gotten appropriate raises. You are also confident in the job because you tend to finish before your co-workers.

If you have a pet peeve it is that people do not know how to communicate. For one thing, people tend to give insufficient details and information when they write and speak. You pride yourself on taking the extra time necessary to say what you mean clearly and precisely, and you also know that people need to get messages more than once, so you reinforce messages by careful repetition of explanations. Although your supervisor has never told you so, you are sure that ER appreciates and respects this quality in you.

Another part of communication is climate. You think that you see a change taking place. The manager formerly was open and relaxed, but now you seem to perceive some tension. He or she does not take as much time with the group as before.

One of the things you enjoy most about this job is that people like one another, and they enjoy socializing as well as working. After all, the work situation is improved when people can relax, be themselves, and have lots of informal interaction. You enjoy sharing jokes with the others, and they seem to respond well to your humor. If the supervisor is really "tensing up," it may be more important than ever to use humor to relax the situation, and you are the one that can do it.

Finally, you have aspirations to move up in the organization, and you are hoping the manager can help you. Consequently, you look forward to today's meeting.

Chapter 11
Discipline Interviews

Correcting an employee, particularly when a penalty must be given, is one of the most unpleasant tasks that many managers face. Disciplining someone is always difficult; it is hard work. By trying to avoid it altogether, you may delay doing it until some crisis forces you into action. Many managers avoid it by having someone else administer it. We know one manager, for example, in a social welfare agency who simply will not discipline. His method is to ask an assistant to do it, and then he schedules himself to be out of the office.

At the other extreme, perhaps, are those people who believe in discipline so strongly that they interpret all corrective situations in terms of discipline. Remember in the last chapter that we tried to point out that discipline and counseling have a similar goal—correction or solving a problem—but the orientation and tactics are different in counseling than in discipline. The fanatic disciplinarian will not recognize the potential for counseling in a situation and seems to have a mental set that makes her or him resort to discipline quickly—sometimes too quickly.

Somewhere in between these two extremes is a sensible approach to discipline. In this chapter we attempt to set out some guidelines that will help you in making discipline effective, even when it is not easy.

A POSITIVE APPROACH TO DISCIPLINE

Discipline can involve very negative behaviors, harsh punishments, win-lose climates, and interpersonal resentment. It is unfortunate, perhaps that we have come to view it from only a negative perspective. James Black has written a book called *Positive Discipline,* in which he tries to construct a more positive frame of reference. The more positive approach treats discipline as a very necessary educational process, the aim of which is to correct undesirable and unacceptable behavior by letting a person know through concrete experience what is expected.

> Discipline should be a constructive, positive force that enables people to work together harmoniously. Consider the work affirmatively and its full meaning becomes evident. Discipline to the scholar is a field of study which, if mastered, hardens or toughens the mind. The football coach refers to a championship team as "well-disciplined," meaning that it executes its plays with precision and skill. A highly trained regiment of soldiers is proud of its reputation for being disciplined; to the soldiers, discipline means that everybody knows his job and each individual works cooperatively with the group to carry out orders.[1]

In developing this frame of reference further, we suggest that self-discipline should also be regarded as a virtue. Therefore, the objective is to get rid of the connotation that discipline is only negative or punitive. In order to do so, we must shift perspectives.

Viewed from the perspective of the person who is being disciplined, there is a natural inclination on the person's part to resist criticism and punishment at the moment that it is being administered. As a manager, however, you may need to keep several things in mind. First, immediate resentments are not always long lasting. There are many occasions when the disciplined person admits that "this was one of the best things that ever happened to me." Consequently, there is a need to consider long-term as well as immediate effects on the individual.

Second, from the perspective of the organization, discipline is the means through which a healthy organization is maintained and problems are overcome. Once again, there may be a necessity for adopting a long-term instead of a short-term perspective. Frequently, the failure to deal with problems immediately leads to some long-term, undesirable effects. Therefore, the real, positive rationale for discipline can be developed in terms of what it accomplishes over the long run, both for the individual and the organization.

[1]James Black, *Positive Discipline* (New York: American Management Association, 1970), p. 27.

Reasons for Disciplinary Actions

Discipline becomes necessary when there are disruptive problems that must be curtailed. Some of the most common problems that warrant disciplinary actions are nonperformance of duties, chronic absenteeism, disobedience or insubordination, disruptive relationships, the damaging of property, carelessness, and the breaking of rules. Obviously, there are many different kinds of problems that might fall within each of these categories, and not all of them would warrant disciplinary actions, but whenever any of them is judged as being serious, discipline should be imposed immediately. It is important, however, to be clear about the positive goals that are to be accomplished by disciplinary action. We should also be clear that the goals may be interpreted quite differently by the manager and the one receiving the discipline.

• *To Be Just.* There is a pervasive sense of justice in our society that demands that people be penalized for doing something wrong. In this sense, people "get what they deserve" or "get what they asked for." We do not disregard the necessity of punishment, even with its negative connotation, but we do suggest that thinking of people's positive accomplishments may be an important perspective for anyone in authority to have. This allows an authority figure frequently to temper justice with mercy and understanding, when it is called for.

• *To Restore the Person to the Discipline of the Organization.*[2] In other words, the manager makes the person a valuable member of the organization again by insisting on changed behavior. The threat of punishment is often the reinforcement necessary to accomplish this.

• *To Protect Proper Procedures.* Of course, no one can write a detailed rule book that is going to cover all situations. However, rules, regulations, and procedures are the glue that holds an organization together. Properly derived, they become necessary for the smooth and efficient working of an organization.

• *To Deter Others from Making the Same Violations.* Frequently, we hear criticism if a manager tries to make an example out of someone. The truth is, however, that people learn from examples. If a rule is not enforced, then it soon becomes evident that no one has to follow it. Consequently, over a period of time it loses its force and cannot be enforced without causing some other problems. For example, you can expect a tremendous uproar if, as a new manager in an office, you try to enforce the "no

[2]James M. Black, *How to Get Results from Interviewing* (New York: McGraw-Hill Book Co., 1970), p. 142.

smoking" signs if the previous supervisor paid no attention to them. Furthermore, sometimes there is no difficulty if one person frequently shows up late for work, but experience shows that if you let one person get away with it, soon others will follow suit. A practice that creates no problems when it is limited to one person may cause major disruptions when others adopt it. Consequently, the first individual may need to be disciplined.

• *To Protect Employees.* Many rules involve safety. Whenever someone gets hurt by violating a rule, the organization may be liable. Therefore, it is the organization's responsibility to coordinate activities, enforce the rules, and prevent dysfunctional behavior. As a manager, you are the enforcer. Recently, we went on a tour of a plant that manufactures housing insulation. In the plant is one machine with whirling blades that has a very elaborate set of rules for operating it. If a supervisor sees the operator violating one of the rules, there is an automatic suspension for a specified time, and the punishment is not negotiable or able to be modified. In this case, the rules are designed to safeguard the arms and hands of the operators, and the danger warrants the enforcement.

• *To Fulfill Your Role as a Manager.* An organization has a right to a well-disciplined, coordinated group of employees, and the management of the organization has the authority to administer discipline in problem situations. As a manager you share this responsibility and authority. Consequently, if you are to fulfill your responsibilities, you must discipline. In a sense, abdicating this responsibility makes you an accessory to the violation.

DIFFERENT MANAGERIAL APPROACHES TO DISCIPLINE

Managers differ greatly in their approaches to discipline, partly because their management styles differ. We assume that there is a general orientation toward management that is going to influence how you will generally approach disciplinary situations. For this reason, we will describe below Robert Blake and Jane Mouton's conceptualizations of discipline within four leadership styles. (See Figure 11.1.)

The task oriented manager (9,1 on the grid® in Figure 11.1) assumes that errors are a result of human error, that discipline enables one to control subordinates closely, and that enforcement of rules not only upholds the rule but also insures predictability of behavior. Such a manager says, "My immediate reaction is to find out who is responsible for the mistake and to mete out the appropriate disciplinary action in a swift and compelling manner. When people know that errors are not tolerated,

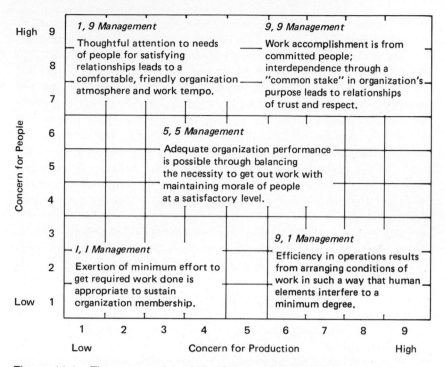

Figure 11.1   The managerial grid®. (Source: Robert R. Blake and Jane S. Mouton, *The New Managerial Grid* (Houston: Gulf Publishing Company, 1978), p. 11.)

they straighten up. If you don't nip such action in the bud, they will take advantage of you."[3]

The people oriented leader (1,9 on the grid) is inclined to avoid strong discipline because it creates embarrassment that in turn will produce resentment. With an inclination to "forgive and forget," such a manager is likely to say, "Well, I know you did the best you could," or "This hurts me more than it does you," or "I don't want to tell you this but my boss says. . . ." The overall approach is one of trying to be nice and to emphasize good human relations.[4]

The compromiser (5,5 on the grid) tries to balance concerns about a task against concerns for people. Consequently, he or she may not insist on the best in either category. Generally, conformity with formal rules and precedents are emphasized heavily. "When disciplinary action does become necessary, it is graduated according to the magnitude and seri-

[3]Robert Blake and Jane Mouton, *The Managerial Grid* (Houston, Gulf Publishing Co., 1969), p. 21.
[4]Ibid, p. 60.

ousness of the error."[5] In disciplining a subordinate, this type of manager will always look for a "carrot" to accompany the "stick" of punishment.

The leader who seeks the most out of employees and their work (9,9 on the grid) is likely to confront employees in a disciplinary situation, but his or her basic orientation is to make the encounter an educational experience. This manager exercises great control about overall objectives but may also permit employees to have some leeway within this overall context. The position of this manager is exemplified by the statement: "I discuss violations with those involved in order to diagnose what the problem is. If the procedure or policy producing the violation is unsound, steps are taken to change it. If it is misconduct, what motivated it needs understanding before corrective action is taken."[6] However, corrective action *is* taken.

Our purpose is not to argue that one of these management styles is necessarily better than another. Nevertheless, Blake and Mouton obviously favor the approach shown as 9,9 on the grid. With its emphasis on confronting disciplinary situations in an educational way, it probably comes closer to the positive discipline suggested by Black than any of the other approaches. As you read this section, it would be useful for you to identify your own management style and your own basic assumptions about discipline.

Obviously, there are subtle nuances that cause disciplinary situations to differ a great deal. Nonetheless, the following guidelines identify key decision points that can make the disciplinary interview a productive, educational experience. Rather than being rules that must be followed, however, they are a checklist of things that should be considered and adapted to your particular inclinations in a particular situation.

PLANNING THE INTERACTION

Unlike other interviews that we have covered, the disciplinary situation sometimes requires an immediate confrontation, with very little planning. We hope that even in these circumstances you will consider some of the guidelines that are listed below. Whenever possible, *delay* your reactions until you have had time to think about what it is that you are doing. Few situations demand an absolutely immediate reaction. Even a few minutes may save you from rash actions.

There are other situations that will allow you to make some elaborate plans. It is for these situations that the following planning guidelines will be most helpful.

1. *Discipline only when necessary.* You must make a judicious decision as to when and what discipline is to the benefit of you, the organiza-

[5]Ibid, p. 113.
[6]Ibid, p. 149.

tion, and the subordinate in the long term. Not every violation or mistake is equally serious; neither do they all warrant your time, attention, and energy. There are times, for example, when a violation is minor or when an employee seems to have a problem that may clear up by itself; in such cases, counseling may be preferable to discipline. On the other hand, gross violations that have important effects on the organization may necessitate immediate and serious discipline. The point is that the decision to have a disciplinary interview with a subordinate calls for your very best judgment.

2. *Learn the facts of the case.* Although it may take time, obtaining full information is absolutely necessary. Know the specifics of who, what, when, where, and with what effect. Be able to point out precisely what was wrong, what rule was broken, and what should have occurred. We emphasize learning the facts for three reasons. First, vague or abstract criticism is very difficult to digest. If the subordinate does not understand, he or she will think that you are being unfair or capricious. To accuse someone of being "disloyal," for example, may leave a subordinate not knowing what he or she needs to do in order for your evaluation to change. Second, you will look foolish if your claims turn out to be based merely on hearsay or unfounded assertions. Being equipped with the facts not only strengthens your case but will also in most cases reduce the amount of denial or reaction that you get from the subordinate. Third, thorough preparation generally heightens the respect for the manager by the subordinate.

3. *Check your own motivations.* Every interview occurs in a broader context, and the previous relationship between the manager and the subordinate has a profound influence on what is likely to take place. A manager may, for example, dislike the subordinate so much that he or she disciplines the subordinate for things that others also do without being disciplined, or sometimes the manager puts a person in a catch-22 situation so that the subordinate is damned if he or she does and damned if he or she does not. Consequently, you must ask yourself, "What is your attitude toward the subordinate?"

4. *Schedule the interview.* Timing may be one of the most important decisions that you make. Basically, you must ask yourself two questions: (1) "When am I likely to get the best results (or the least damage) from this interview?" and (2) "How much time and energy am I willing to spend on this case?" Often these questions are related, because you may have appropriate blocks of time at certain places in your schedule. Nevertheless, there are three major considerations in answering these questions.

First, arrange for the interview as soon as possible after an infraction. The quick follow-up not only prevents a repetition of the behavior but perhaps more importantly, it also makes certain that the punishment is associated with a specific behavior. Long delays allow the subordinate to think that he or she has gotten away with something, and delayed punishment is more likely to be seen as your just "having it in for the person."

Second, minimize the effect of a subordinate's reactions on his or her own productivity and that of others. In order to do this, many managers prefer to schedule discipline interviews at the end of a day or late on a Friday afternoon. The reasons for this are that (1) the employee has finished work and (2) it keeps the subordinate from returning to the work unit and stirring up support and disrupting other people's work. Managers disagree over the impact of the Friday afternoon time. Some say that having the weekend to think about what happened permits the subordinate to analyze the situation and cool down. Others feel that the weekend is too long a period to have to brood about the discipline without being able to react or to interact with the manager. It could well be that the wisdom of either of these choices varies with the particular person being disciplined; therefore, you will have to provide your own rationale for whatever time you set. It need not be acceptable to others—only to you.

Third, arrange for a time when you will have enough time to accomplish your purpose. From a very self-serving point of view, you will make decisions on the basis of how much time and energy you want to spend. Scheduling the interview for the end of the day gives you maximum flexibility in terms of your time and energy. If you wish to conserve your time and energy, you can cut the interview short by saying that you have other commitments. On the other hand, you may have few work pressures, and this may be a time when you could go on indefinitely if you thought the situation warranted it. Still another consideration here is timing the interview so that it is suitable to the subordinate. The end of the day may not give you as much flexibility as you would like if the subordinate is pressured to join a car pool or has other important commitments.

5. *Arrange for privacy.* Criticism is hard to take even privately, but receiving it in front of others will be doubly resented. Even if the infraction occurred in front of others, the interview should occur in private. If there is some punishment to be meted out, the lesson will not be lost on others. In other words, you can provide an example without making a public example of the subordinate. The word will get around.

6. *Check the union contract.* If the infraction and suitable discipline is covered by a union contract, study it to make certain that your own behavior does not violate a rule. Your image will suffer greatly if you try to discipline someone for breaking a rule while you are breaking a rule yourself.

7. *Keep your purposes educational.* Obviously, the general purpose is to discipline the subordinate. Beyond this, however, it is useful to identify exactly what you want to accomplish—what educational value the

interview is to undertake, what advice is going to be given, and what punishment is going to be given. This does not mean that you have to be rigid; you may have some alternatives in mind. However, your purpose and actions need to be thought out clearly.

8. *Reinforce yourself mentally.* Prepare your agenda and your basic approach. Since the discipline interview is likely to be more information giving than information seeking, more directive than nondirective, you will likely be giving an oral presentation. It needs to be clear, and there should be no question or anxiety about what you are setting out to do. Furthermore, since it is likely to involve some unpleasantness, you will need to prepare yourself psychologically to deal with it. This may influence when you decide to conduct the interview. When you can, avoid periods when you are extremely tired or pressured.

ADMINISTERING DISCIPLINE

Once you have made your plans, you are ready to interact with the subordinate by doing the following things.

1. *Act like a manager.* You have a position that involves power and authority. Use it. Some management orientations in recent years have taught people to deemphasize their roles as authority figures. While there are times when doing so may help you achieve your purposes, the discipline interview is not one of them. As we pointed out earlier, the people oriented leader (1,9 on the grid in Figure 11.1) does not handle discipline very well. In order to be a good manager, you must accept the responsibilities of leadership and use your authority wisely without apologizing for it.

One of the most important implications of acting like a manager is that you accept responsibility for the discipline. As a person's immediate supervisor, you are responsible for any corrective strategies. Trying to pass the buck onto someone else weakens the impact of the message, and it has been known to weaken also the employee's respect for the manager.

2. *Be direct.* The discipline interview is one of the cases when trying to build rapport through small talk is inadvisable. The subordinate's anxiety probably builds as he or she waits for the "bomb to drop." Be direct. Give a thorough orientation in the introduction. Explain what the purpose of the interview is and what its outcome is likely to be. It is particularly important here to let the subordinate know what his or her role in the interview is. Is the subordinate allowed to ask questions? Is the subordinate supposed to react in some way?

3. *Seek information.* If the discipline is going to have its maximum impact, you need to know what the subordinate's point of view is. Therefore, you should seek—and listen carefully for—four kinds of information: (1) What actually happened from the subordinate's point of view? (2) Why

did it happen? (3) What was his or her perceptions of the rules, regulations, or circumstances? (4) What is the subordinate's response to the discipline? The first three types of information are valuable in helping you determine how complete your assessment of the situation is. The last type of information simply lets you gauge whether or not you are likely to have some future problems with this individual. Participation by the subordinate in the disciplinary interview may lessen the feeling that he or she has been railroaded. On the other hand, the manager may choose to impose limits on the time and energy that will be expended in listening. Obviously, most subordinates will talk as long as the manager will listen in order to try to change or lessen the penalty.

4. *Review the specific grievance.* Explain exactly how the infraction violates the regulations or your expectations. This is where discipline becomes a form of training, and it is important that this discussion or explanation take place *prior* to the leveling of the penalty. Once the specific penalty is assessed, it may be difficult to be very analytic about the transgression.

5. *Look at the situation as well as at the person.* A characteristic of the task oriented leader (9,1 on the grid in Figure 11.1) is that he or she always looks at error as a result of human error. However, there are times when people are put in situations in which the situations themselves contribute to a failure. Characteristically, people look to themselves as the source of their successes and to the situation as the source for their failures. There is merit in examining the situation to determine to what extent it is a contributing factor.

6. *Separate the action from the person.* Skillful discipline focuses on the specific violation and does not indict the entire person. To say, "You failed to let us know that you couldn't produce the shipment on time" is different in perspective from saying, "You're a failure." Keeping this distinction in mind will help you keep a balanced perspective that avoids overstatement or overkill. If a person has been late four times in one week, it does not make your case very strong to indict the person by saying, "You're always late." The overstatement is obviously false.

7. *Administer a reasonable penalty.* "Inflicting discipline puts the supervisor in a dilemma. How can he [or she] expect his [or her] subordinates to continue to regard him [or her] as a source of help, when discipline is by nature painful?"[7] This is a good question. It may be impossible to impose discipline without generating some resentment, but there are some ways in which you can attempt to lessen it. An analogy may be instructive. If someone touches a hot stove after being warned not to, the penalty is *immediate*, the person has had a *warning*, the penalty is *consis-*

[7]George Strauss and Leonard R. Sayles, *Personnel* (Englewood Cliffs, N.J.: Prentice-Hall, Inc., 1967), p. 311.

tent because all would get the same treatment, and the penalty is *impersonal* in that anyone who touches it will be burned. These are four criteria for good discipline to which we would add two others.

Suit the penalty to the gravity of the error. Serious infractions should not go unpenalized, because excessive leniency can create problems of enforcement later. Neither should the penalty appear to be excessive.

Do not debate, argue, or negotiate the penalty. This is another reason for not setting the penalty until the end of the interview. Be certain that the penalty is fair and then stick with it.

8. *Provide for some follow-up.* This should be the final stage of the interview, and it should give the subordinate a specific orientation as to what is to happen. Plan the follow-up and then actually follow-up. The end of the interview is not necessarily the end of the problem situation. Consequently, you should not only check on the subordinate's progress but also offer encouragement and advice. If the objective of the discipline is in reality to restore the subordinate and to make this an educational experience, you should leave the subordinate not only with a serious assessment of the predicament but also with the hope of being recognized for improvement in the future.

9. *Document the interaction.* It is always wise to keep a record of your interactions. There is an increasing amount of litigation over work relations, and you will need documented proof to protect yourself in case you become involved in a legal action.

SPECIAL PROBLEMS

Even when people admit their guilt, they are not likely to welcome penalties that impose some pain or hardship upon them. There will always be the desire on the part of the disciplined person to protect himself or herself. Consequently, you should be prepared to cope with tension, hostility, anger, and disagreement. Therefore, consider certain special problems.

Silent Hostility

There are some people who react to discipline with dead silence; they understand it, but they do not respond verbally. This can be disconcerting to you, because you simply do not know what is going on inside their heads. Often, they will not respond to any invitation to speak. Lawrence Steinmetz lists four considerations for handling such situations.

1. Recognize when an employee is disaffected or alienated.
2. Encourage the employee to open up, to express his [or her] point of view. . . .You may have to ask him [or her] a point blank question, such as "Bill,

I sense you don't agree with what I'm saying. Would you mind telling me why?" . . . Such efforts usually fail.
3. Try to summarize the points of disagreement.
4. . . . build patiently an atmosphere which will convey to him [or her] a feeling of being a member of the team. If the subordinate does not want to talk, he [or she] should not be forced to. However, the point should be made that by remaining silent he [or she] is not contributing to the problem-solving situation.[8]

Open Hostility

The fact that two people exchange views is no guarantee that they can solve their problems. However, the open display of hostility, in contrast to the silent treatment, at least lets you know what is going on in the subordinate's head. It may be irrational, or your viewpoints may be polarized, but at least you know where you stand. If you both can talk openly, there is a greater likelihood—but no guarantee—that problems can be solved. How should you respond?

First, control yourself. Do not resonate the other person's hostility. Avoid the pendulum effect, in which your behavior is only in reaction to what the other person says or does. Avoid this trap by setting the climate yourself.

Second, recognize that some people need to ventilate their feelings before they can view a problem soberly. It is your choice, of course, as to how far you will permit the subordinate to ventilate his or her feelings. Many superiors feel that it is completely inappropriate to have a subordinate display any feelings. It is permissible to talk about feelings, but it is not permissible to display them. We acknowledge your right to establish the bounds. Nevertheless, the patience to tolerate someone's catharsis on occasion may be a valuable means of restoring the individual to a healthy attitude.

Third, focus on facts.

Fourth, use your power and authority as a last resort. Avoid using it unless it is absolutely necessary.

Disciplining in Front of Others

You may have a real problem if you discover a subordinate violating a rule or making a mistake in front of other people. Should you give the discipline in front of the people? What you do is going to vary with the infraction. A good rule of thumb, however, is to discipline in private whenever possible. Whether there is an infraction of a "no smoking" rule or insubordination in front of others, you can indicate a reprimand is coming. Then call the subordinate in for a discussion of the violation. The

[8]Lawrence Steinmetz, *Interviewing Skills for Supervisory Personnel* (Reading, Mass: Addison-Wesley Publishing Co., Inc., 1971), p. 70.

word will get around to others later. In the meantime, however, you have allowed the subordinate to save face in front of his or her peers, and you can have a more beneficial discussion in private than in front of others.

Disciplining More Than One Person at a Time

Sometimes two or more people are guilty of the same violation, and the question arises as to what is the best way of handling the situation. To talk to both people at the same time would in fact save you some energy, but we think that there is an overriding factor involved. It has been demonstrated in research with small groups that it is more difficult to change a person's mind if there is someone else in the group that supports his or her position. If you try to discipline both people at the same time, the two of them probably will try to ally themselves against you. This creates two problems: (1) There is something intimidating about being outnumbered, particularly in highly emotional situations; (2) It is more difficult to tailor the interview to the particular individual if someone else is there. Consequently, it may be more beneficial to you to have separate interviews but the same punishment for each person.

Tears

Having a subordinate begin to cry is a traumatic moment for many managers. The natural inclination is to try to console the person and to stop the crying. For this reason, many managers find themselves in compromising situations as they try to alleviate the pain, and frequently they make concessions that they later regret. The proper reaction to tears is to give the person time to regain control and to offer the person a tissue. Some even allow the interviewee to go freshen up, but if you allow the person to leave the room, there is the danger of breaking the chain of thought in a way that it cannot be regained.

Postdisciplinary Relationships

What is going to happen after the discipline? The relationship should return to normal. Once a person has paid for a mistake, forget it. Do not freeze your evaluation so that you refer back to the incident. It is the poor supervisor who makes the subordinate pay continually for past mistakes. In such cases, discipline becomes vindictive rather than educational.

THE ULTIMATE DISCIPLINE

The ultimate discipline is to remove a person from a position, either because of gross misconduct or lack of adequate performance. Of these two reasons, misconduct is easier to justify, because the subordinate is likely to know the danger. For lack of adequate performance, however, hope springs eternal, and people usually remain optimistic about their improvement. For both of these situations, the following guidelines will be helpful to you.

1. *Be direct.* Indirectness here gives the impression that your mind is not made up. Whenever you come to the interview, you should have examined your facts and your motives thoroughly, and you should be convinced that firing the employee is the best alternative. Proceed with a short statement of what your action is and why you have taken it. Do not hedge or "beat around the bush."

2. *Do not turn this into a counseling session.* The employee is likely to want to press for further explanation and will want to ask questions. He or she may even plead with you. At this point, however, "you have passed the remedial stage."[9]

3. *Expect the subordinate to be shocked and control your response.* Above all, do not give in to any guilt you may be feeling. We have been told so often that we must empathize with other people that we feel that something is wrong with ourselves when all does not work out well in our relationships. Feeling guilty, however, for removing an employee results in your saying and doing things that might turn out to be inappropriate.

4. *Plan the immediate future.* Terminations take many forms, depending on the nature of jobs. Some managers want to refer a subordinate to the personnel department for details; others try to describe the implications of removal. Some managers go through a lengthy discussion; others keep it short. Some try to salvage the self-image of the person by explaining that anyone can be placed in a situation in which he or she is going to fail; therefore, it is useful to look for the kind of situation in which the person can succeed. Such managers may offer help in locating another job. Other managers would never make such overtures. The lengths that you go to in helping the subordinate is a personal judgment, but it is important that you give the subordinate some ideas about the kind of recommendation he or she can expect from you and when the relationship with the organization must be terminated. It is probably wise also to have a personnel representative talk to the subordinate about final pay, insurance benefits, and final check-out procedures.

PROJECTS

1. Interview several managers in an attempt to discover what strategies they use in disciplining their subordinates. What do they find as being the most frequent problems? How do they handle subordinates' reactions?

[9]Walter Mahler, *How Effective Executives Interview* (Homewood, Ill.: Dow Jones-Richard D. Irwin, Inc., 1976), p. 177.

2. Devise strategies for handling each of the following:
   a. Someone is smoking in a "no smoking" zone where there are chemicals present.
   b. Someone is not wearing safety goggles in an area where it is required that they be worn.
   c. Two receptionists spend too much time talking to one another and are not very friendly with clients.
   d. A worker refuses to comply with one of your orders in front of other workers.
   e. An accountant has made several mathematical errors recently. You have talked with her, but you have just read a report in which you caught three more errors.

3. Role-play the situation of Joe/Jo Smith and the supervisor, which appears at the end of this chapter.

4. How would you handle the case that follows the role playing exercise at the end of this chapter if you were the supervisor? What guidelines would you follow?

DISCIPLINE ROLE-PLAY

PERSONNEL MANAGER

Joe/Jo Smith was hired by our general employment office during a time of "clerical crisis." The employment personnel indicated that his/her tests were not very good but that he/she was a very willing worker and a likable person. We decided to try Joe/Jo, a high school graduate from Wichita, on a clerical inventory job.

Under union rules the employees are subject to a salary increase after three months of employment. During the first few months, Joe/Jo worked closely with another clerk who was very capable. Although we knew Joe /Jo was not very good, we granted him/her a salary increase after the three-month period.

During the next three months Joe/Jo worked alone, and the error rate was extremely high. Twice during this period he/she was told about unsatisfactory work. At the end of six months we denied the second salary increase.

During the next two months his/her efficiency never improved.

After eight months we have gained nothing from the employment of this clerk. We are ready to discharge Joe/Jo Smith. Yesterday, you called the employee and set up an appointment for 4 P.M. today.

JOE/JO SMITH

You are a high school graduate from Wichita. As a student, you were average. Eight months ago you applied for a job with the Bigdone Company, and you wanted to work desperately. Even during high school you had worked part-time as a salesperson.

During the time you applied for the job, you thought your chances were pretty good because you had gotten along well with previous employers. Also, according to the newspapers, there was at that time a shortage of workers to be employed.

The general employment office of the Bigdone Company gave you several tests, indicated that you passed them with an average score, and hired you.

You were put to work on a clerical inventory job. You worked with another clerk, X, who was very capable and very helpful to you. After three months you received a salary increase. The raise pleased you, but you were upset when you were separated from X and had to work alone.

For five months you have worked alone, and you have not been doing as well. Twice your supervisor has called attention to some errors and called your work "unsatisfactory." You thought, however, that the errors were rather minor ones that anyone might have made. At any rate, you resolved to improve and think that you have. You hope to work into a better job with the company.

Two things have upset you. (1) Two months ago a merchant told you that they are going to take legal action against you because you failed to pay your bills. Naturally, you intended to pay them and have asked for an extension of time. The merchant still has you worried, and you find yourself thinking about this more and more. (2) Things have not been going well between you and your fiance(e).

Yesterday the personnel manager called for an appointment at 4 P.M. today. You still have a lot of work to do, but it must be important if the personnel manager made an appointment with you.

CASE

ORGANIZATIONAL FUNCTION—COMPUTER OPERATIONS SUPPORT

1. Staff's responsibility: computer production recovery; technical advice to development group; quality control of new computer systems.
2. Staff: 12 people on three shifts, six days per week.
3. Individual: black male, approximately 25 years old, with no degree, highly intelligent, hard worker, very knowledgeable about his work. Married.
4. Problem: arrives late and leaves early 60 percent of the time. Work has been completed during this time period.

    I am his fourth boss in three years. His previous supervisors have not approached the problem head on but, rather, have chosen to speak briefly to him about his attendance. About every three or four months he does not report to work, and no excuses are made on his part.

    When I was promoted to the position of supervisor two months ago, I spoke to Larry concerning his attendance and how I felt about working hours. He listened but did not react. During the next four weeks he was no more than 15 minutes late when he was late. Then he missed three days without notice. I docked him two days pay and placed him on a 60-day probation. This was done in the form of a written document, which we discussed and he signed.

    If he is true to form he will go back to his old ways after 60 days. What should I do then?

Be explicit in giving the rationale behind what you would do. What considerations did you take into account?

Chapter 12
Exit Interviews

The United States has a very mobile society in comparison with other societies. People move easily and often change jobs easily. In fact, some employers seem to expect employees to move. A manager we know once half-jokingly welcomed a new employee with the words, "Welcome to the first of your five miserable jobs." A study made by Marvin Dunnette and his associates reported that "many companies lose nearly 50 percent of their college graduates during the first four or five years of post college employment."[1] Our purpose in this chapter is to identify the problems for managers in those organizations that have a high turnover among its employees.

First, turnover is expensive. Each time an employee quits a job, the costs of recruiting and training someone new may reach several thousand dollars, and the higher the new person is in the organization, the more expensive the costs will be.

Second, high turnover historically has been associated with low morale, which most managers want to avoid. If good people are leaving,

[1]Marvin D. Dunnette, Richard D. Avery, and Paul A. Banas, "Why Do They Leave," *Personnel* 50 (May–June 1973): 25.

there should be the suspicion that something is wrong with the organization. Third. while no one argues that an organization wishes to keep every individual who is working for it, the employees who often have the opportunities to leave voluntarily are the most capable—the ones that most organizations would like to retain. In the exit interview the manager investigates attrition in the company to determine whether the right people are staying and the marginal ones are leaving.

TWO PURPOSES OF EXIT INTERVIEWS

The exit interview, which is now used by eight out of ten firms in the United States,[2] is an attempt to exert some control over the attrition and perhaps reduce the costs of losing good employees. There are a number of alternative procedures that are billed as exit interviews, but basically they are designed to accomplish two things.

The first purpose is to process the removal of the employee in an orderly, efficient way. Each departing employee needs to be given information about pay, insurance ramifications of leaving, and what will go on his or her record. To review this with the employee is a matter of good administration.

The second purpose of the exit interview is to collect information that will be usable to the organization. At a minimum, the interviewer will assess who is leaving, why the person is leaving, and whether the person's leaving is a plus or a minus to the organization.[3] In other words, the data from an exit interview serves as a means of organizational diagnosis.

Unfortunately, managers and personnel representatives often equate exit interviewing only with the second purpose. We emphasize, however, that accomplishing both purposes is desirable. The first is necessary for smooth transitions, and the second offers data that can be of value to the organization.

USEFULNESS OF AN EXIT INTERVIEW

At a very basic level, the report resulting from an exit interview serves as an organizational record of a particular employee's leaving the organization. A periodic analysis of this data, however, can also provide the organization with some immensely rich information.

1. In a sense, data from the exit interview can help refine selection procedures. For example, because a large hospital was concerned about the turnover in one department, the administration brought in a consul-

---

[2]Felix M. Lopez, *Personnel Interviewing* (New York: McGraw-Hill Book Co., 1975), p. 319.
[3]John R. Hinrichs, "Employees Coming and Going: The Exit Interview," in Richard C. Huseman et al. (Eds.), *Readings in Interpersonal and Organizational Behavior* (Boston: Holbrook Press. Inc., 1977), p. 454.

tant to help. Among the things that the consultant did was to institute a program of exit interviews. The consultant collected data from many former employees' records and analyzed them. After a while, a trend emerged that explained why certain people left and why others stayed. This information was then incorporated in the selection procedures of the hospital, and turnover actually decreased. Similarly, a large airline is currently working on this problem among its flight attendants. Apparently, many people take the job as an entrée into the airline with the hope of eventually moving into management positions. Such opportunities are very limited, so these particular employees often become dissatisfied and leave. Because of information analyzed from the exit interviews, the airline is now looking for ways of weeding out such people in the initial selection process. They want to identify and hire people who will be content to work as flight attendants.

2. Data from exit interviews are also useful in identifying problem areas in the organization, which may then be corrected. For example, consistently high turnover in a particular work unit could alert management, but management would not know exactly what the specific problem is. It could be the nature of the work itself, poor supervision, a low pay scale in comparison to similar work in other organizations, or lack of opportunities for advancement. Any one of these problems can be worked on, but first management must decide which of these is a problem. Data from the exit interview may help to identify it.

3. Data from exit interviews provide management with a means of monitoring attrition. It is part of a general personnel function to know who is leaving, why they are leaving, and whether their leaving is a detriment or an asset to the organization.

4. Exit interviews document employees' reasons for leaving, and this is an important function. The documentation provides a *permanent* record for management, which has legal implications if the termination is ever questioned. Since research shows that employees who are leaving a company apparently skew their answers or change their minds about why they are leaving, it is useful to have a record of what they said at the time of departure. Then, management has a complete file on each employee.

THE PROBLEM OF VALIDITY

As we have stated, one objective for holding exit interviews is to find out why people leave their jobs. However, there is considerable evidence that departing employees do not necessarily reveal their reasons for changing jobs. In fact, some knowledgeable interviewers have claimed that there are always two reasons for leaving a job: the stated one and the real one. The following studies present this problem in graphic terms.

Joel Lefkowitz and Myron Katz conducted a study in which 164 female employees of a lingerie company were given exit interviews before they left their jobs. A list of reasons for termination was made, and later a questionnaire was mailed to them to discover why they left. Two of their results indicate a problem.

> The most frequently given reason for termination at the time of the exit interview is the general "needed at home" explanation. At the time of the follow-up, the most frequent reason involves the inability to cope with production pressures.[4]
>
> [The women] who, during the exit interview, said they were resigning "for no specific reason" *all* listed specific reasons at the time of the follow-up. Half of these reasons were related to problems in personal relations—with peers or supervisors, and about which they would not discuss at the time.[5]

Had these ladies lied? Were the latter reasons mere rationalizations? Or had the ladies, in fact, changed their minds so that all answers were correct *at the time*? We do not know, but the difference does pose a problem for us intellectually.

Hinrichs corroborated these findings when he contrasted reasons given months later when consultants re-interviewed the same people:

> There was no mention of conflict with management in the exit interview reports, but this factor emerged as important in 14% of the interviews conducted by the consultant.
>
> Dissatisfaction with advancement came out as a significant factor in the consultant's interviews but not in the exit interviews. The exit interviews more frequently cited higher earnings in the new job as a reason for leaving than did the consultant interviewees.
>
> All told, the consultant's interviews revealed a less favorable evaluation of the former position than did exit interviews. . . .[6]

All of this evidence raises good questions about the value of the exit interview. There seems to be something at work that permits or encourages employees to give inconsistent information.

At the time of termination, there is an apparent tendency to identify causes over which the organization has no control, such as family obligations and better offers. The research shows, however, that later they list motives for leaving over which management might have had some control, such as relationships, travel, pay, and promotions. The validity of the exit interview data is in question, and unless the manager attempts to determine the real from the stated reasons for leaving, there is not much point in having an exit interview.

Unfortunately, no ultimate criteria for judging the validity of infor-

[4]Joel Lefkowitz and Myron Katz, "Validity of Exit Interviews," *Personnel Psychology* 22 (1969): 449.
[5]Ibid., p. 451.
[6]Hinrichs, "Exit Interview, p. 456.

mation taken from exit interviews exist. We realize, of course, that not all systems for holding exit interviews are functioning in the best way. Many are conducted in a perfunctory manner, sometimes by unskilled interviewers. In some cases interns or very new employees are assigned the task without having had any prior training. In other cases the exit interview involves only a form that the former employee fills out. In the remaining part of this chapter we will describe the considerations that would make it possible to implement an effective exit interview.

ALTERNATIVE PROCEDURES

A number of different procedures are included under the umbrella term of "exit interviews": (1) questionnaires, (2) preliminary exit interviews, (3) postexit interviews, (4) voluntary exit interviews, and (5) involuntary exit interviews.

Many organizations do not give an interview at all but simply ask the employee to volunteer to complete a standard questionnaire for their files. Examples of such questionnaires are included in Figures 12.1 and 12.2. Such a procedure does not give the manager much detailed information, but it may be adequate for the organization's purposes.

A popular variation is to use a questionnaire in conjunction with an interview. The questionnaire is filled out first and then becomes the basis for discussion in the interview.

What is sometimes called a preliminary exit interview may not be an exit interview in the truest sense. It refers to the interview that occurs before a person has actually decided to leave the organization. Supposedly, a perceptive supervisor will recognize the subtle indications that occur when an employee begins to lose interest in the job and looks for another.

> Managers conducting exit interviews stated that, on the average, the employee's dissatisfaction became apparent only two or three weeks prior to his [or her] resignation. In the interview with the consultant, however, the average employee stated that he [or she] had approached his [or her] manager several months prior to taking the extreme step of resigning.[7]

Nevertheless, if a supervisor detects that an employee is vacillating between going or staying, the supervisor can attempt to salvage the worker by exploring his or her thinking in an interview and persuading the worker to stay. The interest shown by just setting up the interview would be quite persuasive.

The postexit interview occurs after the employee actually has left the job. Typically, a questionnaire is mailed to the former employee, or a consultant is hired to interview a group of them. While this practice has

[7]Ibid.

the advantage of perhaps letting people speak more freely, since the ties with the organization have been severed, these practices suffer in two regards. First, the former employees may no longer be interested enough to grant the interview or fill out the questionnaire, and second, the experiences since termination could easily reshape their views of termination so that the information is not what was actually used in making the decisions to leave.

Involuntary exit interviews are those that occur when a person has been fired. Even under these circumstances, it is desirable to make the separation as smooth as possible and to clear up any loose details. The relevant material for this kind of interview is covered in Chapter 11.

NAME _____ DATE _____

JOB TITLE _____ DEPARTMENT_____

SUPERVISOR _____

1. When you started working for the company, did you intend to stay permanently?   Yes _____   No _____

2. Why are you leaving? _____
_____
_____

3. Do you have another job opportunity?   Yes _____   No _____
Where? _____

4. Are there any changes management could have made to prevent your leaving?
_____

5. If you had the opportunity to be in charge of our company, what changes would you make? _____
_____

Please rate the following.

6.	Your supervisor	Excellent	Good	Average	Poor
7.	Wages	Excellent	Good	Average	Poor
8.	Hours of Work	Excellent	Good	Average	Poor
9.	Training received	Excellent	Good	Average	Poor
10.	Promotional opportunities	Excellent	Good	Average	Poor
11.	Grievances you might have had	Excellent	Good	Average	Poor

_____
Signed by Interviewer

_____
Signed by Employee

Figure 12.1   Employee exit interview.

NAME   DEPARTMENT DATE OF TERMINATION

FORWARDING ADDRESS   ELIGIBLE TO REHIRE
            Yes   No

REASON FOR LEAVING

VOLUNTARY RESIGNATION	UNCONTROLLABLE RESIGNATION	INVOLUNTARY TERMINATION
___ Returning to School	___ Death	___ Poor Quality/
___ Family Obligations	___ Health Reasons	Quantity
___ Better Job Opportunity	___ Moving	___ Habitually
___ Supervision	___ Retirement	Absent or
___ Lack of Advancement/	___ Spouse	Tardy
Development	Transferred	___ Insubordination
___ Leaving Area	___ Other	___ Staff Reduction
___ Salary		___ Other
___ Working Conditions		
___ Other		

POSITIVE ASPECTS OF THE JOB

NEGATIVE ASPECTS OF THE JOB

COMPENSATION AND WORKING CONDITIONS

SUPERVISION RECEIVED

CHECKLIST OF INFORMATION DISCUSSED

____ Department management contacted
____ Disposition of final paycheck
____ Effects on retirement pay
____ Fringe Benefits (health insurance, etc.)
____ Return of company property (Identification card, keys, equipment)

INTERVIEWER COMMENTS

DATE _____ INTERVIEWER _____

Figure 12.2 Exit interview record.

Voluntary exit interviews are by far the most common. They occur after the employee announces an intention to resign of his or her own accord. It is these for which the following guidelines are suggested.

Thorough Preparation Necessary

As we have indicated throughout this book, preparation is essential. Six major considerations need to guide you in preparing for an employee's exit interview. Unlike other interviews, however, it need not be necessarily tailored to a particular individual.

1. *Decide who can best conduct the exit interview.* (a) For low-level employees, a personnel representative is often used. In fact, this interview is often the one that is relegated to a college intern or a part-time worker. (b) Some firms have the immediate supervisor conduct the interview, but this practice is quite controversial. It is true that the immediate supervisor is often the most knowledgeable about the employee and can, therefore, assess the employee's answers well. On the other hand, the relationship with the supervisor is often a reason for leaving, and departing employees are generally unwilling to tell this to the supervisor's face. Furthermore, people in the same work unit may have a common blind spot. Having the immediate supervisor conduct the interview is most viable when employees at high-level positions leave. (c) A third alternative is to use selection interviewers. They generally are skilled interviewers, and having them conduct the exit interviews would increase the likelihood that the information obtained could influence the selection procedures.

2. *Schedule the interview within the last two weeks.* Never wait until the last day. Generally, a person is too busy and too psychologically involved with other things to want to take the time for an interview on the last day. In scheduling the interview, make a definite appointment with the employee that allows for more time than you think you will need.

3. *Respect privacy.* Reasons for leaving sometimes are intensely personal, so it is necessary that no one overhears or interrupts the discussion and that provisions be made to keep the information confidential. The reasons often given co-workers are not the same as those given in an exit interview.

4. *Be aware of the multiple purposes.* Keep in mind that the exit interview is an information giving interview as well as an information receiving interview.

5. *Prepare an agenda.* The agenda should be divided into two parts to reflect the two different purposes of the interview. First, assemble all of the employee's records and prepare a checklist of all items that need to be covered. The following list suggests some information that would be pertinent in many cases.

insurance
pensions
vacation pay
time schedule
organizational expectations until departure
type of reference employee can expect
checking-out procedures (keys, equipment, etc.)

Second, we advocate the use of an interview schedule for receiving information, too, in which you identify all the areas that you wish to explore. If trends are to be discovered, you must explore the same areas with all terminating employees. A good way to begin this part of the interview is to review the person's job assignment. Beyond this, you can make a checklist of the most common reasons that people leave jobs and explore each area to see if it has any bearing on this person. In any attempt to understand why someone is leaving, you will need to discover what the individual liked and disliked about his or her specific job. Consequently, you can make a checklist, such as the following, of items to cover.

Was the work challenging?
Was the work too routine?
Were you compensated fairly?
How well informed were you kept?
How much participation did you have in your job?
How free were you to offer suggestions?
How helpful were training programs and educational opportunities?
Was there a reasonable opportunity for promotion?
How did your job fit into your general career plans?
Was your performance reviewed well and fairly?

Specific items like these will enable you to review the employee's perspective about his or her job. Most of them will probably be answered positively and almost routinely.

6. *Structure the interview.* Research on exit interviews indicate that, in general, structured ones are more effective than unstructured ones.[8] Three key observations about structure will be helpful.

First, the information giving portion of the interview should come at the beginning. "The very normality of advising an employee on such routine subjects as what benefits he [or she] will receive and where and how he [or she] will get his [or her] last salary check breaks down preinterview tension and usually enables you to establish a satisfactory climate

[8]C. Bahn, "Expanded Use of the Exit Interview," *Personnel Journal* 44 (December 1965): 620.

in which, at the right time, you can confidently enter the other more difficult section. . . ."[9]

Second, use a funnel structure for this information seeking part of the interview. In other words, start out with the most general questions, so that you do not structure the employee's thinking or answers. For example, let us suppose that you have a list of specific items to which you want the employee to respond. These items might include such things as working conditions, supervision, benefits, and relation with other workers. It would be preferable to ask the following questions before you start probing to get reactions to the spcifics.

1. Can you tell me why you decided to leave?
2. What did you find most satisfying about working here?
3. What did you find least satisfying about working here?

Using this funnel structure gives the respondent maximum flexibility in deciding how to answer. It may also have the advantage of forcing the person to reveal something about his or her priorities.

Third, you must be flexible.

> The exit interview is very much like a jig-saw puzzle. The experienced interviewer realizes that his search for information is similar to a treasure hunt; a small clue here or a sign there turn up unexpectedly. Some chance remark by an interviewee, some unguarded comment on a trivial aspect of his past job may be exploring at great length, and if the exploration is successful highly valuable information can be discovered.[10]

MANAGING THE INTERVIEW

1. *Explain your purpose thoroughly.* Hopefully, an explanation of how the information is going to be used will motivate the interviewee to respond readily. Furthermore, you are going to have to be somewhat persuasive. Since the employee is leaving, he or she is likely to be on guard, particularly if you are the direct superior. At any rate, the employee will want to avoid saying anything that can be used against him or her either now or later. The person may want some references from you later and does not want to jeopardize this by parading criticisms of your organization. Essentially, then, you can explain your purpose in such a way that this employee is persuaded that *you need his or her help*.

2. *Set a personable, but business-like atmosphere.* Keep in mind that the first part of the interview in which you are giving information is for the employee's benefit but that all the answers to your questions are for your benefit, not his or hers. Consequently, you may need to reduce your

[9]James M. Black, *How to Get Results from Interviewing* (New York: McGraw-Hill Book Co., 1970), p. 156.
[10]Ibid., p. 160.

authority and develop a particularly warm manner here. After all, you cannot force the employee to reveal his or her thoughts. An open climate will cause the respondent to answer you honestly, rather than safely.

3. *Avoid the tendency to counsel the employee or attempt to persuade the employee to stay.* It is possible that you might make an extra effort to keep a particularly good employee, but we assume generally that the exit interview takes place after a definite decision to fire the employee has been made. Attempts to persuade at this juncture run the risk of heightening the employee's anxiety about the interview itself.

4. *Be a good listener.* Avoid the tendency to confirm or deny the employee's information. Above all, do not agree or disagree with the employee. It has been found that supervisors typically will agree with information that is not critical of the organization, but they become defensive in the face of critical information. While you might well want to check the consistency of the interviewee's information with the facts later, your role in the interview itself is not to set the record straight but rather to diagnose the situation as the employee sees it. You are a data-collector, a recorder, a listener. Your questions should be designed to keep the employee talking while the conversation rolls along comfortably.

5. *Probe thoroughly.* Do not be content with the first answer given as a reason for leaving. The employee may not want to say things explicitly, so you have to watch carefully for implicit information. We have maintained throughout this book that skillful probing differentiates effective interviewers from ineffective ones. Nowhere is this more true than in the exit interview. As we reviewed earlier in this chapter, people are often quite reluctant to reveal their true reasons for leaving. Sometimes they will hint at the real reason while skewing their answer to be very palatable to the interviewer. These hints ought to be probed.

6. *Conclude positively.* When the interviewee signals that he or she has said all that needs to be said, terminate the interview. Since your objective is to end the relationship on a positive note, wish the employee well and express your appreciation for his or her contributions to your organization. If the employee has been particularly capable, you may even offer your help in the future if he or she ever needs it. Above all, you want the employee to leave thinking that your organization is a good one and that he or she has been appreciated.

7. *Record the information.* Verbatim quotations can be very valuable for later analysis, but access to this record should be seriously limited. After your interview, your records should include: (a) reasons given for leaving, (b) information about problems or suggestions for improving the operation, and (c) impressions of the interviewee and his or her information. Be certain to record the latter as "impressions" so that you do not confuse them with the facts of the case later. They are listed merely to help you interpret the facts.

THIS CHAPTER IN PERSPECTIVE

Exit interviews perform an administrative function in that they provide an easy transition in terminating an employee. All individuals should know clearly what the ramifications and expectations are.

The interviews also provide useful information if they are done well and if there is a consistent exit system. One individual interview is not very helpful as a data gathering device. The information is only truly helpful when it is analyzed periodically along with data from other interviews to determine whether or not there is some pattern developing in terms of why people leave. Consequently, unless you are interested only in mere documentation, and unless you make a concerted effort to make the overall analysis, spending much time in exit investigations is a waste of time and talent.

PROJECTS

1. Interview personnel representatives at four different organizations to determine what their practices are in regard to exit interviews. Look particularly at the ways they (a) collect and (b) use information.

2. Interview someone who recently changed jobs to determine why the person left. What challenges did you have in getting the person to talk about it?

3. Earlier in this book we gave an example similar to the one below. Evaluate the various probes.

INTERVIEWER: Mary, we're sorry that you're going to be leaving us next week. It's important to us to know why people leave. Sometimes where we have been at fault, we can do something to prevent it from happening in the future. Could you tell me why you're leaving?

MARY: Well, I just got this opportunity to work at Johnson's.

Potential Responses of the interviewer:
1. What makes Johnson's better than your opportunities here?
2. What made you decide to take it?
3. Are you getting more money there?
4. What made you apply there in the first place?
5. Didn't you like it here?
6. We're particularly interested in why you were willing to leave here and move there. Could you tell me something about that?
7. (Silence).
8. Other _____ .

4. Perform an experiment in which you conduct exit interviews for an organization. Keep careful records. Then schedule another interview with the same individuals two or three weeks later to see if their answers vary.

5. What would (or have been) your motivations in being the interviewee in an exit interview? Are most people like you?

6. Compile a comprehensive list of why people leave jobs voluntarily and frame relevant questions for each.

7. Tape-record several of your exit interviews (with the interviewee's permission) and analyze your techniques.

8. Conduct a survey in which you discover how people feel about the exit interviews and why they have participated in them.

Chapter 13
Persuasion
and Negotiation
Interviews

The ability to influence another person is one of the most valued skills in our society. The best salespeople, the most mobile managers, the most effective union negotiators, the most successful teachers, and even some of the most sought after counselors earn their money and prestige because they are able to alter someone's viewpoint and behavior better than their colleagues or competitors. Therefore, in this chapter we will probe into this conscious, deliberate process of influencing people so that you can maximize your own skills. To a degree, much of the material about other types of interviews has concentrated on persuasive strategies. The tell-and-sell appraisal, the directive counseling technique, and even the selection interview all involve a persuasive attempt to "sell" a person or an idea.

It is perhaps unusual to combine *persuasion* and *negotiation*, but we do it in this chapter because their common aim is influence. Persuasion has been defined as "communication designed to influence others by modifying their beliefs, values, or attitudes."[1] This is exactly what takes

[1]Herbert W. Simons, *Persuasion* (Reading, Mass.: Addison-Wesley Publishing Co., Inc., 1976), p. 21.

place in bargaining or negotiation situations. Maybe an apt description of negotiation is mutual persuasion, since each person tries to influence the other to modify a position.

Actually, much of our communication is persuasive both in terms of intent and in terms of the strategies that are used. There are those times when the attempt is very obvious because the interaction calls for it. For example, when Mary B. tries to sell a client insurance, she actually is negotiating with the client over what kind of insurance to buy and how much; when Bill M. is offered a job in a university, he announces the salary range that he would find acceptable and then negotiates a contract; Charles D., a consultant, knows that he must sell a company on the idea that he can do the training that they need or conduct a survey in which they are interested. On the other hand, there are many situations that call for negotiation in more subtle ways. Managers and subordinates, for example, frequently negotiate. When Jane L. wants to get some additional training, she has to convince her superior to let her leave work for a week to go away for the training; furthermore, she has to convince her superior that he should pay for it. When Robert W. wants to adopt a new system in his office, he has to persuade his employees that the change would be useful in the long run. As these two examples indicate, the persuasion attempts involve superiors trying to influence subordinates and vice versa. In fact, one of the most often asked questions in communication training sessions for managers is, "How can I persuade my boss to listen to my ideas and accept them?" This is a very difficult question to answer.

Negotiation and persuasion, of course, take place in many different contexts; therefore, there will be some unique features and strategies that should be adapted to these different situations. Nevertheless, people are alike in many ways, and there are many characteristics that all of these contexts share, which will be the focal point of this chapter.

Two limitations are superimposed on the discussion. First, we are concerned primarily with negotiation and persuasion in one-on-one interviews. While this severely limits the more common scope of group negotiation, there are some special advantages to negotiating with one other person, and there are many opportunities to do so. Charles Stewart and W. B. Cash list several advantages of such persuasive interviews: the message can be tailored to one person, feedback is immediate, adaptation to different nuances within the interview is easier, and there are no other parties to obstruct or counteract your persuasive effort. Finally, the "persuadee has more difficulty terminating a face-to-face encounter than a mass media encounter."[2]

Second, persuasion and negotiation are viewed in terms of the inter-

[2]Charles Stewart and William B. Cash, *Interviewing* (Dubuque, Iowa: William C. Brown Company, Publishers, 1974), p. 203.

viewee's having a freedom of choice in the discussion. This rules out the consideration of coercion. If a superior commands a subordinate to do something and then has the power to force this person to do it, this is influence based on power and does not fit our description of persuasion. This limitation is not meant to *eliminate* coercion as a legitimate managerial function; obviously, it is available and is used often. We just choose to focus on situations that call for persuasion where coercion is not an alternative.

So now you want to persuade someone. How should you do it? What is the formula for success? What can you do that will guarantee effectiveness? There are many opportunists who advertise that they have the key to persuasion or that they have the ultimate negotiating strategy. Well, you *can* learn to have more influence, but there is no magic formula. The truth is that "after twenty years of study of bargaining tactics and strategies, no one superior strategy emerges."[3] "It is obvious that various characteristics of the bargainers and of the bargaining situation play a large part in determining whether a particular bargaining strategy will be effective."[4] This simply means that the real key to success is *your own ability to analyze each new situation that you face* and to adapt your presentation to the unique features of the situation.

In order to furnish you with an orientation to persuasion and negotiation interviews, the discussion will revolve around the following topics: (1) stages of negotiation, (2) planning the interview, (3) building a case, (4) managing the interview, and (5) dealing with specific problems.

STAGES OF NEGOTIATION

Many people have studied what happens in all kinds of negotiations, and there seems to be a rather standard pattern that most negotiations follow. In a real sense, most persuasive situations may involve these same phases. Consequently, before you begin to make your move toward a specific persuasive attempt, it might be helpful for you to review the overall process that is generally involved in negotiations.

Phase 1: Establishing the Bargaining Range[5]

Sometimes in persuasive negotiations there is a rather lengthy period during which both sides state their cases. They each express their assessment of the situation. Normally, these first statements reveal the ideal

---

[3]W. Clay Hamner and Gary A. Yukl, "The Effectiveness of Different Offer Strategies in Bargaining," in Daniel Druckman (Ed.), *Negotiations* (Beverly Hills, Calif.: Sage Publications, Inc., 1977), p. 157.

[4]Ibid.

[5]Ann Douglas, "The Peaceful Settlement of Bilateral and Intergroup Disputes," *Journal of Conflict Resolution* 1 (1956): 69.

settlement from the person's own perspective. In the case of labor negotiations, these first statements are public positions that will be expected to be negotiated downward in private. Nevertheless, it is important to make the initial overture. The expert negotiator knows, of course, that this initial statement may reveal a great deal about your own level of sophistication and the negotiation strategies you will use later. Many of you have had the experience, for example, of having traveled in a country where bargaining over prices is the standard operating procedure in the shops. These shopkeepers are experienced in the process, and your first statement can tell them much about your negotiating skill. This is one reason why they frequently ask you to make an offer before they will state their price.

In terms of setting the bargaining range, negotiations tend to follow one of four basic strategies: (1) a tough general offer and bargaining approach, (2) a moderately tough general offer and negotiating approach, (3) a soft general offer and negotiating approach, and (4) a fair offer and negotiating approach. The decision as to which general offer you should use will also determine the basic tactics that you will use, and they can also have a direct bearing on the length of the negotiations and rate of success.

The tough general offer is characterized by an initial high demand, high minimum expectations, and an unyielding stance. It is quite conceivable that a person using this approach might not, in fact, alter his or her negotiating position in response to concessions by the other individual. W. Clay Hammer and Gary A. Yukl report that the tough initial offer reduces the opponent's expectations by indicating that you will not give in easily.[6] If you are able to maintain a tough bargaining stance and reach a settlement, the settlement will probably be more favorable to you. This approach does run the risk of prolonging the negotiations and also of leading to a situation in which agreement or compromise cannot be reached. *The rewards may be greater, but the risk of failure is also greater.* Practitioners of the tough approach often develop an image of being unreasonable, inflexible, but perhaps highly successful. When both sides in a negotiation take the tough strategy and misread their opponent's commitment, then the chances of agreement are significantly reduced. From this discussion, it becomes apparent that *the success of any bargaining approach rests entirely on the other person's reaction to it.*

A moderately tough initial offer often induces the other person to make concessions that may also force you to make some reciprocal concessions. Since concessions pull parties together, both in terms of messages and relationships, the chances for success increase. This simply means that you must know what you are willing to give up. Being prepared to do so may be a wise strategy, because as this discussion suggests, making a

---

[6]Hamner and Yukl, "Different Offer Strategies," p. 141.

concession can be a very persuasive strategy in itself. The moderately tough approach generally leaves room for maneuvering. One goal for you is to create a dialogue that allows you to determine the priorities of your opponent; your opponent will also be trying to find this out from you.[7]

The soft initial offer can be dangerous, because it raises the opponent's expectations. He or she may think that you are an easy mark. The soft initial offer is characterized by an initial low demand and low minimum expectations. While it may be made in good faith by you, this approach may cause a problem because your opponent may think that you will reduce your position further. Therfore, it is dangerous to reveal your position too easily because the other person may expect additional negotiating. If your opponent perceives himself or herself as a tough negotiator, then the problem is complicated because the person will need to go through an elaborate bargaining process just to maintain his or her self-image.

The fair initial offer is characterized by an attempt from the outset to find a solution that is mutually advantageous to both parties. It plays a very integrative role in bringing people together, and the very wise persuader will always try to cast his or her own proposals in ways that seem to benefit the other individual. Whereas some of the four approaches seem to be cast in terms of win-lose situations, the fair initial offer is the ultimate attempt to translate the two positions into win-win situations.

Phase 2: Reconnoitering

Once the negotiating range has been identified, there will be a period in which the negotiators or persuaders seek out those areas that hold the greatest promise for discussion and agreement. It is in this period that the negotiators begin to "jockey for position" by developing their own special tactics. Since there can be no progress between two immovable forces, each side may have to pull back from its first position. The degree to which you do this, of course, varies a great deal with how much inequality exists in bargaining power or strength. A salesperson will rarely have the same kind of clout with a client that a manager will have with a subordinate. However, even in the latter case, a manager may sometimes find it necessary to pull back, compromise, and change his or her mind. To a large extent, this reconnoitering period can be described as a time of reality testing after the initial proposals. It is a period when you can discover just what the real issues and the irreducible positions are.

---

[7]Morton Deutsch and Robert Krauss, "Studies of Interpersonal Bargaining," *Journal of Conflict Resolution* 6 (1962): 52–76. These authors point out that the converse can also be true. Sometimes a hard line can produce enough frustration so that the interviewee may respond aggressively and refuse to make concessions.

Phase 3: Precipitating the Decision Making

In persuasion and negotiation, there is often a great deal of uncertainty over outcomes, and often there can be no conclusion attainable without a crisis. In some cases, one party may resolve to end the negotiation if it appears that no agreement can be reached. Another strategy is to set a time limit or a target date by which a decision will be reached. This has the advantage of bringing pressure on the negotiators to work things out. In some persuasive situations, one person will adopt a defensive strategy of continuing the negotiation so long that the other person eventually gives up. This is often a defensive posture that some individuals take against persistent salespeople, and managers have been known to use it with some of their employees. It is important, however, that some means eventually be used to insist on a decision. Ann Douglas describes this period of resolution as follows:

> The design in bargaining is to force the opponent into making a decision, and for this purpose, it is necessary to narrow more and more the channel through which a party can move, to seal off the tangents which might tempt it to digress, to lure its attention in the desired direction, and to apply pressures which will speed it along toward the ending of the deliberations.[8]

The stages above are descriptive of most persuasive situations, not just formal bargaining sessions. Further, it is useful to remember that we are forever negotiating about jobs, promotions, products, ideas, and positions. Managers obviously have an advantage in negotiating with subordinates on the job, but a knowledge of this process can be useful to you in operating in persuasive situations whether your role is that of a manager or a subordinate. With a knowledge of the overall persuasive and negotiating process in mind, you can now begin to think about a specific instance in which you want to persuade someone. The first step is to plan the interview.

PLANNING THE INTERVIEW

Influence sometimes happens accidentally or with a minimum of effort, but you cannot rely on such happy circumstances. You are much more likely to be successful if you have calculated the variables that are important in each situation.

Determining the Basis for Persuasion or Negotiation

In order to avoid wasting time, determine whether or not there is a basis for your persuasive efforts. If there does not appear to be one, you would be wise not to bring up the topic. If you know, for example, that there is

[8]Ann Douglas, "Peaceful Settlement," p. 81.

no way that your superior is going to buy an idea, your situation will remain better if you do not give your superior the opportunity to turn it down. If, on the other hand, you think that some persuasion may be successful, then make every effort to accomplish it. A key factor is your ability to gauge what is possible, but keep in mind that persuasion sometimes occurs in small increments. The important thing is that it does occur.

Phrasing Your Exact Purpose

At one level, the first objective of negotiation or persuasion is to reach a successful agreement that allows all parties to feel that they have benefitted. In other words, the goal is to make everyone win, or, at least, to make them think that they have won something important. If one party feels that he or she has lost everything and has nothing to gain by supporting the idea or the agreement, then there is a likelihood that it will be violated. Normally, people try to maximize their own interests, and they negotiate to win something for themselves. Sometimes people view the role of persuasion in a very competitive way, and they measure success or failure by how much they have won and the other person has lost. This may not seem as socially acceptable when you read it in print, but it certainly describes the behaviors of many negotiators. Therefore, you ought to recognize that it does exist—and it may be your own orientation. How acceptable this is frequently depends upon your own power and position. In the final analysis, we predict that most persuaders are motivated by a certain selfish aim, and this raises a number of ethical issues about your relationships with other people.

Whichever philosophy of negotiation characterizes you, you need to know exactly what you want from the other party in terms of a change in attitude, belief, or behavior. Generally speaking, it is preferable to select a single specific purpose that you can realistically expect the other person to accept. The more specific the purpose is, the more tightly you can build your case. Furthermore, it is worth repeating that it is probably unwise for you to expect dramatic or sweeping changes on the basis of one interview; realistically, persuasion involves small changes with each new interaction. For this reason, you may need to differentiate between what you really hope to achieve and what you are willing to accept. When negotiations first open, each party may state a position that simply initiates the discussion.

Understanding Your Opponent

One of the most important elements in any negotiation is how much each side knows about the other's value system. The communication maxim to be "receiver oriented" is especially appropriate here. The other party has something that you want—a change in attitude, belief, or behavior—and, therefore, everything that you do must be geared to the other party. In Chapter 2 each person in the interview process was described as being a unique filter of communication, and so it is worth emphasizing that what works in persuading one individual may not work with another. This simple fact dicates that your final strategies must be specially chosen for this individual.

In order to adapt to a person, you must first collect some data about the person. Your overall task is to determine what personal characteristics are relevant to your negotiations and then find out all that you can. In some cases, you will have had prior experiences with the person so that you can calculate how he or she will respond; in other cases, you will need to make a considerable effort to discover the information that you need. Some areas that others have found to be relevant are discussed below.

PHYSICAL CHARACTERISTICS

Age, sex, race, appearance, and build may give you some information about the kinds of experiences that the individual (your opponent) is likely to have had. Age, for example, can be a major influence on the tactics of an insurance salesperson. When you deal with a subordinate, coupling age with an identification of the person's position in the organization may indicate something about the individual's ambitions.

MENTAL CAPACITY

There is probably no more important bit of information that you can know about another person in a negotiating situation than how mentally adept that person is. Your vocabulary, the depth of your explanation, and even the kinds of appeals that you make should be based on a broad assessment of the person's intellectual ability. In other words, how well can this person follow your train of thought, and how might you develop your case so that the person can fully understand and accept it?

ORIENTATION TOWARD SUBJECT MATTER

Has the person been involved in similar negotiations so that you can isolate the person's prevailing opinion? How much does this individual *know* about the subject? How interested is this person in the subject? Some of the best indicators of political, social, or economic beliefs are the reference groups to which a person belongs. Therefore, it could be very important to know the political, social, and economic performances associated with the person's work organization. The reason for knowing the orientation to the subject, perhaps, is obvious. You would make different overtures to someone who opposes your point of view than you would make to someone who already supports it or is neutral.

PAST RESPONSES TO PERSUASION

It will be most helpful for you in predicting future responses to know how the person has responded on similar matters before. People do seem to behave in patterns. Sometimes, you can even discover what strategies they have used in the past or what kinds of objections they are likely to make. In your work situation, it is likely that you can do a fairly credible job of describing just how people with whom you work react in a number of situations. Therefore, you should be aware of it and use it in your planning.

NEEDS

Persuasion seems to be most effective when it satisfies some need that the other party has. Review the needs that are listed in Chapter 2 and associate them with different motivational strategies. For example, whether or not a client will buy may depend upon how well you relate your product to the client's needs. Please note, however, that a seller is not just a need-filler. The exceptional seller is a need creator—someone who makes a person want things so badly that the person develops a psychological need for them. Finally, it is not just the needs of the other party with which you must be concerned. Many negotiators represent constituencies; therefore, you must pay attention to how your product or idea will meet their needs, too.

SOCIOECONOMIC BACKGROUND

Data about group memberships, previous work experiences, job relationships, educational level, and geographical experiences can be invaluable in helping you to determine your opponent's frame of reference. They will also tell you what kinds of experiences you can draw upon in making your case. Finally, they have a great deal of potential for indicating the interviewee's point of view about a variety of subjects.

ATTITUDE TOWARD YOU

Some people are persuaded to accept an idea, not because of the inherent value of the idea, but because of a favorable disposition toward the person proposing the idea. This kind of *source credibility* is invaluable, because it is one of the most powerful persuaders. Give some thought to the other person's image of you; if it is good, use it. Conversely, some good ideas or products are rejected because of the buyer's attitude toward the seller. This often happens also in work situations where the atmosphere is quite competitive or when one of the parties is very insecure. Sometimes, it is not so much that the person is resented as it is that the department or the group whom the person represents is resented. The stereotype in union-management negotiations is such that each representative may be wary of what the other side proposes. They may appreciate and respect

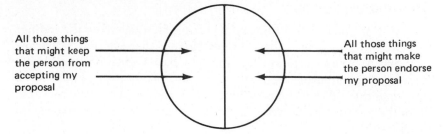

Figure 13.1   Psychological field of a person.

one another as individuals but remain suspicious in the negotiations. Landowners frequently deal quite harshly with right-of-way agents, not because they do not like the agent personally, but because they do not like the organization that the agent represents or the power the organization has to do something against them.

Credibility is so important that you need to develop ways of cultivating it both in and out of the interview situation.

Analyzing Your Own Position

Being thoroughly prepared involves not only being able to support your position but also being able to predict some of the negative arguments that can be used against you, that is, anticipating the objections and the problems. As a strategy, it is useful to acknowledge legitimate objections and then to demonstrate that they are not as important as some of the items that you support. Sometimes we talk about a person's *psychological field.* This simply refers to all the forces within a person's "field" that tend to sway the person one way or the other. For important situations you could represent the person's psychological field as shown in Figure 13.1. For example, suppose that you are trying to get a subordinate to transfer from the Kansas City offices of the company in which you are working to the headquarters in New York City. You might begin to anticipate some objections the subordinate might make, such as higher cost of living, longer commuting time, separation from family, increased taxes, and so on. At the same time, you might begin to make the transfer attractive by emphasizing the prestige of the position, excitement of the city, higher pay, and so forth.

A concentrated effort should be made to determine your opponent's high and low positions. This will help you refine your own position. It is clearly a great coup to learn what your opponent will settle for prior to any negotiation. You can then negotiate with force and persuade the person to accept his or her bottom position without fear of breaking off the negotiation.

Choosing the Setting

Not every persuader has the luxury of making decisions about the setting. Salespeople, for example, have to get clients wherever and whenever they can. As a manager, however, you may have a great deal of leeway. Even as a subordinate, there are times and places that may be more propitious than others for approaching your superior. Whenever possible, make the setting work for you. The following are some things you can do to achieve this.

First, ensure concentration and undivided attention both for yourself and the other person. The ideal situation is to be free from interruptions and to have enough time to explore one another's thinking in detail.

Second, choose a time that is mutually convenient. It is a wise tactic never to introduce an idea until you actually have time to sell it. There have been many people who unfortunately injected an idea when they knew they could not develop it fully, and then later on, when they came back to it, the other person said, "We've already discussed that."

Third, where you have the meeting may influence the interaction. Having it on your own turf may save you time and money and may also be psychologically intimidating to the other person. This gives you the upper hand and it is why many managers choose to use their own offices. An additional advantage is that you have all your materials right at your fingertips.

Meeting in a neutral setting may give the impression of bargaining from good faith. It generally reduces the pressures and may give the appearance of fairness. It is easier to develop rapport with the other party under these circumstances. Meeting away from your office can be used deliberately to give yourself a built-in excuse for delay. Then, you can avoid an immediate response by saying that you "need time to check out some other materials."

After you have made some of the plans that have been discussed above, you are ready to build your specific case for the actual encounter.

BUILDING A CASE

The very essence of persuasion is case-building and the ability to explain the case to someone else in an effective manner. Much of your case can come from your initial planning, but also much if it will have to be fashioned from within the interview itself as the two of you interact. As you begin to think about your case, keep the following principles in mind.

1. In the most successful persuasion and negotiation situations, most people think of themselves as winners.
2. People look out for their own best interests. Everyone is the center of his or her own world, and each person's perceptions and

interests differ from one another. Consequently, if you want to persuade someone, use that person's reasons and interests, not your reasons and your interests.

3. People are persuaded in a variety of ways: (a) by the credibility of the source, (b) through emotional appeals with which they can identify, and (c) by logical or rational facts that can be used to back up a position.

Selecting the Strongest Arguments

If you have already made a comprehensive analysis of the other party, you will have identified some approaches that will be stronger than others. Omit those that you particularly like but that the other party is not likely to accept. Furthermore, listen analytically during the interview to see how the other party is reacting to specific points.

Using a Variety of Supporting Materials

There is an advantage in having more than one way to support a point. It makes your argument more interesting and more convincing. Furthermore, you will find that you can adapt better to a given individual if you are prepared to support your point from several different directions. Consequently, several common ways of building support are listed below.

FACTUAL INFORMATION
It is difficult to argue against empirical data and statistics. Your research should give you the latest numerical data as well as fortify you with some specific instances of things that have happened. Above all, your materials should be up to date.

EXAMPLES
Particular instances not only give concrete data but also have an emotional appeal associated with them. For example, while a survey about accidents has a certain logical impact, knowing about John Smith's specific accident may make a stronger and more emotional impact. Examples have a way of making your point more interesting, too.

COMPARISONS AND CONTRASTS
There is utility in pointing out how two situations are alike or different. Making comparisons can be particularly useful in helping an individual gain some insight into a new area. Suppose, for example, that you know topic X very well but that you have had no experience with topic Y. Anyone trying to persuade you about Y would do well to show how Y compares with X.

TESTIMONY

One of the most frequently used ways of making ideas credible is to be able to report that someone else supports it. Because you will frequently want to build a case outside your own recognized expertise, you may find it useful to collect statements from authorities who agree with you. They may agree with your position entirely, but they may be effective because their expertise is recognized while yours is not. This is how many organizations use consultants—to give credence to something that someone in the organization wants to do.

If you choose to use testimony, be certain that the other party recognizes the person testifying as an expert. Currently, it seems that you can find an expert to reinforce almost any position on any topic.

VISUAL AIDS

A picture or a diagram often helps to simplify verbal explanations, and the number and the quality of visual aids are often used as a gauge of your professionalism. Research has demonstrated that two channels are better than one in communicating. If your opponent can see your case as well as hear it, the message is likely to be better understood. Consequently, pictures, graphs, and visual explanations should be one of your greatest tools in building a case.

While these ways of supporting your case represent different kinds of materials, no one of them has any special magic. You must judge their adequacy in terms of several dimensions: (1) they need to be timely—the most recent evidence that is available; (2) they must be sufficient in the sense that they carry enough weight to make an impact; (3) they need to be the best evidence available; (4) they need to take into consideration that the topic has more than one side. While you need not treat both sides equally, your evidence will be more acceptable to intelligent, well-educated people and those who disagree with you if you at least recognize that the other side does exist. One-sided arguments seem to work well with the uneducated and the people who already agree with you.

Structuring the Evidence

Setting the agenda is important. You determine what will be presented and in what order. It is the means by which you focus on the things you will present that are most likely to sell your case and minimize its weaknesses, if any.

Since persuasion and negotiation focus essentially on solving a problem, the Dewey reflective thinking pattern may be very useful for both your analysis and your presentation:

Define the problem.
Analyze the major issues.

List alternative solutions.
Suggest criteria for effectiveness.
Choose the best alternative as your solution.

Another useful strategy is to raise questions first and supply answers later. In this way, you may find out something about the other party's feelings before you begin to make your "pitch."

One of the most basic considerations in building your case is to keep it clear by presenting one point at a time. Too many people confuse their clients by trying to cover everything at once so that each point is covered superficially.

MANAGING THE INTERVIEW

Planning and building a case are important strategies that will provide the kind of fortification you will need for a persuasive interaction. Your ultimate success, however, will depend upon how well you can manage the interview, and your management of the interview will depend upon how well you can develop certain communication skills that are discussed below.

Building Rapport

Your relationship with your opponent has a persuasive impact on the negotiating process, and rapport is the good feeling or warmth that exists between two people. Although it may be present because of some prior interactions, it should be strengthened from the very beginning of the interview. Obviously, there are times when the two parties are quite antagonistic, too. Nevertheless, a degree of rapport may be instrumental in achieving a basis for negotiation or persuasion. One way that you can try to achieve it is by establishing some common ground with the other person. Basically, this happens when you can call attention to ways in which you and the other person are similar. These similarities may be shared beliefs or values, shared experiences, shared reference groups, or shared goals. They can be nonwork related as well as work related. The fact is that most of us tend to be receptive to people who are "like us" in important ways, and this is often a potent force in building up some common identification. You can also call attention to similarities in such subtle ways as by complimenting the person (thus showing that you have similar tastes) or by identifying a common gripe (such as government interference).

There are two specific methods of establishing a common ground, which have been identified from studies on persuasion, and these are widely used.

The "yes-yes" and the "yes-but" approaches are variants of the same technique. In both cases, little or no hint of any disagreement . . . is expressed until after a whole string of assertions is communicated about which agreement is sure. The object is to establish a habit of assent, to get receivers nodding "Yes," "That's right," "You said it" either aloud or to themselves. Once this is done, the audience will presumably be receptive to more controversial assertions.

Using the "yes-but" approach, persuaders begin by noting those arguments of the opposition with which they can agree, and then having shown how fair minded they are, they offer a series of "buts" that constitute the heart of their case.[9]

Stressing Your Credibility

If you attempt to persuade someone, you are in fact a seller, and you must remember that one of the most potent forces in selling is who you are. In the interaction within an interview, you may need to build your own credibility, and there are several ways in which you can do this.

SHOWING CONSIDERATION FOR YOUR CLIENT

Any sign that you have your client's best interests at heart is likely to increase your standing with that individual. Little things like offering coffee or making the interviewee comfortable have an impact. You can also use questions to show your consideration. For example, even if you have an appointment, you might still check with the other person by asking, "Is this still a convenient time for you?" Another question that compliments the other person is, "I have heard you are really good at _____, and I'm really interested in that. How did you develop this interest?" If the person is a stranger to you, even asking questions about the person's experiences and interests is a means of getting the person to talk about himself or herself and of developing rapport. In this way, you demonstrate a respect for the person as an individual.

DEMONSTRATING YOUR EXPERTISE

You need not be a braggart to let the other person know that you have some expertise. One of the best ways of demonstrating this is by showing a thorough knowledge and understanding of the problem area. It is useful, however, to introduce other references to your experiences and talents rather casually, too, unless it is really blatant. An example would be, "When I was working on a similar problem with TWA, we found _____." In addition to making a statement about the problem, you have let the other person know that you have some experience in the area.

[9]Simons, *Persuasion*, p. 143.

Focusing the Interview

Limiting the agenda is a widely used tactic to keep the interactions within specific bounds. In effect, you try to include items that will benefit your position and to minimize those that would strengthen the other person's position. Mutually agreeing to avoid a topic is a tactic used by negotiators who are representing sides with deep philosophical divisions but who must come to terms to work together. This was done during World War II when the United States and Russia felt it necessary to cooperate in order to defeat Germany.

Another dimension to this problem is to control digressions. It is important that you channel the discussion. The person who controls the topics being discussed actually controls the interview.

Choosing the Best Approach

While there are an infinite variety of approaches to influence people, they generally fall on a continuum between a *hard-sell* and a *soft-sell* approach. Neither is inherently better than the other. We all have preferences about what makes us comfortable, but the final selection needs to be made on the basis of what will work with the other party.

Basically, the hard-sell approach is characterized as aggressive and evangelistic: The pace is quick, considerable pressure is applied, and the person virtually barrages the client with evidence and arguments. Usually, not much attention is paid to objections or to other issues, but the person's main points are restated and reinforced over and over again. Frequently, the hard-sell approach works through sheer force, since people are intimidated by it. Finally, it proceeds from an arrangement in which the persuader states exactly what he or she wants to achieve.

In the soft-sell approach the client is likely to be encouraged to talk more, his or her objections are explored more deeply, and the persuader *suggests* new information in a relaxed, low-pressured way. The structure may be more inductive, since the persuader tries to lead the other person to draw a conclusion for himself or herself. Such interviews are likely to take more time than those allowed in the hard-sell approach. Clearly, there are times when the soft-sell approach works, and they may be circumstances when the persuader already has high credibility so that whatever is said carries a lot of weight.

Articulating Your Case

If you have planned well, you should be quite articulate about your ideas, and you should be able to present them clearly. A persuasive interview is not a speech that can be programmed and rehearsed thoroughly; however, many people have found it useful to practice through role playing.

In this way you are forced to articulate your ideas, and you discover some of the gaps that you may not have anticipated. It does not take much time and effort to write out a description of the client's role for a colleague or a friend to play, and the results may be well worth the time that you take to do so.

Confidence and Persistence

Generally, you cannot be bashful and very persuasive at the same time. Therefore, your manner needs to reflect a certain degree of confidence in your ideas and in yourself. A part of your confidence will enable you to overcome a number of "stoppers" that people have learned to use, such as the following:

> "We've tried that before and it didn't work."
> "We don't have time."
> "I know that this just will not work."
> "Management would never buy this."
> "Why don't we give this more thought later."
> "This sounds good in theory, but. . . ."
> "I don't want to be bothered with this."
> "We're doing all right the way we are."

How would you react if someone made these statements to you just as you started explaining one of your "best" ideas? The example below describes the actual experience of one engineer.

> During a meeting in which I was describing a problem, my supervisor told me to "shut up." He then added, "You are wrong. The unit department head told me that there is no problem. Therefore, this meeting is over." All four people left.
>
> After thinking about the incident for 30 minutes, I went back to his office and stated, "George, hear me out. You always listen to both sides of a story before you make up your mind, and that's why you are a good manager. I know that you have personal problems and you're upset, but you shouldn't let that affect your job." He sat back and told me about his problems with his son. After he completed the story, he apologized and rescheduled the meeting for later that day. At the beginning of the meeting he apologized to all of us, explaining that personal problems had clouded his thinking. I then presented my case, and the other section heads confirmed my analysis.

Not every situation turns out this well, and it is apparent that every persuader takes some risk in being persistent. You will note that the person made some very strategic comments when he approached his superior. He complimented him and also referred to the fact that he knew something else was bothering him. These two overtures seemed to build a little source credibility with the superior, who then became more responsive.

Listening and Probing

The persuader is often cast as the one who does most of the talking, but this is not necessarily the case. In fact, Dean Pruitt and Steven Lewis found a positive correlation between successful negotiation and the frequency with which negotiators ask each other for their reactions to proposals.[10] Feedback is important to any persuader, because a persuader constantly needs to address his or her remarks to what the other party is thinking, accepting, or rejecting at the moment. Sometimes you must probe in order to get this feedback, and the skill with which you probe gives the impression that you are indeed listening and are attempting to understand the other person's position better.

Listening is very important in another sense. Sometimes persuaders mistakenly feel that nothing is happening unless they are talking. This view overlooks the fact that people often have to work through a problem for themselves and that they need time and silence to do the thinking. Furthermore, a lot of persuasion occurs when the opponent has to articulate his or her own ideas. This is one of the dangers of the hard-sell approach: it may not give a person the time required to deal with the problem internally. For example, a marketing manager for a television company reinforced this point very well with her statement, "One of the things you have to learn and also one of the hardest to teach is when to shut up. At some point, the client just has to deal with it himself, and the more you say, the worse it gets."

DEALING WITH PROBLEMS

Persuasive and negotiation interviews have special problems that arise. The following are ones that tend to occur frequently.

Talking Down

Wanting to be persuasive or win a negotiation often causes one party to try to attain power or an upper hand over the other. You will note that this is directly contradictory to what we said about using source credibility as a persuasive tool. Nevertheless, it does occur, and people begin to com-

[10]Dean G. Pruitt and Steven A. Lewis, "The Psychology of Integrative Bargaining," in Druckman (Ed.), *Negotiations*, p. 157.

municate in ways that actually become obstacles to achieving their goals. One of the most common devices is to begin to "talk down" to the interviewee. This is done by a combination of tone of voice and special phrases. While taking away the condescending tone of voice may render the following phrases more neutral, it would still be instructive for you to examine them.

1. "You do understand this, don't you?"
2. "Of course, you know that. . . . "
3. "*Obviously,* this is not possible."
4. "You *certainly* don't expect us to. . . . "
5. "Everybody knows that. . . . "
6. "This plan was developed by highly qualified people."
7. "Let me tell you this much."
8. "I'm authorized to allow you. . . . "
9. "Now, let's be *honest* with each other."
10. "I'll explain that again."[11]

The problem may lie not so much with the meanings of the words as with the attitudes that they betray. Most people resist being thought of as inferior; therefore, they would be very reluctant to establish rapport with or to be persuaded by anyone who tries, consciously or unconsciously, to make them feel inferior. Therefore, you need to omit phrases that inadvertently talk down to the other person.

Rushing

A good persuader must be patient. It takes time for a person to reorient himself or herself. You may need to plant the seed in an interview, feed it in another, and reap the final harvest at a later time.

SEPARATING THE INTERPARTY AND THE INTERPERSONAL CLIMATE

Conflict is often the reason for negotiation. Sometimes you may represent one group in negotiating with a representative of another group. The intergroup antagonisms and differences may be great, but the emotions between the individual negotiators need to be controlled.[12] The negotiators need to be civil and respectful, while persuading as vigorously as possible.

[11]Charles Pyron, *Communication and Negotiation* (American Right of Way Association, Inc., 1972), p. 300.
[12]Ann Douglas, "What Can Research Tell You About Mediation?" *Labor Law Journal* (August 1955): 548.

Use of a Third Party

It is common practice to rely on a third party when crucial negotiations break down. This person can be a friend, a fellow employee, an ombudsman, a counselor, a mediator, or a judge. You will note an increasing order of formality in this list. Our intent is not to tell you how to work with a neutral third party; this is a study in itself. However, it is useful to keep in mind that bringing in a moderator is a well-respected technique.

One specific way in which a third party is used by subordinates was discovered by Cal Downs and Charles Conrad.[13] Subordinates who are successful in confronting their bosses are the ones who could bring in a respected third person to corroborate their views.

Overstatement

Be careful that you are judicious in making your claims. One poor overstatement may reduce your credibility so that all of your arguments are perceived as tainted. For this reason, it is advisable to be very careful about using words like "all," "never," and "everybody." Generally, you should be able to find some way of qualifying what you say and still be forceful.

SPECIAL PERSUASIVE TACTICS

There are a number of tactics that persuaders attempt to use on one another. They are described below in a nonjudgmental way. Whether or not they fit your own ethical orientation, they have been effective on some people. On the other hand, these descriptions can serve the purpose of identifying tactics that are frequently used *on you*. Therefore, it may be helpful to you to recognize exactly what is happening.

Apparent Withdrawal

Apparent withdrawal is a bluffing tactic designed to make the other person believe that you are prepared to terminate the negotiations because you have other alternatives. One example of this occurs when a subordinate lets his or her superior know that he or she is discussing a job with another company when asking for a raise or a promotion with the hope that the superior will assume that he or she will leave if certain concessions are not obtained. Sometimes the best uses of apparent withdrawal occur when the other person finds out your alternatives by "accident."

[13]Cal W. Downs and Charles Conrad, "A Critical Incident Study of Superior-Subordinate Relations," an unpublished paper delivered to the Academy of Management, San Francisco, 1978.

For example, a union negotiator might order strike signs from the same printer that deals with the company.

Waiting Game

When one of the negotiators makes an offer or states a position, the other person may try not to respond quickly. He or she may ask some questions but will not state a negotiating position. The silence or the lack of a response may induce the other party to keep talking and to change position. This is commonly used in salary negotiations. Once the offer has been made, the subordinate may avoid a quick response. Frequently, the offer is revised upward.

Asking for More Than You Want

Because they realize that they are not likely to get all that they ask for, many people pad their initial request. This allows them to trade-off some of their requests for concessions with the negotiator. We suspect that most budget requests are made on this basis.

Leading the Respondent

Through the choice of words and leading questions, a negotiator can often direct the other party to the position that he or she wants the person to take. If a person does not like a certain idea, you can use words with negative connotations to describe it so that the other person will feel negative about it, too. Similarly, giving a person only two choices when in reality there are more is a way of leading the person. A lot of salespeople try this technique.

Getting on the Bandwagon

Sometimes negotiators attempt to get people to do or to accept something because others are doing it or accepting it. Sometimes, persuaders even quote statistics to show that a majority of people are doing it or accepting it. Sometimes, it is enough just to choose a few respected people. For example, we know a company that is very sensitve to what IBM and American Express do in a certain category. If you want to sell them on an idea, all you need to do is point out that these two companies are doing it.

Rhetorical Questions

The persuader may ask a question and then answer it for the other party. A series of these questions can be used to advance an entire argument.

THIS CHAPTER IN PERSPECTIVE

Persuasion and negotiation exist in an infinite number of varieties, and you will probably engage in these processes frequently. Therefore, it will be well for you to think about the best way of approaching each situation. In a sense, this chapter merely represents the beginning of your study of these topics, for there is a great deal of literature about persuasion, conflict resolution, bargaining, and negotiation that can be studied with profit. We encourage you to do so.

As you try to put this chapter in perspective, there are four points that need to be kept in mind.

1. Conflict is not necessarily dysfunctional. Frequently, it brings out the best in people and leads them to the most refined conclusions that can be reached. There will be an element of conflict in most periods of negotiation and persuasion, and hopefully you will be able to view it positively.

2. Two important variables in persuasive situations are (a) the ambiguity of the issue or situation and (b) the power relationships between individuals. As you try to map your persuasive strategies, try to take into account the differences of ambiguity and power.

3. Persuasion can be planned. We frequently think of it in terms of major advertising and sales campaigns. Nevertheless, it is possible to relate much of what we know about persuasion to interpersonal relations. Therefore, you can choose among alternative strategies and tactics.

4. Perhaps a good way of ending this chapter is to raise ethical questions about what you do. To what extent are you taking unfair advantage of others? If you were the other person, would you want the person to do the same thing to you? There are lots of questions to be asked, but there are few easy answers. Furthermore, our experience has taught us that we would not all agree on the answers either. Nevertheless, it is something for you to think about as a backdrop for your interactions.

PROJECTS

1. Survey a group of salespeople to identify the kinds of persuasive strategies that they find effective.

2. Discuss the ethical considerations that ought to guide a person's persuasion or negotiation. To what extent do situational variables make a difference?

3. Analyze your own receptivity to persuasion. Are you influenced more by facts, people's credibility, or emotional considerations?

4. Prepare a report on the research findings in conflict resolution.

5. How much information should you reveal when you are trying to persuade someone? Should you tell them everything on both sides?

6. Survey a group of subordinates to discover what techniques they have found to be useful in persuading their superiors. How does the power relationship affect their choices?

7. Write role playing situations for the following situations and have people role play them.
   a. asking for a raise
   b. selling a subordinate on a lateral transfer involving a move to another city
   c. selling a product, such as a book or a car
   d. persuading a subordinate to change a procedure in his or her job
   e. negotiating a settlement of a grievance with an employee

8. You may find it useful to take each of the situations above and analyze the different strategies on the basis of the important variables in each situation.

Part III
THE INTERVIEWS
USED IN
THE MASS MEDIA

The following three chapters deal with specialized interview formats
and techniques utilized by people in the mass media—magazines
newspapers, radio, and television. The chapters approach the interview
situation from the point of view of the person who holds the balance
of power or controls the interview situation. The role of the interviewer
dominates the chapters on journalistic interviewing and interviewing
for radio and television. The interviewee, however, becomes the
dominant figure in the chapter on the news conference, because this is a
unique situation and the unwritten contract entered into between the
interviewer and the interviewee does not necessarily hold true in this
particular situation. The contract is generally an unspoken one, but the
assumption is that if an interview is granted, there will be cooperation
in most areas and answers to most of the questions asked.

   We fear that the three chapters may become the exclusive reading
of journalists until a crisis emerges at corporate headquarters.
Businesspeople, lawyers, and doctors can see immediate relevancy in
the other chapters but not in the following three chapters devoted to
interviewing for the mass media. However, during 1978, attorneys and

executives from Ford Motor Company and Firestone Tire and Rubber Company faced hostile media situations when the two firms were charged with covering up major product defects that resulted in highway fatalities. In most of the encounters the attorneys or the company executives came off second best, or even worse.

The point to be made, but not belabored, is that journalists interview someone. This someone could be you the businessperson, attorney, or doctor who is thrust into a newsworthy situation and now must respond to the public media. We are relatively sure that the pathologist at the Parkland Memorial Hospital in Dallas, Texas, in November 1964, probably assumed that he would never have a major contact with journalists or be involved in a news conference. Lee Harvey Oswald certainly changed this perception.

Chapter 14
Journalistic Interviews

Whatever his title, no journalist ever forgets he is basically a reporter. And no reporter ever forgets he is basically an interviewer.[1]

Hugh Sherwood

Journalists spend the majority of their working hours gathering information for news and feature stories. The information for these news and feature stories comes from (1) direct observation of an event, (2) secondary or primary sources, such as police records and reports, (3) unsolicited information, such as press releases or people calling with tips or story ideas, and (4) the journalistic interview.[2] Journalists train themselves to use public records and to observe carefully, but too often they neglect to train themselves in the craft of interviewing (assuming they already know how). This is wrong, because even some experienced reporters still do not understand that interviewing is a craft that can be learned, polished, and improved through practice. The journalistic interview is an integral part of the news reporting process from those first casual interviews when the journalist ascertains that there really is a story to the final rewrite when the story is virtually completed but the journalist is looking for quotes or anecdotes that will illustrate the facts and flesh out the story. The jour-

[1]Hugh Sherwood, *The Journalistic Interview* (New York: Harper & Row, Publishers, 1972).
[2]Eugene J. Webb and Jerry Salancik, "The Interview or the Only Wheel in Town," *Journalism Monographs* II (November 1966): 1.

nalistic interview is the primary way of gathering those bits and pieces of information and fact that form a news story.

Journalistic interviews fall into three broad types:

1. information gathering
2. quotation and anecdote gathering
3. personality or creative interviews

Journalists constantly interview people in order to gather information even when they are unaware that they are doing it. Virtually all news is based on a type of authority, and journalists are always trying to talk to people who were involved in some event or can speak with authority. Just taking a simple police report over the telephone involves interviewing the police clerk. The clerk is asked the traditional questions: Who, What, Where, When, How, and Why? The questioning is so casual that it is considered merely a routine telephone conversation and not an interview, but it is an interview.

The second type of interview that journalists are constantly conducting is quote and anecdote gathering. Quotes and anecdotes flesh out a news or a feature story by revealing the human elements, emotions, and feelings that others experience as they watch or participate in an event. Reading or hearing how others reacted and felt involves people in the news or feature story in a way that reporting simple facts cannot do. Readers are able to identify with the feelings and emotions of other people. The historian Bruce Catton makes the Civil War live in a way that few historians can because he describes history through the eyes of people who were there by using their own words (quotations) and personal stories (anecdotes). Gathering quotes and anecdotes is generally considered an extension of the information gathering interview. The reporter at the scene of a bank robbery or an accident quickly gathers the five W's for the story framework and then finds eyewitnesses or people involved in the event who can talk about what happened and how they reacted when they witnessed the accident or bank robbery. Others then can experience the news story vicariously through the eyes and emotions of people who were there.

The third type of interview that journalists conduct is the personality or creative interview. This interview emphasizes the personality, opinions, emotions, and feelings of an individual rather than specific facts or events, although facts and events may be important. This type of interview will go into great depth and may be conducted over a period of days, weeks, or even months. *Playboy Magazine's* interviews with prominent people may take weeks or months to complete, and the interviewer probes deeply into the character and opinions of the person being interviewed. During these long, creative interview sessions, the interviewer may develop such a strong rapport with the interviewee that barriers are dropped and great insights may be gained. Such was the case when a president-elect admitted to having "lust in his heart" or when a senator admitted his deep fears of being assassinated.[3]

The three basic types of interviews are similar in many respects, and they are not mutually exclusive. All three interviews have the overall goal of gaining information, and the interviewer must go through the same steps in preparing for either of the three types of interviews. The differences among the interviews lies in their specific goals and what will be done with the information. Information gathering interviews are primarily looking for the facts—the traditional five W's of journalism. Once the facts are gathered, the interviewer might extend the interview and try to get quotes or anecdotes that illustrate the facts or make the story more interesting. The personality or creative interview is designed to explore an individual's attitudes, feelings, and desires. Tonight's lead story in the newspaper stressing hard news could contain the results of information gathering interviews. A feature story or an in-depth story inside the newspaper might contain information gathering interviews and quotations or anecdotes to liven up a news story that might otherwise be dull or stodgy if the story only presented facts. The results of a creative or a personality interview can be seen in *Playboy, More,* or *People* magazines.

THE ROLE OF THE INTERVIEWER

Hugh Sherwood says that the interviewer's role is to be a "catalyst" who provides the right questions at the right time to get facts, anecdotes, and emotional responses from the person being interviewed.[4] The interviewer is the key element in determining if the interview fails or succeeds. To someone observing the successful reporter-interviewer, the interview may look and feel like a casual conversation. It is not. The successful reporter-interviewer has a specific purpose for conducting the interview and guides the interview with this purpose in mind: probing areas, shaping and forming questions, and listening intently to the interviewee's answers for hints and clues for follow-up questions to ask or areas to probe. The reporter-interviewer is the reader's surrogate and as such he or she must never forget that success, in large part, is measured by the ability to gain and conduct good interviews.

SIX STEPS TO SUCCESSFUL INTERVIEWS

Conducting a successful journalistic interview is not a mechanical procedure, but there seem to be certain basic steps that lead to success more often than not. The steps that many journalists use are (1) defining the purpose of the interview, (2) obtaining the interview, (3) researching the

---

[3]"Interview with Jimmy Carter," *Playboy* (November 1976): 86.
[4]Sherwood, *Journalistic Interview*, p. 19.

interview topic or the person to be interviewed, (4) meeting the interviewee and establishing rapport, (5) determining strategies and questions, and (6) ending the interview.

Defining the Purpose

As elementary as it may seem, it is surprising how many journalists walk into an interview without a clearly defined purpose other than to question the interviewee. The interviewer may know whom they are going to interview and the background of the person, but he or she may not have a purpose other than to get a few good quotations. This situation occurs most when the interviewee is prominent or widely known or when the reporter is assigned an interview and thinks that there is not enough time to prepare.

Define the specific purpose for interviewing someone in concrete terms. Being able to write down the general and specific purpose for an interview will give you the mental direction you need to research the topic or person and construct questions that will cover the areas you wish to discuss. A clearly defined purpose will make the five steps in the interview process easier to accomplish. Without clearly defining the purpose for the interview, you stand a chance of becoming involved in a rambling conversation that covers a lot of ground without getting into much depth in any one area. You may come away with a usable story, but this will be due to luck or the fact that the interviewee is experienced in being interviewed and knows the process better than you do. Without a clearly defined purpose, you cannot do an effective job of research and questioning and this means that the interviewee will be able to control the interview and lead you into specific areas he or she wishes to discuss.

For example, let us say that your editor assigns you to interview the heavyweight boxing champion Leon Spinks. Spinks, a 24-year-old fighter with limited professional boxing experience, defeated Mohammed Ali, a boxer of great skill who had been heavyweight champion for 15 years before losing the title in 1978. Spinks won the boxing title but was later stripped of the boxing crown by the World Boxing Council for not signing a contract to fight the ranking heavyweight contender, Ken Norton. However, the rival World Boxing Association continued to recognize Spinks as the world heavyweight champion. While all of this maneuvering was going on, Spinks was evicted from his St. Louis, Missouri, apartment for allegedly not paying his rent, he was arrested several times for traffic violations, and he was also charged by police with having marijuana and cocaine in his car. (Spinks was later found innocent of the drug charges).

There would be so much to talk about that a two- or three-hour interview with Leon Spinks could end up being a superficial one if you tried to discuss everything. You would first have to limit the areas you wished to cover by defining the purpose. A quick analysis of the situation would indicate that many journalists have already written about Spinks winning the title and how he trained, so this would be old ground to dig in. There also have been several major news stories about Spinks's boyhood in St. Louis, so this too would be old news. However, a new area to cover in an interview with Spinks might be his life after he won the heavyweight boxing title. You might create a list of ideas that related to your overall purpose of (1) writing a news story about Leon Spinks and (2) obtaining an interview with Leon Spinks. A sample outline is shown below.

I. (General Purpose) Get fresh information, feelings, anecdotes illustrating the changes in Spinks's life-style and goals following his boxing match with Mohammed Ali.
A. (Specific Purpose) Discuss changes in Spinks's life-style.
B. (Specific Purpose) Discuss reasons for Spinks's troubles with the law.
C. (Specific Purpose) Explore Spinks's feelings about the future as a boxer and as a human being.

A well-defined statement of purpose would provide you with an overall guide or outline that could be expanded to include specific areas to discuss, as well as specific questions to ask.

Obtaining the Interview

The best way to go about getting an interview is to ask for it. As obvious as this is, it is surprising how often interesting people who might be willing to give an interview are never asked. The reporter may feel that the subject or situation is so sensitive that the person would not want to be interviewed, but you never know until you ask and give the person a chance to accept or refuse. A few years ago a rather bizarre murder case came to a close when a prominent, certified public accountant was convicted of murdering another accountant. The newspapers, radio, and television stations in the city all carried major stories on the preliminary hearing, trial, and verdict. Only one television station had an interview with the convicted man as he sat in his cell a few hours after being sentenced to death. The interview was very dramatic. The camera showed the convicted man sitting on his bunk, his feet up, chain-smoking cigarettes while he answered all of the reporter's questions in a slow, quiet voice.

The reporters covering the trial later said that they never thought they could get into the jail or that the man would be willing to talk so they never bothered to ask for an interview. The television reporter who got the interview said he had not known if it could be done but he had thought he would ask. The County Sheriff had said it was okay with him if the convicted man agreed to the interview. The reporter said he could not believe how easy it was.

When asking for an interview, a journalist should

1. identify himself or herself
2. identify the news organization that the journalist represents
3. state the purpose for the interview
4. tell how the interview will be used
5. confirm where the interview will take place

A telephone call requesting an appointment for an interview might sound like this:

INTERVIEWEE: Hello, Mr. Jones speaking.

INTERVIEWER: Mr. Jones, my name is Phil Brown and I'm a news reporter for the *Saline Free Press*.

INTERVIEWEE: Yes . . .

INTERVIEWER: The reason for my call is that we are going to be doing a series of newspaper stories on the school bond levy that comes before the voters this November. I have already talked with school superintendent Smith about the levy and now I would like to talk with you for our story sometime next week, if possible. I would need about an hour for the interview. My schedule is flexible, and I could meet you whenever you prefer.

INTERVIEWEE: Now, this is for your story on the bond levy, right?

INTERVIEWER: Yes sir, that's right.

INTERVIEWEE: Well, you know, I had a reporter from your paper talk with me about a year ago, and the story got twisted and she quoted me as saying things that I never said.

INTERVIEWER: Mr. Jones, I don't know what you were interviewed about, but I'm not in the habit of making mistakes and I want to represent your feelings on this issue. I really don't think the story would be complete and accurate unless I was able to talk with you and include what you think about the bond levy.

INTERVIEWEE: Hmmm. Well, how about my office this Tuesday at 9:00 A.M.

INTERVIEWER: That's fine. Your office this Tuesday at 9:00 in the morning. Now, is your office still in the Dudley Towers?

INTERVIEWEE: No. We moved about two months ago to the new shopping center on Oak Street.

INTERVIEWER: Okay, I know where that is. Thank you, Mr. Jones. I'll see you at nine on Tuesday.

Since you are requesting the interview, the time and location of the interview should be at the interviewee's convenience. Meeting on territory familiar to the interviewee would also put the person at ease and make your job easier.

One technique for getting to talk with a busy executive or politician who is never "in" is to telephone the person person-to-person, long distance. Long-distance telephone calls seem urgent, and most secretaries or switchboard operators will transfer a long-distance call to the person you are trying to reach rather than say the person is not available at the moment. One Washington, D.C., reporter drives into the Maryland suburbs to call politicians in Washington just so the long-distance operator will place the telephone call and deal with the politician's secretary or assistant. This reporter says that it almost always works, and once the politician gets on the telephone the reporter can usually convince the politician to meet for an interview.

Be prepared to sell the idea of an interview or a meeting, although in the vast majority of instances obtaining an interview is as easy as writing a letter or telephoning and asking for the interview. Many people like to be interviewed, and they are flattered that a reporter thinks enough of them or their opinion to put their ideas or opinions in the newspaper. It satisfies a need that most people have to express their viewpoints. Many prominent people, especially politicians, are used to being interviewed, and they consider it a part of their life. These people would probably be worried if reporters stopped asking for interviews, because it would indicate that their opinions and ideas were not esteemed or wanted. There are those people, however, who are afraid of being interviewed or do not want to be brought to the public's attention. These people may not have been interviewed before, and they fear the experience because they do not know what is expected of them or how to act. The person on whom you may have to use your greatest sales technique is the person who has been involved in an embarrassing situation or experience that he or she would prefer not to talk about. Leon Spinks, for example, might refuse an interview because he knows that eventually he would be questioned about his driving problems or his being charged with possession of marijuana and cocaine.

Try to think of reasons why someone might refuse you an interview and then think up answers or strategies for overcoming their reasons before you contact the person. There are some basic reasons, though, why people consent to being interviewed by journalists:

1. to get personal recognition or publicity
2. to tell their side of the story or controversy
3. to tell the truth or to clarify an issue
4. to educate or espouse a particular cause
5. to help the reporter who needs accurate information
6. to help the reporter who may get in trouble if he or she cannot get an interview

A common reason that people give interviews is to gain personal recognition or publicity for a cause, organization, or charity. Politicians and labor leaders, for example, know that their personal popularity can mean continuation in their present position or help in winning a political or labor battle. An author or actor knows that personal popularity can mean selling more books or greater box office receipts. Personal recognition or publicity for a charitable cause is another strong motivating factor as to why people give interviews. Actor-comic Jerry Lewis consents to interviews, personal appearances, and television interviews every year to gain publicity for the muscular dystrophy campaign.

Telling their side of a controversy is a major motivation for people consenting to talk with reporters. Whenever there is a controversy that gets news coverage, the people involved in the controversy generally want to explain their side of the issue to clarify issues or explain what happened. Usually, the greater the conflict or the issue is, the more people want to speak out on the issue and make sure that others know how they think and feel.

Politicians, teachers, experts in certain areas, or people pushing a particular cause or philosophy may be motivated to give interviews if they think it is a chance to educate or influence others. A union leader trying to get a four-day work week for union members would probably welcome a chance to educate people why the four-day work week would be better than the present five-day work week. If you approach this person correctly and explain that many people do not understand the issues involved, the union leader would probably consent to being interviewed.

For almost any individual there is some motivational key that would get the person to grant an interview. It might be an appeal to their honesty, patriotism, or a chance to educate, gain publicity, or tell his or her side of the story. One strategy that has worked occasionally is getting the interviewee to feel sorry for you: "My editor is going to kill me if I don't get to interview you" is about as old as "Haven't we met before?" but it still works.

Once you know some of the basic reasons people consent to give interviews, you can be prepared to meet and overcome objections if they refuse to give you an interview.

A number of years ago, several police officers in a midwestern city were charged with taking bribes, and they were suspended from their jobs. The suspended police officers initially refused to talk with reporters, and for several days the newspapers, radio, and television reports contained only statements from the city attorney and the policy department representatives. Finally, a persuasive newspaper reporter convinced one of the suspended officers to talk about the situation so people could hear and understand both sides of the issue. Many journalists use the same argument and say to someone reluctant to be interviewed, "Look, I have one side of this story and I want to be fair and give you the chance to answer these charges and tell your side of the story." This strategy is amazingly effective.

Bluffing or lying is a strategy that some reporters use to get interviews. In their book, *All the President's Men,* Carl Bernstein and Bob Woodward tell how they used a bluff to get interviews with people who worked at the Committee to Re-elect the President. Most of these people were afraid to talk with Bernstein and Woodward and usually refused to provide leads or discuss Watergate. The bluff that the two reporters used was to say to prospective interviewees "a friend at the committee told us that you were disturbed by some of the things you saw going on there, that you would be a good person to talk to . . . that you were absolutely straight and honest and didn't know quite what to do. . . ." Whenever the person asked who the friend was, Woodward or Bernstein would refuse to give the individual's name, and this reassured the person that the reporter would protect his or her identity.[5]

Lying about your identity can get you an interview, but it can also get you in trouble. There are many stories about Harry Romanoff, a Chicago newspaper reporter, who used to call people on the telephone and impersonate someone else to get an interview or information. Romanoff honed this technique to an art form that awed other reporters and created a legend, but even Harry got caught once. Romanoff needed to find out the condition of a wounded police officer, so he called the hospital and asked to speak to the ranking police official on the floor where the wounded officer was being treated. Romanoff identified himself as the police commissioner and demanded to know the condition of the officer. The man at the other end of the telephone paused, identified himself as the police commissioner and told Harry that he had been expecting his call.

Some journalists say that the best way to get an interview is not to mention that you want an interview and that if you need an interview you should call the person you wish to talk with and explain that you are doing a story and need help because you do not understand all of the issues involved. They suggest that you ask for a meeting so you can gain the background necessary for writing the story. An offshoot to this strategy is to telephone a person and explain that you are doing a story and have received information but you need help to determine if it is accurate. Asking for help to determine the validity of your information may get you inside the door and into an interview. A sample conversation is provided below.

INTERVIEWER: Mr. Jones, I'm Phil Brown of the Metropolitan Free Press.

5Carl Bernstein and Robert Woodward, *All the President's Men* (New York: Simon & Schuster, 1974), p. 60.

INTERVIEWEE: Yes . . .

INTERVIEWER: I've been assigned to do a story on the school bond levy that's coming up for voter action this November. I've studied some of the financial aspects of the levy and I've even talked with the school superintendent. I just don't understand the financial aspects of this levy. I need help understanding what's going on, and George Green said that you have studied the issue and could explain it to me.

INTERVIEWER: Well, its no wonder you don't understand the levy. Hardly anyone does, and it's so complex that most of the voters won't understand it either. That's part of the reason I'm against the levy.

INTERVIEWER: I understand that you are leading the opposition to the levy. I'd like to hear more about why you think it should not be approved.

INTERVIEWEE: Well, I'd be glad to explain the levy to you. When?

INTERVIEWER: Well, the sooner the better, because I'm supposed to do a story on the levy next week.

INTERVIEWEE: I'm free this Tuesday morning at 9:00. Is that a good time for you?

INTERVIEWER: Yes, it is, Mr. Jones. I'll see you at 9:00 this Tuesday . . . and thanks.

If your initial approaches for gaining an interview are not successful, try to get a mutual friend or an acquaintance to intercede and try to convince the person you wish to talk with to meet with you. A mutual friend might be able to convince the interviewee that it is to his or her benefit to be interviewed. If you want to interview someone in government or industry, the public relations department can do a great deal of your work and arrange an interview. Many business executives feel that they are too busy to give interviews or that they are afraid of being interviewed. The public relations director will realize the benefit for good publicity and will, in some instances, work to help you get an interview. It is best to remember, however, that the public relations director owes his or her allegiance to the employer, not to you. Secretaries are also another way of getting to people who profess to be too busy to be interviewed. Properly approached, the secretary may be able to tell you the best times to call or the place to "accidentally" run into the person you wish to interview.

Researching the Interview Topic or Person

Q: Just what do you do, sir?

A: Are you kidding? If you don't know, why are you here pretending to interview me and taking up my time?

It is a sad fact of journalistic life that the most inane, superficial, or outright dumb questions come from reporters who fail to do even elementary research on the topic or the person they are interviewing. Most journalists know of at least one instance when an unprepared interviewer asked the wrong question and created an embarrassing situation or alienated the interviewee to the point where the interview was called off. It is just common courtesy to be prepared for an interview before taking up the interviewee's time. You should be as well prepared as you can be before you sit down and ask your first question. There are times, though, when the purpose of the interview is to provide elementary knowledge, but even then you should know the background of the person you are talking with and as much about the topic as you were able to find and understand. Even if you do not understand the topic, your questions will reflect the amount of research and preparation you have done.

Research is of the utmost importance if you expect to produce good interviews. Some reporters say this is the most important step, because it puts the interviewer on equal ground, or as near equal as possible, with the interviewee. Raymond P. Brandt of the *St. Louis Post-Dispatch* says the "best approach for an interviewer is to know as much about the subject as the interviewee.[6] You may not always be able to know as much about the subject as the interviewee, but you should have done enough research so that you know which areas may lead to a good in-depth interview. Research will show you the areas to cover briefly and the areas to probe and reprobe. John Brady in *The Craft of Interviewing* says it is better to be overprepared than underprepared, especially when you are dealing with people who may try to deceive you.[7]

Good research prior to the interview will allow you to make the best use of your interview time, and this is especially important when you are dealing with busy people on tight schedules who can spare only 30 minutes to an hour. If you do your research well, you will be able to talk the interviewee's language, understand his or her technical jargon and probe those answers that are superficial. Research will help you focus on the parts of the interview that will be the most productive. Research also can do something else: it can warn you about possible areas to avoid or to approach head on, and it can tell you about the person you are going to interview. David Frost virtually went into training for his marathon television interviews with former President Richard Nixon. Frost and his staff read the Watergate transcripts, studied all available evidence on Watergate, and tried to ascertain the psychological makeup of Richard Nixon before the interview. Frost was able to talk Nixon's language, know when he was being evasive, and focus on those areas or topics that needed to be

[6]Stewart Harrall, *Keys to Successful Interviewing* (Norman, Okla.: University of Oklahoma Press, 1954), p. 162.
[7]John Brady, *The Craft of Interviewing* (New York: Vintage Books, 1977), p. 37.

probed. At the end of each day's interview session, Frost and his associates studied that day's videotapes to prepare follow-up questions for the next interview session. It was a team effort that required a massive amount of research and analysis prior to the interview sessions and during those breaks between interviews.[8]

There is no set answer on how much research is enough. The best thing to do is spend as much time researching as you can or until you feel comfortable enough so that you cannot be lied to or deceived.

Many journalists prepare a list of possible questions and areas to probe as they research the subject or the person. Good research should lead to specific questions and elicit specific types of information. Ken Metzler suggests in *Creative Interviewing* that as you jot down questions during your research, you should also prepare for specific responses and then prepare the follow-up questions.[9]

Adequate research will give you the information needed to help you build an interview outline showing the areas you wish to cover in the order they will probably be discussed. This outline can be nothing more than a series of key words, or it can be detailed, showing topics and the precise wording of questions. The type of outline a journalist constructs for an interview should fit his or her particular style of interviewing. Some journalists can work from a bare-bones outline, while others need to write out each question. Many journalists, though, say that when you have an extremely sensitive, precise question to ask, write it out or memorize the question.

How to conduct research for an interview is not as simple or clear-cut as why research should be done. Every journalist develops a particular style or a method of finding information. Some good general sources to use are

> statistical yearbooks
> encyclopedias
> almanacs
> *The New York Times Index*
> *Reader's Guide to Periodic Literature*
> *Who's Who in America* (or your state)
> biography indexes

These sources will either give you some background or point you toward books or articles that will provide background information about a person or a topic.

One source of information that many journalists overlook is their local college or university. Lodged in one area are a group of people who

---

[8]"Interview with David Frost," *Playboy* (April 1978): 76–78.
[9]Ken Metzler, *Creative Interviewing* (Englewood Cliffs, N.J.: Prentice-Hall, Inc., 1977), pp. 58–59.

have devoted their lives to the study of a particular discipline or a subject and who can give you background information (during an informal interview) or tell you where to find the information you need. Federal, state, and local governments also employ a variety of experts who can be interviewed or who may help you find information for a story. In the 1960s the police department in a large midwestern city was investigating a series of homicides that seemed to be linked. A local newspaper reporter called the local university and was referred to a psychiatrist who had worked for the state Department of Mental Health. The doctor had worked at the state's hospital for the criminally insane for 20 years and was an expert in deviant behavior and forensic medicine. During an interview the psychiatrist profiled the type of person who might commit a series of murders similar to those the police were investigating. Eventually, police arrested a person who was convicted of the murders, and the psychiatrist's profile proved to be very accurate.

A reference librarian is also a valuable asset when you are doing research. A librarian can save a lot of research time, and this person's friendship is worth cultivating. Other sources of information may be individuals who work in public relations departments, hobbiests who have developed specific interests, and friends or other reporters who have some information about a topic. Just asking around the newsroom can probably provide a file of press releases or tips on questions to ask or areas to probe. The thing to remember is that you cannot be an expert on every topic, but you should be expert enough to know where to find enough information on the topic to talk intelligently with experts.

Meeting and Establishing Rapport

Some research dealing with rapport and first impressions indicates that when strangers meet, the first few minutes are critical. A bad impression or an awkward start in the first few minutes can lead to mistrust or interview failure. Your first job is to put the interviewee at ease, gain the person's trust, and establish rapport. The interviewee must not only like or respect you but also must trust your journalistic judgments and professional integrity.

Show respect for the interviewee by being prompt and dressing to fit the situation. Style of dress and promptness are external signs to the interviewee of how he or she is regarded by you. Lateness and inappropriate dress indicate that you do not think much of the interviewee or what the interviewee stands for. Dress to match the situation and the journalistic role you are playing. If you are doing a farm story, clean levis and boots might be appropriate if you are doing interviews in the farmyard or in the fields. If you are assigned to interview the Nigerian ambassador and the only time an interview can be arranged is during a formal reception, then you should dress formally. The *Front Page* image of the journalist with open tie, cigarette hanging out of his mouth, bottle in the back pocket, and hat slouched back on the head is not appropriate. You should dress neatly and well. If you are not a good judge of color and style, there are several good books available on how to dress and convey the image you want.

Being friendly but not overly familiar is good advice during the initial stages of an interview. Do not treat the interviewee as a long-lost friend. Familiarity is one area where it is best to let the interviewee take the lead and set the pace. When you meet the interviewee, show your willingness to be friendly by warmly shaking hands and expressing your pleasure at meeting or for granting the interview. Greet the interviewee as Mr., Mrs., Ms., Miss, Dr., Congressman, Congresswoman, Senator, or Mayor, and so forth, and continue this formal address unless the interviewee asks you to use his or her first name. Reestablish the reason for your being there and summarize your intent and how much time you need for the interview.

During the first few minutes of the meeting, before the formal interview, try to establish some common interests and build rapport. Your research may indicate that the interviewee is an avid sportsperson or has some deep interest. You may be able to establish a friendly relationship with the interviewee by referring to sports, asking about something you know the person is interested in, or exhibiting common likes or dislikes. Look around the office or room for signs of what the interviewee cherishes. People exhibit their trophies or desires in many ways. A photograph of two children on a sailboat says something about what the person holds dear. A golf trophy or a plaque honoring the person for public service, or a charity are symbols to help you establish a friendly relationship with the person you are going to interview.

Some strategies that can help you establish rapport and put the interviewee at ease are to hold the interview on the interviewee's home ground. People are more assured of themselves in their own office or living room. Interview one person at a time and avoid talking with a group of people, because you cannot retain control. Try to be alone with the person you intend to interview. If family or friends linger in the background and create disturbances, move to a new location or take a walk with the interviewee. If other people are present during an interview, both you and the interviewee may feel obligated to include those other people in the conversation and you will not be able to concentrate on each other. Other people may inhibit the interviewee by correcting his or her answers or interrupting to add comments. The best advice is to be alone in comfortable surroundings where there are few distractions. Avoid situations where the power distribution between you and the interviewee is off balance. Try to sit level with the interviewee, because if he or she is sitting higher and looking down at you it will give the interviewee a psychological feeling of superiority. Do not let massive furniture (desks or counters) separate you from the interviewee, because the person can feel protected and may psychologically hide behind the barrier. Try to sit facing each other in a comfortable, natural type of setting without a lot of distracting lights or noises. It would not be presumptuous for you to ask a very busy person if his or her secretary could hold telephone calls for a period of time if the telephone calls would be a constant distraction.

Do not be sarcastic or overly humorous unless you are prepared to find out that the interviewee may be a very sober person who has no sense of humor. Your job is not to elicit laughs; it is to interview someone, and a friendly business-like manner is the best way to build confidence and rapport.

Determining Strategies and Asking Questions

It is impossible to discuss the technique of questioning without discussing strategy, because the two are so closely related. How and when you ask a specific question during the interview is both a matter of questioning and strategy. Some strategy decisions that have to be made before the interview are:

1. how to move from the initial rapport building stage to the interview itself without damaging rapport
2. what your journalistic role or style of questioning will be
3. which specific questioning strategies to use, such as whether to approach sensitive areas directly or indirectly
4. how to handle evasions or lies
5. how to ask the high-risk or tough question

Moving from the opening rapport building stage of the meeting to the interview itself must be done carefully. It is important to establish rapport during the opening stages, and you should try to carry this feeling over into the interview. Some journalists establish good rapport but break this mood by coldly and abruptly saying "Well, it's time to get down to work." In effect, they are saying to the interviewee that it was nice to be friendly and talk, but now they have to get down to work and friendship has to be put aside, so be careful. This is precisely what you want to avoid. Your strategy should be to establish and maintain rapport in the initial meeting and carry it over into the interview.

Timing is important in moving from the opening stage into the interview. You do not want to spend too much time establishing rapport and risk cutting short the interview, but, at the same time, you do not want to rush into the interview until you have established trust. One good way to make the transition to the interview when you feel the time is right is to say, "You know, talking with you is really enjoyable, but I promised you that I would only take one hour of your time. Why don't we just continue this same conversation and I'll start taking notes." Another way to make the transition is to say, "This is exactly what I was looking for, I'm going to take notes on what you said before I forget."

Another strategic decision you must make is how to act during the interview. Some journalists say the best way to act is neutral and natural: do not agree or disagree with whatever the person says. If the interviewee confesses to murdering her husband, do not evaluate the response by condoning or disagreeing with the act, but rather follow-up her answer with a probing question. Journalists who advise you to remain neutral say that if you lose your objectivity and agree or disagree with the interviewee you can affect the answers, because some interviewees may then tell you what they think you want to hear.

Other journalists, however, take a different view and say that the worst thing to do is to act natural and neutral during an interview. These journalists advise the interviewer to determine which role best fits the situation and then play that role. You can play the role of a confessor or a devil's advocate who disagrees with the interviewee's philosophy and challenges the interviewee to convince you he or she is right. You can argue gently with the interviewee or ask the interviewee with a slight air of disbelief if he or she really believes what was just said.[10]

In order to decide whether or not to act natural and be neutral you will have to try both methods and see what works for you in situations. You may have trouble playing a role, and because of this you might have to be natural and neutral. Use whatever strategy feels comfortable for you and produces good results.

There is an old journalistic saying that "there are no improper questions, only improper answers." This may be true, but there are some questioning strategies that seem to be better than others and produce better results. The strategy of asking questions is obviously important in continuing the rapport that was established in the initial meeting. Do not grill the interviewee as a prosecuting attorney might do. Ask questions in a conversational manner, because your purpose is to hold a conversation with someone who has knowledge or has experienced something that you want to know about. Holding a conversation implies a certain amount of give and take during the interview. Make sure that you are asking questions and not making statements that do not call for answers. Keep your questions short and understandable. Long questions or two-part questions are hard to understand and may be confusing. Start with open end general questions that allow the interviewee to talk easily about general topics and get comfortable in the interview situation. This initial question-

[10]Brady, *Craft of Interviewing*, pp. 79–80, 89–95.

ing will allow the interviewee to establish a pattern of question and response that will probably continue even as your questioning becomes more specific and probing. If you want specific information, make sure your questions are specific and precise. When you ask a question that has several possible answers, either give all of the alternatives or none of the alternatives. Do not be afraid to ask what you are wondering: "How did you feel? Why did you do that? What was your reaction?" If you want to know the answer to something, 90 percent of the time the listener or the reader would also like to know.

Sooner or later we all run into the person who lies or tries to evade questions by giving vague answers or giving incomplete answers. Do not accept generalizations or incomplete answers. Probe. Ask the question again, and if the interviewee continues to evade the issue, pursue the issue at that moment or wait until later in the interview to bring up the same question. One journalist says that when she gets evasions she asks "Possibly you misunderstood the question, I asked. . . ." If the interviewee still evades the question, she drops the issue and goes on with the interview, looking for another time and another way to ask the question either directly or indirectly. One television reporter who interviewed a suspended police officer kept getting a "no comment" to many of his questions. After a number of "no comments" the reporter refused to accept the evasions and asked why the suspended police officer could not comment on the questions. The answer was simply that the police officer's attorney did not want his client to talk about specific issues because they were going to file a suit against the city. By asking why and refusing to accept evasive answers, the interviewer came away with a solid interview and an exclusive story about the lawsuit. Remember, too, that sometimes even when you know a question will not be answered, a "no comment" answer might be the whole story. Sometimes you can stop evasions or incomplete answers by simply letting the interviewee know that you know more about the topic than he or she suspects and that evasive answers will lead to tough, precise questioning. Former President Nixon, who is an attorney, was evasive when David Frost asked a question regarding obstruction of justice. Frost, who had just read the legal statute on obstruction of justice, explained the legal issue to Nixon. Frost apparently astounded Nixon with the fact that he knew the legal issues involved in obstruction of justice and that he had read the statute as part of his research for the interview.

There are times when a reporter wants to ask a high-risk question without taking direct responsibility for the question. This could be because the interviewer is embarrassed to ask the question or because the interviewer is afraid of damaging rapport. One strategy is to ask the question but shift the responsibility by saying "Some people are saying that. . . ." or "It is being said that. . . ." These are devices that allow you to ask a tough question or state a position without becoming personally involved in the controversy. The tough question is asked, but the interviewer disclaims responsibility by saying that others are talking about the issue and want to know.

New reporters usually have problems asking tough or embarrassing questions and they may even avoid asking these questions to save themselves from embarrassment. There is no doubt that it takes a certain amount of gall to ask someone if he or she stole the money, killed her husband, or got drunk and ran over a neighbor's child. The thing you must remember is that if someone consents to an interview, the person knows that tough questions may be coming and may be looking forward to either denying the act or justifying what he or she did. By failing to ask the question, you deny the interviewee the opportunity to discuss the issue. William M. Ringle, chief correspondent for the Gannett News Service in Washington recounts the story of Senator Edward Kennedy giving a devastating and witty appraisal of President Nixon's Watergate problems. Kennedy made morality an issue and yet not one of the reporters present asked the obvious question about Kennedy's own moral conduct at Chappaquidick. One of Kennedy's advisors later told Ringle that Kennedy expected the question, had an answer ready, and was astonished that no one asked the question.[11]

There are some general rules that will help you ask tough or embarrassing questions:

1. Ask a tough question in a conversational tone of voice.
2. Ask a tough question late in the interview.
3. Establish rapport and a pattern of question and response before asking a tough question.
4. Reestablish rapport after you have asked a tough question.
5. Consider asking a "trial balloon" tough question.
6. Ask a tough question indirectly if you are unable to ask it directly.

The trick in asking a tough question in a conversational tone of voice is to make the question appear like all the other questions you have asked. You can virtually ask any question if you ask it in the proper tone of voice and after you have established a pattern of question and response. You want to avoid sounding antagonistic after you have carefully built up a conversational pattern.

Save the tough questions for the end of the interview so that if the interviewee gets angry and terminates the interview, you already have most of your information. If you are asked to leave, this obviously means that you cannot reestablish rapport. If the interviewee accepts the tough

[11]William M. Ringle, "Get the Interview as Readers Surrogate," *The Gannetter* 30 (June 1974): 1–3.

question and responds, you should continue the interview even though you may have everything you want. Continue to ask questions of a softer nature and try to reestablish the rapport that you carefully built up prior to the interview.

Using a "trial balloon" tough question is merely a way of determining how the interviewee will respond when you ask the real tough or embarrassing question. The "trial balloon" question is one for which you already know the answer, but it allows you to see how the interviewee reacts and if you can trust his or her response to the real tough or embarrassing question.

If you cannot bring yourself to ask a tough or embarrassing question, then you can be subtle and ask the question indirectly. In some interviews concerning sensitive topics, the indirect question may be the best and most productive approach. For example, instead of asking the attorney why he violated his code of ethics in the Watergate scandal, you might ask a general question about morality in government and business. In the course of the answer, the attorney might bring up his violation of ethics as an example and discuss the matter more candidly and in greater detail than if you had asked the question directly. This indirect technique has been used by journalists dealing with rape victims or homosexuals who might respond poorly to a direct question.

Another tactic in questioning is to ask for examples or anecdotes that will illustrate what the interviewee is talking about. You must remember that facts are fine, but examples and anecdotes flesh out the facts and make your copy enjoyable to read or hear. If an answer seems vague or if you do not understand what is being said, ask for clarification or an example that will help you understand. There is no disgrace in admitting that you do not understand something, but there is disgrace in walking out of the interview still not understanding what the interviewee tried to say. You certainly could not explain something to your viewers or readers if you did not understand what you were writing about.

One tactic that many journalists fail to use is simply listening to what the interviewee is saying and how it is being said. You should be quiet and observant while the interviewee is talking. William Hazlitt, an eighteenth-century British writer, said that "silence is one great art of conversation," and it is axiomatic that you cannot listen to someone else while you are talking. Listen to what the interviewee is saying and key your follow-up questions to the interviewee's answers. Even though you are using an outline, you should be flexible enough to pursue interesting answers or ideas even if they are not listed on your outline. Look at the interviewee when he or she is talking and try to read what the interviewee is saying with his or her body as well as with his or her mouth. Use silence creatively by not jumping in with another question as soon as the interviewee finishes an answer. Let the silence last for a moment; in many instances the interviewees will continue with an example or another idea. Many times silence will lead the interviewees into talking about things that he or she had not planned to discuss. Physically react to the interviewee by nodding your head, smiling at funny anecdotes or verbally agreeing as the interviewee talks. You must always remember that an interview is a two-way conversation and that you must do more than simply ask questions and record answers. You must listen to the interviewee and watch the eyes and body language to determine reactions to questions and the way the interviewee responds.

One way to get a reluctant interviewee to talk is to make an inaccurate statement and let the person correct the error. Paul Leech of the *Chicago Daily News* tried for several hours to interview Herbert Hoover without much success. Finally, Leech purposefully made an incorrect statement. Hoover corrected Leech and then continued to talk for several hours about the nation and the presidency. An offshoot of this strategy is to present someone with a statement or information and ask them to confirm or deny it.[12]

Closing the Interview

For some novice interviewers, closing the interview always creates a little hesitancy or embarrassment. You want the close of the interview to be as smooth as the opening stages. This can be done by keeping in mind some points of etiquette for closing the interview.

1. Set a time limit prior to the interview.
2. Say that you have a few more questions.
3. Review your questions.
4. Remember the interview does not stop once you turn off your tape recorder or shut your notebook.
5. Leave with a compliment.
6. Send the interviewee a copy of your story with a personal note.

Closing the interview may not be a problem. If you agreed to a time limit when you arranged for the interview, then when your time is up you should make moves to terminate the interview. You should always live up to your agreement or indicate your willingness to do so. Many times, if the interview has gone well and you have established good rapport with the interviewee, the interviewee may invite you to continue with your questioning. The important thing is not to overstay your welcome. If the interviewee gives off signals that your time is up, finish your questioning quickly, thank the person for giving his or her time, and depart. Some obvious signals that the interviewee may give you are increased inatten-

[12]Harral, *Successful Interviewing*, p. 3.

tion to your questions, short, brusque answers, nervousness or impatience, or glancing several times at his or her watch.

There are many ways to indicate that you are done with the interview without jumping up and leaving abruptly. Probably one of the best ways to signal that you are nearly done is by saying, "I just have a few more questions dealing with . . . and we'll be done." Another way is to pause; review your notes verbally, indicating that you have covered the areas you wanted to discuss, and say you have just one more question. Some journalists recommend using the verbal review and then asking the interviewee if there were any major points missed during the interview or any questions that should have been asked but were not. This involves the interviewee in the review process, and he or she might have something interesting to add.

Remember that the interview does not stop once you have closed your notebook or turned off your tape recorder. As a matter of fact, many times after your notebook is closed and as you stand in the doorway ready to leave, the interviewee will say something interesting. The interviewee may feel less pressured without the tape recorder going or without your notebook open and respond in an animated way or add an interesting comment. All of this information is part of the interview, and you should automatically assume that anything said is all right to publish. Treat this information casually, though, and do not open your notebook or restart your tape recorder. Just remember what was said until you are outside and can jot down the quote, statement, or anecdote.

As you leave, always thank the person for giving you their time and information. At this point some journalists try to compliment the interviewee by saying that it was a good interview, that he or she particularly liked the way the interviewee spoke on an issue, or that an anecdote was funny and supported a particular point very well. Even the most experienced interviewees may be sensitive about their performance in the interview and would like to be reassured that they did a good job and answered your questions. A compliment at the end of an interview will also make it easier for you to come back for another interview at a later time. It is a good idea to leave on a friendly basis so that you can call again for another interview or to clarify a point.

Another strategy that can cement relations between you and the interviewee is to send the person a copy of your story or notify the person when the story will be run. Do not ask for the interviewee's approval, however.

HAZARDS OF INTERVIEWING

There are many types of interview hazards a journalist can run into, from angry dogs to amorous interviewee's. The most common hazards, though, are

1. matching times and schedules with the interviewee
2. maintaining control over content
3. determining what is "on" and "off" the record and what "off the record" means
4. maintaining source confidentiality
5. taking accurate notes

The biggest hazard in journalistic interviewing is trying to match your schedule with the schedule of the person you want to interview. Because you are requesting the interview, you are at the mercy of the interviewee's schedule. If the interviewee is a night owl, for example, and thinks best after midnight, you may have to take an afternoon nap and adjust your schedule if you want to talk with this person. If the person you want to interview is extremely busy, you may have to conduct your interview in the back seat of a car on the way to an airport or in a hallway with people looking on. Some great political interviews have been done in the back seats of limousines as the politician was being rushed to a speaking engagement or a meeting. The back seat of a limousine may be the only place you can get the interviewee alone for 10 or 15 minutes. The back seat of a car also offers some protection to the interviewer who asks a tough or embarrassing question. Although it is not inconceivable, most interviewees would probably not stop the car and ask you to get out on a busy highway.

One other hazard for the journalist is the interviewee who wants "right of review" on finished newspaper or magazine stories before publication. Some interviewees make "right of review" a prerequisite for granting interviews. In most instances, you should resist this intrusion into your journalistic responsibilities. However, there are times when you may give the interviewee "right of review" in order to get an interview. Before any agreement is made, however, both the interviewer and the interviewee should be clear about the terms of the agreement. You may give the interviewee "right of review" to correct errors, but the interviewee may assume the right to change quotes, content, or your interpretation.

What information is "on" or "off the record" frequently has become a major point of contention between the interviewer and the interviewee. More than one journalist can relate a story of getting a terrific interview filled with good solid quotes and witty responses only to have the interviewee say at the end of the interview that "of course, this is all off the record." At this point, the journalist has to decide whether or not to honor the belated request for confidentiality or to deny it. Most journalists would probably deny a request to keep information "off the record" unless the agreement was made before the information was received. If you honored every belated request for confidentiality to keep some embarrassing statement off the record, all of your stories would be bland and without attribution. There are times, however, when you might decide to honor a belated request for confidentiality or to keep something off the record.

Never ask the interviewee if the information he or she is giving you is "on" or "off the record." Always assume that whatever you are being told is "on the record" and can be used with attribution. If you ask, the obvious response if the information might be controversial or embarrassing is for the interviewee to say it is "off the record."

Make sure that both you and the interviewee understand what "on" or "off the record" means and how it can bind you. Someone may say something is "off the record" and really mean that you can use the information but not the person's name as the source of the information. One journalistic strategy when getting "off the record" information is to go to someone else and get this other person to confirm what you have received and then use the second person as the source. This can be done in a straightforward manner by telling someone you have the information and ask the person to confirm or deny it. However, if the information you have is not confirmed with evidence or other interviews, you may have to be devious to get confirmation or verification that what you have is true. If, for example, a reliable source tells you "off the record" that the mayor of your city has accepted a $10,000 bribe from the Fly-by-Night Construction Company to let the firm do the work without going through the process of bidding, you may have to be devious to get confirmation. One method of seeking verification might be to get an interview with the mayor and near the end of the interview casually ask him or her, "Mayor, the Fly-by-Night Construction Company reports they paid you $10,000 last year. What did you do to earn that money?" The mayor probably would not admit to taking a bribe, but he might admit to being on their payroll, and once that is verified you can start to analyze other aspects. You could also reverse the process and ask the president of the Fly-by-Night Construction Company for an interview and then ask: "Mayor Jones's income tax forms show that the sum of $10,000 was received from your firm last year. What did Mayor Jones do to earn that money?" If you get confirmation that the mayor did, in fact, receive $10,000 from the Fly-by-Night Construction Company, then you may have the basis for a good story and you have kept the source of your original information confidential.

Confidentiality of sources also provides another hazard for the journalist. The courts recognize only a few privileged relationships, and the journalist's source is not one of those relationships protected by law. What is said between a doctor-patient, priest-confessor, or attorney-client is confidential and protected by law. The journalist is on his or her own and, in some instances, journalists have been jailed for refusing to reveal where they received information. In other instances, prosecutors have demanded reporters' notes or film taken during interviews. Although some states have enacted shield laws, not all states protect journalists and allow them to keep their sources of information confidential. Whenever you are asked to keep a source confidential, you should be aware that if you later refuse to identify the source of your information, it can lead to a contempt of court citation and a jail term for you. If you agree to keep a source confidential, you should be prepared to back up your pledge.

One constant hazard for journalists is how to record or keep track of what was said during the interview. Research indicates that this is a problem area for most journalists and that note-taking can be an area where distortions or omissions take place, which can change the whole context of what was said during the interview. There are a number of techniques for recording an interview.

Copious Note-taking

Whenever you take a lot of notes during an interview you may have problems later in transcribing the notes or deciphering what you wrote down when you were in a hurry. Taking copious notes leads to a reliance on your reporter's notebook instead of your own memory.

Brief Note-taking

Taking brief notes that are later used to jog your memory as you reconstruct the interview is a good technique only if immediately following the interview you go to your typewriter and reconstruct the interview. The longer the time period is between the interview and when you write down what happened, the greater the chance is for distortion or forgetting.

Memory

One technique that most journalists fear trying is to listen intently without taking notes and then later reconstruct the interview. This technique also relies on reconstructing the interview immediately following the interview and not allowing too much time to lapse. Author Truman Capote prefers this memory technique, and he has trained himself to remember very accurately. Those journalists who rely on memory say that note-taking inhibits a good interview, because the journalist is always writing things down and not watching the interviewee and listening for clues and hints to follow-up.

Most journalists prefer taking notes to relying on memory, although the use of small audio cassette tape recorders is growing. The cassette recorders do away with the problem of people claiming that they were misquoted, and it does lead to greater accuracy. Transcribing an audio tape interview, though, is very time consuming. Note-takers, on the other hand, edit as they take notes, and they are able to start writing their story after a short period of organization. A method that has the accuracy of audio tape recorders and the quickness of note-taking is a combination of the two techniques. The journalist records the interview on audio cassette tape and keeps brief notes that indicate tape recorder numbers when various quotes are recorded or when certain topics are discussed. The journalist must still transcribe the audio tape, but it can be done selectively and a lot of material can be left out of the transcript.

If you decide that note-taking is the best way to record interviews, here are some general rules that can help you take good notes and reduce any chances for error:

1. Learn shorthand or some method of speedwriting.
2. Do not try to record everything that is said. Be selective and edit as you write.
3. Be exacting with specific quotes, names, dates, facts, and spelling.
4. If you get behind in your note-taking, ask a general question that allows you time to catch up while the interviewee is talking.
5. Do not make a big show out of note-taking, because it can inhibit the interviewee.
6. Use a page in your notebook for each question and answer. This will allow you to rip the pages out of the notebook and easily organize your material after the interview is over.
7. As soon as possible, fully reconstruct the interview from your notes and memory. The longer you wait before reconstructing the interview, the greater the chance is that you will forget important parts of the interview or let distortions creep into your story.

THIS CHAPTER IN PERSPECTIVE

The key to successful journalistic interviewing is the preparation and use of a structured approach to the interview process. Preparation forces the journalist to think about the interview, the interviewee, and the relationship between them. In many ways the journalist becomes an amateur psychologist who must place himself or herself in the position of the prospective interviewee. This may include analyzing possible motives that will lead the reluctant interviewee to grant an interview or determine the correct strategy and tactics to use during the interview. However, even the best laid plans go awry, and flexibility needs to be part of your journalistic repertoire.

PROJECTS

1. Role-play a journalistic interview in class. The instructor assigns the roles, and both people (the interviewer and the interviewee) do research on the person so that a realistic interview can be simulated. The interviewer must go through all the steps necessary for conducting a journalistic interview: research, define the purpose, obtain the interview, determine strategies and questions, meet and establish rapport, and close the interview.

The class observes the interview process and writes a critique of the interview.

2. The instructor assigns everyone in the class to conduct a journalistic interview while the students are at home during one of the school vacations. Students should provide the instructor with (1) research notes, (2) the purpose of the interview, (3) a transcript of the interview, (4) an analysis of the interview, and (5) an explanation of who the interviewee is and the steps taken to establish rapport.

If there are journalism students in the class, the instructor may require some of these students to use the interview in a story they write for a class assignment.

3. Read and critique a journalistic interview found in some major news magazines. Some suggested sources for good interviews are *Playboy Magazine, More Magazine, U.S. News & World Report,* and *Newsweek*.

4. Each class member should select one of the following individuals and prepare for an interview with the person selected. The preparation should include defining the purpose, research, and preparing strategies, questions, and an interview outline.

Idi Amin, president of Uganda, Africa
Roman Polanski, motion-picture director
Robert Mitchum, motion-picture actor
Edmund Muskie, U.S. senator
Alice Cooper, rock star
Fred Silverman, television programmer/executive
Jane Fonda, motion-picture actress
Others, as approved by the instructor

Chapter 15
Broadcast Interviews

Well done, live television interviewing is simply more difficult than print interviewing.[1]

Richard Reeves

The newspaper editor or publisher decides how large each day's newspaper will be based on the amount of news available and how much advertising has been sold. The newspaper may be 24 or 48 pages long, depending on the day's volume of news and advertising. Television and radio programmers, on the other hand, start with a set amount of time they must fill and then fit program material into the predetermined slot. Filling a half-hour newscast or program slot may, at times, take on an air of desperation. The pressure to fill time is constant, and on one day a programmer may frantically try to cut 45 minutes of program material down to 30 minutes and the next day try to stretch 23 minutes of material to fit a 30-minute program slot.

Television and radio stations are huge consumers of program material, and a lot of station resources are devoted to producing or purchasing programs to fill their schedules. Radio has developed music formats that rely on repetition of recorded music, and this, to some extent, alleviates

[1]Richard Reeves, "I Used to Be Dick Reeves," *TV Guide* (October 4, 1975): 16.

the need for station resources to be used to produce programs. Television, though, has a voracious appetite for local and network programs that lose much of their appeal once they have been played. The pressure to fill program time sometimes leads to mediocre programs. Local and network television programmers are constantly looking for program types that are quick and easy to produce and inexpensive. Interview based programs, which do not require script writers, actors, technicians, and stage hands to build sets, meet the needs of television and radio programmers. Interviews are not only inexpensive and easy to produce but also interesting and entertaining.

Because of radio and television's unique ability to come into the home and entertain, broadcast interviewing takes on an entertainment aspect that is usually not found in magazine or newspaper interviewing. Certainly, broadcast interviews are done to elicit information or to explore ideas and personalities but, at the same time, they take on an entertainment function because the audience is participating as the interview is being done or later when it is being replayed on the air. Television viewers can experience the interview, feel tension build, laugh at funny moments or comments, feel discomfort as the interviewee gropes for an answer, and see the interviewee's body language as he or she answers tough questions. This participation in the interview is the reason interviews carry an emotional wallop that newspaper or magazine interviews cannot convey. Newspapers or magazines present a great amount of detail, but television and radio allow viewers and listeners to feel and see for themselves. In no other medium except television could an interview allow people to experience the anguish of a West Virginian who had just lost eight relatives when a power plant scafford collapsed killing 51 workers.

The goals of the broadcast interviewer are not just to conduct an interview and to elicit information. The interviewer must conduct an interview that fits the technological, journalistic, and artistic demands of radio and television. The interviewer must be able to break down barriers, get the interviewee to relax, forget about the recording technology, and engage in a witty, revealing conversation that borders on being a performance. If the broadcast interviewer cannot stimulate the interviewee into giving a revealing performance, then he or she must direct the interview into areas where information will outweigh what the audience will perceive as a drab personality. In other words, the interviewer must satisfy the audience's need for interesting or entertaining material.

There are three basic types of broadcast interviews, and each type has certain distinct characteristics and problems. These three types are: (1) the news interview, (2) the in-depth recorded interview, and (3) the live in-depth interview.

THE NEWS INTERVIEW

Radio and television news programs rely heavily on the recorded interview to fill the allotted news time, because eyewitness accounts of incidents are much more believable than a straight newscast. If there is a hierarchy of believability in broadcast news, it would be: (1) an interview excerpt with a participant or an eyewitness, (2) a report from the reporter at the scene of an event, (3) an in-studio report from a reporter who gathered the information or talked with eyewitnesses, and (4) the newscaster reading the story.

Because news reporters are seldom able to be at the scene of a news event, interviews help reconstruct the event. It is quite common for a news reporter to arrive at the scene of a story and try to interview eyewitnesses or people involved in the incident.

Radio and television news stations also try to get interviews just for the visual or aural change in the newscast. A 30-minute television newscast would be awfully dull if there were no visuals other than the news announcer reading the news. Broadcast interviews have a production value whether or not they have a news value. This aspect of seeking visual or aural change has at times been a major criticism of broadcast news. Critics have charged that broadcast news producers and reporters cover visual or aural news stories whether or not they are good stories and merit film or tape coverage. A number of studies have been done to validate this criticism. News editors and producers were asked to evaluate two stories of equal merit—one with film or tape and the other without visual or aural reinforcement. Inevitably, the story with film or tape was chosen because of its aural or visual impact compared with the nonvisual or aural story.

Radio News

The radio news interviewer may spend much time interviewing people by telephone. Because most radio news teams are small when compared with television news departments, radio newspeople usually cover more jobs and have less time. In one work day, the radio newsperson may cover a beat, write news stories for several newscasts, interview several newsmakers, anchor several newscasts, and cover a local government meeting. Because of this type of schedule, most radio interviews are done over the telephone because it saves time and the telephone also has some advantages over face-to-face interviewing. Many busy people will answer the telephone and talk for five minutes, although they would turn down a formal appointment for an interview in their office. The telephone can get into places where a reporter, in person, might not be able to go.

Most radio newsrooms are arranged for easy telephone interviewing.

Telephones are hooked up directly to tape recorders, and to record an interview all the interviewer needs to do is to start the tape recorder, set voice levels, open a switch, and start to talk. Some general rules about interviewing by telephone are (1) set the voice levels and (2) have the equipment working before you make the telephone call. This will avoid having the interviewee wait while you set up the equipment. As soon as you get hold of the person you wish to interview, identify yourself and your station and ask the person for permission to record the interview for replay on your newscast. If the person agrees to a recorded interview, start the tape recorder and reask the question so that you have the agreement on audio tape if later the interviewee changes his or her mind and says he or she did not know you were taping the conversation you have proof to the contrary. Always notify someone when you want to tape an interview, because failure to get permission to tape a conversation for replay on radio may be a violation of FCC regulations or state or federal law.

Radio news has some obvious advantages over television news, which relies on heavy, bulky videotape or film equipment. First of all, audio tape recording equipment is lighter and more portable than television news recording equipment. One person can easily handle an audio tape recorder or cassette tape recorder and conduct an interview. Audio tape is also much easier to edit than videotape or film. The radio news interview can be edited and prepared for use in a newscast within 15 or 20 minutes. An interesting aspect of recording telephone conversations is that the interviewee cannot see the tape recorder and so there is less chance of the interviewee "freezing" during the interview. We are all used to talking on the telephone, and this natural situation is not likely to inhibit the interviewee.

Radio news interviewing by telephone does have some disadvantages. The interviewer cannot see the interviewee, so an important visual element is lost to both parties. Since we communicate visually as well as verbally, the interviewer and interviewee are not able to see what each is saying or take body language cues that would be given off in a face-to-face conversation. The interviewer also loses the ability to control the interview during a telephone conversation. Since you cannot see what the interviewee is doing or who else might be present, there may be distractions.

Television News

The television news interviewer is burdened with a lot of heavy equipment that requires constant attention, proper lighting levels, and some type of power source. In the days before the widespread use of videotape and electronic news gathering equipment, the television interviewer also had the constraints of a film magazine that held about 12 minutes of film, so almost all interviews were conducted in less than 12 minutes. The videotape camera and recorder has liberated the television news interviewer from the 12-minute interview, but film and electronic news gathering equipment need a power source, so if batteries have to be used, the battery life can be a controlling factor. Unless the power source is AC, a rechargeable battery that lasts about 1 hour may be the only power source available. In many ways, the television technology dictates story length and even on occasions story content.

The television interviewer, unlike the radio news interviewer, normally conducts interviews face-to-face. This requires arranging appointments in advance, driving to and from locations, adjusting time schedules to match the interviewee's schedule, and making sure there is a power source nearby or that batteries are charged and ready to go. A further complication may arise in small television news operations where the reporter may have to share a photographer with several other reporters and the photographer's schedule has to be matched with the interviewee's schedule.

Most television interviewers try to set up interviews in realistic surroundings to avoid too many "talking head" interviews which show a tight shot of the interviewee's head and shoulders. Watching a "talking head" newscaster lead to a "talking head" film or videotape interview is dull television. A great deal of time and effort is and should be spent trying to avoid this type of interview. Reporters will try to get the interviewee to meet at good visual locations that will reinforce the story content. For example, instead of interviewing the city commissioner in charge of traffic safety in his or her office, the interviewer might set up the interview at the busiest, most dangerous intersection in the community. In this way, the photographer can also shoot silent film or videotape of the intersection, which can be used with the interview to support or illustrate what is being said.

While there are obvious differences between the radio news interviewer and the television news interviewer, the nature of broadcasting and broadcast journalism imposes some similar problems on both. For example, both radio and television news interviewers have awesome deadlines and strict time limitations on the amount of material they can use.

For the radio news reporter, there may be a deadline every hour of the day and there is constant pressure to provide the newscaster with different audio tape for each newscast. Since radio news has so many deadlines during the day, however, missing a radio news deadline has less severe consequences than missing a television news deadline. Radio news is generally run for a short time every hour, so if the radio newsperson cannot get the interview back to the station on time, the interview can certainly be back at the station in time for the next scheduled newscast. Missing the 6:00 P.M. television news deadline, however, means that the film or videotape story will not be run until the late night news at 10 P.M. or 11:00 P.M. Television news is run less frequently during the day than radio news, but television newscasts generally run 30 minutes long and are a major production and journalistic effort.

If the television news interviewer fails to make a deadline, the producer or news editor will be faced with revising the newscast at the last minute and creating terrific production problems. Failure to make a deadline in television news is a major offense. If given a choice, most television news editors or producers would probably prefer using a mediocre story or an interview that is on time and fits into the assigned newscast than a great story that is too late for the assigned newscast. Television news is a balance between quality and deadlines.

Television news editors and producers work with people and equipment that are not nearly as portable as radio reporters and audio tape equipment. Most television reporters can cover one or possibly two stories during a day. These stories are assigned in the morning, and the news editor or producer starts planning the content of the evening newscast shortly after making assignments. Throughout the day, the news editor's plans are based on the interviewer completing the assignment and coming back with usable film or videotape. If the reporter fails to cover a story or do an interview that is usable, the news editor will lose a visual segment of the newscast, and this can create major timing or planning problems. Television news editors generally assign safe stories that they know will provide usable film or videotape. Because there is so much pressure to produce visual stories, the news editor cannot afford to assign risky stories that may not produce good film or videotape.

Because of the deadlines and constant pressure to finish one story and move on to the next story, most broadcast news reporters cannot devote too much time to research and this leads to shallow interviewing. The format restrictions of radio and television news dictates that interviews be very short. It is not uncommon for a radio news audio tape to be 15 or 20 seconds long. Because of the small amount of air time devoted to individual film or videotape stories, the broadcast interviewer generally tries to get short summary statements from the interviewee. Very seldom can the news interviewer go into complex issues or in-depth topics, because they will run longer than the air time allotted for the story. Because of the demand for short, succinct, witty statements that summarize issues, it is very easy for individuals to prepare canned answers and dominate or control the interview. Many experienced politicians may even ask the reporter how long a statement is wanted on a particular topic and be able to extemporize a statement that is within five or ten seconds of the time specified.

Because of the nature of radio and television news, many stories are virtually written before the interview takes place, and the interviewer merely wants the interviewee to make the "right" statement that fits the story. This is especially common when one of the wire services— Associated Press or United Press International—carries a story that contains a quote or several statements. Radio news reporters will call the individual quoted in the wire story and try to get the person to say on audio tape what was written in the wire service story. Television reporters, with all their bulky equipment, are slower and have to make appointments and arrive at the location for the interview. Because of the time lapse between when the story clears the wire and when the videotape or film will be aired, television reporters try to update a story or get the interviewee to project into the future so the news story will not seem like old news.

An example of the difference between radio and television news is shown in the following situation. Suppose at 10 A.M. the wire services carry a story about a local police officer arresting a man who is wanted in connection with a murder and armed robbery. The local radio reporter might call the police department at 10:05 A.M. and get a telephone interview with the police officer, which would be used on the 11:00 A.M. news. The local television reporter, however, may not get to the police station until 1:00 P.M. and by this time the arrest is already three hours old. The television interviewer might try to update the story by finding something new in the case. He or she might try to get a statement from the district attorney about the arraignment procedure, bail or bond possibilities, or some unusual aspect of the case that the radio and newspaper reporters may have missed.

This type of hard news interview is conducted under severe time limitations and deadlines with virtually no opportunity for research except reading the wire story or talking with the arresting officer for a few minutes before the interview. This is the worst type of journalistic interviewing, and normally it will produce shallow interviews and summary statements. The technology, competitive factors, and the fear of being different leads to this type of interviewing being common in broadcast news.

THE IN-DEPTH RECORDED INTERVIEW

The in-depth recorded broadcast interview is very similar to the journalistic interview except for the recording equipment. This type of interview is usually best handled when it is done over a period of days or weeks, as David Frost did when he interviewed former President Richard Nixon. Frost and his team recorded Nixon for 16 hours and then cut the videotape down to 4 programs each of which was 90 minutes in length.[2]

[2]David Frost, *I Gave Them a Sword* (New York: William Morrow & Co., Inc., 1978), pp. 20–21.

This type of interviewing, when it is spaced out over a period of time, gives the interviewer time to view the videotape or film of each session, check facts, and in later interviews confront the interviewee with distortions, lies, or position changes. David Frost's outlines for his series of interviews with Nixon contained: (1) questions that had to be asked, (2) general areas to experiment with, and (3) verbatim quotes from Nixon or others that could be used to confront the former president during the interview.[3]

In-depth recorded interviewing is much safer than live interviewing and there is a lot less pressure involved. Both the interviewer and the interviewee are more relaxed because they do not have to worry about errors, long pauses, timing, or pacing. All of these elements can be cleaned up by editing. The recorded interview is structured and built in the editing room by the producer or the editor. The editing process is designed to shape and to add continuity to an interview that may have wandered around and touched on the same topic several times. The pacing will be improved by editing, and the interview will be cut to fit a predetermined time slot.

THE IN-DEPTH LIVE INTERVIEW

Live radio and television interviewing is exhausting, risky, and intense. It is also very rewarding and fun when it goes well and the interviewer and interviewee forget about the technology and have a good conversation. The live radio or television interview is a cross between the brief news interview and the in-depth recorded interview. Mike Wallace says of the live television interviewer; "He is not only reporting, he is actually editing and publishing at the same time."[4]

The performance aspect is constantly present in live broadcast interviewing. The interviewer must never forget that he or she is "on camera" or "on mike" or he or she could lose control of the interview and miss important time or commercial cues. A live radio or television interview is a performance, and people who do live broadcast interviewing for a living can become stars.

Asking high-risk questions during a live interview may also be very embarrassing. Former Governor Lester Maddox walked off the set during an interview with Dick Cavett when Maddox demanded and did not receive an apology for something Cavett said. Fortunately, Cavett had another guest on the program and they were able to fill the program time. Barbara Walters probed into Bert Reynolds's divorce, and Reynolds then turned the tables and asked her if she cared to talk about her recent

[3]Ibid.
[4]Hugh Downs and Mike Wallace, "The Craft of Interviewing," *Television Quarterly* 4 (Summer 1965): 10.

marital separation. Asking high-risk questions is truly a risk on live television or radio. The interviewer must always be poised for the unexpected response and hope that he or she can cope with the answer or provide a retort.

Most of the time interviewees on live television programs are prescreened by a member of the program staff. A member of the "Tonight Show," for example, screens all prospective interviewees and makes a list of questions and possible responses for Johnny Carson to use when he conducts the interview. Prescreening prospective interviewees can open unique lines of questioning or point out high-risk areas to avoid. Prescreening may also point up other possible problems, such as a problem talker or a person who might freeze before the camera.

One technique that many live radio and television interviewers use is to educate viewers or listeners as the interview progresses. Many times, the question during a live interview serves two purposes; it gives history or background and it elicits specific information. The interviewer makes sure that the listener or the viewer understands the significance of the question by providing historical or background information as part of the question. An example of this technique follows.

INTERVIEWER: Now, Mr. Jones, you've been an attorney for the American Civil Association for close to 30 years. During this time, you've defended the rights of Communists to speak out in public and be a member of the Communist party. You've defended the rights of Ku Klux Klan members to march in the South. Why do you now oppose the ACA's defense of the American Nazi party's right to march in Skokie, Illinois? What is the difference?

Another related technique used by radio and television interviewers is to summarize periodically what has been said, especially after an answer to a question has wandered a bit or is not very clear. If the interviewer summarizes what he or she thinks was said, this clarifies the question and answer and gives the interviewee a chance to agree or to correct any misconceptions. An example of this technique follows.

INTERVIEWER: In effect, you are saying that teachers have lost control of what takes place in their classrooms because school administrators keep their jobs only as long as the public is content, and they want to avoid disciplining or failing a student whose parents might create a public stir?

INTERVIEWEE: Yes, that's basically it. When a few angry parents show up at a school board meeting to complain that their children failed a grade at school, the school board members, who are elected, tell the school administrators to keep things smooth. If it means passing a student who should have failed, well, then so be it.

TYPES OF INTERVIEW PROGRAMS

There are many different types of interview formats that are used to fill television and radio schedules. Some of these are:

1. game and quiz shows
2. public-affairs and public-service programs
3. magazine programs
4. news programs
5. interview programs

Game and Quiz Shows

These shows rely on an initial short interview to build rapport between host, contestants, and audience. Once superficial information is gained and rapport established, the quiz or game part of the program is introduced. Some of the best quiz and game show formats encourage a continuing conversation/interview between host and contestants during the game part of the program. This allows continued rapport between contestants and audience and enables the host to pace the program by lengthening or shortening the conversations as necessary.

Public Affairs and Public Service Programs

Most television and radio stations produce some type of public affairs program that deals with news-related topics or that delves into local/regional social, political, and economic issues. A common format is to have one host/interviewer question several guests about a particular topic. This type of program normally focuses on one or two specific areas and is informational in nature.

Another approach is to have several reporter/interviewers question one guest, such as is done on "Meet the Press" or "Face the Nation." This type of format works best when the interviewee is well known, able to talk intelligently about many different topics, and able to sustain the pressure of an extended interview with several questioners.

Magazine Programs

In this type of program several unrelated segments or elements are held together by a host or several hosts. "Sixty Minutes," "AM America," "The Today Show" and "The Merv Griffin Show" are examples of the magazine format. In all magazine-type programs the interview is an important element, and the hosts are generally very good interviewers. The interviews are generally short, focusing mainly on personalities, although, in some of these type of programs there are news interviews that disperse information as well.

News Programs

For a variety of reasons, many television or radio stations in the United States purchase most of their local programs from outside sources. The only local type of programming that these stations produce are daily newscasts. News programs on radio or television almost always will contain some type of recorded material: audio tape, videotape, or film. Much of this recorded material will be short excerpts of interviews conducted by reporters over the telephone or in the field where the news is happening. A five-minute radio newscast will normally contain two to five short interview excerpts; a half-hour television newscast, on the other hand, may contain as many as six or eight short interview excerpts.

Interview Programs

Straight interview programs are generally only successful if the interviewer is dynamic and can become a personality or a star in his or her own right. Tom Snyder, Johnny Carson, and Dick Cavett are personalities who draw an audience no matter who their guests are. Even though these interviewers are stars themselves, the selection of people they will interview is extremely important. Snyder and Cavett cannot carry the whole program or maintain interest without controversial, witty, intelligent interviewees.

BROADCAST INTERVIEWING STRATEGIES

Broadcast interviewing is a combination of the best and the worst of journalistic interviewing. The same basic principles used in journalistic interviews are also used in broadcast interviews, but in broadcast interviews there are technological, legal, and artistic factors that affect the interview. The broadcast interviewer must be an entertainer who can make the performance look easy. The best broadcast interviewers seem to make things go so smoothly and effortlessly that many people wonder why they get paid so much money for doing nothing.

Many of the strategies learned in journalistic interviewing are used in broadcast interviewing. However, the technology and demands of the medium place other requirements on the broadcast interviewer. As we have discussed, the broadcast interviewer has to retain control of the interview, cope with the technology, and appear to be totally at ease. There are certain strategies that broadcast interviewers use, though, whether the interview is taped or live:

1. intense concentration
2. interview structure
3. body language

4. silent or dead air
5. rehearsals
6. general strategies

Intensity of Concentration

Broadcast interviews demand an intense amount of concentration by the interviewer. In a newspaper or a magazine interview, the interviewer can allow the interviewee to wander over many topics for several hours and then go back to the newsroom and edit and structure the story. In contrast, the broadcast interview is edited and structured as it occurs, and the editor is the interviewer. The broadcast interviewer must be careful to keep the interview on track and yet follow up leads given by the interviewee, must make sure the pace and interest level is maintained, and make everything look easy and casual. The broadcast interviewer must be able to edit or compress the interview into a short time period and not appear to be hurrying the interviewee. All of this involves a great amount of concentration and skill to conduct the interview, to cope with the technology and time limitations, and to appear poised and in complete control of the situation.

Interview Structure

Mike Wallace, CBS newscaster, says that all broadcast interviews should have a "story line" or a structure.[5] Broadcast interviews tend to be structured more tightly than other journalistic interviews because of the time and technology demands of radio and television. Broadcast journalists tend to get to the heart of the interview and the high-risk question faster than newspaper journalists do because they do not have the time to build slowly to the high-risk question.

One strategy many broadcast interviewers use to get into the heart of the interview faster is to ask the first few low-risk questions off-camera or before the interview starts. They may spend a few minutes chatting and establishing rapport off-camera and by the time the interview starts they have already moved halfway to the high-risk question.

Body Language

Broadcast journalists tend to use body language and their own body responses to help build a communication link with the interviewee. Barbara Walters, for example, tends to lean forward toward her guest in an effort to increase communication and help the interviewee forget there are cameras and other people present.

[5]Ibid.

Eye contact is also very important in communication. When a person is interested in what someone else is saying, he or she tends to look the other person in the eye to encourage the person to keep talking. If the interviewer leans forward toward the interviewee and at the same makes eye contact, the interviewer also indicates a desire to get closer to find out more intimate information. The interviewer hopes that during the interview there may come a moment when their eyes lock, when the camera or tape recorder is forgotten, and when the interviewee opens up and talks freely.

Dead Air

Dead air is the broadcast interviewer's way of punctuating, adding drama, or stimulating the interviewee to talk about something in greater detail. Dead air, or the deliberate failure of the interviewer to ask a question immediately following an answer, tends to stimulate the interviewee to fill the "dead space" and keep on talking, sometimes revealing intimate or important information. An example of this follows.

> INTERVIEWEE: I never really had contact with him about the construction project except for payroll accounting matters. So I didn't know what he planned to do or really what he did until after he was indicted by the Grand Jury. . . .
>
> INTERVIEWER: (Pause 4–5 seconds. Interviewee nods head encouragingly.)
>
> INTERVIEWEE: Well (nervously), I'm sure that initially he didn't plan to use substandard concrete in the foundation. . . .
>
> INTERVIEWER: (Pause 3–4 seconds)
>
> INTERVIEWEE: I mean . . . well . . . he told me that the concrete was good and would hold. But, I don't know about that stuff . . . I'm an accountant, not a contractor.
>
> INTERVIEWER: Let's go back a moment. At first you say you didn't even talk about the construction project. Now you have just said that he did talk with you about the concrete quality. You can't have it both ways. Which is it . . . did you know or didn't you?

Hugh Downs recalls the time when Jack Parr sat quietly without saying a word and Mickey Rooney punctuated the silence by talking and talking and talking. Downs says Rooney spent 25 minutes digging himself into a hole 50-feet deep. Mike Wallace uses dead air when he gets half an answer; frequently the interviewee will feel uncomfortable and keep on talking.[6]

---

[6]Ibid.

Rehearsals

Most broadcast interviewers will tell you not to rehearse your interview totally or it will sound rehearsed and have a dull, mechanical quality. Other interviewers say that a general discussion of topics and general questions and possible answers help the interviewee determine how to answer questions and where the interviewer will lead the interview. If the rehearsal is more of a general discussion, it can probably be beneficial, but to rehearse specific questions and answers is probably a dangerous technique.

General Strategies

Broadcast interviewers have developed other general techniques or strategies for live or taped interviews. These techniques were developed to fit the unique problems of broadcasting and have specific reasons for being adhered to.

1. *Always have the next question ready.* Occassionally, the interviewee will cut an answer short and catch the interviewer unprepared for the next question and a long silence will occur. To avoid dead air and an awkward situation, always have the next question ready while you concentrate on the interviewee's answer.

2. *Ask questions that most people would ask if they met the interviewee or had a chance to do the interview.* One complaint that many people have is that broadcast interviewers forget to ask the question that they would like to know about. Remember, you are the audience's surrogate, and your job is to ask those questions that members of the audience would like to ask. You are also a professional, though, so make sure that after you ask those general questions of interest you also probe beneath the surface.

3. *Ask questions that the interviewee would like to be asked.* This is an ego builder for the interviewee, and it also produces good information. If you are interviewing a powerful businesswoman, for instance, ask her a question that will allow her to talk about her rise to power and the barriers she has had to overcome. The answer probably will be very interesting and will reveal a great deal about the woman's character and determination. Most people who have risen to powerful positions are not bashful about their struggles, and many of them are proud of their accomplishments.

4. *Do not refer to a question or a comment made before the interview started.* This question is out of the audience's frame of reference, and they will feel left out of things if you constantly refer back to another conversation. Referring back to a conversation that the audience has not heard or seen is also very confusing. Do not refer to the audience in "television or

radio land" during the interview or say "members of our audience would like to know." Members of the audience should be eavesdroppers on the conversation, and by constantly reminding the interviewee of the audience you may inhibit his or her answers or induce him or her to freeze during responses.

5. *Do not interrupt the interviewee with meaningless phrases or sounds, such as, "I see" or "uh uh."* These do not really encourage the person to talk; they are repetitious, sound bad, and make the film or tape difficult to edit.

HAZARDS OF BROADCAST INTERVIEWING

Government regulation of broadcasting places a burden on the broadcast interviewer who must know and comply with Federal Communications Commission regulations dealing with indecency, political broadcasting, the "Fairness Doctrine" and personal attack. The broadcast interviewer must not only know how to interview but also must be part lawyer and know how to steer clear of areas that could involve the station in a legal suit or demands for equal time. An example of this follows.

> INTERVIEWER: What will it take to straighten out the problems in the city welfare office?
>
> INTERVIEWEE: I'm glad you asked that question, because it is something I am vitally concerned with. I think it will take a new philosophy of government. And the person best able to do that job is. . . .
>
> INTERVIEWER: (Interrupting) That is an interesting topic— philosophies of government. But, with the elections next week, we want to avoid taking sides in the election or endorsing one candidate over another. What else could be done to straighten out the city welfare office problems?
>
> INTERVIEWEE: Well, probably a new procedure for screening those who apply for welfare would cut out a lot of paperwork and areas for mismanagement. For example. . . .

Although there are several different types of broadcast interview situations, there are certain basic problems that most broadcast interviewers have to cope with.

1. time factors
2. technology shock
3. technological problems
4. fear of being recorded
5. freezing on the air
6. problem talkers

7. the interviewee taking control
8. lying by the interviewee
9. failure to prepare adequately
10. professions that are difficult to interview

Time Factors

Time in radio and television is very costly. WCAU Television, Philadelphia, Pennsylvania, for example, sells 10-second commercials in prime time for $900 and 30-second commercials for $2100.[7] Time is so important that normally everything that is played on a radio or television station is tightly formatted, structured, and timed to avoid running long and interfering with commercial or program time.

Whether interviews are done live or recorded and edited, they must normally fit into a very tight, predetermined time slot. For example, a news interviewer may conduct a 15- or 20-minute interview covering several different topic areas. The producer may assign a 90-second time slot for the story, so the reporter must fit the interview and script into the allotted time. In many instances, the choice is not what story to tell but how much to tell in the time available. Former NBC news correspondent Ron Nessen gives the example of a reporter who tells his producer that he has a good story that needs 3 minutes to explain. The producer counters by saying she has 45 seconds for the story. An interviewer doing a live interview in a magazine program also has time restrictions and must be able to conduct the interview and bring it to a natural conclusion in the allotted time. If the interview is scheduled for 8 minutes and it runs 2 minutes long, some other element in the magazine program will have to be shortened or eliminated.

Technology Shock

People who are not familiar with television or radio can easily be overwhelmed by the studios, equipment, and technology needed to record a broadcast interview. (Radio suffers less from this problem than television because there is no need for lights and cameras as in television.) The broadcast interviewer must be aware of technological shock and be able to overcome the interviewee's fears and inhibitions.

Experienced television interviewers often will take an inexperienced interviewee on a studio tour before sitting down on the set for the interview. It is also a good idea to get the inexperienced interviewee on the set 5 or 10 minutes before the live interview starts so that he or she can get

[7]*Television Factbook* (Washington, D.C.: Television Digest, Inc., 1977), p. 692b.

used to the lights and movements of the technical people. Sometimes a tour reduces anxiety to the point at which during the interview the interviewee may forget that the cameras and other people are present. If the interview is being filmed or taped, assurances that major mistakes or flaws can be edited out may also ease the novice interviewee's mind. Be careful, however, that you do not let the interviewee think that he or she has the right to ask for content changes.

Technological Problems

One thing that always is running through the minds of the radio and television interviewer is, "Is the equipment working?" Because broadcasting relies so heavily on electrical and film recording equipment, it is only a matter of time before equipment problems occur.

Losing an interview because of technological problems can create several problems. First of all, the program producer or news producer already may have scheduled the interview for that day's newscast or show, so now other program material will have to be found quickly to fill the hole. Second, the interviewer may be embarrassed because now he or she must·go back to the interviewee and ask for another interview appointment.

Fear of Being Recorded

Both radio and television interviewers constantly run into people who consent to interviews but balk when they see the recording equipment. Some people fear that they will make errors or look bad and have to be coaxed into being interviewed on camera or tape. One reporter says that he tells people who resist being interviewed that he is not there to make them look bad. He just wants information that the interviewee has and he will edit out the bloopers or bad spots. Cindy Schoepner, KLWN news director, says she can usually convince someone to allow her to tape the interview by telling the person, "Someone is going to have to explain this issue on the air. It's going to be you or me; now who do you want to do the explaining?"

Some people fear being recorded because film or tape leaves little doubt about what was said. It is virtually impossible for an interviewee to claim that he or she was misquoted if the reporter has the film or videotape to prove what was actually said. In newspaper or magazine interviews, when they are not audio tape recorded, the interviewee can claim that he or she was misunderstood, was misquoted, or did not make the statement at all.

Freezing on the Air

The camera or tape recorder inhibits most people, and some are inhibited to the point where they are speechless. If the interview is being taped, this situation can be overcome by turning off the equipment and reducing the interviewee's fears. Many experienced interviewers say freezing normally occurs if the interviewee does not understand what is expected of him or her. To avoid this situation, it is best to tell the interviewee to ignore the equipment and technical personnel and just concentrate on the interviewer and carry on a normal conversation.

Freezing is not uncommon, but it can be overcome with patience and time. If the interview is live, however, patience and time may not be available. Most people, though, do not freeze to the point at which they are speechless. The most common occurrence is when someone is witty and verbal off-camera and then very uncommunicative when the camera or tape recorder is turned on. Again, proper conditioning before the interview is the best defense against the interviewee freezing on camera.

Problem Talkers

Problems occur most when an extroverted person who has a lot to say does not understand the dynamics of a broadcast interview. The best way to avoid this problem is to explain before the interview that you will lead the interview and that the interviewee should keep his or her answers relatively brief and to the point. You have to do this with some subtlety because you do not want to inhibit the interviewee and create a situation in which the interviewee is afraid to answer questions fully or to talk about interesting areas that you fail to mention. A good way to explain what you want is by going over your interview outline and discussing general responses or areas for response.

Despite your best precautions, however, some interviewees will still be problems on the air or in front of the camera, and you must be prepared to deal with the situation diplomatically. If the interview is being taped, you can let the person ramble on if you have enough tape in your camera or tape recorder. If you do not have an unlimited supply of tape or film, you will either have to interrupt or signal the camera operator to turn off the equipment. If the interview is live, you will have to interrupt and gain control of the interview. One way to stop a problem talker from rambling on is simply to put your hand on the person's arm; this generally will stop the person from going on. If you have commercial breaks in the program, you can take those minutes to explain that the interview is going far off track and into areas that are not productive or that answers are running way too long and must be shorter.

The Interviewee Taking Control

In live situations or when you have limited supplies of film or videotape, it is very easy for the interviewee to monopolize the interview and take control. This is usually done by those interviewees who are aware of broadcasting's limitations and are sophisticated in using the media. Nearly every broadcast reporter has experienced the situation in which he or she asked a politician a question and received an answer that did not relate to what was asked, because the politician had a statement to make no matter what the question. The only thing that can be done in such a situation is to signal the camera operator to turn off the camera or let the film or videotape run and then re-ask the same question. An example of this type of situation follows.

> INTERVIEWER: Senator, why did you support the Stoker Amendment, which would raise personal property taxes, when it appears your constituents favor a tax cut?
>
> INTERVIEWEE: I'm glad you asked that question because I do favor a lid on spending. The taxpayer is tired of the government overspending billions of dollars each year. Just look at the Air Force buying planes that don't fly and the Navy purchasing ships that can't sail. When I was on the committee that investigated the Department of Defense, we found terrible waste . . .
>
> INTERVIEWER: (Interrupting) Excuse me, but . . .
>
> INTERVIEWEE: (Continues over interviewer) and I promise you who are listening to me that I will continue to fight for your rights in Washington and watch your money to make sure that is is being wisely spent . . .
>
> INTERVIEWER: (Interrupting) Ah . . . Senator . . . we just ran out of film.
>
> INTERVIEWEE: You're welcome. Glad to talk with the press anytime.

If you are on the air live when this happens you cannot do anything unless you want to make a major issue out of the incident and confront the politician with the evasion. You can re-ask the question and hope for an answer or you can just go on with the interview and hope to lead the person back to areas you want to discuss.

Some interviewers have a technique that reduces the chances of the interviewee taking control. It appears harsh, and occasionally the interviewer is accused of badgering the interviewee, but the technique is effective. The interviewer simply stops the person in mid-sentence and says, "Your answer does not relate to the question I asked; your answer seems self-serving." This usually embarrasses the interviewee into responding to the question, but it can make enemies, and the listener or viewer may not like the way the interviewer handled the situation.

Lying by the Interviewee

Richard Reeves points out that newspaper interviewers can go back to their offices and at leisure check facts to make sure that the interviewee was telling the truth. The broadcast interviewer, on the other hand, has to be well prepared and able to catch lies or distortions immediately and confront the interviewee.

How many times have CBS viewers watched Mike Wallace lead an interviewee on a certain line of questioning and then suddenly confront the person with an inconsistency, a statement from the past, or evidence that contradicts the answer? Wallace's technique is devastating, and it indicates that he knows as much, if not more, about the particular topic than the interviewee does. Catching the interviewee lying or distorting the truth can only be done by a broadcast interviewer who has researched the topic and the interviewee's background and knows what answer to expect.

Failure to Prepare Adequately

As a group, broadcast interviewers tend to be not as well prepared for an interview as newspaper and magazine journalists. This is because broadcast interviewers may have to interview more people in one day than print journalists, so the interviewer simply does not have enough time to research and to prepare adequately for the interview. It is not uncommon in some news operations for a broadcast journalist to interview two or three people on different topics during one work day. Preparation may consist of reading a brief news release, talking over possible questions with the photographer, or discussing for a few minutes with the news editor or other reporters.

Professions That Are Difficult to Interview

Radio and television interviewers quickly learn that there are certain professional people who generally are more difficult to interview than others. Professors, doctors, lawyers, and scientists may be awkward to interview because they use technical jargon and are very concerned with how they are viewed by other members of their profession. Members of these professional groups tend to talk in a specialized language and to speak very carefully and formally. There are obvious well-known exceptions to this rule, such as Dr. Joyce Brothers and Dr. Carl Sagan, but, on the whole, members of these professional groups tend to be more difficult to interview than members of some other professions.

One television reporter says that he tells doctors, scientists, and professors to explain complex issues to him as they might explain them to a 12-year-old child. This sometimes reminds the interviewee that the item is very complex and that the interviewee needs to take special care with the answer. The reporter says this technique works sometimes but, too often, as soon as the camera and the lights are turned on, the interviewee slips back into the public, professional role and his or her answers become complex and formal.

THIS CHAPTER IN PERSPECTIVE

The technological and live demands of broadcast interviewing set it apart from the typical journalistic interview. Some of the basic strategies and techniques are similar to the journalistic interview, but there is always the element of entertainment present. The broadcast interview must be highly structured and carefully planned, but these are the two areas most commonly overlooked by the broadcast interviewer. The novice interviewer watches the casual performance of the experienced interviewer and wrongly assumes that the relaxed atmosphere indicates no appreciable planning or research. The broadcast interview is like an iceberg in that only a small portion of the whole is seen.

PROJECTS

1. Read the broadcast news interview at the end of this chapter and write a critique of the interviewer's strategy and tactics. Try to answer the following questions:
    a. Was the interviewer prepared for this interview? From your evaluation, were the questions carefully prepared? Was the interview structured? Had the interviewer prepared for the interview with enough research?
    b. Who had control of the interview; the interviewee or the interviewer?
    c. In general, was this a good interview example. Why? Why not?
2. Listen to a radio newscast and view a television newscast. Then critique the way in which the interviews were used. Attention should be paid to the content, the supporting materials in the script leading to the interview, and the length of the interview.
3. Critique a local television interview program. Then compare it with "Bill Moyers Journal," "Wall Street Week," "Firing Line," or Tom Snyder on "Tomorrow."
4. Visit a television station and view the production of an interview program.
5. Interview a radio or a television reporter. Ask the reporter how he or she prepares for each interview and whether or not there are special techniques that he or she uses.
6. For practice, interview someone about a book that that person has read recently.
7. Discuss the various audiences that a television interviewer is trying to address. (Often, for example, there is a studio audience in addition to the televi-

sion audience.) Every reporter has a very special audience of peers and management.

8. Discuss how far a reporter should go to get the interviewee to disclose information that the interviewee obviously does not want to disclose.

9. What is the appropriate balance between interviewer and interviewee participation in a broadcast interview?

SAMPLE BROADCAST INTERVIEW[8]

Interviewee: My name is Anita Tassinari and my title is executive director of the Alachua County Older Americans Council.

Interviewer: Okay, would you please tell me basically what your Meals
on Wheels program consists of?

Interviewee: Yes, when it started in March of 1974 we were serving 65
home delivered meals each day in the Gainesville area among
elderly people, 60 and older, who needed this help either temporarily or sometimes permanently recommended to us by their friends,
family, their neighbors or by themselves or their doctors or even
social workers or perhaps somebody in the hospital where they
had been for treatment of a broken bone, operation, and illness.
But the doctor had said "Yes you may go home, but who is going to
look after you when you get there?" Then, that's where we came in.

Interviewer: Do all the hospitals in the Alachua County have your
number and know of you?

Interviewee: Yes, yes they do. And most of the hospitals have social
workers who are quite well aware of us.

Interviewer: Okay, and to qualify for this, there is really no qualification.
All they have to do is just call you?

Interviewee: That's right, but we make home visits, of course, and it's
up to us to make the determination, if there's a waiting list, and
there usually is a small waiting list. Ah . . . we can serve 80 meals
that are under our grant. And then because of local assistance and
other ways we're able to add another 10 meals. Ah . . . so we're
usually sending 90 meals out a day. Part of it is dependent upon
volunteers who are willing to come in and deliver these meals. So it
breaks down to about 10 routes of 8 or 9 trays per route and, ah . . .
2 volunteers to a route, who come only once a week, therefore, it
takes 20 a day or 100 a week for delivery. And, of course, we're
very fortunate some of the people we've had are ones who've
started coming in 1974 and are continuing to come even after 4½
years of assisting us once a week. Ummm . . . and there are others
who have dropped out and had to be replaced. We find the
churches very helpful in helping us fill these needs and at the very
beginning, before we had any volunteers, we went to the churches.
In fact, just to get off the ground and get started back in '74 we
asked each church denomination to take one day as their responsibility and try and fill it with all the volunteers we needed for that
day. So for a while we had a day called "Catholic day" or the

[8]Anita Tassinari, Executive Director of the Alachua County Older Americans Council,
interviewed for WRUF Radio, Gainesville, Florida, by news reporter Susan Brooks.

"Methodist day" or the "Presbyterian day" or the "Baptist day" or whatever day, but now that isn't so any more. We get people from every organization, just calling up and volunteering. We have mothers bring their little children by the hand, 2-year-olds, and we have couples who are retired who are delivering. One time somebody called us up and said . . . ah . . . and was feeling in a jolly mood, I guess, and he said "You know the people who delivered me my meal to me today, I think are older than I am."

Interviewer: (Laughter)

Interviewee: And this could happen because we've had people in their 70s delivering meals for us.

Interviewer: Could you tell me a little bit about the food you serve? How is it prepared? Hmm . . . and how do you determine what types of meals to make?

Interviewee: Yes, of course. Well, we have our own kitchen, and we have . . . ah . . . a menu cycle that we repeat. Ummm . . . its probably a four-week cycle that is repeated two or three times before we change it . . . as seasonal changes. We have diets in our home delivery phase, low-salt, low-sugar, and bland, as well as regular diet. All these diets, menus, are prepared by registered dieticians and checked by a second registered dietician in Gallahassee under HRS before it is approved for us to use, so it is about a six-week process before we can get the menu prepared for a four-week period. . . . We have an advisory council made up of people who are participants in our program. . . . So it is a really well-balanced, full meal.

Interviewer: Uh huh. Do you feel that workers who are delivering the food are also giving those people companionship as well as the food they need?

Interviewee: Yes. Absolutely. In fact, it is equally important with the food. And some people have told us it is more important. Those receiving the meals say to us "We like the food but it's even nicer seeing, knowing I can count on seeing someone every day." And looking forward. . . . Of course, as I've mentioned, people come and go on routes. Many are there temporarily while they are ill and recuperating and too weak to shop and cook for themselves because they live alone. Others stay on longer. But they do look forward to these visits, and the visits mean as much to them as anything. . . . It isn't just a hot-food program.

Interviewer: Okay . . . um . . . let's see. How do the family members of the recipient feel about your program? And do you have any contact with the family members?

Interviewee: Oh, yes. Often we are serving two people in one home. We've served all kinds of combinations. We've served two sisters, sister and a brother—all elderly of course—husband and wife, um . . . many combinations, ah . . . two men in a home, younger members, the children who are married, are often not living in _____. But they will send us money from wherever they are. We receive checks from California to pay on a meal we have been delivering to that person's mother to assist with the cost of the meal. . . . And everyone is given that opportunity to give, to donate, whatever they can but there is no . . . ah . . . specific charge per meal. Ummm the sit-down meals, the congregate meals in our four dining rooms . . . the cost is to us . . . $1.55. For the home delivered meals, because of the diets and the fact that we use a very fine . . . insulated tray costs $1.70.

Interviewer: Oh . . . do these people pay for these meals?

Interviewee: Well, that is what I was pointing out. There is no specific charge because most everyone that we are serving needs our help, and also the government has given us guidelines to go by. But we are allowed to indicate the cost to us. . . . But we also accept food stamps; we are approved for food stamps. And these turn into cash for us and any money that is donated in this manner is put into an escrow account in the bank, and we follow federal guidelines and then at the end of the first year we use whatever has been collected from our participants as the initial part of our food program budget for the second year. And this has been followed each year. We . . . ah . . . reached about $10,000 each year. Ummmm, this past year we hope to exceed that and maybe get to $12,000 . . . donations this year. Just from the participants alone, now this is not counting money donated by churches and other organizations, which assist us very much, particularly with our Meals on Wheels.

Interviewer: How severe would you say that the problem of the elderly and poverty is in Alachua County? Is it a major problem?

Interviewee: Well, of course, when we think about the poor countries of the world, I guess that we can't say it is a major problem. I think, ever since 1930, when Social Security was started by the government. . . . And I am sure there are elderly people who over a period of years have not been able to eat right, and perhaps that has contributed to their death. I would hate to think that anyone in the United States would actually die of starvation.

Interviewer: Can you tell me about any other services that your organization provides for the elderly?

Interviewee: Yes. We don't stop with just food. We ask first that our volunteers—because they are the ones going each day to the homes—be sure and always come back to report to us any needs that they see or feel that we can further assist our people. Of course, our staff are making regular visits to these homes, too. We never take on anyone into our program without knowing them personally and having visited in their homes first to know exactly what they need. But after we get them on the program, we are concerned about other problems that may arise. . . . We have the ability to send a handyman out to assist an older person in their home. . . . We've even changed light bulbs. . . . If a person needs help with a Social Security problem, food stamp certification, ahhh, getting glasses fixed, any kind of service that we see, that may be needed we stand ready to assist the person with.

Interviewer: Is this program restricted just to Gainesville, or is it more extensive than that?

Interviewee: Yes, our name is Alachua County Older Americans Council. It was organized 7½ years ago by a group of people living in this area, some of them living in the small towns of the county. Organized mainly by retirees, some retired teachers, members of the mental health association, some retired ministers—and I always like to say that I was pleased that . . . ah . . . that we thought of it from the county . . . ah . . . broader context than just Gainesville. Also, I was pleased that members of the board came from both the black and white community in all our endeavors. Also we've gotten good support from the small towns of the county. We conduct programs in every small town of Alachua county, regularly, on a weekly and monthly basis. And we've been doing this for four years. . . . These programs are quite varied; some are simply singing and recreation. Many of them are informative; we invite the fire department, the police department, the food stamp people, social workers, the Bureau of the Blind. We invite people to talk on nutrition, and a great deal of information can be learned over a period of time with these little, short 10- or 15-minute programs that precede the lunch.

Interviewer: I notice there is a stereo with an album and a table full of games over there, as well as a scale. It seems like you are trying to combine enjoyment with health. Is that correct?

Interviewee: I am glad you brought that up. The health I haven't really touched on, and it's important. It is our objective to get out health information and to provide health services. Here we are living in, the center really. I feel that _____ is becoming the center of health service because we have four fine hospitals. . . . Health is a very important concern of older people. They want to know more, and we try to provide them information. How to reach services and even give them free services and also free transportation if that is what it takes to get them to a health care facility.

Chapter 16
News Conferences

The news conference is basically a modern-day public relations/publicity device designed to generate favorable news coverage. Daniel Boorstin would call the news conference a pseudo event, because it is not spontaneous; rather, it is planned in order to get press coverage, and many of the announcements made in a news conference become self-fulfilling prophecies.[1] Most news conferences are planned and controlled by the person who will be the focus of the press conference. For example, a business executive, politician, or actress might call a news conference to announce the successful launching of a new product line, a political campaign, or a film venture. The news conference certainly is not spontaneous; it is designed to generate good publicity for the business executive, the politician, or the actress, and the announcement of the "successful" venture may be a self-fulfilling prophecy if the venture is successful. In effect, the interviewee tries to control the situation and gain publicity to help the venture by monopolizing events so that they appear to be newsworthy.

[1]Daniel Boorstin, *The Image* (New York: Atheneum Publishers, 1972), pp. 9–12.

TYPES OF NEWS CONFERENCES

There are three basic types of news conferences:

1. formal
2. spontaneous
3. background

Each of these news conferences serves a different and important function in the flow of information between the interviewee and the reporters who represent the general public. The news reporter/interviewer is basically a conduit who passes along information and acts as a gatekeeper in the flow of information between the news maker and the public.

Formal News Conferences

Formal news conferences generally are arranged and controlled by the interviewee, and they are designed to satisfy one or more reasons for holding a news conference. The purpose for the news conference should be very precise, such as to rebut a specific rumor, introduce a new product line, or make a major announcement of general interest. Generally, in a formal news conference the topic is focused on by the interviewee through an announcement, a statement, or a news release given to the reporters at the start of the news conference.

The initial announcement or news release will normally focus the questioning on the areas that necessitated calling the press conference. For example, if the president of a major corporation and the mayor call a press conference to announce the expansion of a major business in the area, which will result in 120 new jobs and a payroll of $15 million, then most of the questioning will probably revolve around this topic. A sample initial announcement may sound like this:

> INTERVIEWEE: Good afternoon. I'm John Watkins, president of the XYZ Manufacturing Corporation. I think I know many of you . . . at least your faces are familiar, so I've seen many of you at various business or civic affairs. The reason I have called this news conference is to announce a major expansion of our company. You should have all received a packet of information when you came in. It contains a news release, an architect's drawing of the new facility, and some facts and figures relating to the expansion.
>
> To summarize the news release quickly, we plan to build a 40,000 square-foot facility adjacent to our present plant. The new facility will cost $2.1 million to build. When completed—and we estimate that will be 22 months from today—we will employ 120

new employees to produce the new and improved XYZ gidget, which we hope will become a household word. The new facility will double our gidget production capacity and allow us to become a national firm that can supply 60,000 gidgets a month.

The opening news announcement did several things:

1. It announced a major expansion.
2. It focused the reporters on this topic.
3. It got a plug in for gidgets.
4. It reminded everyone how important gidgets are for the local economy.

It would be considered bad form for a reporter to ask Mr. Watkins about another topic during the formal question-and-answer session following the announcement of the expansion. This is not to say, however, that a reporter would not ask Mr. Watkins about some other topic later after the formal question-and-answer session was completed. In many instances, great stories have been obtained after the formal news conference was completed and everyone was standing around drinking coffee and chatting about a variety of topics. The follow-up questions to the announcement probably would focus on the announcement and its impact on the local community. Because most reporters would ask questions containing local ramifications, part of the initial decision making to expand, hire more people, expand production, and build the complex should be made with an eye toward local public relations values. This could mean, for example, that if local people were not capable of handling the sophisticated gidget machinery, instead of going outside the market to hire gidget producers it would be better public relations to hire local people and train them to operate the gidget machines. This would result in local people benefiting from the expansion. A local firm could be hired to construct the new building, and the contract might specify that local subcontractors could be used or, if the construction firm is from outside the region, that they could employ a specific number of local people.

Some likely follow-up questions to the opening news announcement would be:

1. One hundred and twenty new employees would generate how much of a payroll for this area?
2. Are you going to hire locally?
3. Who will build the plant?
4. Is there a market for 60,000 gidgets a month?
5. Will this benefit other local businesses, such as transportation, packaging, and so on?

Spontaneous News Conferences

A spontaneous news conference can either mean that the news conference is not focused and ranges over a wide variety of topics or that the news conference is not a planned one and has come about spontaneously. In either case, the questioning will range over a number of areas, and the interviewee has much less control of events or topics than he or she would if it were a formal news conference. A good example of this type of news conference would be when the president of the United States meets periodically with news reporters. The president may make an announcement at the beginning of the news conference, but following the announcement the questioning may range over a wide variety of topics.

A spontaneous news conference may be controlled by the interviewee or it may also be controlled by the news reporters. The interviewee might have regular news conferences but set certain guidelines, such as a specific time limit, no direct quotes, and no cameras or recording instruments. If a spontaneous press conference is centered on an event, then the news reporters may exert some control over the situation. An example would be if a business executive comes out of a closed Senate hearing and finds himself or herself surrounded by newspaper, radio, and television reporters. A hypothetical dialogue follows.

> INTERVIEWER: Mr. Watkins, you have just testified behind closed doors for three hours before the Senate Monopoly Committee. What did you tell them regarding charges that XYZ gidgets have monopolized the gidget market?
>
> INTERVIEWEE: Well, much of what was said and the questions asked cannot be repeated at this time. At least, I do not think I have the right to reveal that information, but I can say that I rebutted the monopoly charges. It is true that we have acquired several small gidget firms in the past few years, but these were marginal firms that were in or near bankruptcy. The firms that we purchased would have gone out of business and put several hundred people out of work. The reason they were not economically sound was because they had old, out-dated equipment, and we invested several million dollars in each gidget firm to make the firm productive and economically stable.
>
> INTERVIEWER: That's fine, but did you monopolize the market and drive others out of business?
>
> INTERVIEWEE: No, we did not. There are three other gidget firms in the country. We just build a better gidget for a lower cost, and so we are tough competitors. Would you rather we not build a good gidget at a price lower than other gidget builders?

The business executive, Mr. Watkins, did a number of things in the impromptu news conference outside the Senate hearing on monopolistic practices:

1. He rebutted the monopoly charges.
2. He presented to the public his firm's side of the argument.
3. He got in a plug for XYZ gidgets and pointed out that they are good and less expensive than competitive gidgets.
4. He put the reporter on the defensive with a question that really has only one answer.

This type of news conference is a spontaneous event over which both the interviewee and the reporters exert control. The interviewee may decide to withhold information or not talk with the reporters, whereas the reporters may badger the person into speaking with them and answering questions.

Background News Conferences

The background news conference serves the purpose of transmitting news from the interviewee to the interviewers without the high-risk stakes of a formal or a spontaneous news conference. The background news conference usually concerns itself with general background information that reporters need to interpret events correctly and to write about them with insight. The background news conference is not very common in business, but it is a common occurrence in Washington, D.C., where government officials give information to reporters that is not immediately useful for a story but that is useful as a background to understand future events.

The background news conference generally has very formal or rigid guidelines. Many times the interviewee will stipulate that everything is "off the record" and that no recordings can be made or that no direct quotes or direct attributions can be made. In this way the interviewee is put in a position in which he or she can comment freely without fear of seeing direct quotes or attributions in the next day's newspaper or on the evening news. The general information can be used by the reporter, but the reporter cannot reveal the source of the information. Many stories in which the news reporter says "informed sources" or a "high government official" came out of background news conferences.

The background news conference can be initiated by the interviewee who wishes to transmit information to reporters or by reporters who, feeling the need for a greater understanding, can pressure a government official, for example, to hold a background news conference. An example of this would be when the president announces that he is taking a trip to Saudi Arabia or some other foreign country. Members of the news media want to know not only the official reasons for the trip but also the unofficial reasons, and they might pressure the State Department or the president's press secretary for a background briefing. During the background briefing, the government representative might "leak" to reporters that one unannounced goal of the trip is to discuss Soviet and Cuban involvement in the Horn of Africa and how it might affect the Arab nations.

The background news conference is useful because it provides government or industry leaders with a way of "leaking" information to the public without being held responsible for the information. Because the event is off the record, information is transmitted, but reporters have agreed prior to the news conference that only general information can be used and that no direct quotes or attributions can be used. Some government officials use the background news conference to see what public or press reaction might be to a proposal or an idea without publicly committing themselves to the idea. A government official, for example, might wish to see what the public's reaction would be to the system of National Health Care before she comes out publicly and supports the program. She could, during a background news conference, mention that her department supports the plan and then watch to see what reactions occur after the story is used by newspapers, radio, and television. In this way the official can avoid supporting an unpopular public program.

An example of a business executive using an off-the-record background news conference occurs when an industry or a business wishes to support or to fight a government action. The business executive could call reporters together and tell them, off the record, how much a proposed government action could hurt the business and eventually how much of an impact it would have on the local economy if operations are curtailed. The story would be published or broadcast, but the business executive would not be named as the source.

The background briefing has been a constant source of irritation to news reporters, because clearly it is a way for the interviewee to use the media. Some reporters do not want to be put in the position of attending sessions where everything is off the record because they feel that they are being used by the interviewee. Several newspapers or news organizations have policies that their reporters will not attend off-the-record sessions. Their philosophy is that they are in the business of getting and reporting news, not just gathering it for their own personal benefit.

REASONS FOR HOLDING A NEWS CONFERENCE

There are many reasons people hold news conferences and expose themselves to the risk of meeting with news reporters. Some of the reasons are in the public interest, whereas others are self-serving or egoistic:

1. to transmit legitimate news or information
2. to see his or her name in print or his or her face on television

3. to generate publicity for an event, person, firm, or idea
4. to tell his or her side of a controversy
5. to rebut rumors
6. to remove pressure from reporters for a news conference or a personal meeting

Transmission of News

News conferences frequently are used by people in government and business to transmit legitimate information to all news organizations at the same time. Someone might call a news conference to announce a new product line or a business expansion that would have a major economic impact on the community, or a government official might call a news conference to release the details of a new highway system or the construction of a new federal building. The information is new, newsworthy, and of legitimate interest to the general public and the news media. This type of informational news conference provides an efficient method of transmitting information to all interested parties at the same time and avoids duplication of effort, since most reporters would want the same basic information. Without a formal news conference, a representative might have to meet individually with 12 or 15 reporters and spend several days being asked the same question and giving the same basic information.

Strictly internal operations of a firm or a government agency seldom are interesting enough to justify calling a news conference. News conferences should not be called to announce an internal reorganization, promotions, or awards unless the event has a major impact on the community. If a person wants to obtain publicity for these types of events, he or she should go to the public relations department and ask them to send out a news release and see if any reporter is interested enough to follow-up the story. To call a news conference and announce matters of internal importance normally are counterproductive, because it irritates reporters by making them feel they have been used for no newsworthy purpose.

Ego Gratification

Ego gratification is one reason people call news conferences, and this venal reason generally pushes them to call a news conference over minor or internal matters that do not interest others outside the organization. Calling or holding a news conference for ego gratification generally works against the corporate image and can damage the credibility of a public relations staff. Many good public relations specialists have lost the respect of people in the news media because they were asked to a news conference that did not impart legitimate information and wasted the reporter's time. Sometimes public relations specialists exercise bad judgment in an effort to get headlines or news coverage of an event; however, many times the public relations person was forced to arrange a press conference knowing full well it was held only to please the superior's ego.

Generation of Publicity

Another reason for calling a news conference is to get publicity or news coverage for an event or a particular situation. The news conference may be part of an overall public relations campaign to generate publicity for a product, an event, or a person. Most corporations and prominent individuals employ public relations specialists in an effort to manage the news generated about them and to coordinate efforts and events that might get news coverage. For example, General Motors and Ford Motor Company engage in massive publicity campaigns every year when they introduce their new car models. These firms purchase advertising in almost all the media, but also they make an effort to generate free news coverage in newspapers and magazines and obtain free air time on radio and television stations. These firms hold massive parties for newspeople, and they invite writers from automobile magazines to parties where the new car models are shown and executives talk with reporters to stimulate good publicity or news coverage.

Telling His or Her Side of a Controversy

Anytime there is a controversy in a community that involves divergent viewpoints, the people involved in the controversy try to present their side of the issue to the public and justify their position. Many times, if the issue is highly controversial or emotional, like busing, nuclear power, or abortion, people will call a news conference.

In general, business and industrial leaders have ducked their responsibilities by failing to present their company or industry position adequately to the press. Often chief executive officers try to back out of a public fight, fearing that it is a no-win situation and that there might be contact with the news media. In effect, they fail to represent their company and to protect the firm's reputation and image. Backing out of a public fight does not stop the fight; it just gives the field (news media) to the other side. Most reporters want to express both positions in a controversy, but if an executive fails to uphold his or her responsibility and meet with reporters to express the company point of view, then the reporters must either present a biased story or try to summarize the executive's viewpoint without his or her help.

Rebuttal

Many times rumors circulate about individuals, companies, or situations and a news conference is called to issue an official statement designed to discount these rumors. A company president, for example, might call a news conference to rebut rumors that his or her firm has made bad investments and is going into bankruptcy. This type of rumor, if it is not stopped, could lead to a loss of confidence in the firm, and stock prices could fall and the firm forced into bankruptcy by a false rumor. A news conference, if it is well planned, should present the company point of view, stop the rumor, and reestablish confidence in the company.

Reaction to Pressure to Hold a News Conference

Often when there is a major controversy or a serious rumor about a firm or an individual, members of the news media will generate the impetus for a news conference. If rumors about a company's financial health are circulating, news reporters will start calling the public relations department or various contacts inside the firm to find out what is going on. Rather than have several different stories emanating from the company, it may be decided that it is better to have one representative meet with all members of the news media and answer all of the questions at once.

This type of pressure is rather common. Every time a public utility asks for a rate hike rumors start circulating as to what it will mean, and usually the rate hike creates quite a bit of controversy. In many instances, though, the chief executive officer tries to remain out of the spotlight until he or she must answer or try to stop the rumors rather than simply presenting the firm's point of view at the outset and halt potential rumors before they start. At this point, the company is involved in remedial actions and is on the defensive rather than being positive and aggressively presenting the company's viewpoint.

ADVANTAGES AND DISADVANTAGES OF NEWS CONFERENCES

Holding a news conference has some advantages over individual meetings with every news reporter who wants information, but there also are hazards that the interviewee should be aware of before committing himself or herself to the rigors of a meeting with members of the news media. Some of the advantages are the following:

1. Reporters are treated equally.
2. There is a better usage of the interviewee's time.
3. The interviewee can focus the news conference or limit the areas of questioning.

Some of the disadvantages are:

1. The interviewee may lose control and not be able to limit the areas of questioning.
2. The interviewee may be forced to give speculative answers.
3. Syntax and language suffer under questioning.

An advantage of holding a news conference is that every news reporter is treated equally. Everyone has a chance to attend the news conference and everyone attending has an opportunity to ask questions and get answers to their questions. If there is supplemental information, such as a press kit, everyone attending the news conference gets the same press kit. This equal treatment reduces the possibility that a news reporter will charge later that the interviewee or the firm favors one particular station or newspaper over another. Calling a news conference and inviting everyone in the news media reduces the chance that someone will think the interviewee is playing favorites.

The interviewee can also make better use of his or her time by calling one meeting with reporters rather than meeting alone with each reporter. However, as the number of reporters increases so does the pressure to perform. There is also the fact to consider, however, that if you make an error in front of many reporters, the error is compounded and can be widely disseminated. Holding a press conference does increase risk and the amount of pressure on the interviewee. A classic example of an error getting more coverage than a statement of substance is when former President Gerald Ford, during an election visit to Iowa State University, said that he was glad to be at "Ohio State University." The error got more news coverage than the substance of his speech, which dealt with farm policy.

Another thing that can happen during a news conference is that the interviewee might be forced to speculate about events outside his or her control. This should be avoided, although most news reporters will try to induce the interviewee to speculate about how something might happen or if it would happen at all. The best way to avoid speculative answers is to say that there are so many things that could happen that it would be unwise to speculate. If pressed on the issue, the interviewee should always assume that others involved in the situation will do the honorable or right thing. Do not speculate, in public, about the motives of someone else or assume that they will do something negative. If you must give a speculative answer, be positive and assume that individuals, firms, or countries will uphold their responsibilities and do what they have agreed to do. For example, if you are pressed to answer whether or not a local contractor will complete a construction project on time, you should always publicly assume that the contractor will perform as expected and complete the job on time. You might hedge your answer, though, by saying that while you feel the contractor will finish on time, the contract does contain a penalty clause if the project is not completed as scheduled.

Language use or syntax usually suffers during a news conference unless the interviewee is well prepared for the news conference and had had considerable experience with news conferences. It is understandable that under the pressure of being questioned, filmed, recorded, and examined minutely by a number of reporters an answer may wander or sentences and ideas may be garbled unless they are well rehearsed. Even the most polished performer may stumble or say the wrong thing. Former President Gerald Ford fumbled an answer during his televised debates with Jimmy Carter. Ford said that Poland was not under Soviet dominance when he really meant to say that the United States did not recognize the fact that Poland was dominated by the Soviet Union. President Jimmy Carter's statement about "ethnic purity" sounded radical, but, as was later explained, it referred to the way many cities or communities have ethnic areas that retain their foreign cultural flavor and customs.

PLANNING STRATEGIES AND TACTICS

News conference planning and strategies are hard to separate into discreet categories. Planning involves strategy decisions, and vice versa.

Planning

Despite the high risks involved in a news conference, it is surprising how many news conferences or meetings with the press are left to chance. Chief executive officers who would spend days preparing for a high-level staff meeting or a board meeting walk into news conferences with little or no preparation. In this type of situation, is it any wonder that they run into hostile questioning or face questions that they cannot answer? This is no place to learn on the job, because one bad experience could hurt an executive's image (hence the company image) and make the individual wary of ever again meeting with news reporters.

In many instances, news conferences are planned only after there has been negative publicity, and the news conference is a defensive one and is designed to answer charges. In such a situation it is best if the company's public relations plan is positive and aggressive in telling the company's side of the story. Ideally, the news conference should be part of an active public relations plan.

Executives, businesspeople, politicians, or government officials who know that they will constantly have to meet with news reporters should train themselves in news conference techniques and strategies. This is one area where learning on the job can be disastrous, and a planned, controlled situation should be created where you can experiment, learn, and be critiqued on your performance.

There are a number of individuals, consultants, or public relations firms that can provide training on news conference techniques and strategies. The most realistic way of approaching this situation is to rehearse and role-play the interviewee in a news conference setting. This should be done in front of lights, television cameras, audio tape recorders and, in some instances, hostile questioning from people who are role-playing news reporters. The news conference can be videotaped, so that the interviewee can see how he or she performed and can listen to his or her own answers in response to the hostile questioning. Becoming familiar with the physical setting of a news conference will give the interviewee confidence in his or her abilities. Once the interviewee is familiar with the physical setting, he or she can concentrate on formulating answers, thinking under pressure, and learning how to handle tough questions. If a formal training session cannot be arranged, the public relations department can at least simulate a news conference setting to give you some familiarization with it before you have to face the real thing.

Short-term planning for a news conference is based on the assumption that the interviewee can physically handle the news conference and retain some control. With this assumption, the public relations specialist should go through the following checklist with the interviewee.

1. Determine precisely the news conference goal. This should lead to a determination of which content areas will be covered and which areas will not be covered by the interviewee.
2. Prepare a list of possible questions and draft responses to the questions.
3. Determine who will be invited and the physical setting for the news conference.
4. Determine how the news conference will be terminated.
5. Prepare supporting materials. This should include a press kit containing a news release and visual materials.
6. Have the interviewee memorize the questions and answers and then rehearse the news conference.
7. Make sure that company officials with specialized knowledge are at the news conference to answer technical questions.

Strategies

With this seven-point checklist in mind, you should now consider how each one of these points will be handled.

DETERMINING GOALS

Many times the goals for a news conference are set by circumstances. External events create the need for a news conference, and the news conference is called to meet those needs. Rumors, controversy, or the introduction of a new product line set their own general goals for the news conference. Determining specific goals will lead to a decision on what content areas will be included in the news conference and which areas to avoid. Two examples might be:

rebut and stop rumors about the financial status of the company
reestablish confidence in the company by showing that its financial
status is good

This could be accomplished by doing the following.

1. Be the only company voice on this matter. This means that all statements about the rumor would come from the chief executive's office after consultation with attorneys and the public relations director.
2. Clearly and simply rebut the rumor and present your side of the issue.
3. Provide supporting evidence to rebut the rumor and support your position.
4. Explain the significance of the evidence verbally and/or visually.
5. Establish a general feeling of confidence in the interviewee's character and control of the situation through manner, language, and supporting materials. This will create a halo effect that will carry over to the company image.
6. Explain how the rumor or problem may have started, if this can be determined.
7. Limit the news conference to a single purpose or the impact of the news conference will be diluted.

Once the goals are clearly outlined, content areas will generally fall into place. For example, you might decide to talk about the following things at the news conference.

1. sales of new gidgets introduced in the market last year
2. last audit by an outside accounting firm
3. investments made during the past year
4. the specific rumors

Furthermore, you may decide not to talk about the following:

1. the recent fire in plant 3
2. the firing of a union steward for insubordination
3. the fact that the chairman of the board is dating a 17-year-old movie starlet.

The interviewee can try to limit questioning in several different ways. The most popular method is simply to focus the news conference by means of an opening statement and by saying that questions about the opening statement will be answered but questions about other topics will not be answered. If there are questions about other content areas, indicate you will arrange another news conference or individual meeting to answer those questions.

PREPARING QUESTIONS AND ANSWERS

Preparing questions and answers is rather easy to do and should not take a competent public relations staff more than a few days to complete. The best way to start this task is by reviewing all the news coverage about the firm and all recent press contacts. This information will show what various members of the news media feel is important, so the staff can assume that some questions will be asked on these topics. Careful analysis of the goal and the content areas of the news conference will also lead to potential questions.

The staff should always assume that embarrassing questions will be asked or that reporters will automatically assume the role of devil's advocate. Careful responses should be worked out by the staff that would either answer these questions or turn the news conference back to desired areas.

DETERMINING CIRCUMSTANCES OF A NEWS CONFERENCE

Since most news conferences are designed to get maximum news coverage, normally everyone in the local and regional news media is invited. However, there may be times when only specific reporters who specialize in a topic might be invited to the news conference. If the content is specialized, then the news conference may be limited to those who can talk specific jargon and understand the topic.

Timing of the newscast is important, because the various newspapers and radio and television stations have different deadlines. For example, the evening newspaper may have a deadline of 11:00 A.M. for its early edition. The television stations may have a 4:00 P.M. deadline for their early evening newscasts and a 9:00 P.M. deadline for their late newscasts. Radio is more flexible because stations generally have a newscast every hour, so missing one deadline is not as serious as missing a television or a newspaper deadline.

Where the news conference is going to be held should be determined by two things. The first of these is that the interviewee should have control and should be in a comfortable setting, which will help the interviewee gain a psychological or a physical edge. This should take into account whether or not the interviewee will stand up, sit down, stand behind a podium or a lectern, or sit behind a desk. These are issues that have a direct bearing on the way the interviewee will be perceived by reporters and those viewing the videotape or film.

A desk or a podium can be a psychological barrier between the interviewee and the news reporters. The interviewee may prefer being behind a podium or a desk because it offers psychological protection, and this can reduce anxiety or the fear of being totally exposed to strangers. A desk or a podium may be necessary for notes, holding microphones, or psychological support. Standing at a podium tends to make the interviewee more imposing, distant, and authoritarian. Standing behind a podium can also give the interviewee a psychological edge in controlling the news conference. While the reporters sit in a group, the interviewee stands behind a podium facing them from an elevated position. Sitting down behind a desk is less formal and imposing than standing. The interviewee and news reporters are closer together and they are looking at each other eye to eye. The sitting down news conference is probably smaller (four to ten reporters) and more relaxed, and this seems to reduce pressure on the interviewee to perform well and control the news conference. When the interviewee sits down at a table or a desk with reporters, he or she is psychologically doing away with some formalities and is allowing the reporters to gain more control and meet him or her on equal terms.

Select carefully the room in which the news conference will be held. Rooms with a lot of windows or fluorescent lights should be avoided, because this poses problems for the television photographers who must control lighting. If the room has windows, make sure that shades or blinds can be drawn to control sunlight. Also make sure that there is no music or loud noise from something such as an air conditioner, because this would affect sound amplifiers and tape recorders. If there is music or a hum from an air conditioner, make sure that maintenance personnel are available to turn off the music or air conditioner during the news conference. Another good idea is to make sure that you have a number of electrical outlets or long extension cords for the television and radio reporters who must set up lights and need electrical power for their equipment.

ENDING THE NEWS CONFERENCE

News conferences can be ended in two ways: (1) planned and (2) unplanned. It is obviously best to plan the way the news conference will end, because this gives the interviewee greater control over the situation. The best way to end a press conference is to have the press aide or a public relations person stop the news conference at a predetermined time or at a predetermined signal from the interviewee. Limiting the time of the news conference also limits the number of questions and answers that can be given. President Carter, for example, prepares answers for 25–50 questions, but during a normal news conference only 18–20 questions can be asked and answered. A few business executives and politicians have developed a technique that creates a favorable attitude on the part of the press. At a predetermined time in the news conference the press aide or the public relations specialist will announce that the news conference is over and that the interviewee has an extremely important appointment that must be kept. This now leaves the interviewee either to agree and leave or to say that he or she can put off the important appointment for ten more minutes. The reporters will go away from the news conference with the feeling that the interviewee is a fine person because he or she put off a very important appointment just to continue answering their questions. It may sound corny, but it is amazing how often it is used with good results. Like all techniques, however, if it is overused it soon loses its effectiveness.

After the news conference is over, try to provide a situation where news reporters and the interviewee can mix informally and talk. A good method is to provide coffee, cokes, and light snacks in an area adjacent to the news conference. The interviewee and the news reporters can talk in a less pressured atmosphere, although the interviewee should be warned that even though the news conference is over he or she is still being interviewed and can be quoted. During this informal meeting, reporters will continue to ask questions and elicit information. Some reporters who are working on an exclusive story like to save some of their best questions for this informal session when other news people will not overhear their questions and the interviewee's answers.

PREPARING VISUAL AIDS
If possible, always prepare visual aids and a press kit to reinforce the content of the news conference and to illustrate items that are difficult to explain orally. Press kits should contain a news release, photographs, slides, drawings, maps, and any other items that could help reporters understand and visualize the story. Visual aids are good devices to use in a news conference because they help others to understand and because television camera operators are always looking for something visually exciting to photograph. Always employ a television graphic artist to prepare visual aids or you will probably waste time and money. Special techniques and knowledge are necessary to produce graphics that look good on television. An artist's sketch or a model of a building or a bridge is visually appealing to the television photographer or the newspaper photo journalist. An average story with exciting visuals may get more newspaper space and television time merely because the visuals are good.

REHEARSING THE NEWS CONFERENCE
Rehearsing takes time and is generally overlooked in the hurry to get a news conference organized. This, however, is a critical step that should not be eliminated. The interviewee should first read all of the possible questions and answers and then, with the public relations specialist, revise answers in light of company policy and goals. Next, the questions and answers should be memorized with special attention paid to high-risk questions and answers that probably will be asked. Once the questions and answers have been memorized, the interviewee should rehearse the news conference in the room where it will be held. The room lights and physical setting should be arranged as they will be during the actual news

conference to give the interviewee a feel for the real situation. People should be brought in to act as reporters and ask the questions that will probably be asked the next day. Since many people have a tendency to ask their superior easy questions, it might be a good idea to hire a few outside people to act as hostile, badgering reporters who pursue embarrassing lines of questioning.

A rehearsal also will give the interviewee a chance to work with the visual materials to make sure that he or she can physically handle them. Sometimes the visuals are complex, and a public relations specialist may have to handle charts, maps, or chalkboards. This type of situation is best found out prior to the news conference.

AVAILABILITY OF SPECIALIZED INFORMATION

Many company chief executives, politicians, hospital administrators are primarily managers, not technicians. The executive, for example, may have started out in engineering, production, or marketing, but as a manager he or she deals with personnel problems and concepts rather than with specific techniques. When the topic of a news conference is highly technical, the interviewee always should have technical people present who can answer technical questions.

Do not let the interviewee try to fumble through a technical answer for which he or she is not qualified to answer. He or she is better off explaining that the specifics of the problem are very technical and that the project engineer or the director of development are present to handle some of the highly technical questions. It is better to admit a lack of technical background than to fumble through an answer and have some reporter later discover that the answer was wrong.

Tactics

In all meetings between news reporters and the interviewee there is a balance of power. Sometimes the interviewee dominates the situation, but at other times the reporters may be so commanding that they gain total control. Usually, the balance of power is fairly evenly divided during the interview or news conference.

Clearly, the balance of power is a bargaining point in many meetings between news reporters and interviewee.[2] A news reporter may do a newspaper or a television story favorable to an individual in expectation that the person will provide other information in the future or provide access to information or individuals. Many reporters continually do this

[2]Stewart Harral, *Keys to Successful Interviewing* (Norman, Okla.: University of Oklahoma Press, 1954), p. 91; and Leon V. Sigal, *Reporters and Officials* (Lexington, Mass.: D. C. Heath & Company, 1973).

when they need specific information. This is a method of favoring an individual and strengthening the contact or bond between interviewer and interviewee. This does present problems occasionally if the interviewer and the interviewee become too friendly and the interviewer loses objectivity or the ability to report bad news that might affect or hurt the interviewee.

Dr. Joyce Brothers, a psychologist, notes that reporters are disadvantaged in a news conference situation, especially in a presidential news conference. She cites the fact that the president has an aura of power that intimidates and that reporters are further disadvantaged because there are 200 to 400 people who want to ask questions and only 18 or 20 will have that opportunity to do so.[3] A contrary view is held by Deputy Press Secretary Walter Wurfel who thinks that the balance of power is not tipped towards the president:

> I think it's debatable which entity dominates the news conference. Whether the President does or the press. Now I'm confident that if you talked to three network correspondents they'd say "oh, the President dominates it," because after all it is his answer to give or withhold. But, it is the correspondents who choose the topics and choose whether they can be dropped quickly or pursued at some length. And so I think there is some kind of balance.[4]

Wurfel points out further that there are certain aggressive reporters who will always be able to ask their questions of the president, even if they are not called upon. They will stand up and ask the question in a loud, aggressive manner and intimidate into silence the reporter who was called upon by the president.

The interviewee can use a few tactics that will give him or her greater control over the news conference. These tactics are planting easy questions, requiring questions in advance, and handling the problem question.

The planted question is a technique that is commonly used in a news conference. A public relations specialist will approach a friendly reporter and convince the reporter to ask a particular question. The interviewee knows who will ask the question and can plan when he or she will call on the friendly reporter. Planted questions and opening statements are generally used as devices to get positive information out when it appears that members of the press may ignore the particular topic or question. Sometimes a planted question can be used by the interviewee to make a startling announcement or to send up a "trial balloon." An example of this

---

[3]Dr. Joyce Brothers, "The President and the Press," *TV Guide* (September 23, 1972): 8.
[4]Walter Wurfel, White House Deputy Press Secretary, private interview held during meeting of regional Radio Television News Directors Association Convention, Lawrence, Kansas, 1978.

would be if a public relations specialist asked a reporter to ask Congress-woman Y what her election plans are. The answer might be that she is considering running for the presidency because she has received numer-ous offers of support and financial assistance for a campaign. The planted question elicits a startling response that probably will be the evening's lead television and newspaper story. The politician also gets the opportu-nity to see how others respond to her "trial balloon" before she formally commits herself to the campaign.

Another tactic that should be employed is always to identify specific reporters who ask easy questions or questions that can be easily an-swered. If, during the news conference, the interviewee is pressed hard in sensitive areas or on embarrassing topics, he or she can change the track of questioning by recognizing the reporter who will ask as easy or a noncontroversial question. This maneuver will either change the track of questioning completely or give the interviewee time to regain compo-sure.

One news conference tactic that reporters despise occurs when the interviewee demands that all questions be submitted in writing before the news conference. This technique virtually leaves control totally in the hands of the interviewee, who selects which questions will be answered and which questions will not be answered. The interviewee can prepare answers that best service his or her interests. Many reporters refuse to participate in such a news conference because they feel it is purely a public relations ploy and not worthy of news coverage. However, there are some people who are so important or famous that they can use this technique and reporters will attend the news conference despite their personal feelings. A few people who could get away with this technique would be the late Howard Hughes, President Carter, or some distin-guished foreign leader. French President Charles deGaulle always de-manded that questions be submitted in advance to the dismay of the press corps who grumbled about the practice but continued to attend the news conferences. There are stories that deGaulle used to sit behind his desk in front of reporters and thumb casually through the pile of questions until he found one he wanted to answer. Some reporters, anxious to see how their questions fared in deGaulle's hands, resorted to writing their ques-tions on colored paper so they could be spotted as the French president leafed through the stack of questions.

THE PROBLEM QUESTION

Questions that come out of left field can destroy any control the inter-viewee has over the news conference and lead to many problems. If the interviewee loses his or her composure, even easy questions can pose problems, and the interviewee then may talk too much, become emo-tional, or say the wrong thing. Such problem questions can never totally be prepared for, but some strategies or techniques for fielding them can be learned by the interviewee.

The best way to handle a problem question is to have foreseen the possibility of its being asked and to have prepared an answer. If you are a well-known person and you have just been sued for divorce, for example, you should expect questions about the divorce and your relations with your wife. Plan your answers in advance and you will retain control of the news conference and your own composure.

If a problem question is asked and you do not have a prepared statement, you can simply say that at this moment you cannot comment on the issue but that as soon as you can you will be happy to discuss the matter. If you decide not to comment on a question or a topic, also be prepared to explain why you will not comment, because the next question probably will be "Why?" News reporters are trained to probe, and the basic probing question is "Why?" If you do not know an answer to a question, do not be afraid of saying you do not know the answer but you will find out. President Carter is one of the few politicians who will tell a reporter that he does not know an answer, and it is refreshing to hear him admit this. Be careful, though, of using "I don't know" too frequently, because people can start to wonder about your competence if you use this technique too often.

Another way of handling the problem question is to start to answer the question and then lead your answer off to a side issue that you are prepared to discuss. This is done frequently, and most good speakers are rather adept at using this technique. This technique can also be used when you have specific information that you want to present and a reporter asks a question that allows you to lead into the area you wanted to discuss. Once you start discussing the side issue, however, you should avoid follow-up questions about the original topic, since a follow-up question will only point out that you did not answer the question. If the original question is repeated, it can be devastating. Former President John Kennedy would occasionally take any question and give the answer or information he wanted to give out. This can be a dangerous technique, though, because a news conference is designed to impart news, not propaganda, and if the press feels the news conference is a propaganda ploy, it can hurt your public image.

LYING TO THE PRESS

One technique that some people use to retain control of the news conference and to avoid embarrassing situations is to lie or distort the truth. This is generally a risky strategy, because if the interviewee is caught in a lie everything he or she has ever said suddenly becomes suspect. Reporters, like elephants, have long memories, and one lie or distortion can open the interviewee up to the most intense examination and investigation. Despite their sometimes gruff exteriors and caustic wits, most reporters basically are idealists who believe very strongly that an informed public is an integral part of our democratic system. Lying to a reporter is, in effect, lying to the public. Lying is possibly the worst thing that can be done to a reporter. Some people have wondered if President Nixon could have survived Watergate if he simply admitted his errors and promised to clean up the scandal. Many people were more upset about his lies to the nation and the press than they were about any actual involvement in the Watergate scandal.

Rather than avoid a question by lying, you can answer a question and still retain your moral credibility with reporters by saying you cannot comment on the issue. You have put off the issue but at least you have not lied. If you decide not to comment, one good response is to say that you do not have all the facts and until you do, it would be unwise or unfair to comment.

IMAGE VERSUS CONTENT

During the past 10 or 15 years, more and more people have become interested in a public person's image. Studies have been made to determine why one person may seem more dominant than another if personalities are basically equal. The 1960 Kennedy-Nixon television debates also focused researchers' attention to what was said, who won, and who dominated. Although there were many psychological variables involved in the debate, many researchers remarked that Kennedy's poise and general style was a factor that impressed many viewers. Some researchers even went so far as saying that the Kennedy image may have been more important than what he actually said. Kennedy had an image, a style, class, an aura, and a mystique that impressed others and allowed him to dominate older and powerful people.

There are three basic areas that an interviewee should be concerned with that are related to general image: personal grooming, language, and body language or poise.

The interviewee's body language and general body movement also projects an image to people watching and evaluating. An athletic movement carries a different message than a ponderous, heavy movement. Being bent over as opposed to standing erect also says something about the interviewee. The best thing for the interviewee to remember is to move naturally and calmly and avoid nervous hand, eye, or facial gestures that indicate nervousness or lack of poise. Our body movements carry a message, and to those who know what to look for, the body message may have more meaning than what is being said. Studies have shown that when a person shakes his or her head, indicating "No" while saying "Yes," the majority of people would believe what they see rather than what they hear.

Our style of speech and speaking also affects our image. Presidential candidate Al Smith may have been an intelligent, adept politician, but he sounded like a New York gangster and this obviously hurt his image and chances for attaining the presidency. On the other hand, John Kennedy's New England accent worked for him and gave him an image of sophistication and good breeding. Your style of speaking and general speech is much harder to change than the color of your clothes, but, if your speech is a handicap, voice training may be able to improve the image you project. To a certain extent, voice and diction patterns are a product of where you have lived, have gone to school, and your family background. Your speech can be modified, but it takes willpower and formal training.

EXAMPLES OF NEWS CONFERENCES

At the end of this chapter are three examples of news conferences taken from different presidential press conferences. President Carter uses a different opening strategy in each of the examples. The questions and the president's responses were chosen to illustrate the give and take of a news conference.

Read the transcripts of the press conferences and try to analyze the strategy and tactics used by the reporters and President Carter.

Try to answer the following questions:

1. Judging from the opening remarks (if any), in what type of news conference was the president involved?
2. Analyze individual questions and presidential responses. Were questions relevant, and did the president respond fully to the questions or did he avoid giving answers? If he avoided questions, was he successful?
3. Were there any specific questions that were predictable?
4. If there were predictable questions, judging from the president's responses were the answers carefully structured in advance to avoid sensitive issues?

PROJECTS

1. Role-play a news conference with members of the class taking the role of reporters and someone from outside the class assuming the role of the interviewee. Both reporters and interviewee will have to do significant research to make the experience realistic.

2. Observe a news conference. Local newspaper editors or radio and television news assignment editors can tell you in advance when and where news conferences are going to be held.

3. Invite a local business executive or a public official into the class for a news conference. This should be audio taped or videotaped for later analysis.

4. Watch a televised presidential news conference and analyze the dynamics taking place.

OF THE
PRESIDENT OF THE UNITED STATES

at 3:00 P.M. EST
April 25, 1978
Tuesday

In Room 450
Old Executive Office Building

The President: Before I became President I realized and was warned that dealing with the federal bureaucracy would be one of the worst problems I would have to face. It has been even worse than I had anticipated. Of all the steps that we can take to make government more efficient and effective, reforming the civil service system is the most important of all.

The civil service reform proposals which I submitted last month will return the civil service to some system of reward and incentive for the tens of thousands of superb public servants who want to do a good job for the American people.

This will also give managers a chance to manage. It will reward excellence, good service, dedication, and will protect employees' vital and legitimate rights.

It will also expand the protection against political abuse that employees need in order to do their jobs well, and will make our civil service one of the most dependable and one of the most effective and honest in the whole world.

Nearly everyone in our country will benefit from the civil-service reform proposals. For those in private business, it will mean faster government action, less intrusion in the private sector of our economy. For taxpayers, it will mean that we get more for the money that we pay. For those who depend on government for help, it will mean better services to them, quicker, more effective.

And most of all, for the civil-service employees, for the government employees, it will mean that they can do their jobs better and more effectively. They only have one life to live, and sometimes in a sacrificial way they want to dedicate their lives to public service, and this will let them do a better job.

When criticism and debate in the Congress lead to a stronger plan, then I will support those changes. But I will object very strenuously to weakening our proposal, and I do object also very strenuously to false accusations, specifically one that has been raised recently that this will intrude into the privacy of public servants and inject politics and possible abuse into the system to damage those who serve the government. In fact, to the creation of a Merit Protection Board and an Office of Special Counsel, political abuse is specifically removed.

I know that everyone wants a better government, particularly those of us like myself who are responsible for leadership and management of the United States Government.

In a way, I believe that our nation is being tested these days. We have a period of relative calm, free from great crisis or threat to our national security. And we are being tested to see whether or not we can take advantage of this opportunity for improvement.

It will reveal, I think, whether we can deal with conflicting narrow special interests and act in the national interest of our country.

Civil service reform is now before the Congress. It will test me and the Congress as well, and I believe that the Congress will give the right answer to the question: Can we have a better government? I think we can.

Question: Mr. President, where do you stand now on the possibility of imposing by Executive Order or administrative action, oil import fees, and how soon might you act?

I understand that a couple of your advisers are suggesting a May 1 deadline.

The President: Well, no one has suggested a deadline that early. As a matter of fact, we have just finished the fourth major element of a five-part comprehensive fuel or energy program with natural gas deregulation. And now this is being recommended to the complete Conference Committee.

The next step is the crude-oil equalization tax which will be addressed by the Finance Committee in the Senate and the Ways and Means Committee in the House, representatives of them in the Conference Committee.

I have talked to the chairmen of both those committees about the crude-oil equalization tax, the fifth element of our major proposals.

It is too early, I think, to consider administrative action. I still hope and expect that the Congress will act and will complete the fifth element of our energy plan and present the entire package as it would be to the Congress in one body.

Question: Mr. President, President Brezhnev has offered to not build the neutron bomb if you agree or the U. S. agrees to do likewise.

Is that the word you are looking for to halt the program?

The President: No. The Soviets know and President Brezhnev knows that the neutron weapon is designed to be used against massive and perhaps overwhelming tank forces in the Western and Eastern European areas.

The Soviets, over a period of years, have greatly built up their tank forces and others stronger than have the NATO allies.

The neutron weapons are designed to equalize that inequality, along with many other steps that our country is now taking. The Soviets have no use for a neutron weapon, so the offer by Brezhnev to refrain from building the neutron weapon has no significance in the European theatre. And he knows this.

We are strengthening NATO in other ways. Ourselves, our NATO allies, will meet here in Washington the last of May with a recommitment, which is already well in progress, for a long-range strengthening of NATO and all its aspects.

But this statement by Brezhnev concerning the neutron weapon has no significance at all. . . .

Question: Mr. President, just to follow up on the Middle-East thing, I would like to pursue it just a little bit more maybe from a slightly different angle. The Israeli Foreign Minister, Mr. Dayan, has suggested that Israel might be willing to give up its own fighter planes in your package, if the sales were stopped to Saudi Arabia and Egypt.

In the light of your own professed interest in cutting back on foreign arms sales, would you consider withdrawing the entire package to prevent a new escalation of the arms race in the Middle East?

The President: No, I would not. As I said earlier, the process through which we sell arms—and this sales proposal, would be completed five years in the future, by—I think the last deliveries would be 1983—is initiated by a request of arms to them. As I said earlier, we committed ourselves to help Saudi Arabia with arms sales to protect themselves in September of 1975.

At the same time, approximately, in the fall of 1975, our government committed to help Israel with their proposal, by making arms sales available to them. Obviously, if any nation withdrew its request for arms sales, that would change the entire procedure.

I have never heard of Foreign Minister Dayan's statement that they did not need the weapons or would withdraw their request for weapons until today. Mr. Dayan is on the way to our country. He will be meeting shortly with the Secretary of State and others, and I think only after very close consultations with them can we determine whether or not Israel desires to go ahead with the arms sales commitment that I have made to them.

But I do not intend to withdraw the arms sales proposals after they are submitted to the Congress, and I do not intend to delay.

Question: If Mr. Dayan did in fact tell you that Israel would withdraw its request, would you then be willing to pull back the whole package?

The President: I can't imagine that happening, and I would rather not answer a hypothetical question of that kind. . . .

PRESS CONFERENCE NO. 28

OF THE
PRESIDENT OF THE UNITED STATES

9:00 A.M (Local Time)
March 30, 1978

Ballroom
Hotel Nacional
Brasilia, Brazil

The President: Good morning, ladies and gentlemen. I am very delighted to be here in Brasilia to participate in a live press conference, and I will alternate questions from the Brazilian and the American press.

I will begin with Mr. Bonfim.

Question: Mr. President, at the beginning of your administration there was a clear tendency to isolate and treat Brazil coldly in favor of democratically elected governments, elected by the people.

Yesterday at the airport you stressed the need for cooperation between Brazil and the United States as equal partners. Who has changed: Brazil or you?

The President: I certainly have not changed. The experience that I have had in Brazil as Governor of Georgia before I became President made Brazil the most important country to me. I and my wife visited it frequently. We had a partnership arrangement between my own state and the state of Pernambuco.

We studied the background, the history, the culture, and the government of Brazil, and there has not ever been any inclination on my part or the part of my administration to underestimate the extreme importance of Brazil as a major world power, nor to underestimate the extreme importance of very close and harmonious relationships between the United States and Brazil.

There are some differences of opinion between ourselves and Brazil which have been very highly publicized.

But on the long scale of things, both in the past history and in the future, the major factors which bind us in harmony with Brazil far transcends—are much more important than the differences that have been published between our approach to human rights, for instance, and the subject of nonproliferation weapons. But our commitment to Brazil as a friend, our need for Brazil as a partner and a friend has always been the case and is presently very important to us and will always be that important in the future.

Question: Mr. President, despite some jawboning pressure from your administration, U. S. Steel has raised its prices again. How does that fit in with your overall plans on inflation that is going to have some substantial impact nationwide?

The President: It fits in very poorly. (Laughter) I think the prices announced by U. S. Steel, as their plans, are excessive, and although I have not been thoroughly briefed on what the Council on Wage and Price Stability has recommended, I will get that report today, but I think any such increase as I have heard, approximately $10 a ton, is excessive and does cause additional, very serious inflationary pressures in our country, and I think is much greater than would be warranted by the recent coal settlement.

Question: The restraint of your public words until now, your specific desire to meet with the new President, all these facts amount to a virtual blessing of the Brazilian mission. Is your interest in civil rights and political dissidents fading away, or are American economic interests in this country so strong that Brazil is already a special case?

The President: I might say that the history, the culture, the common defense requirements, trade, common purpose bind the people of Brazil, all bind the people of Brazil and the people of the United States together in an unbreakable commitment regardless of the identity of the leaders in our own country or yours. The people of Brazil and the United States are bound together. There is no lessening of our commitment to the principles that you described. The basic freedoms to democratic government, to the protection of human rights, to the prevention of nuclear proliferation, these commitments are also very deep for us.

Obviously, the overwhelming responsibility when I come to a foreign country, no matter where it is, is to meet with the leaders who are in office. But I also will be visiting the Congress this morning. I am sure that I will be meeting with the Chairman of a Foreign Relations Committee who is also a candidate for President.

We have already pointed out I will be meeting with religious leaders and I hope that in this process that I will have a chance to get views from all elements, at least some of the major elements of the Brazilian society. But I am not endorsing any candidates, and I think that the overwhelming sense of my visit already has been that the strength of our friendship and the mutuality of our purposes now and in the future far override any sharply expressed differences of opinion on even the major and very important issues of human rights, nonproliferation, trade, and so forth.

Mr. Cormier (AP) : Thank you, Mr. President.

PRESS CONFERENCE NO. 29

OF THE
PRESIDENT OF THE UNITED STATES

1:55 P.M. EST
April 11, 1978

International Ballroom West
Washington Hilton
Washington, D.C.

Question: Jean Alice Small, the Daily Journal, Kankakee, Illinois.

Mr. President, recently it was reported that Secretary of Agriculture Bergland is considering resignation from his Cabinet post because of your position on agriculture and the farm bill. May I ask if this is true? And in reference to your Cabinet, do you plan to make any Cabinet changes in the near future or after the election?

The President: That report was absolutely erroneous. There was no basis for it at all. There has not been any difference of opinion between myself and Bob Bergland about agricultural policy. At the Cabinet meeting Monday morning, Bob Bergland said that, as was the case when Mark Twain said the report of his own death had been exaggerated, he had never comtemplated resigning from the Cabinet. As a matter of fact, if Bob Bergland and I have ever disagreed on a basic agricultural policy, I am not aware of it. I contemplate no changes in my Cabinet. Nothing would please me better than to finish four years with the same Cabinet I presently have.

Question: Thank you for straightening it out.

The President: Thank you.

Frank Cormier (AP) : Thank you, Mr. President.

(Applause)

Part IV
THE INTERVIEW
AS A RESEARCH
TOOL

The interview is one of the most commonly used techniques for conducting research of all kinds. Therefore, you can read this section regardless of whether you are a manager, an academic researcher, a marketing specialist, a private consultant, or a student in an interviewing class. Furthermore, you can read it with two goals in mind: first, the ideas discussed can help you in any research project that you are engaged in; second, since most of you consume more research than you actually conduct, you can read it with an eye toward becoming a better, more critical researcher.

The goal of Part IV is to give you an introduction to three types of research interviews: survey interviews, telephone interviews, and focus-group interviews. Each of these has some unique aspects that need attention. There are projects that call for a great deal of sophistication in analytic and statistical tools, and we have deliberately neglected these. Such information abounds in numerous statistics books. The treatment of the dynamics of these types of interviews have not received as much attention, however, so we feel that these chapters are ones that will be valuable to you.

The final chapter in this part deals more with a context than a method or a technique. Organizational analysis through interviews has become so widespread that professional managers need to know some of the possibilities for its use, and professional consultants or interviewers need to know how to plan and implement it. No occupation has grown more rapidly than that of "organizational consultant." There are, of course, a lot of good ones and a lot of bad ones. Therefore, the more knowledgeable you are about the procedures of analysis, the more you will be able to discriminate among the best and the less useful analyses.

Chapter 17
Survey Interviews

Research has become almost a way of life in the United States, as people try to collect data about other people's sex lives, their buying habits, their impressions of politicians, their feelings about social issues, their satisfaction levels with their jobs, and their opinions about products. The ability to obtain information in systematic ways has a high priority in most kinds of organizations, and the interview has become one of the techniques used most often to obtain this information. It is the means by which students and faculties in universities collect much of their empirical data; it is the means by which many service organizations try to discover normative behavior; and it is the means by which more and more organizations are obtaining crucial information that helps them contend with their external and internal problems.

Because they are operating in a volatile environment, businesses particularly are finding it increasingly useful to monitor the marketplace. Quite simply, research reduces the areas of subjectivity and increases the areas of objectivity in making management decisions. Through survey interviews, you can investigate (1) where you have been by analyzing and interpreting the past, (2) where you are now by examining present services and markets, (3) where you might go in the future by investigating desires for new directions, and (4) what you have to do to accomplish your goals.

The following list suggests some of the areas for which the survey interview is helpful in obtaining information.

> to determine the demographic information about people who use a certain product or a service: age, sex, educational level, income, and geographical location
>
> to determine who listens to a particular television or radio station and who reads a certain newspaper or magazine
>
> to determine the "share of market" for any consumer product or service
>
> to discover the effects of charges in product or services upon sales
>
> to evaluate television programs in light of viewer preferences
>
> to compile salary ranges for a particular kind of job
>
> to evaluate themes and approaches for advertising a new product
>
> to describe the kinds of training practices within organizations
>
> to project the future of a market by analyzing the expectancies of experts
>
> to determine the voter images of a political candidate

This list could be expanded greatly, but at least it represents some of the many ways that survey interviews can be used.

ADVANTAGES AND DISADVANTAGES OF SURVEY INTERVIEWS

The interview, of course, is only one research technique; there are others that are used widely, too. Nevertheless, in comparison to the others, the survey interview does have several advantages.

Face-to-face contact allows increased rapport with a respondent; therefore, it is easier to gain respondent cooperation. The interviewer can actually sell potential respondents on the idea of cooperating. Furthermore, the face-to-face environment allows the interviewer to observe the difficulties and irritations that occur in the interview and to adjust the interview accordingly.

In a personal interview, it is more difficult for the respondent to terminate the interview. Therefore, there are fewer refusals and terminations with personal interviews than with other methods. In a telephone interview, for example, the respondent can hang up without any repercussions, but it is often difficult for a respondent to ask a person sitting in his or her living room to leave. If rapport can be established, the personal interview generally lasts longer than other methods do.

One of the major advantages to the personal interview is the potential for using visual aids, which allow you to ask more complicated questions. Not only can you get more information, but you also can reduce the potential for distortion in the results.

Personal interviews also allow a great flexibility in the types of questions that can be asked. Because you can show the interviewee questions as well as ask them orally, you can use a mixture of rating scales, projective techniques, and card sorts in addition to the standard question format.

Finally, probing is generally more thorough in the personal interview. This is not even possible with questionnaires, and the amount of probing time is severely limited with telephone surveys. Consequently, the personal interview has a distinct advantage in facilitating discussion of open questions.

Because of these advantages, personal interviewing by skilled personnel is normally credited with being the most accurate data gathering instrument and with being the one that also gives the most complete information. There are, on the other hand, a few limitations to the personal interview.

Interviewer bias is perhaps the greatest obstacle to be overcome. Unless you are very skilled, you may attempt to obtain complete information in ways that lead the respondent. Furthermore, the face-to-face situation provides more opportunities for you to communicate your own biases by ad-libbed comments or nonverbal expressions. *Modeling effects* are sources of bias in any research, and they appear when the interviewer consciously or unconsciously projects his or her own views on the respondent. This can be done verbally, but it can also be done through gestures, shifts of posture, tone of voice, and intensity of expression. Obviously, modeling effects are greatest in the face-to-face interview when the interviewer and the interviewee are confronting one another.[1]

One severe limitation of personal interviewing involves the *sampling plan*. This is the selection of the specific persons to be measured from the total possible respondents. Generally, a sampling of respondents must be selected in advance, and this is often done using meticulous methods. However, the sampling is done without taking into account the percentage of potential respondents who will not be at home. Usually return visits are attempted, but they are very expensive both in time and money.

The next limitation is similar to the sampling plan. The high crime rate in cities has made many potential respondents very reticent to open their doors to strangers. Since these people are the ones who are most likely to have elaborate security devices, it is often difficult to reach people in the upper-socioeconomic classes and the inner-city ghettos.

Personal interviewing is not an economical or an expedient way of covering large geographical areas. To do so would require too much time

[1]Derek L. Phillips and Kevin Clancy, "Modeling Effects in Survey Research," *Public Opinion Quarterly* (Summer 1972): 246.

and travel. Therefore, telephone interviews and mailed questionnaires can cover large areas more quickly and more economically.

When compared with other methods, personal interviews generally require extensive procedural controls and supervisory management. The selection, supervision, training, and controlling of interviewers in the field can be a complex maneuver, and a number of difficulties may be encountered. These can be time consuming.

Perhaps the biggest disadvantage or limitation is the cost of collecting the data. The cost per response is much greater than the cost of other methods, partly because of interviewer fees for time and travel. Additionally, supervisory fees often run as high as 50 percent of the cost of the project.

In summary, the personal interview has some real advantages, but it also has some limitations. As you plot your research strategies, you should weigh them in order to determine which of your several research techniques will be most suitable to your project. Specifically, you should make your decision on the criteria of (1) depth of answers needed, (2) ease of tabulation of answers, (3) time, (4) costs, and (5) potential problems. If you do, in fact, select to use personal interviews, then you can begin to make your plans.

PLANNING THE INTERVIEW

The research interview, like the other types of interviews discussed in this book, needs considerable planning. However, there is one difference that needs to be pointed out. In the discussions about the interview as a tool in management and in the mass media, we emphasized that you must adapt the interview to the respondent. In the research interview, you should not do this. In fact, in order to be rigorous about obtaining information, you are encouraged to treat everyone alike: do not vary the questions, and do not vary the style. With this difference in mind, you can now begin to plan your interviews.

Defining the Problem

The first step in good research is to define the problem and determine the specific information you need. Many marketing research projects fail because the problem was inadequately conceptualized from the beginning. It is only when you know the specific problem areas that you want to investigate that you will begin to design a questionnaire or an interview outline that can be usable.

Refining Your Questions

Write out an outline of questions for each problem area that you want to cover. This becomes a content framework for the particular problem area.

The outline of questions will show precisely the information that is required.

STRUCTURED QUESTIONS

Decide on the types of questions that can best get you the information that you need. *Structured questions* include questions of fact, knowledge, or opinion, for example, "Did you watch the six o'clock news on WXXX last night?" (fact) or "What station shows the program 'Happy Days?' " (knowledge) or "Here is a list of statements some people have made about the way Walter Cronkite presents the news. Please select the one with which you most agree" (opinion). Structured questions can also fall into the categories of single-response or multiple-response questions. An example of a single-response question is "What is your age?" An example of a multiple-response question is "Within the past week, which television stations have you watched for local news?" The important rule of thumb for writing good structured questions is to be certain that you offer a full range of alternatives for the respondent.

Structured questions can use one of the following types of scaling techniques for the answer.

• *Paired Comparisons.* In *paired comparisons* the respondent is asked to make a choice between two alternatives, for example, "Which of the television stations have the friendliest anchor personalities on the news? _____ NBC _____ CBS."

• *Semantic Differential.* In a *semantic differential* respondents are exposed to a series of bipolar adjectives for which they can indicate their relative degrees of feeling. The question below illustrates one way it can be used. The respondents would be asked to show, for example, how they feel about Jimmy Carter. If you want to know how Jimmy Carter compares with another candidate, you could ask the respondents to judge "Candidate X" on the same scales.

warm	____	____	____	____	____	____	____	____	cold
competent	____	____	____	____	____	____	____	____	incompetent
liberal	____	____	____	____	____	____	____	____	conservative
active	____	____	____	____	____	____	____	____	passive

Once the respondent has checked one of the blanks on each line, you can then explore through the personal interview why he or she made the choices. Ultimately, the answer to the question "why" may be more valuable to you than the choice itself.

• *Rank Order.* For a number of items the *rank order* can be used to assess people's priorities. You could, for example, give a person a list of three potential candidates for the presidency and ask that they be ranked in order of preference.

• *Rating Scales.* Through the use of *rating scales* respondents are asked to use a numerical scale in answering a question. You could ask, for example, "How strongly do you feel that the federal government needs to balance its budget?" and offer a scale like the following.

very strong   1   2   3   4   5   not strong

Rating scales like this one have several advantages. They are easy for respondents to use; they give direct information about respondents' degree of preference; they give more information than paired comparisons do about the general level of preferences; and they allow for more sophisticated statistical methods in analysis.[2]

• *Card Sorting.* *Card sorting* is a method that has grown in popularity. The respondents are given a variety of cards with particular concepts or statements of attitude on them. As they read these concepts or statements on the cards they are asked to divide the cards into piles on a board, with each pile representing different degrees of agreement or disagreement. This method allows the gathering of information from a large number of "questions" within a relatively short period of time.[3] This is one of the reasons it has been used extensively in academic research as well as in marketing research.

Unstructured Questions

Unstructured questions (or open questions) have an important place in personal interviews, too, because they allow for in-depth answers and for extensive probing. In addition to the standard open question, word associations, sentence completions, and projective devices are often used when it is felt that a direct question will telegraph what the interviewer wants or when it is felt that a direct question will not uncover the true feelings of the respondent.

The final step in refining questions is to determine the exact wording of the question that will eliminate ambiguity and bias. Unambiguous communication requires that the question as understood by the interviewer be the same as the question as understood by the respondent; it also requires that the answer as understood by the respondent be the same as the answer as understood by the interviewer. For example, "Do you like Michelob?" is not necessarily the same as "Do you like the taste of Michelob?"

---

[2]Richard Seaton, "Why Ratings Are Better Than Comparisons," *Journal of Advertising Research* (February 1974): 47.
[3]Everett F. Cataldo, et al., "Cardsorting as a Technique for Survey Interviews," *Public Opinion Quarterly* (Summer 1971): 202–215.

Structuring the Questions

Arranging the questions in a logical sequence not only makes administration more convenient but also decreases respondent fatigue. Generally, you can plan a definite sequence for the questions using either the funnel, the inverted funnel, or the tunnel structure. The format in which the questions are laid out on the questionnaire or interview outline is not the most important consideration that you have, but there are ways of doing it to make your use of it unobtrusive. For example, you should avoid splitting a question at the end of a page so that asking the question and recording the response are not awkward.

Finalizing the Questionnaire or Interview Outline

One of the most important aspects of planning is to pretest the questions. Usually a pretest consists of 15–20 interviews that constitute a "dress rehearsal" for the survey. It is your final means of omitting errors, refining questions, and testing the adequacy of the structure. The pretests should be conducted in the same manner as is anticipated for the full-scale survey. In other words, avoid the tendency to treat the pretest as just a test, because you may not be as alert in noticing things as you should be. Treat it as the real thing.

On the basis of the pretest, revise the questionnaire and prepare the final draft. Whenever possible, precode the possible answers for the questions. By placing coding blanks in the right-hand margin, for example, you can greatly reduce the cost in the data processing phase of the research.

CHOOSING RESPONDENTS

Most surveys are conducted so that the researchers can make some kind of generalized statement about a population of people, that is, a total group of people, such as Americans or Republicans. Obviously, it would be impossible to survey or to interview all of these people. Therefore, a sample of the population is chosen as being representative of the group; they are surveyed, and if they were selected scientifically, then their responses would be assumed to be representative of the total group. Most research studies are conducted in this manner, and the process has worked very well.

Choosing an adequate sample is one of the most important considerations that you will have, and there are two very basic considerations in making your selection. (1) You must decide on the number of people needed to be able to make your generalization about the population. It would be impossible to set down all of the guidelines to be used in making this decision because of the tremendous variety of them among studies. You can consult an advisor or a manual for these. In terms of numbers, however, there are scientific procedures that are used that enable pollsters to select 1000–2000 respondents and then generalize to broad areas of the country. (2) You must decide who the specific respondents are to be. The rest of this discussion focuses on a variety of methodologies that are appropriate for selecting people.

"Start-Point" Probability Sampling Technique

A sampling method used extensively in media studies involves selecting city blocks, sometimes randomly and sometimes because they fall within certain districts. After the city blocks are selected, the interviewers are assigned age and sex quotas on each block identified by the sampling method. This sampling design is based on the use of "start points" in the area to be surveyed. From each start point, a given number of interviews (such as four) are conducted according to a systematic plan.

A table of random numbers is often utilized in choosing the "start point" addresses. Then interviewers are given explicit instructions and diagrams for the selection of interview households around the "start point." In single-unit dwelling areas, interviewers begin at a household and proceed counterclockwise around the block, knocking on every other door until they have made the necessary number of contacts. If there is no one home at any of the homes, one return visit is made per house. If after this return visit an interview at each address has still not been completed, the interviewers continue around the block, knocking on every other door until the necessary number of interviews from this "start point" have been completed. If there are insufficient households on this block, then the interviewers go to the household directly across the street from the "start point" and proceed with the same counterclockwise, every-other-house pattern.

If the "start-point" household is in a predominantly multiple-dwelling area, the second interview can take place in the building next door to this household. In such a case you should choose an apartment either one story higher or lower than the "start point." As you continue in the counterclockwise direction, the third interview should be on a different story of the next building. This procedure is continued until four contacts are completed.

It is important that you keep meticulous records on your contacts. Generally, an audit sheet should be provided for you to list the addresses of all households contacted and the results of the contacts, such as "interview completed," "no one at home," "ineligible respondent," or "interview refused."

Given the randomly selected interview households, interviewers are generally instructed to conduct interviews with respondents falling into prescribed categories of age, sex, or race. The proportion of respondents falling into each category is established by referring to the most recent census information for that area. It is also useful to specify respondents in more than one category. For example, by specifying both the age and the sex of respondents, you can avoid drawing a sample in which the age characteristics of either sex grouping fails to reflect the age characteristics (parameters) found in the total population. You certainly would not want to draw samples that had a disproportionate number of old women, middle-aged men, or young women.

In describing the "start-point" probability sampling technique, we have outlined a basic procedure based on some surveys that have actually been conducted. Obviously, you could obtain more than four contacts in an area, or you could move clockwise rather than counterclockwise. Nevertheless, the principle of trying to obtain some diversity in your respondents is one that needs to be emphasized in whatever specific procedures that you use.

Use of Random Telephone Numbers

An alternative method involves beginning with a list of randomly generated telephone numbers. Select a starting point randomly in the telephone directory and then take every nth name, or use a table of random numbers to determine how far to skip down to the next name. This method has advantages: (1) it establishes a random sample that is faster and more economical than the means described in the first method, and (2) it avoids the problems with clusters of responses in the same neighborhood.[4] This method has the additional advantage of permitting you to call for appointments, but the fact that it spreads out the interview locations means that you must travel greater distances.

In summary, the ultimate objective in sampling is to achieve a representative group of respondents as economically as possible. In doing so, two guidelines are used extensively: (1) some kind of stratified sample is used, which means that you try to cover people in all sex, race, age, or income levels that are important to you (you do not want one group to be so predominant that it slights the others), and (2) within each category you need a random selection, which means that theoretically each person within that group has just as much probability of being selected for an interview as any other person in the category. Planning the sample is often easier than actually obtaining it. Consideration is often given to reducing refusal rates by use of a premium or payment to respondents. Some experiments have found that the offer of an honorarium does not have a serious effect on the acceptance or refusal rates for personal inter-

[4]Matthew Hanck and Michael Cox, "Locating a Sample by Random Digit Dialing," *Public Opinion Quarterly* (Summer 1974): 253–260.

views.[5] However, premiums are used as incentives with focus groups and with mail surveys, and in these instances they do seem to make a difference.

SELECTING INTERVIEWERS

Since surveys involve the compilation of data obtained from many interviewers, it is crucial that they be skilled in obtaining the same kinds of information. In other words, you want to minimize the differences in their filtering, which were described in Chapter 2.

In selecting interviewers, you should consider a number of factors. The person must be able to follow simple sampling instructions and road maps. If he or she is located near the interviewing sites, travel costs will be reduced. Generally, you should attempt to match the race of the interviewer with the racial composition of the geographical area of the survey. In the past it has been found that respondents tend to avoid responses that might offend the interviewer of a different race. Studies show that white respondents are as susceptible to these effects as black respondents are.[6] The impact of race on responses, however, is a very inconsistent phenomenon. Sometimes it seems to have an impact; at other times, it does not. In one experiment, for example, the researchers found that questions dealing with militant protest and hostility toward whites aroused racial tension in the interview. However, dealing with reports of discrimination and basic living conditions, personal background, and social status seemed not to be influenced by the race of the interviewer. Therefore, it would seem that the impact of the race of the interviewer may vary with the type of question asked.[7]

Finally, the interviewers should be experienced in probing techniques in addition to being personable, attractive, and articulate individuals. In order to obtain an interview from a total stranger, interviewers must be the kinds of individual who find it easy to meet people easily and develop a relationship quickly.

TRAINING INTERVIEWERS

In projects with any degree of complexity, it is necessary to train all interviewers before they go into the field. Even people who are already very skilled interviewers need to go through the training so that all inter-

[5]Barbara S. Dohrenwend, "An Experimental Study of Payments to Respondents," *Public Opinion Quarterly* (Winter 1970): 621–624.
[6]Shiirley Hatchett and Howard Schuman, "White Respondents and Race-of-Interviewer Effects," *Public Opinion Quarterly* (Winter 1975): 523–528.
[7]Howard Schuman and Jean Converse, "The Effects of Black and White Interviewers on Black Responses in 1968," *Public Opinion Quarterly* (Spring 1977): 44–48.

viewers are trained consistently. The basic objective of the training session should be to familiarize all interviewers with the questionnaire or interview outline and the sampling procedures. Another objective should be to motivate the interviewers by explaining the purpose of the project and by making them feel that what they are doing is very important. This motivation is extremely important, because sometimes interviewers care so little about their projects that they simply manufacture data without going through the interviews. Generally, it is advisable for the training to be conducted personally by the research project director.

During the training session, each interviewer should be given a handbook, which has been prepared specifically for the project. The handbook should contain: a statement of purpose; a description of all the materials to be used in the field work, such as questionnaires, maps, time sheets, and nonresponse logs; an explanation of the sampling procedures; a basic description of the interviewing methods; instructions for probing beyond the primary questions; and completion deadlines.

One vital part of the training should require interviewers to complete several practice interviews in order to ensure that they understand the instructions and are capable of performing an acceptable interview. During these practice sessions, pay particular attention to how the interviewers introduce themselves, whether or not they ask the questions in the exact forms desired, how accurately they record responses, and how well they probe answers. After the training has been completed, each interviewer should be given an identification card and sent out to do the field work.

SUPERVISING THE INTERVIEWING

It is important to have direct supervision of the interviewers by someone in close contact with them. The guidelines described below should become standard operating procedures.

1. There should be daily collection and checking of interviews from various interviewing locations. It is unwise to allow interviewers to stockpile several days' work. The daily pick-up allows early pinpointing of problems and the taking of immediate corrective actions.

2. Check each completed questionnaire or report for legibility, completeness, and how well your instructions have been followed.

3. Verify interviews. Verification is necessary to determine whether the interviews were actually conducted and whether they were conducted in accordance with your wishes. It is customary to verify at least 10 percent of each interviewer's work. This is done by calling the respondent on the telephone and asking (a) whether the person was actually interviewed on the reported data, (b) how long the interview took, and (c) if the respondent would mind replicating some of the questions covered in

the interview. These questions give you the ability to check the content of the reports and to uncover any attempts to falsify complete interviews. Unfortunately, there have been cases where the interviewers have fabricated complete interviews; these are sometimes called "kitchen-table" or "curb stone" interviews. Another form of falsification occurs when interviewers shorten the period of time required for an interview by asking questions from only the beginning and end of the questionnaire and fabricating some of the answers to questions in the middle. Another tendency to falsify answers occurs when interviewers find that a particular question is difficult or embarrassing to ask. Frequently, they supply the answer that they think the respondent would give in light of the other answers. Some forms of falsification can be detected by a random selection of questions throughout the questionnaire to be verified in your telephone call to the respondent.

CONDUCTING THE INTERVIEW

The procedures for conducting the information getting interview follow the general pattern that we have recommended throughout this book.

1. *Sell the interview.* In most instances the respondents will not know you and will not have volunteered to be interviewed. In a sense, you are an intruder. Therefore, you must be thoroughly prepared to ask for the interview and to convince the respondent that the project is worth his or her time. You must be able to demonstrate that the respondent will get some intrinsic or extrinsic reward for participating. Some of the more common attempts to motivate respondents include saying that (a) a neighbor or friend has participated, (b) the person's opinion is really sought, (c) the report is important enough to be published or to be used in making important decisions, (d) the person can have a copy of the report, or (e) you really need the person's help.

2. *Introduce yourself and the project.* Give the respondent a quick orientation. Try to give a full explanation of its importance before the interviewee has an opportunity to refuse.

3. *Follow the interview outline or questionnaire.* It is crucial that all interviewers follow the same pattern if their data are to be analyzed consistently.

4. *Make it a pleasant communication experience for the interviewee.* Pay attention to the verbal and nonverbal cues. Sometimes respondents want to talk, and you may have to spend some extra time listening. At other times, they may be pressed for time and indicate this to you. In these instances, the situation will be more pleasant if you proceed in a manner that is as efficient as possible.

5. *Probe answers whenever necessary to minimize your own input.* Try to avoid making assumptions about the answers; get the respondent to phrase them as explicitly as possible.

6. *Express appreciation for the respondent's time and cooperation.* Leave the interview in a manner that will make it easy for another interviewer to come along at some other time and be welcomed by the respondent.

ANALYZING THE DATA

While a broad coverage of statistical interpretation of data is beyond the bounds of this book, we would like to emphasize that there are two means of analyzing data—through frequency counts and content analysis.

In frequency counts you may wish to learn merely how many people take one position as opposed to another. If you are doing a market survey, you may wish to find out how many people watch KXXX, as opposed to KZZZ or KYYY. There are times, however, when you may wish to go beyond just the reporting of frequencies. Sometimes, for example, you may wish to know whether two groups are statistically different in their answers: Do women and men differ in their stands on abortion, for example? Well, if you were to do a frequency count, you would find the percentage of women who answered in favor of abortion and contrast this with the percentage of men who answered in favor of it. By consulting a good statistics book, you could find a formula to determine if the two groups were significantly different. You could make the same kinds of contrasts on any kind of demographic data, such as age groups, income groups, race groups, or geographical groups.

You could use also a kind of content analysis to analyze answers. For open or unstructured questions, no categories of responses would be provided to respondents. If, for example respondents were asked why they identify with one candidate for office over another, they might reveal several reasons. At some point, the interviewers will want to analyze all of these open responses to determine whether or not there are certain trends or themes. One way of doing this is to have several people read all of the responses and develop some ad hoc categories into which most of the responses would fall. You might merely build a catalog of reasons for support or rejection. If frequencies are still important, you could determine how many times each category was mentioned. In any kind of content analysis, it is useful for you to check the reliability of the raters. In other words, you would have someone develop the categories and determine how many times the responses fell into each category. Then you would ask someone else to use those same categories to determine how many times the responses fell into the categories. If there were close agreement, then the results would be reliable. If, however, there were not close agreement, you would need to do further analysis, because something would be wrong with the categories or with the way the people were coding them. This is merely another scientific means of checking the adequacy of your results.

PREPARING A REPORT

Every survey is done so that the results can be reported in some fashion. There is no set format for making such a report. However, there are a few guidelines that ought to be followed.

1. Keep it simple. Try to minimize the amount of effort that is needed to interpret the results. Whenever possible, use graphs and charts to make the results clear.
2. Be truthful. Researchers have human frailties and it is easy for them to be tempted to distort results toward their own point of view or to try to please the client or even to invent data to save some time and energy. Besides being unethical, this is not good business practice. One disclosure of falsifying data could ruin a career.
3. Plan the distribution of the report even before the research is done. This helps avoid awkward compromises at the end.
4. Respect confidences. Do not reveal individual responses.

DEALING WITH PROBLEMS

Any survey research project is subject to several sources of error. In this section we will discuss three types of error: sampling error, nonresponse error, and response error.

Sampling Error

Sampling error occurs when the samples are inappropriately drawn and, therefore, cannot be representative of the desired population. Perhaps this can best be explained by using several examples. If you were using a telephone directory to choose respondents, you would have to realize that you would have automatically eliminated the people who do not have telephones and the people who have unlisted numbers. Should there be a significant number of such people (as there have been in the past), then your sample could be inadequate. Or, if you were taking a survey on a college campus and decided to take purely a random sample, you might get an overwhelming number of freshmen. Therefore, their answers might not represent how the upper-class students felt.

It might also be possible to have an error because you did not select a large enough sample. One of the reasons for choosing a sample is to save time, energy, and money that otherwise would be necessary for interviewing a whole population. Frequently, there is a great deal of subjectivity in deciding just how many people should constitute a sample. This is not an easy question, and the answer is always dictated by the amount of rigor you want to put in the project. Generally, it is preferable to plan to have more respondents than you actually need than it is to run the risk of having too few.

Nonresponse Error

Nonresponse error occurs when a person selected to be in a sample is not interviewed for a particular reason, such as the person not being home or outright refusal to cooperate. This presents a problem because a researcher cannot estimate the effect of nonresponse error on the total findings, whereas there are some statistical measurements that might allow the researcher to correct for some sampling errors.

Response Error

Response error occurs when the collection of information is faulty in some respect. It happens when there is a difference between what a respondent actually believes and feels and what is reported to the interviewer. There are several sources of response error. Inaccurate information may come from an inability or unwillingness to provide accurate information. The less salient the question is to the respondent, the more likely an inaccurate answer becomes. An unwillingness of the respondent to answer can be caused by (1) the time required to answer, (2) perceived loss of prestige, (3) invasion of privacy, or (4) perceived conflict with investigator opinions.

Time problems occur when a respondent wishes to complete the interview as quickly as possible. The result often takes the form of hasty answers without much reflection on the question. This problem is accentuated by long questionnaires that fatigue the respondent.

When the information sought involves the possible loss of prestige for the respondent, there is a tendency for the respondent to upgrade the responses, to make them sound better, and to associate them with higher prestige positions. For example, people often like interviewers to feel that their income and educational levels are higher than they really are. Since youthfulness has a positive value in our culture, some people misrepresent their ages. People who live in rural areas or in the suburbs are likely to give the nearest city as a place of residence.

Measuring the amount of inaccuracy that results from prestige bias is very difficult. One approach is to ask for information in two different ways. You could, for example, ask 'What is your age?" early in the interview and then later ask "In what year were you born?" Another way is to try to ask some indirect questions. You might ask "What magazines do you read?" and later ask "What magazines does your neighbor read?"

Invasion of privacy is a sensitive point for many respondents. Some subjects are considered to be taboo or private. In one survey, respondents were asked, "About which of the following matters would you be *least* willing to answer questions?" The responses are as follows.

Subject	Percent
finances and money	29
family life	24
political beliefs	18
religious beliefs	5
job or occupation	1
no single choice	23

Additionally, when asked "Do you believe that most people answer honestly the questions asked by interviewers?" 14 percent said "no" and 20 percent answered "do not know."[8]

Finally, inaccuracies sometimes occur because respondents apparently are responding to certain "cues" from the interviewer. The appearance and manner of the interviewer can exert great influence. In a cosmetics survey, an unexpectedly high usage of luxury cosmetics was found among women from low-income families. One woman had conducted all of the interviews in the low-income area. She was well-dressed and carefully groomed. To check on this possible error, a matronly woman dressed similarly to the respondents called on them the next day and used the same questionnaire. The brands of cosmetics that they reported this time were ones that were much less expensive than those reported in the first survey.[9]

It must also be recognized that the mere fact that a person is being interviewed may affect that person's attitudes and opinions. For example, voter turnout for a primary election was higher for a group that had been surveyed about their political preferences than it was for other groups not surveyed.[10]

THIS CHAPTER IN PERSPECTIVE

Obtaining information through surveys has become big business in the United States. Sometimes, surveys are conducted because people are merely curious about the way others behave: politicians are concerned about how people are thinking; and businesses are concerned about trends that may affect them economically. The result has been an extensive use of information getting personal interviews.

[8]Gideon Sjoberg, "A Questionnaire on Questionnaires," *Public Opinion Quarterly* (Winter 1954): 423–427.
[9]Elizabeth G. Morgan, "The Right Interviewer for the Job," *Journal of Marketing* (October 1951): 201–202.
[10]Robert Kraut and John McConahay, "How Being Interviewed Affects Voting: An Experiment," *Public Opinion Quarterly* (Fall 1973): 398–406.

This chapter has focused on some of the broad concerns for implementing a large survey. The same considerations would be given to almost any small survey that you want to conduct in your school, in your neighborhood, or in your organization.

Another important aspect of this chapter is that problems have been pinpointed that arise not only from the reluctance or the ineffectiveness of the respondents, but also from some relatively unscrupulous practices by interviewers. Consequently, it is useful to end the chapter by printing a Code of Ethics on the following pages for people who are engaged professionally in public research.

CODE OF PROFESSIONAL ETHICS AND PRACTICES

"We, the members of the American Association for Public Opinion Research, subscribe to the principles expressed in the following code. Our goal is to support sound practice in the profession of public opinion research. (By public opinion research we mean studies in which the principal source of information about individual beliefs, preferences, and behavior is a report given by the individual.)

We pledge ourselves to maintain high standards of scientific competency and integrity in our work, and in our relations both with our clients and with the general public. We further pledge ourselves to reject all tasks or assignments that would be inconsistent with the principles of this code."

THE CODE

I.   Principles of Professional Practice in the Conduct of Our Work
  A. We shall exercise due care in gathering and processing data, taking all reasonable steps to assure the accuracy of results.
  B. We shall exercise due care in the development of research designs and in the analysis of data.
    1. We shall employ only research tools and methods of analysis that, in our professional judgments, are well suited to the research problem at hand.
    2. We shall not select research tools and methods of analysis because of their special capacity to yield a desired conclusion.
    3. We shall not knowingly make interpretations of research results, nor shall veracity permit interpretations that are inconsistent with the data available.
    4. We shall not knowingly imply that interpretations should be accorded greater confidence than the data actually warrants.
  C. We shall describe our findings and methods accurately and in appropriate detail in all research reports.
II. Principles of Professional Responsibility in Dealings with People
  A. The Public
    1. We shall protect the anonymity of every respondent. We shall hold as privileged and confidential all information that tends to identify the respondent.
    2. We shall cooperate with legally authorized representatives of the public by describing the methods used in our studies.
    3. We shall withhold the use of our name in connection with the planned publication of research findings unless we have first expressed and approved the material.
  B. Clients or Sponsors
    1. We shall hold confidential all information obtained about the

> client's general business affairs and about the lists of responses for the client.
>
> SOURCE: Adapted from the American Association for Public Opinion Research, "Study of Validation Practices," *Public Opinion Quarterly* (Fall 1960): 529–530.

PROJECTS

1. Write an introduction for an interview on the following.
   a. uses of drugs
   b. dog food purchases.
What are some of the different things that you would have to do under these two circumstances to get people to be interviewed?

2. Get together with a group of five people and plan a complete survey. You may wish to see how people feel about an issue or about a product. You may even wish to experiment with some different ways of asking for information.

3. Interview a professional researcher to discover some of the individual's guidelines for doing research.

4. Construct a representative sample for 400 in-house interviews, using your local telephone directory.

5. Discuss the Code of Professional Ethics and Practices just outlined. Why is there a need for such a code?

6. Collect several research reports and catalog different means of illustrating reports. Discuss your preferences.

Chapter 18
Telephone Interviews

Interviewing by telephone is one of the most commonly used research techniques because it is quick and economical. Therefore, in terms of actual usage, it may be a very good supplement to personal interviews. Before deciding to use it, you ought to be aware of its advantages and limitations.

ADVANTAGES

1. No other data collection technique allows for as quick a turnaround time in the field than the telephone interview. Furthermore, if central location interviewing is used, there is no time lag in bringing the completed interviews from the field to the central office. This savings in time can be translated easily into a savings of money, too.

2. The refusal rate is generally as low as 7 percent in telephone interviewing. Unlike personal interviewing where respondents are concerned about allowing a stranger into their home, telephone interviewing allows respondents anonymity and protection.

3. Sample selection is easy for telephone interviewing. The popula-

tion is virtually defined automatically (homes with telephones), and this includes most of the population. The sample selection is very routine. The only real caution is to be certain that you have an up-to-date directory. Screening questions at the beginning of the telephone interview can isolate efficiently and quickly whatever the population the researcher desires. If a respondent indicates that he or she does not watch television, for example, then you will not complete an interview about programming. Or, if you need people who are in certain age categories and a person's birthdate falls outside this range, then you may choose not to complete the interview. It is a very quick procedure.

4. The telephone also allows control of the geographical area of the sample. In addition to the standard alphabetical white pages, the telephone company publishes a cross-reference telephone directory of names and telephone numbers by address. Using this directory makes it easy to concentrate on a small area if you wish. On the other hand, interviews can be scattered over a wide area of the city or the country at little expense.

5. Follow-up of the interviews is efficient. For additional information from the respondent—whether the initial interview was personal, by telephone, or by questionnaire—the telephone is the most efficient method. As this might suggest, telephone interviewing is often used in conjunction with other forms of data collection. One way the telephone has been used is to determine the variance between respondents and nonrespondents in mailed surveys.

6. People who are difficult to reach in person can be reached by telephone. Households with working men and women must be interviewed at night. Restricted apartment complexes and neighborhoods make it very difficult to contact people personally, but they all answer their telephones.

7. Telephone interviewing permits easier training and supervising of interviewers. Central-location interviewing provides the real benefit of actually being able to supervise interviewers as they conduct the interviews. Correction of problems is instantaneous.

8. The respondent is less likely to feel obliged to answer in a socially desirable way in a telephone interview. The respondent is not as easily tempted to model his or her own point of view after that of the interviewer. Therefore, the feeling of privacy of the telephone is a great advantage.[1]

DISADVANTAGES

While there are many advantages to conducting surveys by telephone,

---

[1]Frederick Wiseman, "Methodological Bias in Public Opinion Surveys," *Public Opinion Quarterly* (Spring 1972): 105–108.

there are some disadvantages, too, which need to be recognized. Sometimes they can be overcome.

1. One of the main disadvantages is that the sample is restricted to households that own a telephone. At the end of every survey, there remains a question about how phone owners and nontelephone owners differ. In general, research shows that the lowest incidence of telephone ownership is among rural and low-income households. While approximately 90 percent of all households in the United States have telephones, there is a heavily increased usage of unlisted telephone numbers; this brings about another sampling problem to achieve representativeness in telephone surveys. Households without telephones and households with unlisted numbers have certain characteristics that can bias the sample. Arbitron Radio estimates significant numbers of unlisted telephone households in major metropolitan areas.[2]

Area	*Unlisted*
Los Angeles	46.9%
Chicago	44.6%
San Francisco	40.5%
Philadelphia	40.3%
Phoenix	36.2%
Atlanta	32.6%
Kansas City	22.9%

Since a significant number of homes would be missed by sampling only those homes in the directory, it is worth noting that the differences between "listed" and "unlisted" homes can be striking. Unlisted telephone heads of households are more likely to

be younger
be single, separated, or divorced
be blue collar or labor union members
have completed less formal schooling
have lower income in lower-income zip codes
rent rather than own a home
reside in an apartment rather than a house
be nonwhite
be recent arrivals in the community
be less likely to vote or participate in community affairs

2. Telephone interviewing is sometimes criticized for not being able to collect highly personal information. Age and income are particularly

[2]Arbitron Radio, "Expanded Sample Frame: A Procedure for Sampling All Telephone Households," *American Research Bureau* (March 1978).

hard to get. Of course, a great deal depends upon the interviewer's ability to establish rapport with respondents. Initially, respondents are suspicious of the identity of the caller and the authenticity of the survey. Salespeople, using the "I am taking a survey" pitch, have made it difficult for legitimate researchers to operate. With personable interviewers, there would probably be no difficulty in collecting most kinds of data.

3. The interview outline or questionnaire must be shorter for telephone use than for personal interviewing. This means that the personal interview is better for in-depth interviews. However, questionnaire length is not a great handicap if the questionnaire is limited to one subject and is carefully written. In general, it is recommended that telephone interviews be kept under 20 minutes, and most of them should average about 10 minutes. Some people will even sit through a 30–45 minute interview if the subject is of great interest to them. The longer the interview, though, the greater is the likelihood of a sudden termination.

4. Complicated explanations and visual aids cannot be used over the telephone. Therefore, concept testing or advertising layouts are not appropriate subjects. Rating scales must also be simplified, and this prevents the use of complete rating scales or rank order questions.

5. Finally, probing of responses is severely curtailed. This is caused partially by the greater difficulty in establishing an interactive rapport with the respondent.

TYPES OF TELEPHONE INTERVIEWS

Central-location Interviews

Central-location interviewing is the use of a group of telephone lines in a single location. All interviews are conducted and supervised within one office or location. Decentralized interviewing allows each interviewer to use a private telephone in the home or office. While central-location interviewing is slightly more expensive, it also has several advantages. Highly trained, full-time interviewers can be used on every study. Interviewers can be briefed easily. Supervision is immediate and constant. Complete observation of any pretesting can be done. All completed interviews are immediately available for supervisors to check for consistency, completeness, and neatness. And information can be quickly passed on to all interviewers doing the fieldwork.

WATS Interviewing

WATS is the acronym of Bell Telephone for Wide Area Telecommunications Service. WATS divides the United States into several bands or regions. Different bands can be rented and calls can be made into any area within the band at no additional expense. Therefore, WATS interviewing is very advantageous when the population for the study is outside your geographical region. For larger-area surveys, WATS can reduce costs over regular "1+" long-distance calling. The cost of WATS can be obtained from your local telephone company. In 1978 the monthly rate for a national (4 band) line in Lawrence, Kansas, was $1500.

DESIGNING A QUESTIONNAIRE

There are some differences between the design of telephone surveys and the design of personal interviews. The introduction is particularly important. While you must introduce yourself and describe the project in general terms, your introduction needs to be brief, because you need to ask the first question as soon as possible. You want to minimize the respondent's opportunities to refuse. Once you have asked the first question the respondent begins to get personal satisfaction from the fact that someone is asking his or her opinion. Nearly 80 percent of refusals occur between the introductory remarks and the first question.

Do not use the word "survey" in the introduction. Use the words "research study" or another substitute. The word "survey" is currently associated with a sales gimmick.

Never ask the respondent, "May we ask your opinion on a few questions?" You do not want to give the interviewee an opportunity to say, "No." You should move directly and quickly into the first question.

Use simple words. Each word in a question is a potential source of error. The greater is the number of words, the more complex the structure of a question must become. Therefore, brevity is a goal. As a general rule of thumb, limit each question to 20 words. Furthermore, the questions must be worded as simply as possible. Orient respondents to the lowest vocabulary level in the sample.

Refine the questions so that you will not be asking two questions as one, such as "What do you consider the most economical and convenient means of travel?" If you want valid responses, ask separate questions.

Avoid ambiguity; be specific. For example, in the question, "Do you listen to KAAA regularly?" it is not clear whether "regularly" means once a day, once a week, or once a month. For the answer to be meaningful, you would have to rephrase the question.

Special care must be taken with rating scales. Generally, they should range from three to five points. The more you get, the more difficult it is for the respondent to keep them in mind. Some examples of the various scales follow.

Three-point Scales

important	fairly important	not important
higher	same	lower
yes	depends	no
above average	average	below average
more than most	like most	less than most

Four-point Scales

many	some	very few	none
excellent	good	fair	poor

Five-point Scales

strongly approve	approve	cannot decide	disapprove	strongly disapprove
absolutely true	possibly true	in doubt	possibly false	absolutely false

Care should also be taken in structuring lists of items. There is a tendency for items appearing first and last in a list to be used as answers more frequently than those in other positions. Order bias—the systematic error caused by positioning items—will render the results less useful. In one study, the top position outdrew middle positions by 6 percent; the bottom position was used more by 2 percent. This is significant because the same items had been rotated to different positions with responses by matched samples of respondents.[3]

SELECTING A SAMPLE OF RESPONDENTS

Sampling for telephone surveys is much easier to design than for other types of surveys. Listed below are several guidelines you should follow when you select a sample from a published directory.

1. Select three times the number of completed interviews you actually want; for example, if you want 400 completed interviews, select 1200–1600 numbers. The refusal rate and the number of unanswered calls warrants this.
2. Determine the number of pages in the directory, and decide how many numbers are needed from each page. For example, the

[3]Stanley L. Payne, *The Art of Asking Questions* (Princeton, N.J.: Princeton University Press, 1951), pp. 84–85.

Atlanta directory contains 1807 pages. If you were looking for 1600 numbers, you might take 1 from each page with occasional random skips.

3. Measure the average number of column inches in the directory. Divide the number of interviews you need from each page into the column inches to select the number to call.

4. Select the numbers and place them on a telephone tally sheet to be used by interviewers.

The idea behind selecting numbers is to spread the selection throughout the directory in a systematic way and to reduce the possibility of bias.

A variation of the procedures outlined above is *random-digit dialing.* The problem of unlisted numbers already has been discussed, and random-digit dialing is a way of trying to get around the problem. By this method, you may get numbers not listed in the directory.

One form of random-digit dialing begins with a selection of central telephone exchanges from the 28,000 central offices in the United States. The number of central exchanges depends on the sample design and the definition of the population. This is followed by the selection of the last four digits from random numbers, usually computer generated sets of four digits.

Another variation is the selection of all seven digits from random numbers. This procedure increases the number of calls necessary to obtain a working number. A third method of random-digit dialing—and a method that is quite economical—is the "1+" random dialing. Numbers are selected directly from the telephone directory, as previously discussed. However, the last digit is changed by adding a constant of 1. This does correct for unlisted numbers. The only potential problem occurs when new exchanges or banks of numbers have been added.

Selecting the proper size sample is extremely important in all survey research. The number will vary, however, with the nature of the individual project, the degree of precision required, and the number of calls you intend to use in tabulation and analysis. Despite what is commonly thought, the size of the sample is not related to the size of the population.

In order to reduce nonsampling errors in surveys, you should do the following:

1. make the survey as simple as possible
2. minimize fatigue by using short questionnaires
3. do not ask questions that respondents cannot answer
4. restrict the questions to essential information

5. use the smallest sample size that is consistent with the objectives of the study.[4]

CONDUCTING THE INTERVIEW

Be thoroughly prepared. Be thoroughly familiar with the interview guide. You should have been through several rehearsals. Furthermore, you should have a positive attitude when the respondent answers the telephone. You are much more likely to obtain the interview if you seem enthusiastic about conferring a privilege upon the respondent, rather than asking the respondent to undergo an ordeal.

Ask questions exactly as they are worded on your outline. This is essential, because the answers are only valid if respondents are asked precisely the same questions.

Never show surprise or disapproval concerning the respondent's answers. To do so might produce a modeling effect, or lead the person to alter an answer. Over the telephone your voice intonation can be a great influence on the kind of results obtained. In an experimental study on this subject, it was found that the number of positive responses from a group was significantly higher when the questions were asked with a rising-voice inflection than when the same questions were asked with a voice-dropping inflection. Additionally, the voice-rising intonation increased the respondent's willingness to answer.[5]

Probe when necessary. This is more difficult to do in telephone interviews than in other types of interviews but it is still necessary because answers may be incomplete or unclear. Your task is to help the respondent answer without leading in any way. An example of probing without leading follows.

> INTERVIEWER: In as much detail as you can, tell me why you used to prefer one radio station but now you prefer another.
> RESPONDENT: The quality of the music.
> INTERVIEWER: Exactly what about the quality of the music made you change?
> RESPONDENT: They used to play slow music, but now it's too fast.
> INTERVIEWER: What else made you change your preference?
> RESPONDENT: Well, I think they began to have too many commercials. Other stations don't have that many.
> INTERVIEWER: What else?
> RESPONDENT: That's all.

[4] Benjamin Lipstein, "In Defense of Small Samples," *Journal of Advertising Research* (February 1975): 33–40.
[5] Arpad Barath and Charles F. Cannel, "Effect of Interviewer's Voice Intonation," *Public Opinion Quarterly* (Fall 1976): 370–373.

Care should be taken to avoid overzealous probing. Some interviewers coerce respondents into mentioning more items in response to open questions than the respondent would normally volunteer.

Never allow yourself to be drawn into the interview. If your own opinion is sought, dodge the question and simply reply that you are interested in the respondent's opinion. In this connection, respondents sometimes begin to ask questions about the client or the underlying purpose of the survey. Keep any responses to this type of questioning very general, because revealing this information often introduces a bias into the interview.

Provide an answer for every response. Never leave a blank space. If the respondent does not know the answer, write "don't know" or some other explanation in the answer space. If the respondent does give an answer, record responses to open questions in the person's own words— profanity, slang, and all.

Expect your interview to be validated. It is done routinely on all good projects to ensure that the work is of a high quality. Usually, verification is made by telephone, and respondents are questioned about the interview length, content, and classification information. If one interview has been proved to be falsified, the whole of that interviewer's work would be disqualified.

Keep a list of numbers before you. Dial the numbers in the order in which they are listed. If no one answers or the line is busy, make a check on your tally sheet. When no one answers or the line is busy, call back twice more on different days and hours. If after a total of three calls you cannot reach the home, abandon the number. If a business number is reached, terminate the interview and abandon the number. For this reason, your tally sheet should contain more numbers than you need to complete. The extra numbers will be used as substitutes. Each time a call is made, something should be marked next to the number on the tally sheet.

Call between 10 A.M. and 9 P.M. Try to avoid calling earlier in the morning or later in the evening, because these are often regarded as private times. Do some calling every day and space the calls throughout the day.

DEALING WITH PROBLEMS

There are many types of problems that can occur with telephone interviews. In this section we will discuss a few of them.

Nonresponse Bias

It is highly unlikely in any survey that your response rate will be 100 percent. The nonresponse rate needs to be checked to determine whether or not it is randomly dispersed throughout all demographic groups. In order to avoid bias, statistical weighting can adjust the survey nonresponse. In short, the result of the individual or the subgroup that is underrepresented is multiplied in order to adjust it with the other group.[6]

Letters sent a week in advance of the interview can lower refusal rates. Advance letters have been known to reduce nonresponse rates by as much as 5 percent. If advance letters are sent, they should explain the survey, explain how names have been chosen, and then invite people to call if they have any questions. Use of incentives or rewards have not been found to be effective in increasing the response rate for telephone interviews.

Verbal Abuse

Any telephone interviewer needs to be prepared mentally for a certain amount of rejection; sometimes this rejection is expressed with verbal enthusiasm. If you are to be successful, you must not let this affect you too much. When you dial the next number, you need to demonstrate your enthusiasm to the next respondent.

THIS CHAPTER IN PERSPECTIVE

Telephone interviewing is one of the most common methods of conducting survey research. Quick fieldwork, low refusal rates, coverage of large geographical areas, efficient follow-up, and the close supervision of interviewers make it highly advantageous.

In reading this chapter, you have not only been presented with an outline of how to conduct interviews over the telephone, but you have also received information that may help you interpret much of the information reported to you each day. In other words, this information can be as helpful to you in judging the adequacy of other people's research as in helping you design your own research.

PROJECTS

1. Interview some professional interviewers to find out their techniques.

2. Design a brief survey. Conduct a personal interview and then a telephone interview in order to contrast the differences. In which interview did you have the most confidence? Which gave you the best results?

3. Examine the transcript of the telephone interview that follows. In what sense is it different from a mailed questionnaire?

4. Examine the questionnaire designed by Martin Research at the end of this chapter. Give a critique of it.

[6]Carol H. Fuller, "Weighting to Adjust for Survey Nonresponse," *Public Opinion Quarterly* (Summer 1974): 239–246.

5. Discuss your own experiences with telephone surveys. What kinds of things did the interviewer do that
    a. made you participate?
    b. caused you to refuse?

6. If you were a supervisor of a group of interviewers, what procedures would you set up to ensure that you got the best quality possible?

TELEPHONE INTERVIEW

What follows is a transcript of an actual telephone interview. The identification of the people and the stations has been changed.

As you read the transcript identify specific times when the interviewer:

1. failed to probe for details and additional information
2. changed the meaning of the question
3. deviated from the exact wording of the question
4. had disturbing verbal mannerisms
5. provided the answer for the respondent

TRANSCRIPT

Interviewer: We're conducting a survey about television news, and we'd like your opinion about some of the television you may have watched. First of all, as I read these age categories, would you tell me in which one you fall? Are you in the 18 to 24, 25 to 34 . . .

Respondent: 18 to 24.

Interviewer: Now, within the past seven days, have you watched a local news program on television . . . that is, a news program about things that are happening in this area?

Respondent: Yes.

Interviewer: Can you get Channel 2, WZZZ, on your television set?

Respondent: Yes.

Interviewer: Do you get an excellent, good, fair, or poor picture?

Respondent: Uh, excuse me, now?

Interviewer: Do you get an excellent, good, fair, or poor picture?

Respondent: Good.

Interviewer: OK, now how about Channel 3?

Respondent: Yes.

Interviewer: Now what's the picture . . . excellent, good, fair . . . ?

Respondent: Fair.

Interviewer: OK, is your TV hooked up to an inside or outside antenna?

Respondent: Uh . . . outside.

Interviewer: OK, uh . . . is the antenna designed for VHF, UHF reception, or both?

Respondent: Both.

Interviewer: Within the past seven days, have you watched a local news program in the early evening, between 6 and 6:30?

Respondent: Yes.

Interviewer: OK, which station did you watch?

Respondent: 2.

Interviewer: Why did you watch Channel 2 for news?

Respondent: Uh . . . force of habit, I guess.

Interviewer: OK, how about at 10 o'clock? Have you watched the news?

Respondent: Yeah.

Interviewer: You also watched 2?

Respondent: Yes.

Interviewer: OK. Why? Just force of habit, huh?

Respondent: Yeah.

Interviewer: Overall, which station would you prefer to watch for news? 2?

Respondent: Yes, 2.

Interviewer: What would improve the news on 3, since you watch 2?

Respondent: Hum . . . I don't know just . . . uh . . . force of habit you already put down. At 5:30 we watch the CBS Evening News. That might be a better answer for 6.

Interviewer: Got it. OK. Now how about at 10 o'clock . . . Is there any reason . . . same reason then too?

Respondent: We just watch it when it comes on.

Interviewer: There's nothing you can think of about 3 to make you watch?

Respondent: No . . . not really.

Interviewer: Do you watch newscasts from Kansas City?

Respondent: Just occasionally.

Interviewer: Occasionally, OK.

Respondent: When there's weather. You know, a storm is coming from Kansas City or something like that.

Interviewer: OK. Is there any station that does a good job with weather, or are all the stations alike in the way they handle the weather?

Respondent: Pretty much the same.

Interviewer: Pretty much the same?

Respondent: Uh huh.

Interviewer: OK. Are you familiar with the use of a device called "weather radar" in this area?

Respondent: Yeah.

Interviewer: Do you think it is a worthwhile thing for a station to use, or is it a gimmick?

Respondent: You mean as far as it comes across?

Interviewer: Uh huh. As far as you're concerned. Do you like it?

Respondent: Useful.

Interviewer: You think it's useful?

Respondent: Not useful.

Interviewer: You don't think it's useful?

Respondent: Right.

Interviewer: Is there any station you feel does a good job covering sports, or are the stations the same in the way they handle the sports?

Respondent: Uh . . . pretty much all the same.

Interviewer: OK. I'm going to read some names of people on news shows. Please tell me if you remember seeing the person on television. First, George Golly . . .

Respondent: You want me to tell you whether I like him?

Interviewer: I want you to tell me if you have . . . if you remember seeing this person. George Golly, he's on 3?

Respondent: Right.

Interviewer: Jerry Wally?

Respondent: Yeah.

Interviewer: Jim Holly?

Respondent: Yeah.

Interviewer: Jerry Bolly?

Respondent: Yeah.

Interviewer: Tom Polly?

Respondent: Yeah.

Interviewer: Ron Rolly?

Respondent: Yeah.

Interviewer: Ron Dolly?

Respondent: Yeah.

Interviewer: Mike Molly?

Respondent: No.

Interviewer: Now, would you describe each of these people you have seen. First, George Golly?

Respondent: He's pretty good. Pretty . . . very concise. He just says his things good. That's about it.

Interviewer: OK. How about Jerry Wally?

Respondent: Always happy.

Interviewer: OK. How about Jim Holly?

Respondent: Jim Holly, uh. I can't think of anything specific.

Interviewer: You like him? Dislike him?

Respondent: Yeah, I like him.

Interviewer: OK. How about Jerry Bolly?

Respondent: He's alright. He's happy-go-lucky like Jerry Wally. I like that.

Interviewer: (Laugh) You like that, OK. Tom Polly?

Respondent: Yeah, he's pretty good. He seems to get the point of the newscast.

Interviewer: OK, how about Ron Rolly?

Respondent: Yeah, he's OK.

Interviewer: OK. Ron Dolly?

Respondent: Uh . . . He's not either way really.

Interviewer: If you were putting together a news show including news, weather, and sports, who would you choose for news?

Respondent: Uh. Bill Colly. He used to be on the air here.

Interviewer: What?

Respondent: He used to be on 2. He lives in Chicago now.

Interviewer: How about weather?

Respondent: John Solly. He's another guy in Chicago.

Interviewer: He what?

Respondent: Chicago.

Interviewer: What station?

Respondent: He's on one of the stations. In the morning.

Interviewer: Wait a minute. He's nationwide?

Respondent: Yeah, about 15 minutes.

Interviewer: On what?

Respondent: I can't remember.

Interviewer: Network? Wait a minute . . . we're confused. OK, how about sports?

Respondent: I like Ron Polly.

Interviewer: You do?

Respondent: Yeah.

Interviewer: OK. As I mention each of the following words, tell me which station . . . modern approach?

Respondent: Modern approach?

Interviewer: Yeah.

Respondent: Is this just local?

Interviewer: Uh huh.

Respondent: Uh . . . 2.

Interviewer: Most carefully investigates news stories?

Respondent: 2.

Interviewer: Presents the news in a way that is easy to understand?

Respondent: Uh, well 2, I guess.

Interviewer: Has the best film showing the news?

Respondent: I'd say 3.

Interviewer: Most concerned about the community?

Respondent: Channel 11.

Interviewer: Who's more professional?

Respondent: Uh, it's a toss-up.

Interviewer: I can put toss-up if you want it to be.

Respondent: Yeah, it's just a toss-up.

Interviewer: Too serious?

Respondent: Oh boy . . . neither really.

Interviewer: Biased?

Respondent: Biased?

Interviewer: Yeah.

Respondent: OK, uh . . . how much?

Interviewer: Most . . . or too.

Respondent: Say 2.

Interviewer: (Laugh) OK. Too many commercials?

Respondent: All.

Interviewer: (Laugh) Has largest news staff?

Respondent: Say all again.

Interviewer: OK. Quickly adopts new and unique things in its local news.

Respondent: New things . . . uh . . . 3.

Interviewer: OK. In general, would you rather watch a newscast that presents a large number of facts about a few stories, or a few facts about a large number of stories?

Respondent: Large number.

Interviewer: The seating arrangement of the news people in the studio and the background arrangement is known as the news set. Does any station, in your opinion, have a particularly attractive news set?

Respondent: Uh . . . no.

Interviewer: Here are some different things involved in television newscasts. Please tell me whether it is very important, somewhat important, or not very important to you in deciding whether a television station does a good job in giving the news. First, whether the person reading the news sounds like an authority?

Respondent: Not very important.

Interviewer: Not very important . . . OK. Coverage of a wide range of subjects?

Respondent: Uh, yeah, it's important.

Interviewer: OK. Having on-the-scene reports from reporters in the field?

Respondent: Important.

Interviewer: A large number of stories covered in each newscast?

Respondent: Important.

Interviewer: Making the newscast different from 6 P.M. to 10 P.M.?

Respondent: Yes, important.

Interviewer: Giving details about what goes on behind the scenes?

Respondent: Somewhat important.

Interviewer: Hearing and seeing the people mentioned in the news?

Respondent: Uh, somewhat important.

Interviewer: Most television stations promote their news. How would you complete this sentence? "I would probably watch a station for news at least once if I saw an ad or commercial that . . .

Respondent: Uh . . . I don't know. In Chicago they had . . . creative, humorous writing.

Interviewer: OK. Which radio stations do you regularly listen to?

Respondent: AM or FM?

Interviewer: Either . . . both.

Respondent: Around here, huh?

Interviewer: Well, uh, (laughter) . . .

Respondent: I just moved here from Chicago and Albuquerque.

Interviewer: Let's say here.

Respondent: Here?

Interviewer: Yeah.

Respondent: 102.

Interviewer: If you could make one suggestion for improving the way the news is presented on Channel 3, KZZZ, what would you suggest?

Respondent: More quality (laugh).

Interviewer: OK. How about for 2?

Respondent: A lot of comedy.

Interviewer: What's the race?

Respondent: White.

Interviewer: What, specifically is your occupation?

Respondent: I'm a welding foreman . . . for the railroad.

Interviewer: Oh, alright. Will you repeat your phone number back to me please?

Respondent: Excuse me?

Interviewer: Will you repeat your phone number back to me?

Respondent: 555-1212.

Interviewer: Thanks for your time.

MARTIN RESEARCH SURVEY RESEARCH

TV Telephone
Final I

INTRODUCTION

Hello . . . we're conducting a survey about television news, and we'd like your opinions about some of the television you may have watched. First of all . . .

SCREENING QUESTIONS

A. As I read these age categories, would you tell me in which one you fall? Are you in the 18–24, 25–34, 35–49, 50–64, or 65 and over age group?
    1._____18–24 2._____25–34 3._____35–49 4._____50–64
    5._____65+ (Discontinue interview.)
B. Within the past seven days, have you watched a *local* news program on television, that is, a news program about things that are happening in this area?
    1._____Yes (Go to question 1.) 2._____No (Discontinue interview.)

1. Can you get Channel 2, WZZZ, on your television set?
    1._____Yes 2._____No (Go to question 2.)
    a. (If "Yes" ask:) Do you get an excellent picture, a good picture, a fair picture, or a poor picture on Channel 2?
    1._____Excellent 2._____Good 3._____Fair
    4._____Poor
2. Can you get Channel 3, KZZZ, on your television set?
    1._____Yes 2._____No (Go to question 3.)
    a. (If "Yes" ask:) Do you get an excellent picture, a good picture, a fair picture, or a poor picture on Channel 3?
    1._____Excellent 2._____Good 3._____Fair
    4._____Poor
3. Is the television set you usually watch hooked up to an inside antenna, an outside antenna, or cable television?
    1._____Inside antenna 2._____Outside antenna
    3._____Cable television (Go to question 4.)
    a. (If "Inside antenna" or "Outside antenna" ask:) Is the antenna designed for reception of VHF stations, UHF stations, or both? (VHF—CH. 2–13; UHF—CH. 14–82)
    1._____VHF only 2._____UHF only 3._____Both

4. Within the past seven days, have you watched a *local* news program in the early evening, between 6 and 6:30 P.M.?
1._____Yes   2._____No (Go to question 5.)
a. (If "Yes" ask:) Which station do you watch most often for *local*
news between 6 and 6:30?
1._____Ch. 2   2._____Ch. 3   3._____Other (Specify
_____)
b. Exactly why do you usually watch this station for *local* news in
the early evening and not another? (Probe.)

5. Now, what about the late evening? Have you watched a *local* news
program in the late evening, between 10 and 10:30 P.M., within the
past seven days?
1._____Yes   2._____No (Go to question 6.)
a. (If "Yes" ask:) Which station do you watch most often for *local*
news between 10 and 10:30?
1._____Ch. 2   2._____Ch. 3   3._____Other (Specify
_____)
b. Exactly why do you usually watch this station for *local* news in
the late evening and not one of the other stations? (Probe.)

6. Now, *overall,* which station would you say you prefer to watch for
local news?
1._____Ch. 2   2._____Ch. 3   3._____Other (Specify
_____?
a. What would improve the way the news is presented
on_____?
(Channel *not* mentioned in question 6.) (Probe.)
b. Do you find yourself often watching newscasts from Kansas
City?
1._____Yes   2._____No (Go to question 7.)
(i) (If "Yes" ask:) Why? (Probe.)

7. Is there any station you feel does a particularly good job covering
weather news, or do all the stations seem more or less alike in the
way they handle the weather?
1._____One particularly good   2._____All alike
a. Which station do you prefer to watch for weather news?
1._____Ch. 2   2._____Ch. 3
3._____Other (Specify_____)
b. What is it about the weather news on_____(station
mentioned in question a) that sets it apart from the others?
(Probe.)
c. Are you familiar with the use of a device called "weather radar"
on any of the stations around here?
1._____Yes   2._____No (Go to question 8.)
(i) (If "Yes" ask:) How do you feel about the use of weather radar
in the weather news? Does it seem like a worthwhile thing for a

station to use, or does it seem like a gimmick that isn't very worthwhile?

     1._____Worthwhile   2._____Gimmick

8. Is there any station you feel does a particularly good job covering sports news, or do all the stations seem more or less alike in the way they handle sports?

    1._____One particularly good   2.All alike (Go to question 9.)

    a. Which station do you prefer to watch for sports news?

      1._____Ch. 2   2._____Ch. 3   3._____Other (Specify _____)

    b. What is it about the sports news on _____(station mentioned in question 8a) that sets it apart from the others? (Probe.)

9. I have a few questions about people who are on local television news shows. I will mention some of these local television news people, and after I read each one please tell me if you remember seeing this person on television.

    1. George Golly on Ch. 3   1._____Yes   2._____No

    2. Jerry Wally on Ch. 2   1._____Yes   2._____No

    3. Jim Holly on Ch. 2   1._____Yes   2._____No

    4. Jerry Bolly on Ch. 3   1._____Yes   2._____No

    5. Tom Polly on Ch. 2   1._____Yes   2._____No

    6. Ron Rolly on Ch. 2   1._____Yes   2._____No

    7. Ron Dolly on Ch. 3   1._____Yes   2._____No

    8. Mike Molly on Ch. 3   1._____Yes   2._____No

10. (Ask the following about each person the respondent indicates having seen in question 9.)

Now, would you describe for me, in any words you want to use, each of these people you have seen? First, what are your reactions to him? (Probe.)

    1. George Golly

    2. Jerry Wally

    3. Jim Holly

    4. Jerry Bolly

    5. Tom Polly

    6. Ron Rolly

    7. Ron Dolly

    8. Mike Molly

11. If you were to put together a news show including news, weather, and sports, which one person would you choose for news, which one for weather, and which one for sports?

    1. _____newscaster

    2. _____weather

    3. _____sports

12. As I mention each of the following words or phrases, please tell me

which area station it *best* seems to describe as far as the station's local news programs are concerned.

1. modern _____
2. most carefully investigates news stories _____
3. presents the news in a way that is easy to understand _____
4. presents the best film showing the news _____
5. most concerned about the community _____
6. professional _____
7. too serious _____
8. biased _____
9. too many commercials _____
10. has largest news staff _____
11. quickly adopts new and unique things in its local news _____

13. In general, would you rather watch a newscast that presents a large number of facts about a few stories, or a few facts about a large number of stories?

    1._____Few stories   2._____Many stories

14. The seating arrangement of the news people in the studio and the background arrangement is known as the "news set." Does any station, in your opinion, have a particularly attractive news set?

    1._____Yes   2._____No (Go to question 15.)

    a. (If "Yes" ask:) Which station is that?

    1._____Ch. 2   2._____Ch. 3

    b. How does its news set differ from that of the other stations? (Probe.)

15. I'm going to read a number of different things involved in television newscasts. Please tell me whether it is very important, somewhat important, or not very important to you in deciding whether a television station does a good job in giving the news.

	VERY IMPORTANT	SOMEWHAT IMPORTANT	NOT VERY IMPORTANT
1. whether the person reading the news sounds like an authority	_____	_____	_____
2. coverage of a wide range of subjects	_____	_____	_____
3. having on-the-scene reports from reporters in the field	_____	_____	_____
4. the large number of stories covered in each newscast	_____	_____	_____
5. making the newscast different from 6 P.M. to 10 P.M.	_____	_____	_____

VERY   SOMEWHAT NOT VERY
IMPORTANT IMPORTANT IMPORTANT

6. giving details about what goes on
   behind the scenes   _____   _____   _____
7. hearing and seeing the people
   mentioned in the news   _____   _____   _____

16. Most television stations promote their news. How would you
    complete this sentence?
    "I would probably watch a station for news at least once if I saw an ad
    or a commercial that _____

17. Which radio stations do you regularly listen to?

    _____ _____ _____

18. If you could make one suggestion for improving the way the news is
    presented on Channel 3, KZZZ, what would that suggestion be?

19. If you could make one suggestion for improving the way the news is
    presented on Channel 2, WZZZ, what would that suggestion be?

20. Sex: (Record without asking)
          1._____Male   2._____Female
21. To which racial or ethnic group do you belong?   _____
22. What, specifically, is your occupation? _____

Date of interview: _____
Phone number: _____
Interview name: _____

Chapter 19
Focus Group Interviews

A focus group interview can be defined as (1) a small group of people (2) brought to a central location for an intensive discussion (3) with a moderator (4) who focuses discussion on various issues in accordance with a general outline of question areas. The purposes are threefold: (1) to probe intensively for *qualitative* data related to specific problem areas; (2) to generate new ideas as a pretesting device prior to a quantitative survey research study; or (3) to have respondents experience and react to a stimulus such as product, a television program, a magazine, a commercial, or an idea that you want to test before proposing it.

Focus group interviewing for such diverse activities has become a popular research methodology in recent years. Its popularity has spread because researchers are seeking qualitative answers that reveal patterns of viewpoints, attitudes, and feelings. We have used this methodology in a number of ways. For example, reader response to a national magazine was evaluated in a focus group. Not only were the respondents asked to respond to the individual articles and authors, but they also were asked to respond to questions about format, title, and appearance. In another case, response to the commercial of a small loan company was contrasted with the reactions to commercials of three competitors. A political candidate wanted to know what the main issues were in a certain city, so she had a researcher conduct some focus group interviews to determine how people were thinking about certain issues. In other cases, focus group interviews were used to design a logo for a bank. Respondents were shown several alternatives and were asked to respond to each. The researcher could modify the logo on the spot to determine what the reactions would be.

The focused interview has a number of distinctive characteristics.

1. Interviewees are known to have been involved in a particular situation (have taken part in an experiment, have seen a film, have heard a radio program, etc.).
2. The investigator has provisionally analyzed the situation and developed hypotheses regarding probable responses to it.
3. Content or situational analysis provides a basis for making an interview guide, setting forth major areas of inquiry, and providing criteria of relevance for interview data.
4. The interview focuses on subjective experiences for the purpose of ascertaining interviewees' definitions of the situation in which they were involved.[1]

This process of focus group interviewing has had little formal study. Most of its use has grown through a trial-and-error approach by commercial research practices in the field. The earliest users were advertising researchers who pretested the effectiveness of commercials, marketing managers who attempted to gain additional qualitative insights into potential customers, television programming decision-makers, and communication researchers specializing in propaganda. Now the method is used for many other purposes, and its potential is unlimited.

RATIONALE FOR FOCUS GROUP INTERVIEWING

Focus group interviews have both disadvantages and advantages when they are compared to door-to-door personal interviews, telephone interviews, and mail questionnaires. The following discussion is designed to tell you about the limitations of focus group interviews and to help you make some choices as to when to use them beneficially.

Advantages

1. Focus group interviews give respondents a chance to talk freely, without the strictures of systematic questioning. Participants often are more likely to voice what is truly on their minds. Similarly, a group of

[1] Robert K. Merton, Majorie Fiske, and Patricia Kendall, *The Focused Interview* (New York: The Free Press, 1961), p. ix.

people chatting together is more natural and relaxed than a single individual being interviewed. This gives the focus group credibility, and clients will act on results from focus groups when they would be reticent to give the same credibility to a limited survey project with the same number of respondents.

They also avoid the sterility of other forms of marketing research. By observing the interactions among the group members, you can learn about the social dynamics and the interpersonal reactions that are related to the topic being discussed. You can see how participants talk about a product or an idea in actual conversation, and it is important to note the vocabulary, phrases, inflections, and subtle nuances that come out in the informal setting. You can do this also in a personal interview, but in a group the interviewees are able to respond in a much more casual manner. Furthermore, as a part of the group dynamics, interviewees may be challenged and "forced" to defend their views with a spontaneity that becomes valuable research data in itself. A good researcher will observe how a controversy comes up and how it is resolved within the group. In marketing applications, this challenge-response format gives insights into the way images are formed in the customers' minds.

Since different members of a group have different levels of knowledge, they begin to learn from one another. This illustrates how product information, for example, is absorbed or resisted and then integrated into the thought processes of potential customers.

2. Focus group interviews are economical if they are substituted for a larger survey project. However, the cost of interviewing a group of ten is likely to be more expensive than interviewing the same number individually.

3. The interaction in a focus group is multiplicative, with each respondent becoming a richer source of information than he or she would be alone. This happens because one interviewee's statement serves as a crystallizing accent and as a springboard for additional comments and ideas.

4. Clients can participate in or observe groups without the rest of the group being aware that they are the clients. This permits them to see and hear respondents as they give their ideas. It can be impressive for them to see people, not as tabular inputs, but as real persons sharing their opinions. The live expression of opinion is stimulating, which adds a sense of conviction in the validity of the methodology.

5. Focus group interviews supply quick results. For example, a nationwide series of group interviews with farmers in eight locations was conducted during an eight-day period. The presentation of results was given five days later. The total field and analysis time was only two weeks. A comparable telephone survey (with corresponding credibility for the client) would have taken a minimum of five weeks.

In summary, the advantages of using focus groups are that they give respondents a chance to talk openly and freely, they are economical, the interaction is multiplicative, clients can observe the groups, and the results are supplied quickly. There are, however, some disadvantages in using focus group interviews.

Disadvantages

1. The sample sizes are very small, and there is a resultant inability to generalize to the total population. By their very nature, focus group interviews involve a small gathering of people. Regardless of the credibility a group appears to have, you must remember that focus group sessions produce no information that can be considered substantially or statistically significant from a rigorous research point of view. Such intensive discussions add insightful explanations to statistical data. For example, if it is known that a particular television news personality is disliked by the audience, focus group discussions could produce several possible reasons for this. These judgments, however, are *possible*, not necessarily *typical*. You cannot assign statistical meaning to these judgments. Nevertheless, these sessions remain a valuable tool for determining in a limited way public attitudes and opinions. They also can be profitable sources of idea generation.

2. Sometimes, focus group interviews are overused. With their current popularity, some market researchers tend to use them for almost every project, substituting this methodology for other types of survey research. Often, little attention is given to the ability of different methodologies to collect necessary information adequately.

3. Because the focus group interaction can increase the participants' awareness of ideas, the interpretation of data must take this into account. It is possible that the researcher would not find the same reactions in the market if interviews were conducted under different circumstances. For example, one participant may pass on information about a political candidate's stance toward an issue that was not known prior to the discussion. The others would then react to this new information. This does not mean that there is a high degree of awareness of the candidate's position on this issue in ordinary situations. Therefore, care must be taken in the analysis.

4. Focus group interviews limit the ability to explore each person's pattern of background and experience extensively. Since a focus group session does not consist of several people being interviewed individually, a single individual's pattern of behavior and attitudes are visible only in pieces and are not pursued as they would be in an individual in-depth interview.

5. Each group has a certain composition of its own that has to function to produce a good discussion. This can create problems. In fact, the

focus group can have any problem that is characteristic of any other group. For example, dominant members who are often opinionated and vocal can intimidate reticent members. Therefore, the value of the group is often determined by the skill and the competence of the moderator and the peculiar life of the particular group.

6. The time available for the focus group interviews generally is limited. Most are conducted within a two-hour limit. Therefore, the value of a group can be limited if a disproportionate amount of time is taken up with idiosyncratic behavior or unproductive ideas.

7. Regardless of the ability of the moderator, it may not be possible to cover topics as systematically as the moderator wishes. There is generally much repetition of voiced opinions, which limits a balanced analysis. With only one or two focus group sessions, it is difficult to determine how representative the groups are. Furthermore, analysis of focus group sessions is hampered by problems of identifying who said what. If possible, it is useful to relate comments made by the same person during various parts of the interview. While it is useful to audiotape the proceedings, parts of the discussion are often hard to follow due to the noise or members talking simultaneously.

8. Some people are often inhibited by the public nature of the group. When topics of a highly personal nature are explored, there is often great pressure for peer approval. It is also advisable to beware of receiving too many socially acceptable responses. There is a need for skillful probing and challenging responses in order to keep the answers from being biased by social acceptability.

9. Individuals who agree to participate may be highly peculiar. You can imagine that many people would respond negatively when a stranger calls on the telephone and offers them $10 to come to a conference room in a motel to discuss television programs or a new product. There is a high percentage of nonresponses to the initial recruiting. This raises several good questions about the samples. Do the people who refuse to cooperate share common characteristics? Are the people who agree to participate more knowledgable, opinionated, or articulate? How representative is the group? At this point, our research cannot answer these questions completely.

CONSIDERATIONS IN FORMING A GROUP

Sampling procedures for focus group interviews constitute a very critical problem area. You want to obtain as representative a small group as you can, because the validity of your results, as well as the way the group functions, depends on the sampling methods. As we just pointed out, encouraging individuals to come to a location away from home is a difficult job. Therefore, the following guidelines are designed to help you form a productive focus group interview.

Selecting Participants

There are several possible methods for selecting participants for focus group interviews. Each of them have some inherent advantages and disadvantages.

Random solicitation of respondents at a shopping center or a mall is a commonly used method. It risks the biases in the traffic patterns of given shopping centers. Therefore, careful attention to the demographic profile of an area can reduce the problem.

Interviewees often are obtained through *random telephone contact.* If you try this method, you can expect to invite 20 to 25 people for every favorable response.

Respondents are often selected from *membership lists* of organizations, clubs, churches, and civic groups with an imposition of quotas through screening questions. This is perhaps the most common form of solicitation. It is very practical and efficient, but it also has several problems. It is not random, and there is always the risk of obtaining professional panelists—people who volunteer every time a request is made. This method also may permit a possible bias in viewpoint, because there is a narrow range of organizations in any one group. For example, you may have only 5 or 6 organizations represented in a group of 12 individuals.

On the other hand, the major advantage of using membership lists is economy. You can secure the cooperation of large numbers of people in a relatively short period of time. Do not forget that many people long for an opportunity to give their opinions. A member of a Kiwanis Club once volunteered to participate because he said, "No one ever asked my opinion before." Finally, the cooperation of recruited members is generally more reliable if the organization receives an honorarium.

Another method is for interviewees to be recruited from *lists of people who have participated in market research studies before.* Most large metropolitan areas have research organizations that will help you set up a group for a fee. They keep files of people who are willing to participate in focus group interviews. If you use this method, you must realize that you are getting some "professional" panelists, and your representativeness for the group may be limited. Nevertheless, many researchers find it very useful.

Finally, the *client may provide a list* of people.

Whatever method you decide to use, you need to get the best possible sample. Therefore, we recommend you use the following procedures.

1. Utilize specific screening questions for each project to qualify the participants. Age, sex, political party preference, income, race, and other relevant classifications can be used to tailor a mixed group. In the past few years, specific problems have occurred because supervisors relied on organizations themselves to fulfill designated quotas or recruited as many of their own acquaintances as they could for groups. This has led to some

unfortunate group compositions, such as identical twins appearing in the same group and the same individuals appearing in different groups on different occasions but for the same project.

2. A specific screening question should prohibit participation by any individual who has been involved in a marketing research project or panel within the last six months.

3. Consider using split locations within a city to provide geographic diversity for the project.

4. Recruit only one participant from each organization for each group. This can reduce the odds of two people in a single focus group knowing each other. There are times, however, when this rule may not apply. For example, several people from the same church were used in a focus group interview about some religious materials that the congregation was using. It was simply impossible to bring together strangers over a wide geographical area to talk about the topic.

5. Always recruit some respondents who are not derived from group lists. At least 25 percent of any single group should be randomly recruited.

Limiting the Size of a Group

Focus group interviews generally are most productive when they have from 8 to 15 people. Any number under 8 is too low, because discussion will be too concentrated. Each member might feel threatened and might feel required to participate whether or not he or she is ready. Furthermore, the small group is too vulnerable to individual personalities and biases.

At the other extreme, more than 15 people is too many. Dispersing such a large group around a room causes dificulties in controlling the conversation. Private conversations, frequent murmuring, and distractions become all too prevalent. As the size of a group increases, the more likely it is that a moderator will be tempted to use a classroom style that involves questioning individuals in turn so that everyone has a vote, asking for a show of hands, or cautioning the group to talk one at a time. Such a style actually hinders the original purpose of the group discussion and does nothing to increase the actual information derived from the group.

Note that the exact number of people who will show up for a group is unpredictable. If you recruit 15 people, then 5, 8, 10, or all 15 may show up. Consequently, it is a good practice to recruit more than you need. The percentage of no-shows can be reduced by using telephone call-backs to confirm the session. For example, if you initially recruit someone five to seven days before the group is scheduled, a confirmation call should be made on the day before the group takes place. By using this method, you can expect almost 100 percent of the people who agree to come to show up.

Regulating the Composition of the Group

The composition of a focus group varies, of course, with the purpose of the project. Sometimes you want a demographically diverse group in order to get an interplay of diverse viewpoints. However, in most research situations, sharp diversity or polarization of the group is hazardous. Instead of the main focus, struggles over age, sex, or class differences can predominate. In other words, it is possible to select a group that has too much diversity.

To obtain the most valuable qualitative information, participants should have some unifying elements out of which true discussion can grow. We have used groups at various times that had the following in common: people without checking accounts; homemakers; women employed outside the home; readers of a certain magazine; members of a certain income group; members of a given political party; and people from the same kind of work.

Choosing a Good Location

Focus group interviews typically are held in such settings as hotels, motels, meeting rooms at churches or fraternal organizations, universities, advertising agency conference rooms, a moderator's home, or occasionally at the client's business. Many marketing research organizations have special group interviewing facilities with built-in audio and videotape equipment and one-way viewing.

In selecting a location, one should give consideration to geographical location within the city, comfort, informality, special needs for viewing visual stimuli, and product display. In cases where groups are used in large cities, it is advantageous to use special group interviewing facilities within research organizations. In smaller localities you must seek out other alternatives.

Scheduling Carefully

Use care in scheduling the day and the time for your interviews. Usually evening sessions, beginning about 7:30 P.M., work well. Consider the commuting patterns in your city, and allow enough time for participants to eat dinner before the session. Friday and Saturday night sessions will increase your nonresponse rates and cause problems in recruitment. Weekday daytime scheduling is admissible if you do not mind having a heavy concentration of homemakers. In fact, for some projects, this might be your best group for testing certain products.

Obviously, the schedule should depend on the nature of your project. A series of focus group sessions conducted for the American Broadcasting Company relating to the subject of early morning television preferences and behavior were conducted in six cities beginning weekdays at 10 A.M. However, early morning television viewers who watched before going to their daytime jobs were not available for participation. On the other hand, could a person respond to visual stimuli designed for early morning consumption at 7:30 P.M.? After due consideration, the morning time was found to be preferable with the clear understanding that the scope of the project was limited to early morning viewing by homemakers.

Finally, you must check out the local situation. If Sunday night church attendance is common in a small town, for example, it is absurd to go against the local pattern and try to recruit for such a time.

Using Premiums

In order to encourage people to accept an invitation for participating in a group session, incentives are necessary. The purpose of premiums is not to buy a person's cooperation necessarily, but it does offer a small incentive to encourage cooperation. It can be paid to the individual or to the individual's sponsoring organization. As of this writing, a $10 bill, enclosed in an envelope, is standard. When money has not been available as a premium, meals, merchandise, or a handshake and a "thank you" have been used effectively. In a nationwide series of interviews with owners of large farm operations, a steak dinner with a few drinks provided the incentive.

Securing Telephone Follow-up

An interesting technique to use is a telephone follow-up interview approximately 24 hours after the session. The purpose of this posttest is to determine changes of opinion or to investigate ideas that the participant has after leaving the immediacy of the group. For example, after a series of focus group interviews were conducted in Kansas City for Bank-Americard, telephone follow-ups sought clarification and changes of opinion after the group pressures were removed. Two or three people from each group voiced an objection to a specific statement made by another member of the group. In the session itself they had been reticent to argue the point directly. Furthermore, the follow-up provided a posttest measure to various logos, color, and thematic considerations that had been explored within the group.

A decision to use telephone follow-up interviews depends on the nature of your project and your budget. It is best if the moderator does the follow-up personally, but this is time consuming and expensive. Nevertheless, if it would be valuable to consider the themes that are best remembered the next day or the changes of opinion that have taken place after reflection or opinions that were not voiced at the session, then the follow-up is very useful.

CONDUCTING THE GROUP INTERVIEW

Each interviewer learns how to moderate a focus group interview that will be consistent with his or her own personality. If you think of it as a small group discussion, then all of the things that are known about the way small groups work can be applied. As the leader of this small group, you will want to lead in terms of process, that is, how the group works, but you will want also to encourage people to introduce any opinions or viewpoints that they care to examine.

In a sense, the focus group interview is a small task oriented group. Moderating it requires careful thought and attention.

Remembering Your Purpose

You are holding a focus group interview to encourage people to give you in-depth qualitative information and to generate ideas. The more that you can find out from them, the better your report will be. To accomplish your purposes, you must (1) go beyond mere surface reactions to explore why people take their relative positions and (2) resist the temptation to insert your own ideas or to guide the discussion so that the ideas are comfortable to you. Social acceptability already has been mentioned, but perhaps it would be useful to state again that your behavior as leader can be a powerful influence over what others say.

Orienting the Group

Before you begin the focus group session check in and seat respondents. Try to achieve a thorough mix in the seating arrangements, separating any individuals who may be even vaguely acquainted. If it is a heterogeneous group, prevent people with similar characteristics from sitting together. This prevents the development of cliques. For example, you would want to prevent all blacks, all women, or all men of comparable ages from sitting together.

After you have done this, provide each member with a name tag or a name plate to put on the table. This helps people to refer to one another by name. Then introduce yourself, and explain the general nature of the research and something about yourself and your firm. It is necessary to establish yourself immediately as a credible person. Explaining the general purpose will prevent the participants from being preoccupied with second-quessing what you are really after. Use as much candor as is feasible in explaining your purpose, but avoid telling them *why* the information is sought. This would cause participants to concentrate immediately on this, so that you would not be able to obtain some very valuable background information. For example, you might tell them that you are collecting data on issues for a political candidate, but you would not want to identify the candidate or the political party.

In a chatty manner, as the moderator you should also tell the group what is expected of them in terms of the discussion. They should be encouraged to discuss without having to raise their hands or take turns talking. They should also be assured that they can feel free to agree or to disagree, since everything that will be discussed is a matter of opinion and, therefore, there are no right or wrong answers.

Record the group, and be candid about it. Tell them that they are being taped in order to aid your own memory of their exact comments so that you can write a better report. Also stress the confidential nature of the research.

Controlling the Interview

You must exert control and leadership without stifling the free flow of ideas. Control is a priority so that all the major points of concern will be covered. You must also exercise control in a way that will keep the respondents relaxed and comfortable.

Control of the interview means that you must keep on top of the discussion, gently nudging it in the direction that is most beneficial to you. It does not mean that you must dominate or stifle responses or particular points of view. Therefore, you must strike a balance between friendly permissiveness and business-like directness, which are necessary to keep the discussion moving along.

One of the best ways to exercise control is to prepare a discussion outline before the session. This outline is simply a list of question areas that you want to cover. By the time the session ends, make certain that each question area has been commented on by a majority of the members.

Another form of control is to judge the relevancy of the discussion at different points in time. Relevance is not always easy to ascertain on the spot as the discussion works around a particular point, so do not be too quick to judge. Nevertheless, you are the final arbiter of whether or not the discussion is proceeding along the lines that will be beneficial to you and your client.

Above all, the control of the group is a function of influencing the group processes. Each group develops its own tone and mood. It is helpful to determine the mood as soon as possible. Sometimes this can be

done by observing the group from behind a one-way mirror as participants arrive. If there is relaxed, easy conversation, you can expect a lively
interaction. If they seem to be unsure and up-tight, you should spend the
first minutes of the discussion relaxing the group.

   The individual dynamics of different groups is an interesting challenge. Some are very determined and task oriented from the start. It
matters little what you do; the discussion goes on. Other groups are
fragile and delicate, and need constant encouragement and direction. The
most difficult challenge is presented by the lethargic group, since the
most common response in this type of group is apathy. Sometimes it can
be cured by raising a dramatic or a controversial subject, by changing
direction, or by taking a short break. At the other extreme is the group
that becomes overstimulated. It is characterized by exaggerated comments, excessive socializing, and sometimes giddiness. A comment about
"getting back to work" may be necessary to bring them back to the task.

   The interviewer in a group setting is like a conductor orchestrating
an improvisation. Much like a musical jam session, the group calls for
awareness of what is going on and what people are doing and feeling.

Dealing with Problem Respondents

Sooner or later you will encounter some problem respondents, with
whom you must deal. As part of your role, you must learn to deal with
them so that they do not deter the group from its task. Listed below are
some of the most frequently encountered problems.

GROUP HOGS

Group hogs are dominant, overly verbal personalities who tend to control
the discussion. They often want to react to every comment made by
someone else. Group hogs usually emerge immediately in the session.
You can deal with them by using their comments as a stimulus for disagreement. For example, you might turn to another participant and ask,
"Do you agree with that?" Or, if you want to encourage disagreement,
you might even resort to a slightly leading question, such as, "You don't
agree with that, do you?" If the problem is really bad, you may just have
to stifle excessive remarks directly.

WALLFLOWERS

Wallflowers are shy individuals who remain silent or merely voice agreement with what others have said. There are two categories of wallflowers:
shy but redeemable contributors and hopeless nonperformers. Try as you
might, some people are almost totally vacuous. You will have to identify
wallflowers early. If, after ten minutes of discussion, the wallflower shows
few signs of coming to life, you may have to forget him or her entirely and

concentrate your efforts elsewhere. One method of getting wallflowers to participate is to require a response to your initial questions from everyone. Begin with a matter-of-fact question, such as asking what television programs the participants watch. Then proceed to opinions. At this point, difficult individuals can be pinpointed. Every group member will feel more comfortable after the ice has been broken.

The redeemable wallflower, basically shy, easily intimidated, but thoughtful, can be encouraged by direct questions. You can be sure that the person who always begins to say something but never quite jumps into the discussion is this type of person. Draw this person out by inviting his or her opinions.

THE AXE BEARER

The *axe bearer* is a unique individual who possesses some characteristics of the hog. You can recognize the axe bearer because he or she has a one-track mind. Regardless of the issue being discussed, this person has one point to be made, which he or she makes again, and again, and again. The result is a great deal of wheel-spinning and a loss of task orientation for the entire group.

Two examples of the axe bearer occurred in a session about prime-time television. First, in one focus group interview an elementary school PTA president referred constantly to the violence on television. It was difficult for this person to look at any other aspect of television programming. Second, in a focus group interview made up of farmers, an organizer for the National Farmers Organization attempted to use the focus group as a recruiting platform for this organization. He attempted to turn every topic into a discussion of why farmers must work together to solve their economic plight. When faced with such an axe bearer, you must be firm and not too subtle. In fact, it might be necessary to point out to the person and to the group exactly what is taking place by this person's contributions. Often the group will be thankful for your control.

THE EAGER BEAVER

The *eager beaver* tries to get his or her ideas spoken before anyone else and does not necessarily want to hog the discussion. In fact, the eager beaver may feel that he or she is helping you out by getting things started. This type of person is really trying to be open and cooperative and, therefore, a great deal of tact is needed. One of the ways to circumvent this problem is to ask questions of other individuals directly to say simply, "Charles, would you start out our discussion on this point." This gives someone else an opportunity to begin the discussion.

THE COMPROMISER

The *compromiser* tends to change his or her opinions to accommodate others. Apparently, the desire for peer approval is so great in this type of person that it makes you wonder whether the person actually has any substance to his or her opinions. Focus group interviews, because of their social chemistry, seem to bring out the compromiser. You should be alert to subtle and overt shifts in position of members. When contradictory positions are evident, direct a question to the compromiser for explanation.

Involving All Members

Try to involve all members in the discussion, because you need all the participants' opinions. It may be necessary at times to call on people directly for participation or to reassure the group that you need participation from everyone. This can be natural and nonthreatening if you address the person directly and make it an offer to participate rather than a command.

So that names will be used throughout the session, provide name tags for each person. Ask the participants to write out the name by which they would like to be addressed. This allows individual participants to set the tone of formality or informality that will make them comfortable.

Sparking Controversy

To be successful, you must serve as a catalyst for generating different viewpoints. Use planned statements of extreme positions, as well as statements of others as springboards. However, it is not generally a good idea to do this in the first 15 minutes of the interview. Allow casual rapport to become established before you risk polarizing the group in controversy. Since some controversies involving opinion cannot be resolved, you must be ready to move on to another topic after you have received the kinds of insights that you need in the ways that people think about the controversial topic.

Cutting Through Superficial Opinions

Your basic objective is to uncover reasons behind an opinion rather than just to discover the opinion itself. The key for unlocking this information is to probe thoroughly for explanations and clarifications. The probing techniques that will be useful here are the same ones that are used in all other interviews. The only difference is that you may need to single one person out of a group momentarily in order to discover that person's thinking. Be certain that you do not do this to the extent, however, that it inhibits the rest of the group.

Keeping a Sense of Progress

The worst thing that can happen to a group is for it to lapse into a state of limbo. You must keep things moving. In order to proceed, sometimes you will need to cut off discussions before the group is ready and explain why you are making the transition to something else. In general, groups appreciate a sense of movement toward some goal.

Taping the Interview

The dynamics of a group need your complete, undivided attention; it is virtually impossible for you to be both a good moderator and a good note-taker. You may, of course, make some notes, but an audio tape will provide you with the kind of verbatim comments that will enrich any report that you make.

Seating Arrangements

The most popular seating arrangement is to have the group sit in a circle, preferably around a table. It is a matter of strategy to seat yourself at the side of the table rather than at the head. You want to exercise leadership, but you also want to avoid having the participants direct all responses to you. Sitting within the group or at the side of a table decreases your prominence and encourages a certain amount of independence.

Concluding the Interview

Make certain that you cover all of the topics you need, but stay within the announced time limits. At the end of the session, you may choose once again to tell the group generally how the information is going to be used. Then thank them for their time and contributions. Keep it cordial, because you may need the participants for some follow-up or for a later interview. One problem sometimes surfaces at the end of the session when people inquire about the conclusions you have drawn. Answer ambiguously that you will need time to think about it. Be friendly, but do not answer the question.

THIS CHAPTER IN PERSPECTIVE

The focus group interview can be a valuable tool for collecting qualitative information in many different areas: marketing, advertising, politics, management, publishing, and communication research. The method can be used in large, analytic research studies like some of the ones described in this chapter, or it can be used rather informally just to generate ideas or reactions. As a manager, you could use it with a group of employees just to see how they are reacting or interpreting a message, a report, or a new system. It can also be used extensively by a communication researcher or a management consultant. Keep in mind that focus group interviews have certain limitations but that they are an excellent means of securing subjective information that has rich explanatory value.

PROJECTS

1. Survey several television stations to determine how focus group interviews are used in connection with their programming.

2. Contact several advertising firms or marketing departments to determine how they use these interviews. Ask to see a report based on these kinds of interviews.

3. Ask permission of someone using a focus interview to attend a session as an observer. Sometimes, consultants are happy to have an assistant.

4. Prepare your own focus group interview. Select a group of people and have them read the same magazine. Then prepare an interview outline in which you intend to find out their reactions to: (a) the title of the magazine, (b) the kind of paper on which is was printed, (c) the general nature of individual articles, (d) the layouts, (e) who they think the magazine appeals to, and (f) at least one specific article. After you have conducted such an interview for 45 minutes, determine what problems you would have in writing a report on the basis of the interview.

5. There is a large amount of information now available about group dynamics. Go to the library and seek out one of the most recent books on this topic to determine some of the things that might be helpful in controlling a focus group interview.

Chapter 20
Organizational Diagnosis
THE INTERNAL SURVEY INTERVIEW

All organizations thrive on information. Whether you are working in a hospital, university, government agency, or an industrial plant, managers need to know the projects that have been completed, the status of those not completed, and any problems that are preventing the accomplishment of the task. This is why so many reports are required to be sent up through the chain of command. This is just one type of information, however, that is important to an organization.

In recent years, managers have been progressively concerned with monitoring how the organization works. They have learned that in order to get the work done, the organization needs to be healthy, to operate efficiently, and to fulfill employee's needs. Therefore, managers seek a self-correcting feedback of information by diagnosing the interaction patterns within their organizations. These diagnoses are variously called *organizational development, human resource development, attitude surveys,* or *organizational audits*. Regardless of what they are called, the analysis is likely to use a series of interviews to get information. Therefore, it is important to consider some of the principles on which such an analysis should be made.

Any organization may find itself wanting to conduct such an analysis. We have conducted them in hospitals, public utilities, manufacturing plants, airlines, military installations, churches, federal agencies, and universities. Sometimes these analyses have examined the total organization; at other times, they have focused on a specific item such as job satisfaction, an appraisal process, or a reaction to a specific channel of communication. You can design your analysis to focus on anything within the organization.

In most organizational analyses, the interview plays a supplementary role. It is used in conjunction with other research techniques. One of the oldest of these is *observation*. By watching people in operation you can take note of how things are being done and analyze how they can be improved. This was the basis for the time-and-motion studies that have been done extensively. There are several variations of the observation technique. The *shadow technique* employs an observer who follows a given person around and makes notations of everything that the individual does. In a *duty study*, the researcher stays in one particular location (such as a head nurse's station) to observe everything that goes on in that location. In still another variation, a group of observers may *invade* several different sections of an organization at a precise time in order to make comparisons about what is going on at that particular time. Data obtained from observations have been very helpful in analyzing organizations. If they are used alone, however, there will always be questions about how representative the observations are and whether the observer influenced the actions of the people being observed.

The *questionnaire* is probably the most frequently used means of diagnosing an organization, and the number of questionnaires used is legion. The types of questionnaires used range from standardized instruments to lists of questions specifically designed for one analysis. Questionnaires are popular because they are a relatively inexpensive means of collecting data from many people in a short period of time. Furthermore, they are limited only by your own imagination. The questionnaire, however, does not allow you to probe answers in depth or to uncover areas that have eluded you before. These limitations of the questionnaire are two of the advantages of an interview. Therefore, the research technique that generally supplements both observations and questionnaires is the interview because it "mines the richest deposits of employee feelings."[1]

The interview is a time consuming means of collecting information, and it is expensive partially because of the time involved. Not only is the cost of using an interviewer expensive, but it is also expensive to take employees away from their jobs to be interviewed. Nevertheless, it allows

[1]Felix M. Lopez, *Personnel Interviewing* (New York: McGraw-Hill Book Company, 1975), p. 294.

you to get information not permitted by any other method, and this makes the time and expense worthwhile.

Data from interviewing is useful only when the information is valid and reliable. You are wasting your time if your data do not meet these criteria. Getting valid, reliable data requires more skill than is often assumed. For example, when a manager assumed responsibility for the house organ in her plant, she decided to conduct a survey of the employees' reactions to it. On the last page of the next issue, she asked, "What do you think of (name of house organ)?" and left several lines for people to write in their answers. Dismayed by the fact that she received only one response out of 3000 employees, she decided to ask the employees the same question in person randomly when she met them during the day. Again, their noncommital answers left her with a feeling that the employees did not really care. Perhaps they did not care, but no one could have been certain on the basis of what had happened so far. This manager made a lot of mistakes, and her effort dramatizes the fact that a good questionnaire and a good interview involve more than "just asking questions." The rest of this chapter outlines some procedures that are important in designing effective interviews.

IDENTIFYING REASONS FOR THE INTERVIEWS

Employee surveys are conducted generally to give management a clear idea of the employees' perceptions, how they feel, and what suggestions they can make. From management's view, obtaining such feedback allows them not only to assess how well the organization is doing in regard to some particular feature but also to identify problems early enough so that they can be remedied before they grow costly and unmanageable.

Surveys are likely to be taken seriously by employees only if two things occur. First, the reasons—even general ones—should be announced publicly. Employees need to be "sold" on the idea. The most effective surveys can come after considerable publicity has been generated about them through the internal communication media. Conversely, in our experiences, the most resistance has come when a top-level manager made a decision to conduct a survey and had interviewers arrive at the plant without anyone knowing about it beforehand; suspicions were great. On the other hand, at another organization of 1300 employees a massive publicity campaign was planned. Not everyone was receptive to the campaign. Nevertheless, more than 80 percent filled out questionnaires, and many employees were volunteering for interviews in addition to those that had been scheduled for interviews.

Second, employees will be more receptive if they feel that something may actually occur as a result of the survey. They hate exercises that are fruitless and that waste time and have made many complaints about either never hearing the results of surveys or never seeing anything occur as a result of them. While management often conducts surveys for its own benefit, there is a need to reward the effort of the employees in some fashion.

CHOOSING INTERVIEWERS

The decision about who to use as the interviewers is an important one, and it should be made on the basis of two questions: (1) who has the necessary skills to get information, and (2) whom will people trust enough to give accurate information. In terms of skills, the interviewers need to be particularly trained; in terms of trust, they need to be people who can ensure confidentiality so that the respondents cannot be made to suffer as a result of their answers.

Based on these criteria of skill and trust it is necessary that the interviewers be somewhat removed from the immediate work situation. Large organizations such as United Airlines, Sears Roebuck, and IBM have in-house consultants who are qualified to conduct surveys. They have special skills that qualify them as experts, and they are generally far enough removed from the immediate work environment that they can be trusted. Many organizations, however, must hire outside consultants to satisfy both criteria. In fact, this need is so great that consulting is one of the fastest growing professions in the United States.

SELECTING INTERVIEWEES

Considerable attention already has been paid in Chapter 17 to sampling techniques. Some of these same considerations apply to organizational research, yet the situation has some major differences, too. Listed below are some of the concerns that should guide you in selecting interviewees. The most general guideline, of course, is to interview those people who can give you the best information suited to your purposes.

1. Sometimes in small organizations or individual work units, it is possible to interview everyone. For example, a three-person committee might be given the responsibility of finding out how their academic department, which consists of 25 people, feels about a certain procedure. In this case, it is an easy decision to have each member of the committee interview one-third of the department. It would have been inadvisable to try taking a sample of such a small group. Furthermore, each member of the department might want to register a reaction.

2. Use a small sample. Obviously, most organizations will be larger than the one just described. If it is larger than 200, it may become too

time consuming and too unwieldy to try to interview everyone. In such cases, you should try to select a smaller number of people that represents the total group.

Some randomization of selection is probably desirable. When you select randomly you *assume* that all sides will be represented and that there will be no inherent bias present. Randomness means basically that each person has as much probability of being selected as any other person. Consultants often find some resistance to random selection, though. For example, a high-level manager may want to pick exactly who he or she wants to be interviewed in one survey. This manager may make the remark, "Interview Smith, Jones, and Hatcher, but don't interview Williams or Johnson because they won't tell you the truth anyway." This manager probably thinks that he or she is being helpful, but if the consultant follows the manager's advice the results will be skewed toward the manager's perceptions, and the validity of any report will be seriously impaired.

There are, on the other hand, two limitations that ought to be placed on randomization. First, it is often useful to select a stratified sample, which ensures that all departments, all levels, and all classifications of people are represented. If you are going to conduct a survey on a college campus, for example, you might select 50 freshmen, 50 sophomores, 50 juniors, and 50 seniors. This ensures that each group is represented, and it is important to do so because research has demonstrated that each of these groups may have different experiences and difference perspectives. Similarly, in an industrial organization you might want to make certain that all departments—production, personnel, industrial relations, and marketing—are well represented. If the numbers in each department are quite different, you might choose to interview the same percentage from each category.

Second, generally it is desirable to interview people in key positions, and a random selection might leave some of them out. In one communication audit of a large organization, it was decided that every member of top management would be interviewed because they could give the best overview of the entire organization. Throughout the rest of the organization, random selection was used.

3. Invite volunteers; let anyone who wishes to be interviewed be interviewed. Obviously, volunteers feel that they have something of value to be communicated. There is a special caution that should be used in analyzing volunteer data, however. These are the people frequently who have problems or who are most upset in the organization, and they volunteer because of their concerns. Special consideration should be given to determine just how widespread these concerns are. In one instance interviewers found that most of the volunteers came from one special clique that did not reflect the opinions of most of the people in the organization.

4. Accessibility is also a key factor in selecting interviewees. Not everyone is equally available to be interviewed. Some will refuse because of a reluctance to commit themselves or because of time pressures; others will be on vacation, on leave, or away on business. Consequently, the selection procedures should be flexible enough to allow for some contingencies.

CHOOSING THE TIME AND THE PLACE

In terms of timing, the best approach is to have a complete timetable made up well in advance so that interviewees will know exactly when they are scheduled and approximately how much time the interviews will take. This allows them to plan their schedules accordingly. In general, employees resist being called suddenly away from their work. If you interrupt them suddenly, you risk having their work pressures compete constantly with your questions.

The length of the interview will vary widely. Normally, you should allow at least one hour per interview, and two hours is preferable if you are interviewing management. Considerable time is necessary for building rapport and trust as well as for getting information, and it is always better to allow more time than is needed than it is to try to cut interviews short or to play "catch-up" all day with your schedule.

Another consideration that has a bearing on time is the work flow. Monday morning is generally not a good time to interview supervisors and managers because they have meetings scheduled, and this is the time that they normally spend getting things organized for the week. Usually early morning is not a good time for planning an informative exchange either, because most people need time to get oriented in their work. These are merely two examples that illustrate the point that you should discover optimum times during a day when people will be most receptive to your interviews.

In earlier chapters we made the point that where an interview takes place can enhance or inhibit the interviewees. In a survey one option is to set up a permanent headquarters and have all interviewees come there. This has the advantage of getting interviewees out of their own immediate work environments to a place where it is easier to relax and talk and where privacy—both physical and psychological—is ensured. In one survey the headquarters was in a glassed-in office in a very large office area. No one in the office could hear the interview, but they could all see the participants. While this did not seem to bother most of the interviewees, there were some who seemed to be aware that their peers were looking at them and knew how long they were in the interview. After this experience, the interviewer concluded that a glassed-in office should be avoided whenever possible.

Another option is to conduct the interview in the interviewee's work space or office. This should be done only if the interviewee has a private office; you should never attempt to interview someone on a production line or in a general work area. The biggest problem with the interviewee's office is that you are vulnerable to many interruptions. Not all interviewees will think of holding calls or even shutting a door, and it is impolitic for you to suggest that he or she do so. In this sense, the interviewee is in control.

A third option is to hold the interview in a conference room, coffee shop, or other nonwork related facility, which would have the advantage of protecting you against interruptions and also of making the exchange more informal.

In conclusion, the time and the place should be selected in order to assure privacy, to stimulate free communication, and to accommodate interviewee preferences. Rather than be dogmatic, it is wise to give the interviewee an option in designating the time and the place. For example, when a consultant schedules an interview with a plant manager, he might simply ask, "Where would you like to have the interview?" The manager might respond immediately by picking up his coat and suggesting, "I don't care but let's get out of here or we'll never get through the interview." The manager might then lead the way to a deserted area where they both can have some coffee and hold a two-hour interview.

REFINING THE INTERVIEW SCHEDULE

The content of any interview is determined by what the interviewer wants to know. Some of the most frequent kinds of information sought in an organizational analysis include: attitudes, opinions, feelings, suggestions, and descriptions of how things work. Listed below are a few sample categories with representative questions for each.

> *Opinion:* How would you describe the management style of your immediate superior? Is it effective?
>
> *Suggestion:* If you could make any changes in the organization, what changes would you like to see?
>
> *Feelings:* How do you feel about the new organizational structure for your department?
>
> *Process:* What are the most frequent kinds of problems that you encounter on your job? When these problems occur, how do they generally get resolved? Give me an example.
>
> *Attitude:* What is most important about your job? What tends to affect your job satisfaction most?

The following guidelines may be helpful in refining your interview schedule.

1. Work out the schedule. This is particularly important when several people are involved as interviewers. It is not necessary perhaps for them to ask questions in the same order, because they will need to adapt to the differences among the interviewees, but it is useful for them to ask questions using a fairly standard wording in the questions. Even though you may spend different amounts of time on various questions, all question areas should be explored by each interviewer.

2. Test the schedule through a pilot study. Get reactions before you actually use it. The objective is to find out whether there are problems in understanding the questions or whether the questions give you the kind of information that you seek. Even pilot tested questions may need later refinements.

3. Structure the interview so that the beginning questions are very open. This allows the interviewees to bring up the areas that are most important to them. For example, if you were interviewing workers in a company about their job satisfaction, you might have seven or eight different areas that you would like to explore in detail. Rather than begin with a question about each, however, you might be wise to ask first, "What are the things that most affect your job satisfaction?" Their answers to this question could give you great insights into their thinking about their jobs and might not be limited necessarily to the areas that you had planned to discuss.

USING MULTIPLE INTERVIEWS

Having more than one interview with the same individual can be very helpful. In fact, for an in-depth organizational analysis, this should be standard practice. In planning a communication audit of a large organization, several consultants in the International Communication Association planned two stages of interviews.

Exploratory Interviews

Exploratory interviews were the means by which the initial information was collected. They were designed primarily to obtain a general orientation to the organization, to identify problem areas, and to determine what additional questions needed to be probed on questionnaires and in later interviews. In other words, it was unlikely that the results of the first group of interviews would be as sharp in analyzing the organization as the results of follow-up interviews.

Follow-up Interviews

Follow-up interviews elicit more precise information. By having obtained information in the first round of interviews, the interviewers now would have a better idea of what should be probed in detail and would have a better perspective for probing in the second round. Care about how this is done, however, should be taken, because sometimes unconsciously interviewers can reveal information from previous interviews.

Sometimes you may want to ask why you have obtained the general results that you obtained in a survey. The following question illustrates such an attempt. After analyzing some questionnaire data, the researchers knew how people felt about the organization but they still did not know why. Consequently, the following question was built into the follow-up schedule.

> In our survey we found some very positive reactions to some questions and identified some areas that needed improving. (This statement was useful in being complimentary, in allaying defensive reactions, but also in suggesting that not everything was positive.) The ratings of your organization's overall communication efforts were not as high as they might have been. Why do you think this occurred?

Another reason for follow-up interviews is to adopt a time perspective. It is useful to ask what changes have occurred since the last interview, because things may have gotten better or worse. In either case, you will not be stuck with a frozen evaluation of the organization based on one group of interviews. Furthermore, you may even know of circumstances or programs that have been changed since the last interview, and it may be profitable to check people's perceptions of them. This can be particularly crucial for consultants who have introduced some interventions into the organization. Figure 20.1 gives an example of a follow-up interview outline.

Outline
I.   For the write-ups, please group your answers not only according to the question (1, 2, 3, etc.) but also according to the following classifications: Administration, Supervisory Classified, and Nonsupervisory Classified.
II. The introduction is very important, because many people want to know how they were selected for the interview. I recommend that you take care of this in the introduction by explaining the following.
     A. Purpose: follow-up to check earlier perceptions and ask more pointed questions, to explore more about strengths and weaknesses. Selection of interviewees was determined by desire to interview some of the same people in order to check earlier information and interview others that would give a broader base than was had before; that is, make certain all areas of the organization are represented.
     B. How information will be used: guarantee anonymity but state that data will help to explain some of the results.
III. The following questions are designed as a broad guide. In some cases, the respondents' answers will make you want to use them in a different sequence. You can also make whatever adaptations in the guide that you feel are needed after the initial interviews.

Questions

1. Have there been any significant changes in the communication patterns in your organization recently?
2. In our survey we found some very positive reactions to some questions and identified some areas that needed improving. The ratings of "Your organization's overall communication efforts" were not as high as they might have been. Why do you think this occurred? How would you explain this?
3. What is motivating people in the organization now? What are their principal concerns? How is the communication here relating to and perhaps satisfying these concerns and needs?
4. Let's look at you as the receiver of information. We'd like to ask you questions about five areas of information that you might receive.
   a. Questions:
      (1) What information in these areas would you like to receive?
      (2) How would you like to get it? From whom?
      (3) Why aren't you getting it now.
   b. Areas:
      (1) progress in job and how you are being judged
      (2) organizational policies
      (3) how organization's decisions are made that affect you
      (4) promotion and advancement opportunities
      (5) important new service or program development
5. Now, let's discuss you as the sender of information.
   a. How do you know what you need to send to others? How do you make the decision to initiate communication? Do you receive many requests for information?
   b. Do you find yourself requesting information to do your job? What kind? Why is this not sent routinely?
   c. Is there any way in which you do not get to participate in an evaluation of superiors or supervisors? Would you find this useful? How high up would you like to evaluate? What would happen if you could?
6. In terms of upward and downward flow of communication, what kinds of filtering are planned in the system? Relate this to the identifying of the chief loci of responsibility in the organization.
7. What happens when you send upward communication to
   a. immediate supervisor?
   b. middle management?
   c. top management?
   d. Where is the greatest lag or block? Why?
8. When there are blocks to communication, what kinds of formal techniques do you use to get around it? What kinds of informal techniques get the best results for you?
9. How much do you use the informal channels? How are they structured? How do people tap them if they want to?
10. Let's turn to your evaluation of other communication sources. What should top management be communicating that they are not?
11. How would you evaluate your immediate supervisor as a communicator?
12. How would you evaluate your departmental meetings in terms of
    a. information?
    b. decisions?
    c. frequency?
13. Are there important differences for you between communicating with x employees and communicating with y employees?

14. How do you get the information needed to do your job? What kinds of information do you need to know is available but not necessarily to receive all the time? How should it be made available?
15. What channels are best at keeping you abreast of the day-to-day operations and happenings in the organization?
16. How does the organization reward excellence in
    a. productivity?
    b. service?
    c. research?
17. Some people have said that there is a need for greater coordination within the organization. How do you feel about this? Are there some examples that you can share?
18. What do you think we are going to find as a result of conducting the audit? What is going to happen as a result of our report?
19. Are there questions that we have not asked that should be explored?

Figure 20.1   Follow-up interview outline and questions

DETERMINING HOW INFORMATION WILL BE USED

Although you can do many things to maximize your success in the interview, there is a major factor over which you may have little control. This factor is how the information is going to be used (or whether it will be used at all) or how similar information has been used in the past. In conducting surveys, you can become accustomed to such questions as "What is going to happen to this information?" and "Are we going to get to see a report on this?" Felix Lopez addresses this point well with his statement:

> An employee survey is no idle pastime. When a company conducts one, it tells its employees that their ideas and their points of view on matters that affect them are wanted, and it promises them action on those items that dissatisfy them. This commitment has deterred some companies from undertaking them; the failure to honor it has destroyed employees' faith in many others.[2]

William Glueck notes that one strong determinant that affects the validity of the survey is "whether the employees feel that the employer is sincerely interested in knowing the truth and will act wherever possible to follow-up on their suggestions."[3] The implication is that you ought to know in advance what is going to happen to the information so that a proper explanation can be made to the interviewees. Furthermore, this should be specified in the contract with the organization. Several options are discussed below.

1. *The results are not publicized.* Many managers will commission a

[2]Ibid., p. 291.
[3]William F. Glueck, *Personnel: A Diagnostic Approach* (Dallas: Business Publications, Inc., 1978), p. 746.

survey simply for their own benefits. They are merely curious, and the information stops with them.

2. *The results are not used.* Sometimes an industrial relations or personnel department will conduct a survey at their own suggestion and feed the results to the appropriate managers. It is then the manager's option to use it or not to use it. Unfortunately, many results are merely shelved.

3. *The results are fed to an implementation committee.* In one instance we know of the results of an audit of a university were given to a special committee, which drafted its own report and circulated it widely to anyone who wanted it. They also began to make suggestions about changes that needed to take place as a result of the information. This survey produced some results because of their efforts.

4. *A general report is given to management with individual reports going to appropriate supervisors.* One of the most effective uses of survey results that we have seen followed this pattern. A supervisor in a camping plant received his report and called all of his department together along with a representative from the industrial relations department. He summarized the results orally and opened the floor for discussion. The opening statement was that "people around here just don't know how to manage." For the next two hours there was a vigorous and productive exchange of viewpoints in which the supervisor received information never before revealed to him. He was unusually brave, and perhaps unusually secure, to go through this process, but it worked well for him.

RECORDING INFORMATION

Organizational analysis generally requires many interviews spread over several days. Consequently, it is imperative that the interviewers not only elicit valid information but also that they register it in some form usable at the end of the project. Memory alone cannot be trusted over such a period. For this reason, the following guidelines are suggested for taking notes.

1. Experiment until you find what method works best for you; for example, take notes during the interview or try to summarize at the end.

2. Write a summary of each interview immediately after the interview. Make notations not only about the answers but also about your perceptions of the interviewee. Avoid the tendency to put it off until later; you can do it best when the information is still fresh.

3. Write down verbatim quotations for important ideas. Exact quotations add a note of credibility to any report.

4. Use an assistant as a recorder. This technique has proven to be particularly effective on occasion. In this technique two people go to the interview—one to conduct the interview and the other to take notes. The

addition of a third party should always be cleared with the interviewee, of course. A good explanation can alleviate any feelings of intimidation that occur.

This procedure has two advantages: it frees you from note-taking so that you can concentrate exclusively on the interaction, and it also allows you to check your perceptions after the interview with those of the recorder. These periods of processing can be both fun and instructive as you both explain the conclusions you have drawn and the evidence supporting these conclusions.

OVERCOMING PROBLEMS

One of the greatest problems is simply that of building trust. After all, you are asking for information that may affect the other person's livelihood, financial security, and relations with others; most people are quite cautious about making statements that might cause problems in any of these areas. On the other hand, when people feel that you can be trusted, there is "more concisely intended disclosure and a greater amount of disclosure."[4]

If you are a consultant, the interviewee probably will not know you. Your task, therefore, is to keep the interviewee from defining this as a risky situation. One approach is to give a thorough orientation in which you establish your own credibility. Introduce yourself, making certain that you emphasize those credentials that will demonstrate your objectivity and expertise. Then explain what you are trying to accomplish, perhaps how you are planning to go about it, and how the information will be reported. Conclude the orientation by offering to answer questions about the procedures.

Even thorough orientations will not always relax everyone, and remember that trust waxes and wanes. In fact, the entire interview may involve a process of building trust. For example, a vice-president in a utility company once talked to a interviewer for 45 minutes before deciding to risk disclosure. When the consultant started to leave, the manager made a decision to trust the consultant and invited the consultant to sit down again. Then the manager provided some very personal information about the organization. Apparently, the manager had a lot at stake and it took some time to decide to trust the consultant.

Keep information confidential. This is a problem that is related to trust. You can assure people of confidentiality and keep the information to yourself. Beware of subtle ways of betraying confidences. Sometimes interviewees unconsciously will prod you to tell them what you are find-

---

[4]Lawrence R. Wheelers and Janis Grotz, "The Measurement of Trust and Its Relationship to Self-Disclosures," *Human Communication Research* 3, no. 3 (Spring 1977): 250.

ing out about a topic or about the other people you have interviewed. If you answer these questions specifically, you may find yourself inadvertently revealing confidential information. Sometimes even the questions that you ask suggest that you have been talking to a certain person. On the other hand, it is not wise to put the interviewee down with "I can't answer that" either, since the interviewee may retaliate by not answering your questions. One way to handle this situation is to give a very neutral response, such as, "We're finding that people have a lot of different viewpoints about almost every question."

Your own enthusiasm can present a problem. If you have obtained new information from someone, you may want to probe deeper and deeper into certain areas. This may even be highly desirable. Nevertheless, your questions must be phrased very carefully, since each question not only asks for information but also reveals what you already know.

Dealing with perceptual differences is also a problem. Since every person looks at the organization in different ways, their assessments of the organization will differ. Some will pinpoint problems in areas that others would describe as working smoothly. At this point, it is very useful to distinguish between opinion and fact. Opinions may be catalogued in terms of how widespread an opinion is. Facts, on the other hand, need to be checked out. Whenever possible, ask people for specific instances to aid you in your checking.

ANALYZING THE DATA

The interview is one of the best means of securing insight into an organization, because the amount and kinds of information obtainable are unlimited. Somehow you must put it all together in ways that make sense to you and your client. The following guidelines will help you in doing this.

1. *Develop a focus.* Be sensitive to the subtle nuances and common threads that run through respondents' answers. Then let the focus of what is important *evolve* from your data rather than be superimposed into a predetermined structure. Too many organizational analysts start out with a limited framework into which they force their analysis. Be flexible and be open.

2. *Make certain that your conclusions are supportable.* Perhaps this point is obvious, but you should remember it in order to prevent your own filtering from leading you to make tenuous conclusions. Develop a list of supporting evidence for each conclusion.

3. *Be aware of your criteria.* As you analyze, develop some criteria for judging success or effectiveness. More often than not, these criteria are not stated, so it is good practice for you to do so. Should you be guided more by your own values and preferences or by those of the organization? Should you be guided more by the stated objectives of the organization or

by the objectives implicit in the way the organization operates? Just what are the earmarks of an effective organization? These are questions that you will need to answer in order to make sound judgments.

MAKING A REPORT

The report is the culmination of your work; it is the reason for your work. Consequently, it is imperative to consider it as the last stage of the analysis. You may find these guidelines helpful in making your report.

1. *Never give the report in written form alone; schedule an information giving interview also.* This is absolutely essential for clarifying statements and letting your interviewees ask questions.

2. *Prearrange the form in which the report is to be given.* If the organization has several work units, for example, it should be agreed upon in advance whether there will be a report on each individual unit or on the organization as a whole. You should also prearrange who is going to see the report.

3. *Offer tentative conclusions.* When you report your findings, it is appropriate to present the hard facts and then suggest several different interpretations. In fact, this interview may be a time in which the interviewees can even clarify some of the findings. At any rate, you are there to supply them with information that must be processed through their filters. At best, you can only be a guide.

4. *Expect cautious reactions.* Often analysts are so engrossed in processing information that they become quite enthusiastic about it, and they may expect the interviewees who are hearing the report to share their enthusiasm. The fact is, however, that the interviewees have not been actively involved with the material before this time, and they may have some difficulty assimilating it. Therefore, they may feel that they need time to go over it in detail.

5. *Keep your report balanced.* In a sense you have been conducting a general performance review for the entire organization. You will remember that most people who are appraised want a proper balance between the good and the bad. Since in any organizational analysis most of the attention is bound to be focused on central administration or upper management, it is wise to remember that they, too, will want a balanced perspective.

6. *Resist becoming defensive.* The report will probably have a lot of your energy invested in it, and you probably have some pride associated with it. This only makes you vulnerable to defensive feelings when people begin to ask questions or try to pinpoint weaknesses in the report. In one report to a top executive, for example, the executive kept claiming that the consultants had somehow manufactured or manipulated the data in detrimental ways. It was very difficult to make the executive see that the

data were actually determined from employee responses and that they were not "dreamed up" by the researchers. In the end, the researchers had to be quite persuasive in their explanations and also very tactful.

THIS CHAPTER IN PERSPECTIVE

In conducting organizational research, you need to use all of the guidelines affecting research in general. There is one big difference, however, between this type of research and the others. What you do and what you report vitally affects the lives of people on the job. In other words, they must live with the results. Therefore, you need to be doubly careful that your approach to the diagnosis is as professional as possible and that you deal in factual information rather than in intuitive guesses. At the same time, organizational research can be one of the most exciting forms of research, because you are not only collecting data, you are also discovering the processes inherent in a living organization. Furthermore, you can see how your information is going to relate to making the organization function better. Therefore, it calls for your best efforts.

PROJECTS

1. Make a collection of questionnaires that have been used to diagnose organizations. Determine what they have in common. If you were conducting such an analysis, what kind of information might you get from interviews to supplement the questionnaires?

2. Contact the organizational communication division of the International Communication Association to get some of the interview guides that have been used in organizational audits.

3. Find out the name of an organizational consulting agency in your city and interview some of the consultants.

4. Find an organization in your city that will let a group come in and conduct a series of interviews. This has been done with mutual benefit to the researchers and the organization. Work out all the details with a company representative.

5. Discuss some of the ethical considerations that should guide you as you conduct these interviews.

6. Discuss some strategies that you might use if you were interviewing someone that you suspect is lying based on contradictory information you have received from other sources.

7. Discuss things that you can do to win the trust of interviewees in an organization. Start by enumerating the reasons that they may not trust you initially.

8. Conduct an interview with a group of workers. Then contrast this experience with the personal interview.

9. What are the major considerations that you would have in feeding back the results of your analysis in an interview with top managers?

Epilogue

One of the underlying premises of this book has been that you as an interviewer can affect the behavior of the interviewee. In a sense, your role gives you a great deal of power. Furthermore, we have emphasized the idea that it is your responsibility to exercise control over the interview. Consequently, it seems useful to end this book by pointing out that wherever there is control, there is the possibility of misuse of control. While one person cannot legislate the morality of another, it would at least be useful for you to think about the ethical guidelines that ought to guide your own behavior. The following is a composite list made up by groups that have discussed the issue of ethics in relation to the interviewer's role as planner, manager, and measurer.

1. Never misrepresent either yourself, your project, or your findings.
2. Respect the importance of the interview for the interviewee.
3. Respect the confidentiality of information. Never betray your sources.
4. Be nonjudgmental about the responses. There are times, of course, when a manager would find this hard. However, for any information getting interview, it is not only ethical but also very practical to be nonjudgmental, since to be judgmental would probably shorten the interview.
5. Do not manipulate the interviewee. In this sense, manipulation refers to taking away the interviewee's right to choose. It also refers to such behavior as coercion and blackmail.
6. Make appropriate explanations about your purposes. Any request for information made by an interviewee needs to be honored in some form.
7. Try to become aware of your own biases and avoid letting them influence you unduly in the interview.
8. Respect all rights of the interviewee.

Perhaps you will not agree with all of these; perhaps there are circumstances in which some of them may not apply; and perhaps there are other ethical statements that you would make about the role of the interviewer. The important thing is that you think about the ethics of what you do. Frequently, you will find that these ethical statements lay an excellent framework for outlining steps in becoming a professional interviewer.

Index